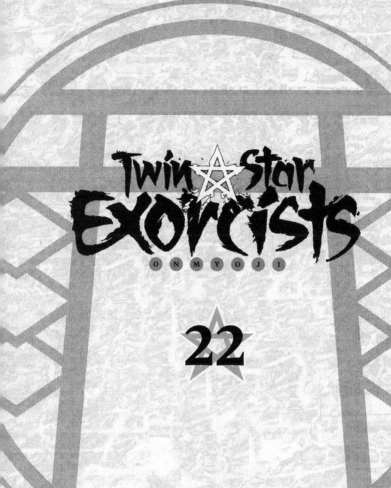

Twin ☆ Star Exorcists

O N M Y O J I

22

STORY & ART
YOSHIAKI SUKENO

Character Introduction

Arimori Tsuchimikado

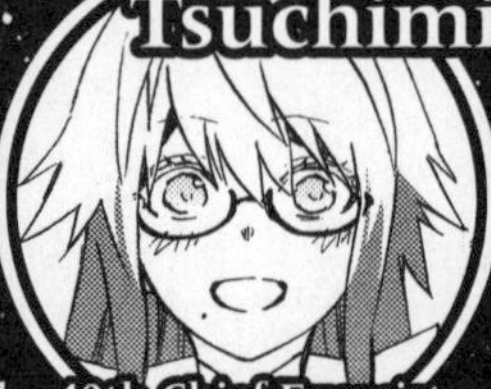

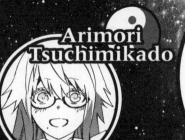

The 40th Chief Exorcist and the son of Arima, the former Chief Exorcist. He used to be a member of the Enmado Clan but he returned to the Tsuchimikado Family after the death of his father.

Kamui

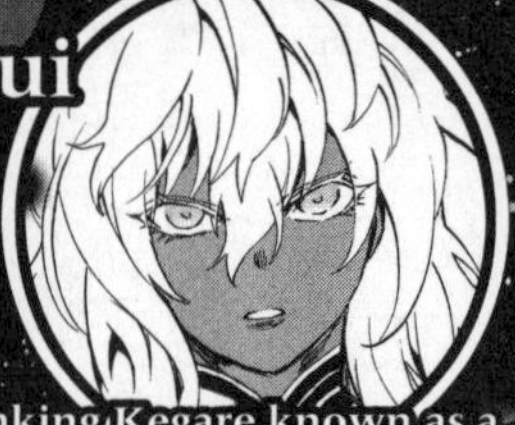

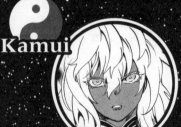

A high-ranking Kegare known as a Basara, a Kegare who speaks. Kamui murdered Benio's parents, but after helping Benio on her journey to regain her powers, he has developed some kind of feelings for her.

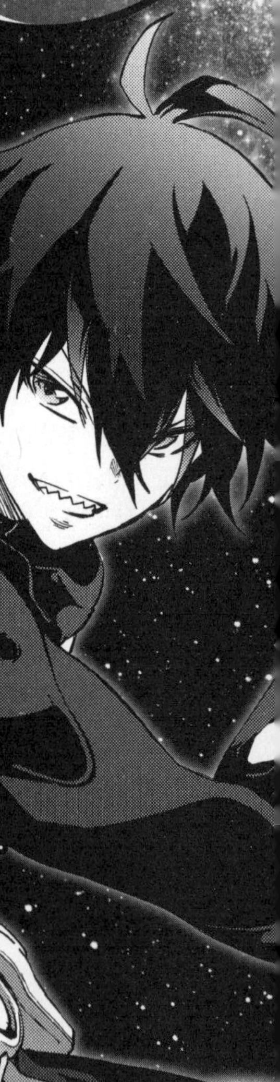

Rokuro Enmado

A brave young man striving to become the most powerful exorcist. He set up his own dynasty, the Enmado Family, on Tsuchimikado Island. At first he and Benio didn't get along, but he gradually fell in love with her.

Story Thus Far...

Kegare are creatures from Magano, the underworld, and it is the duty of an exorcist to hunt, exorcise and purify them. Rokuro and Benio are the Twin Star Exorcists, fated to bear the Prophesied Child who will defeat the Kegare. Their goal in their teens is to go to the exorcist's headquarters on Tsuchimikado Island to train and defeat Yuto, Benio's twin brother and the murderer of Rokuro's childhood friends.

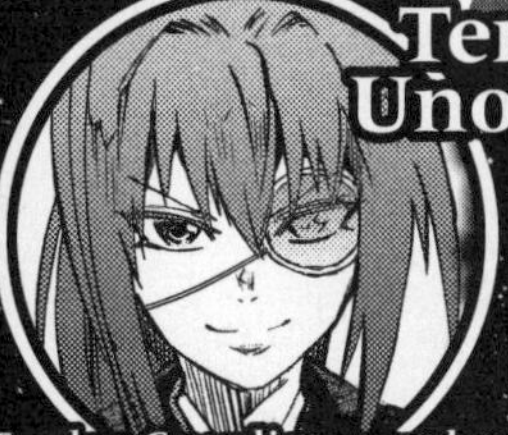

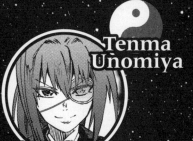

Tenma Unomiya

Twelve Guardian member God of the In-Between. His Spiritual Guardian is all the Great Yins of the past. He too helped Rokuro defeat Yuto.

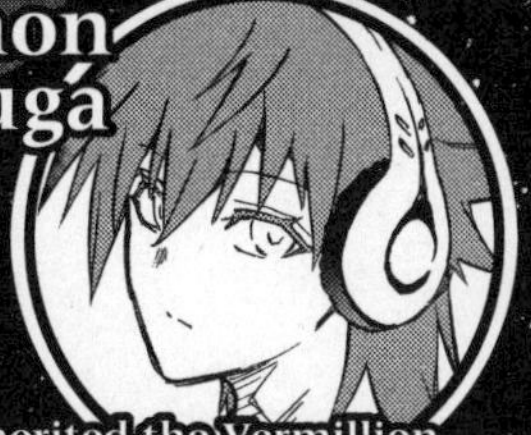

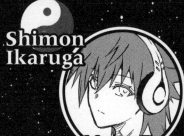

Shimon Ikaruga

He inherited the Vermillion Bird guardian when he was just 14. At the Imperial Tournament, Tenma cut off Shimon's right leg, but he has returned to the front lines of battle with a prosthetic one.

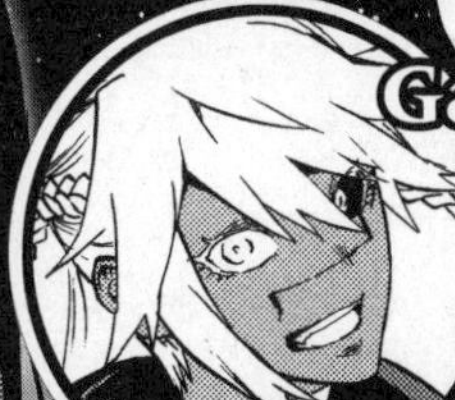

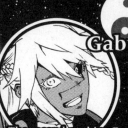

Gabura

The second-ranking Basara, said to currenly be the most powerful Kegare. Aggressive, independent and capricious.

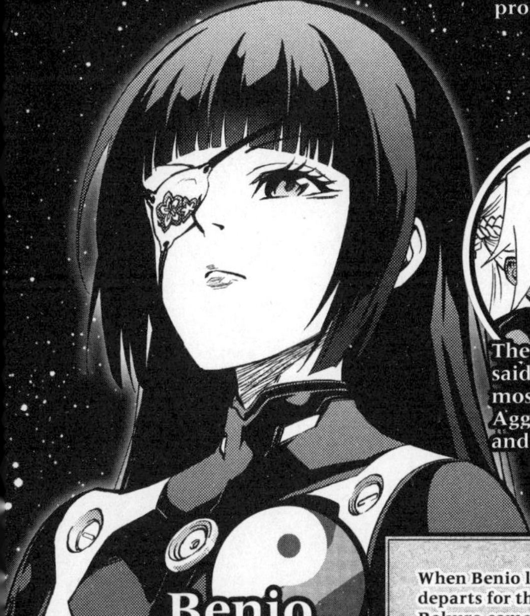

Benio Adashino

The daughter of a once-prestigious family of exorcists who dreams of a world free of Kegare...Her true identity is the Great Yin, the ultimate form of a Kegare. She appeared in the nick of time to help Rokuro defeat her elder brother, Yuto. Now 20, she has agreed to marry Rokuro!

When Benio loses her spiritual power, Rokuro departs for the island alone. Eventually, Rokuro comes face to face with his archenemy, Yuto, and Benio, having claimed her true power as the Great Yin, appears in the nick of time. They fight and defeat Yuto together—as the Twin Star Exorcists.

Four years have passed, and Rokuro and Benio are highly respected on Tsuchimikado Island. They have been living together for quite some time, but their relationship hasn't progressed... Rokuro finally gets an engagement ring and proposes to Benio. She accepts, and the two are finally engaged. But nothing goes smoothly for these two...

Twin Star Exorcists

ONMYOJI

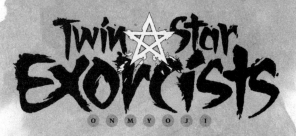

EXORCISMS

22

ONMYOJI have worked for the Imperial Court since the Heian era. In addition to exorcising evil spirits, as civil servants they performed a variety of roles, including advising nobles by foretelling the future, creating the calendar, observing the movements of the stars, measuring time...

#80 Gathering of the Mighty

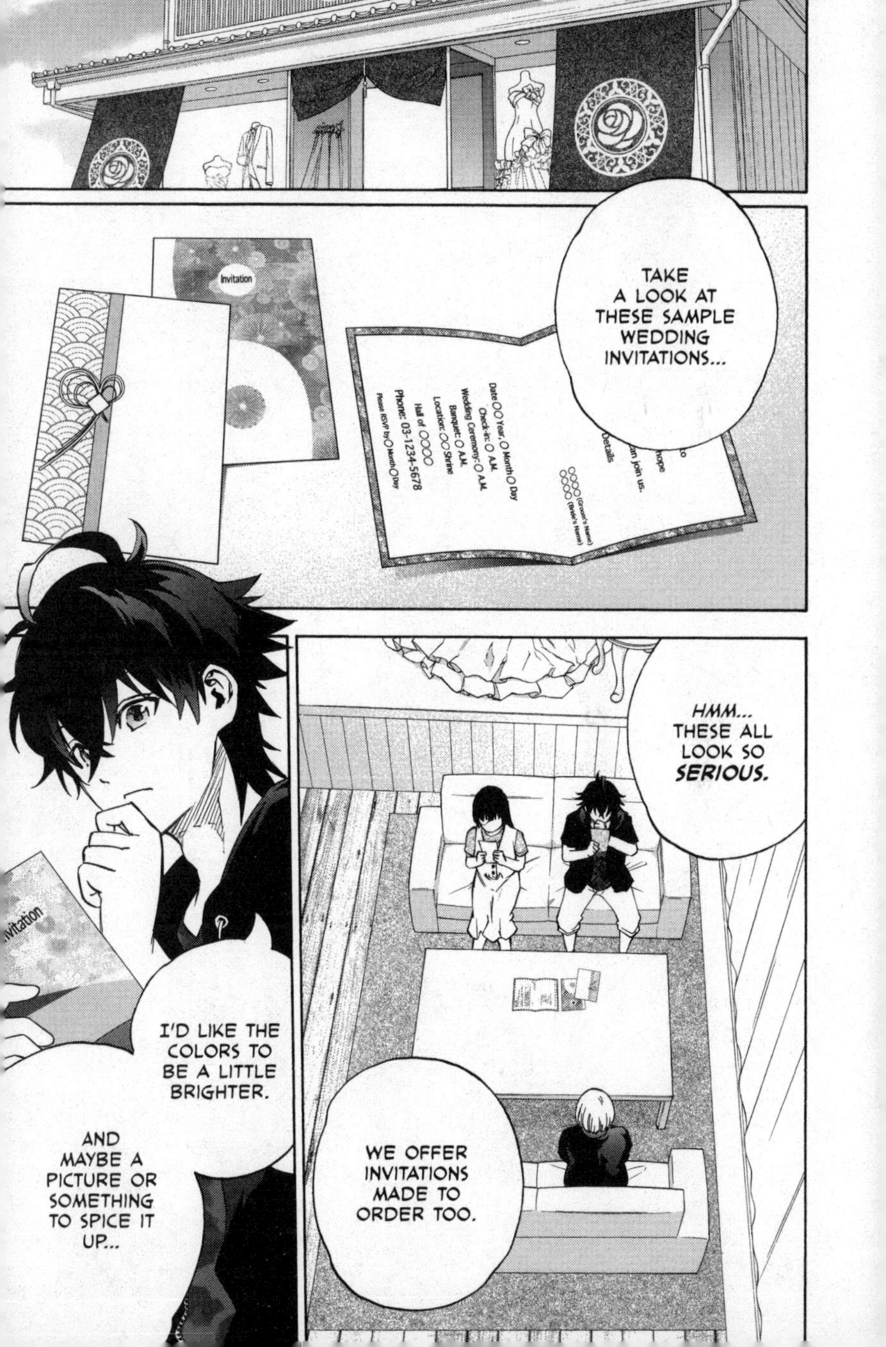
Invitation
TAKE A LOOK AT THESE SAMPLE WEDDING INVITATIONS...
Date ○○ Year, ○ Month ○ Day
Check-in: ○ A.M.
Wedding Ceremony: ○ A.M.
Banquet: ○ A.M.
Location: ○○ Shrine
Hall of ○○○○
Phone: 03-1234-5678
HMM... THESE ALL LOOK SO *SERIOUS.*
Invitation
I'D LIKE THE COLORS TO BE A LITTLE BRIGHTER.
AND MAYBE A PICTURE OR SOMETHING TO SPICE IT UP...
WE OFFER INVITATIONS MADE TO ORDER TOO.

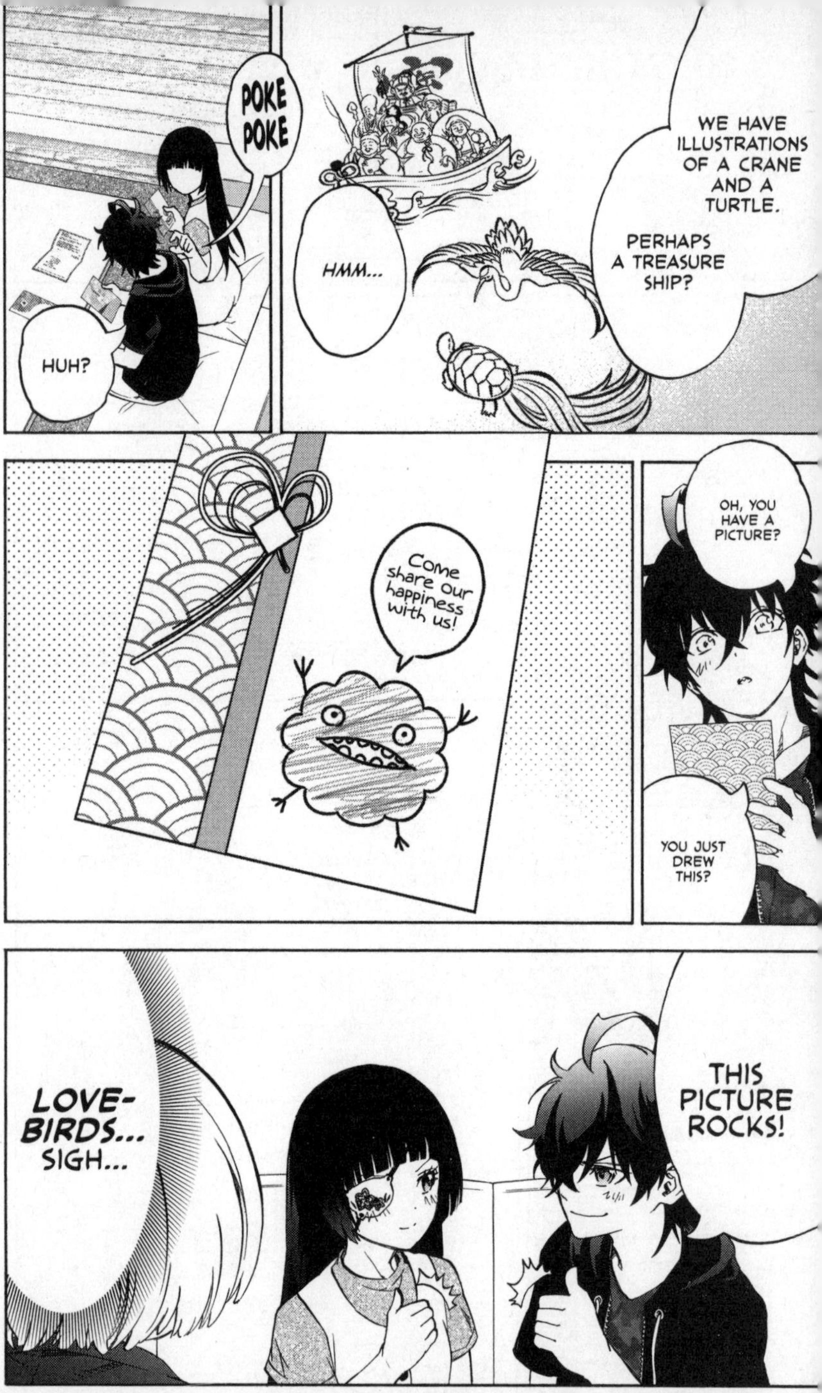
WE HAVE ILLUSTRATIONS OF A CRANE AND A TURTLE.
PERHAPS A TREASURE SHIP?
HMM...
POKE POKE
HUH?
OH, YOU HAVE A PICTURE?
YOU JUST DREW THIS?
Come share our happiness with us!
THIS PICTURE ROCKS!
LOVE-BIRDS... SIGH...

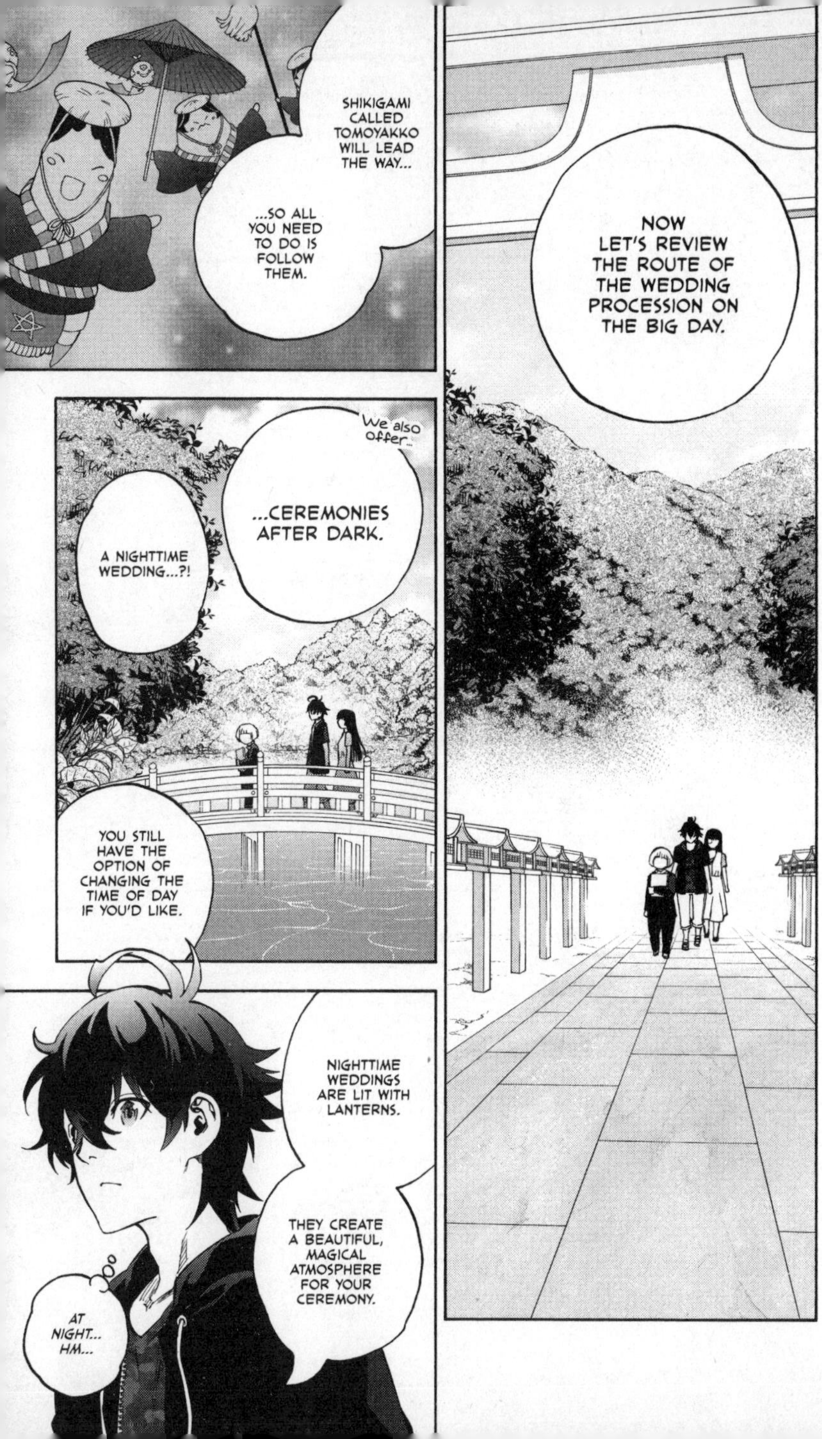
NOW LET'S REVIEW THE ROUTE OF THE WEDDING PROCESSION ON THE BIG DAY.
SHIKIGAMI CALLED TOMOYAKKO WILL LEAD THE WAY...
...SO ALL YOU NEED TO DO IS FOLLOW THEM.
We also offer...
...CEREMONIES AFTER DARK.
A NIGHTTIME WEDDING...?!
YOU STILL HAVE THE OPTION OF CHANGING THE TIME OF DAY IF YOU'D LIKE.
NIGHTTIME WEDDINGS ARE LIT WITH LANTERNS.
THEY CREATE A BEAUTIFUL, MAGICAL ATMOSPHERE FOR YOUR CEREMONY.
AT NIGHT... HM...

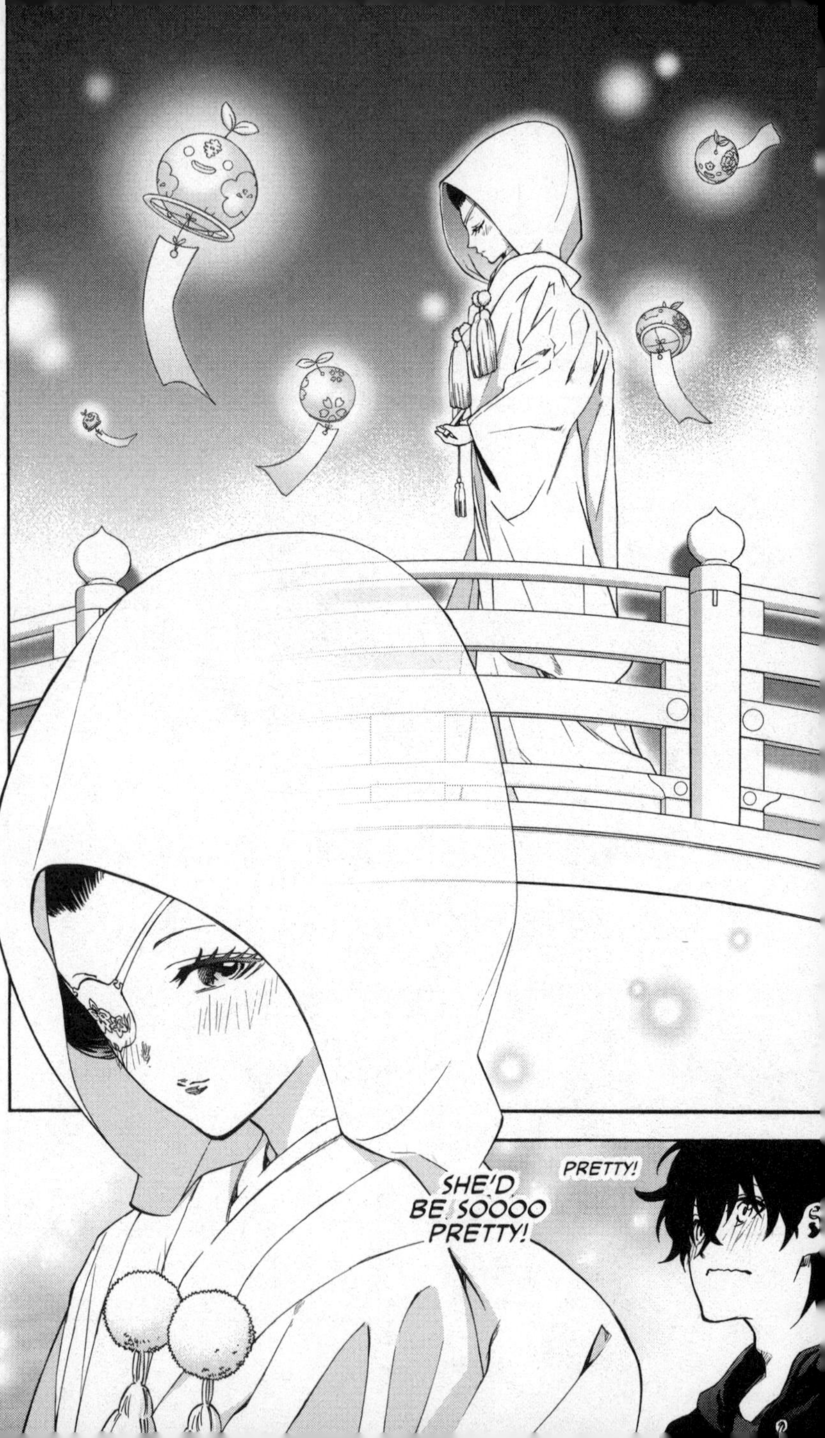
PRETTY!
SHE'D BE SOOOO PRETTY!

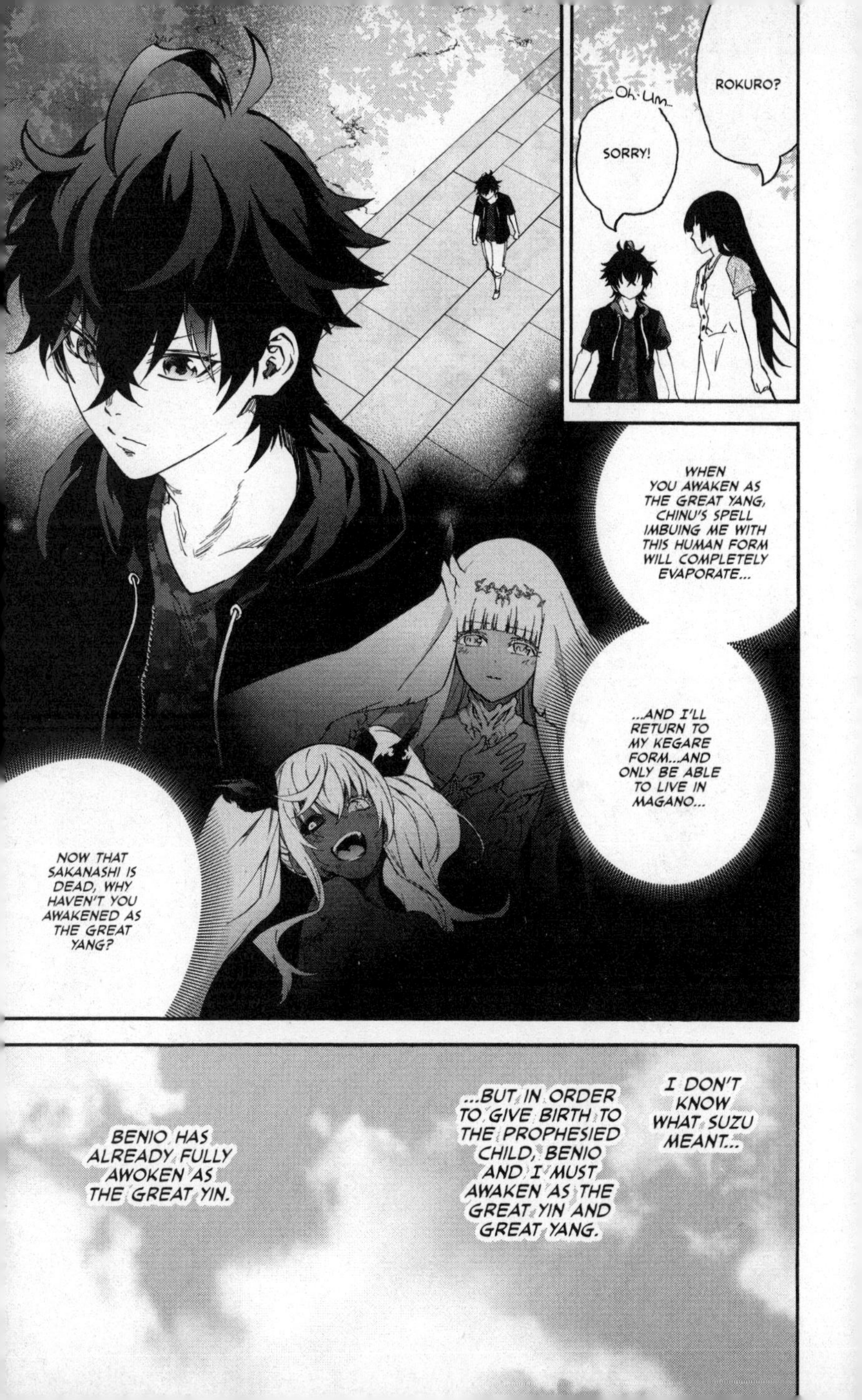
ROKURO?
Oh. Um...
SORRY!
WHEN YOU AWAKEN AS THE GREAT YANG, CHINU'S SPELL IMBUING ME WITH THIS HUMAN FORM WILL COMPLETELY EVAPORATE...
...AND I'LL RETURN TO MY KEGARE FORM...AND ONLY BE ABLE TO LIVE IN MAGANO...
NOW THAT SAKANASHI IS DEAD, WHY HAVEN'T YOU AWAKENED AS THE GREAT YANG?
I DON'T KNOW WHAT SUZU MEANT...
...BUT IN ORDER TO GIVE BIRTH TO THE PROPHESIED CHILD, BENIO AND I MUST AWAKEN AS THE GREAT YIN AND GREAT YANG.
BENIO HAS ALREADY FULLY AWOKEN AS THE GREAT YIN.

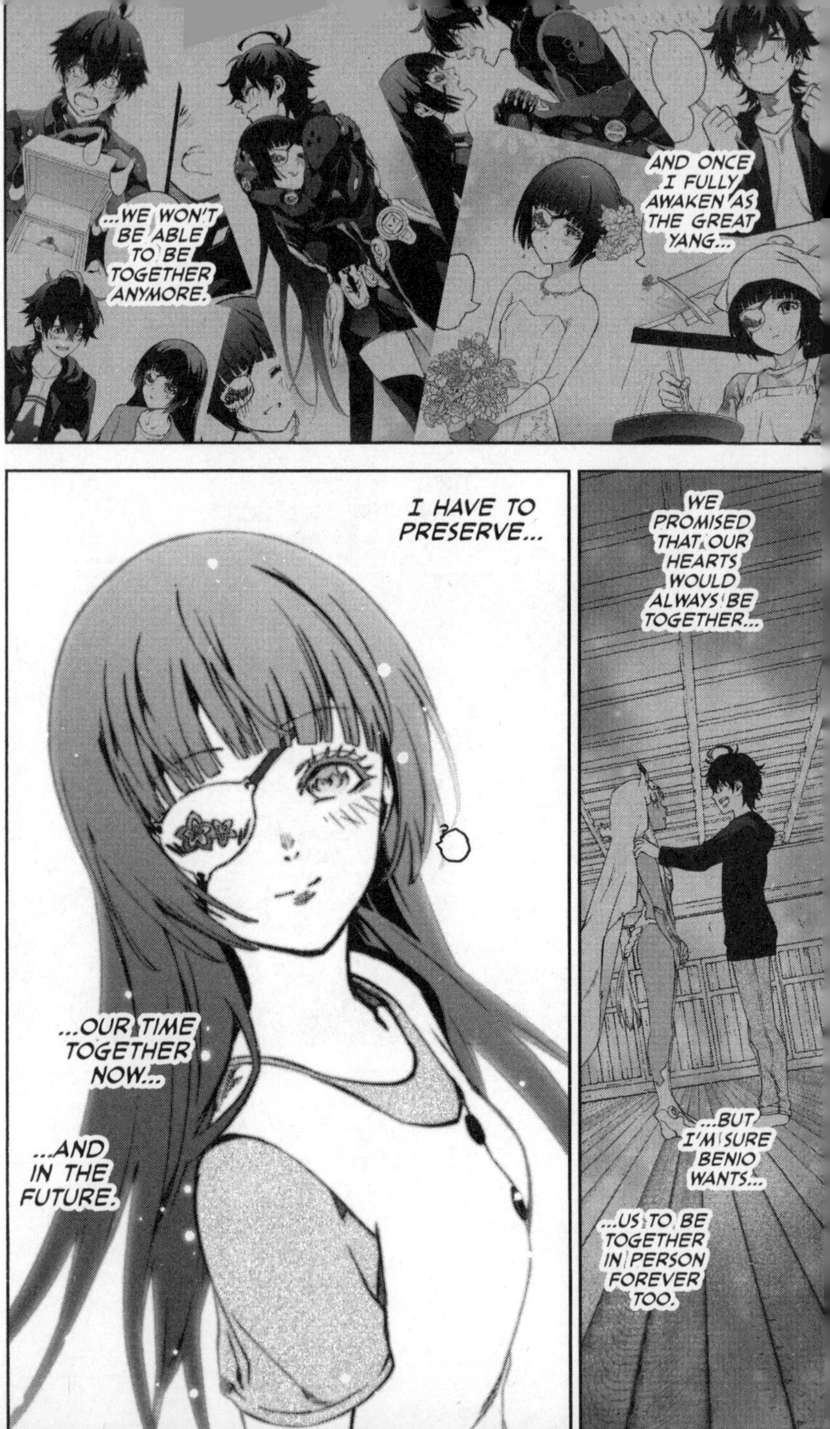
AND ONCE I FULLY AWAKEN AS THE GREAT YANG...
...WE WON'T BE ABLE TO BE TOGETHER ANYMORE.
WE PROMISED THAT OUR HEARTS WOULD ALWAYS BE TOGETHER...
...BUT I'M SURE BENIO WANTS...
...US TO BE TOGETHER IN PERSON FOREVER TOO.
I HAVE TO PRESERVE...
...OUR TIME TOGETHER NOW...
...AND IN THE FUTURE.

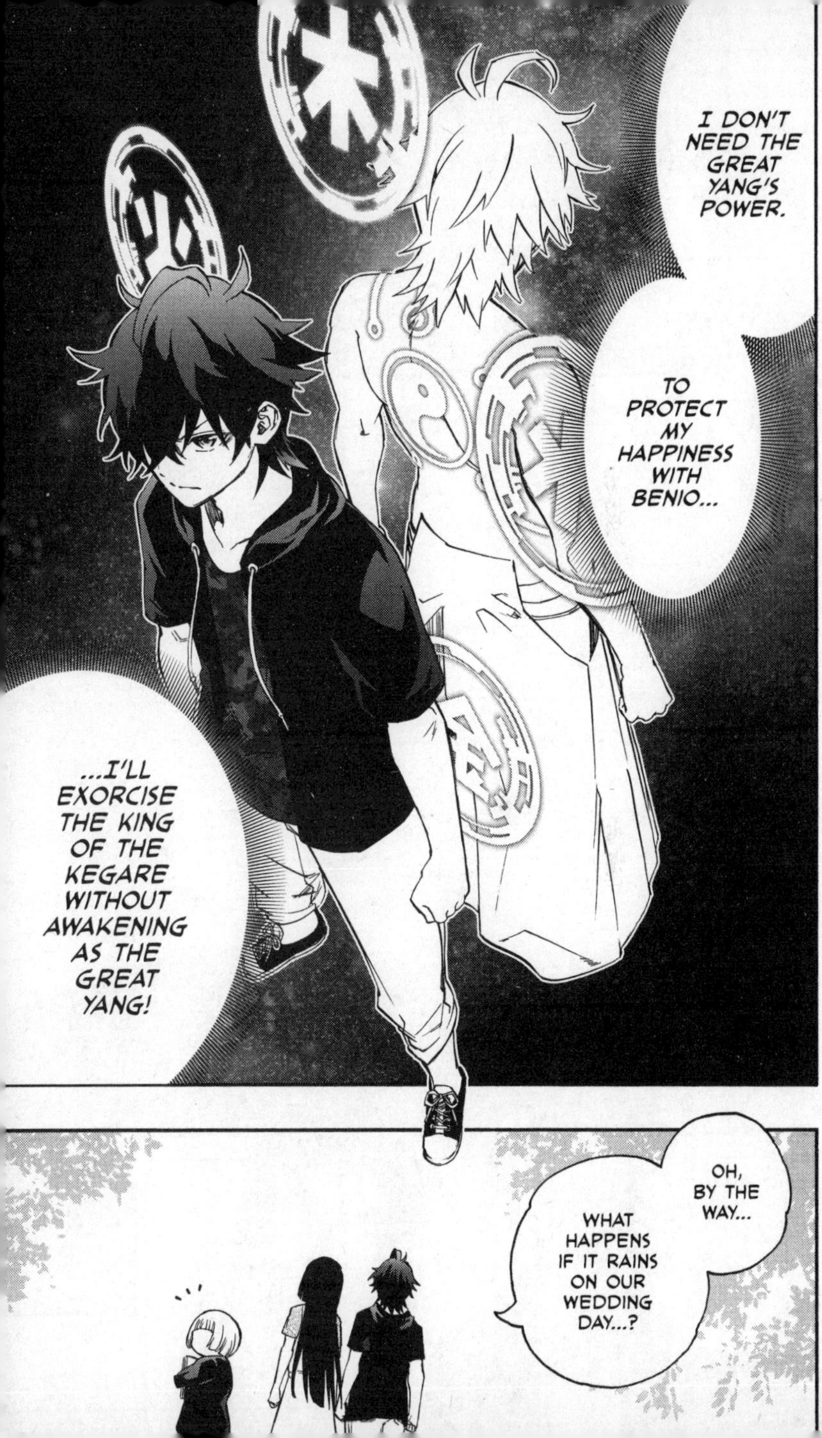
I DON'T NEED THE GREAT YANG'S POWER.
TO PROTECT MY HAPPINESS WITH BENIO...
...I'LL EXORCISE THE KING OF THE KEGARE WITHOUT AWAKENING AS THE GREAT YANG!
OH, BY THE WAY...
WHAT HAPPENS IF IT RAINS ON OUR WEDDING DAY...?

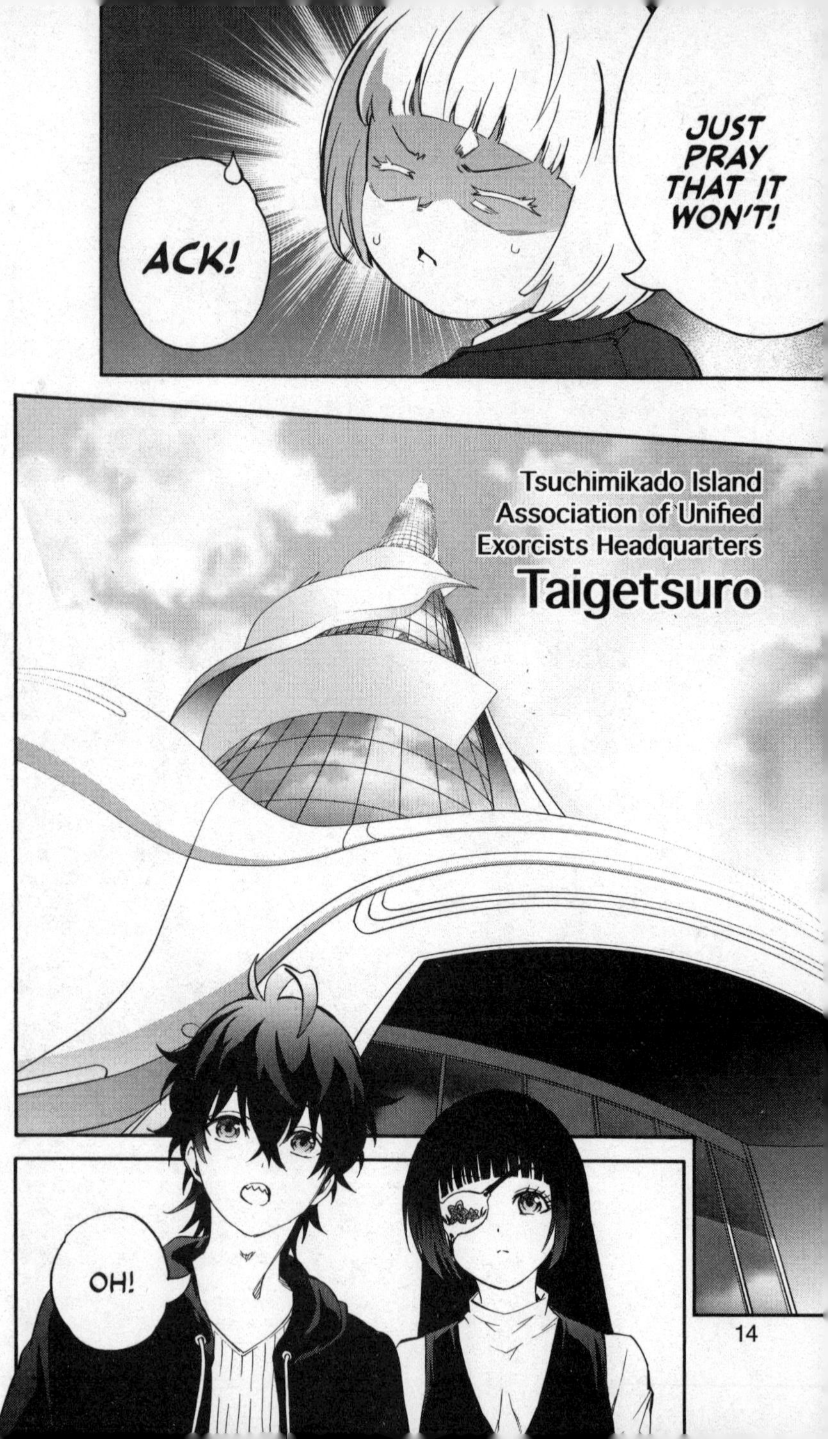
JUST PRAY THAT IT WON'T!
ACK!
Tsuchimikado Island Association of Unified Exorcists Headquarters
Taigetsuro
OH!

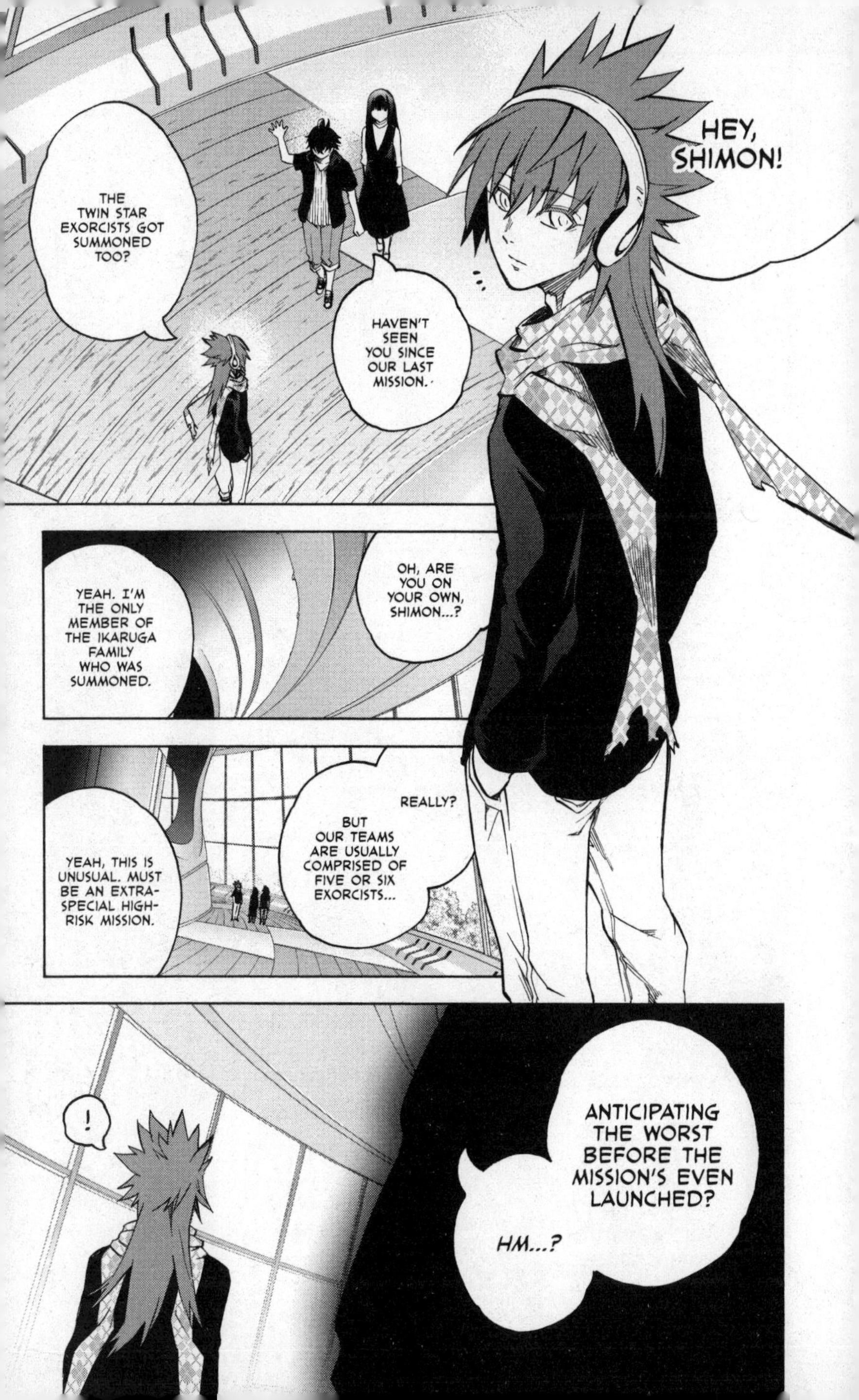

HEY, SHIMON!
...
HAVEN'T SEEN YOU SINCE OUR LAST MISSION.
THE TWIN STAR EXORCISTS GOT SUMMONED TOO?
OH, ARE YOU ON YOUR OWN, SHIMON...?
YEAH. I'M THE ONLY MEMBER OF THE IKARUGA FAMILY WHO WAS SUMMONED.
REALLY?
BUT OUR TEAMS ARE USUALLY COMPRISED OF FIVE OR SIX EXORCISTS...
YEAH, THIS IS UNUSUAL. MUST BE AN EXTRA-SPECIAL HIGH-RISK MISSION.
ANTICIPATING THE WORST BEFORE THE MISSION'S EVEN LAUNCHED?
HM...?
!

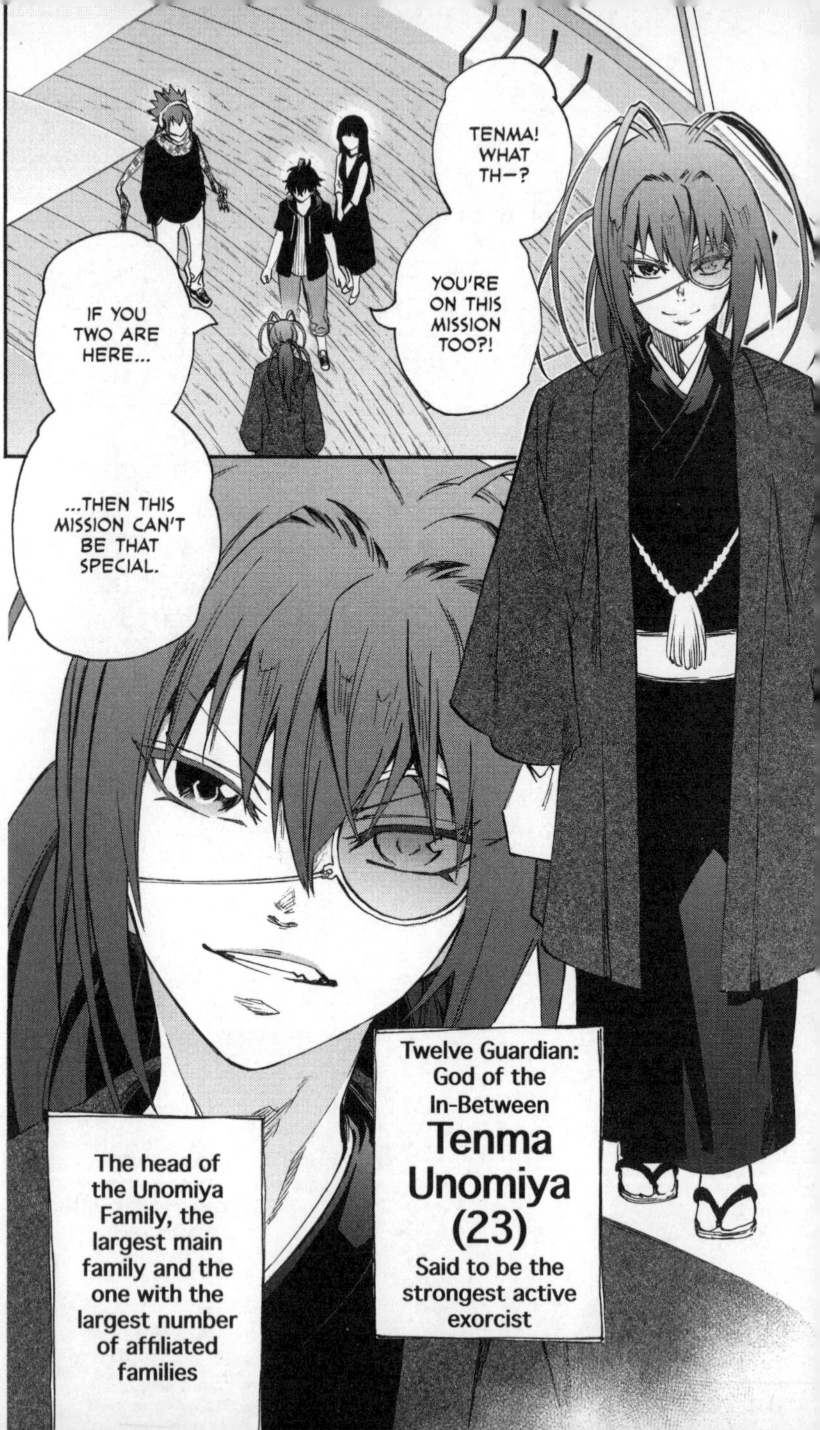
TENMA! WHAT TH—?
YOU'RE ON THIS MISSION TOO?!
IF YOU TWO ARE HERE...
...THEN THIS MISSION CAN'T BE THAT SPECIAL.
Twelve Guardian: God of the In-Between
Tenma Unomiya (23)
Said to be the strongest active exorcist
The head of the Unomiya Family, the largest main family and the one with the largest number of affiliated families

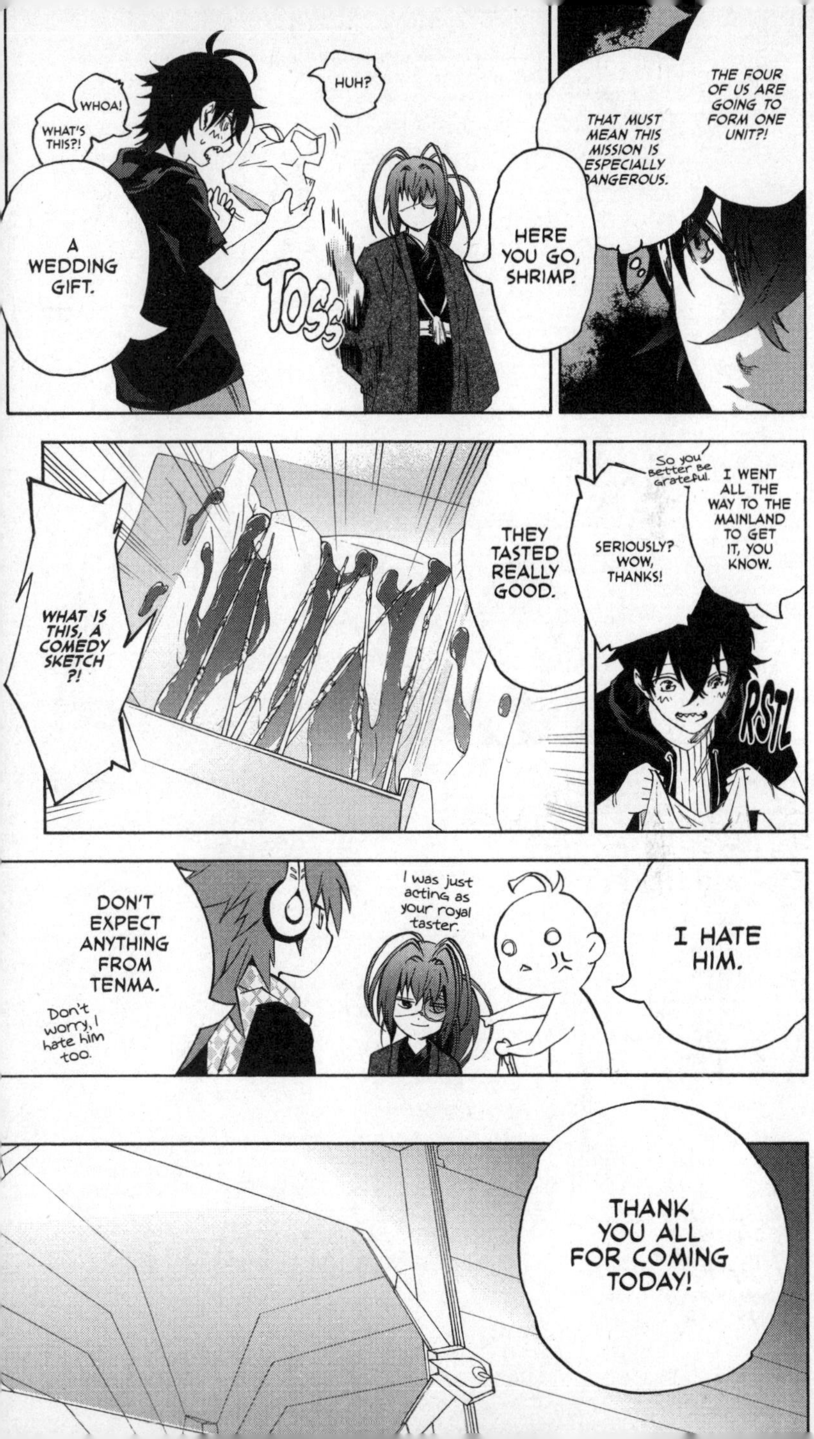
THE FOUR OF US ARE GOING TO FORM ONE UNIT?!
THAT MUST MEAN THIS MISSION IS ESPECIALLY DANGEROUS.
HERE YOU GO, SHRIMP.
HUH?
TOSS
WHOA! WHAT'S THIS?!
A WEDDING GIFT.
I WENT ALL THE WAY TO THE MAINLAND TO GET IT, YOU KNOW.
So you better be grateful.
SERIOUSLY? WOW, THANKS!
RSTL
THEY TASTED REALLY GOOD.
WHAT IS THIS, A COMEDY SKETCH?!
I HATE HIM.
I was just acting as your royal taster.
DON'T EXPECT ANYTHING FROM TENMA.
Don't worry, I hate him too.
THANK YOU ALL FOR COMING TODAY!

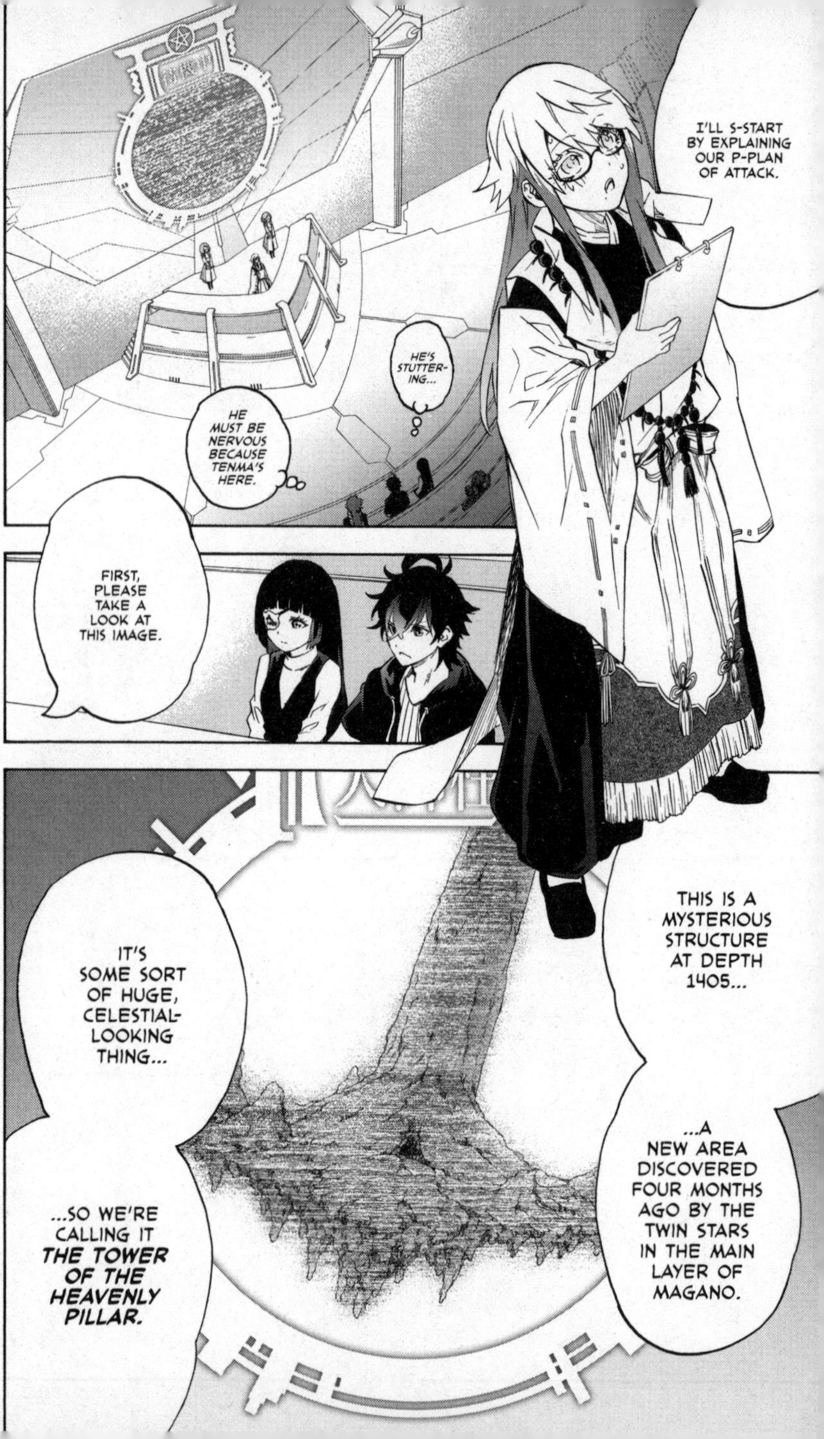
I'LL S-START BY EXPLAINING OUR P-PLAN OF ATTACK.
HE'S STUTTERING...
HE MUST BE NERVOUS BECAUSE TENMA'S HERE.
FIRST, PLEASE TAKE A LOOK AT THIS IMAGE.
THIS IS A MYSTERIOUS STRUCTURE AT DEPTH 1405...
...A NEW AREA DISCOVERED FOUR MONTHS AGO BY THE TWIN STARS IN THE MAIN LAYER OF MAGANO.
IT'S SOME SORT OF HUGE, CELESTIAL-LOOKING THING...
...SO WE'RE CALLING IT *THE TOWER OF THE HEAVENLY PILLAR.*

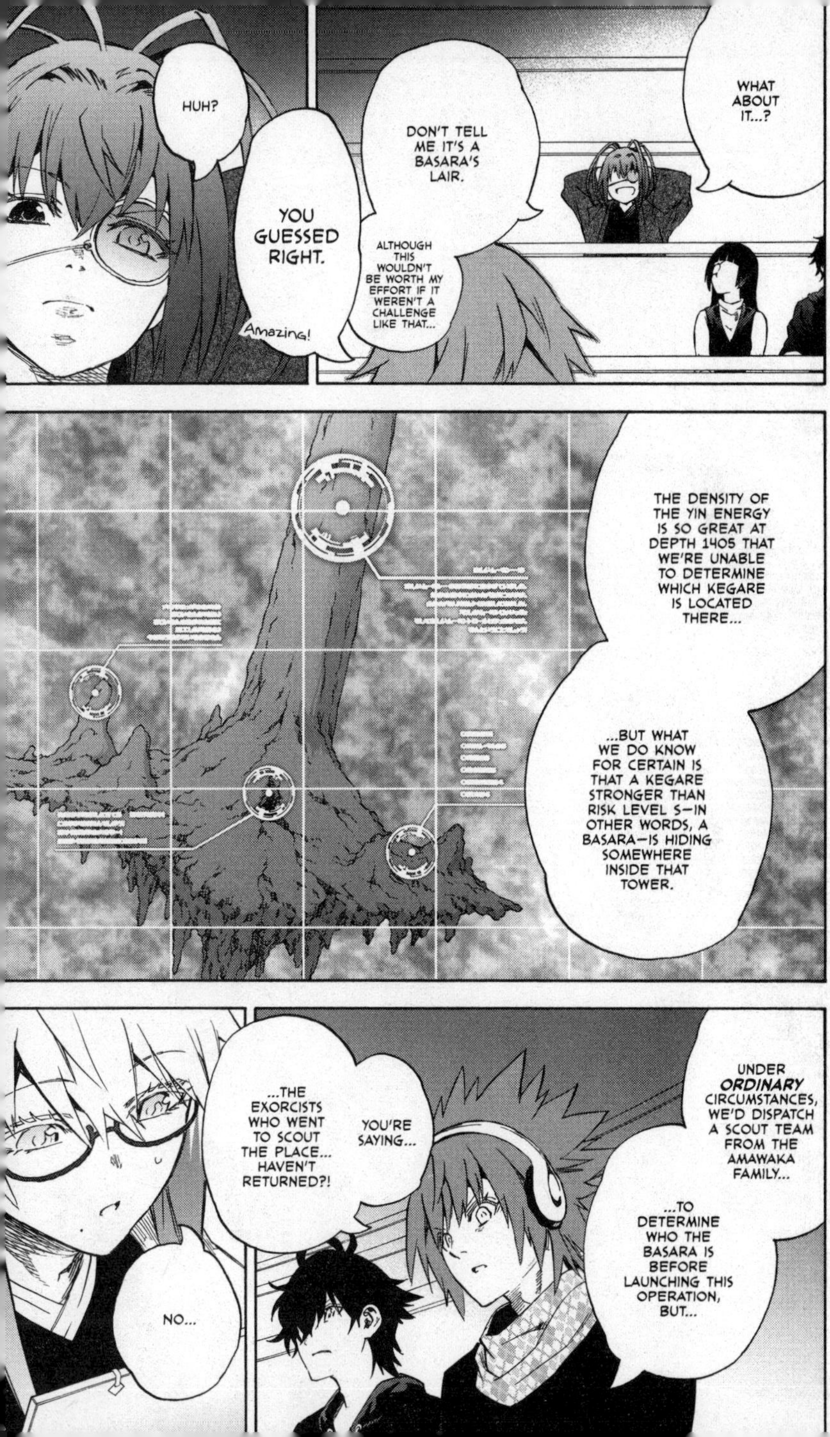
WHAT ABOUT IT...?
DON'T TELL ME IT'S A BASARA'S LAIR.
ALTHOUGH THIS WOULDN'T BE WORTH MY EFFORT IF IT WEREN'T A CHALLENGE LIKE THAT...
HUH?
YOU GUESSED RIGHT.
Amazing!
THE DENSITY OF THE YIN ENERGY IS SO GREAT AT DEPTH 1405 THAT WE'RE UNABLE TO DETERMINE WHICH KEGARE IS LOCATED THERE...
...BUT WHAT WE DO KNOW FOR CERTAIN IS THAT A KEGARE STRONGER THAN RISK LEVEL S—IN OTHER WORDS, A BASARA—IS HIDING SOMEWHERE INSIDE THAT TOWER.
UNDER ***ORDINARY*** CIRCUMSTANCES, WE'D DISPATCH A SCOUT TEAM FROM THE AMAWAKA FAMILY...
...TO DETERMINE WHO THE BASARA IS BEFORE LAUNCHING THIS OPERATION, BUT...
YOU'RE SAYING...
...THE EXORCISTS WHO WENT TO SCOUT THE PLACE... HAVEN'T RETURNED?!
NO...

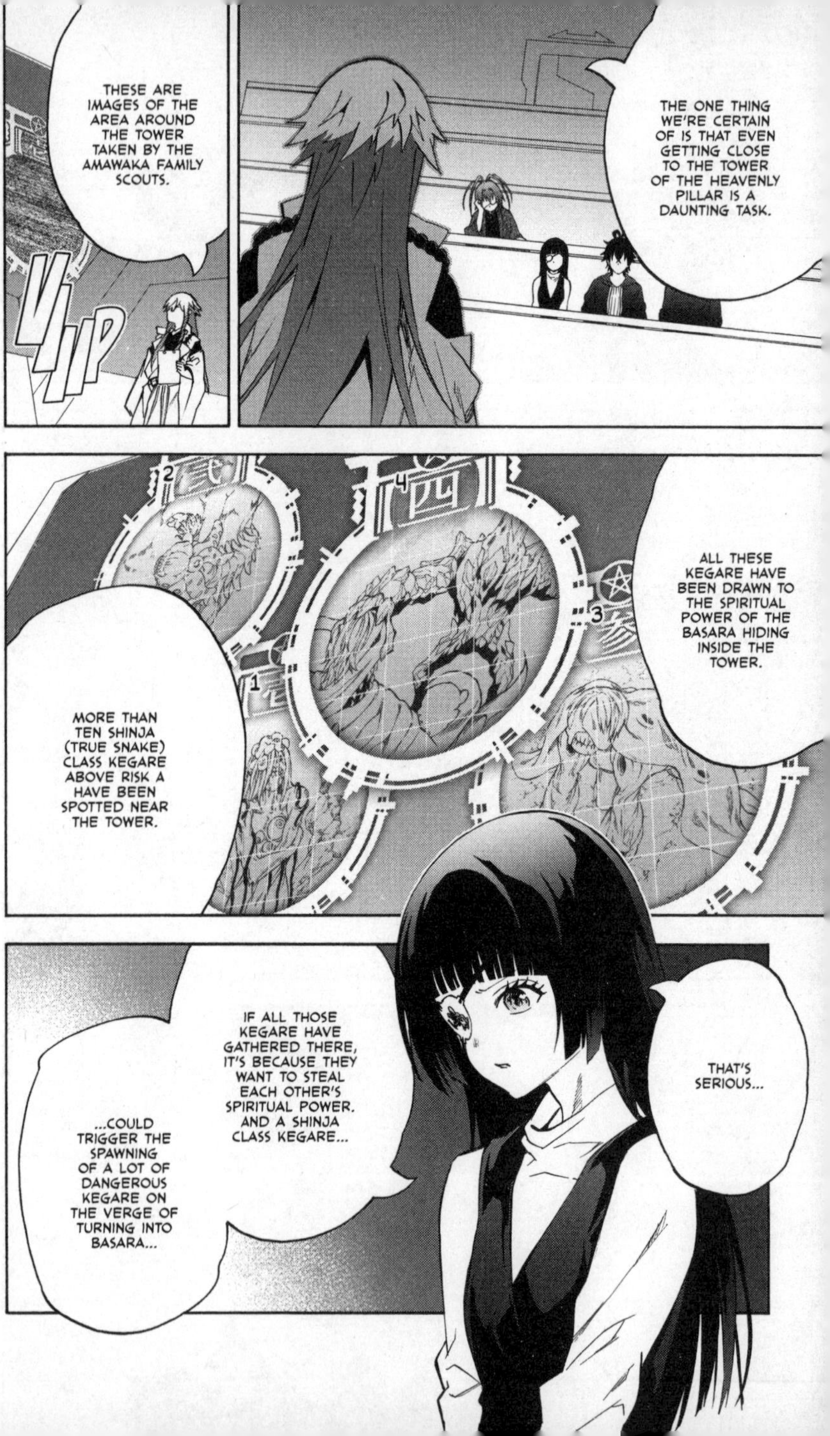
THE ONE THING WE'RE CERTAIN OF IS THAT EVEN GETTING CLOSE TO THE TOWER OF THE HEAVENLY PILLAR IS A DAUNTING TASK.
THESE ARE IMAGES OF THE AREA AROUND THE TOWER TAKEN BY THE AMAWAKA FAMILY SCOUTS.
VIIP
ALL THESE KEGARE HAVE BEEN DRAWN TO THE SPIRITUAL POWER OF THE BASARA HIDING INSIDE THE TOWER.
MORE THAN TEN SHINJA (TRUE SNAKE) CLASS KEGARE ABOVE RISK A HAVE BEEN SPOTTED NEAR THE TOWER.
THAT'S SERIOUS...
IF ALL THOSE KEGARE HAVE GATHERED THERE, IT'S BECAUSE THEY WANT TO STEAL EACH OTHER'S SPIRITUAL POWER. AND A SHINJA CLASS KEGARE...
...COULD TRIGGER THE SPAWNING OF A LOT OF DANGEROUS KEGARE ON THE VERGE OF TURNING INTO BASARA...

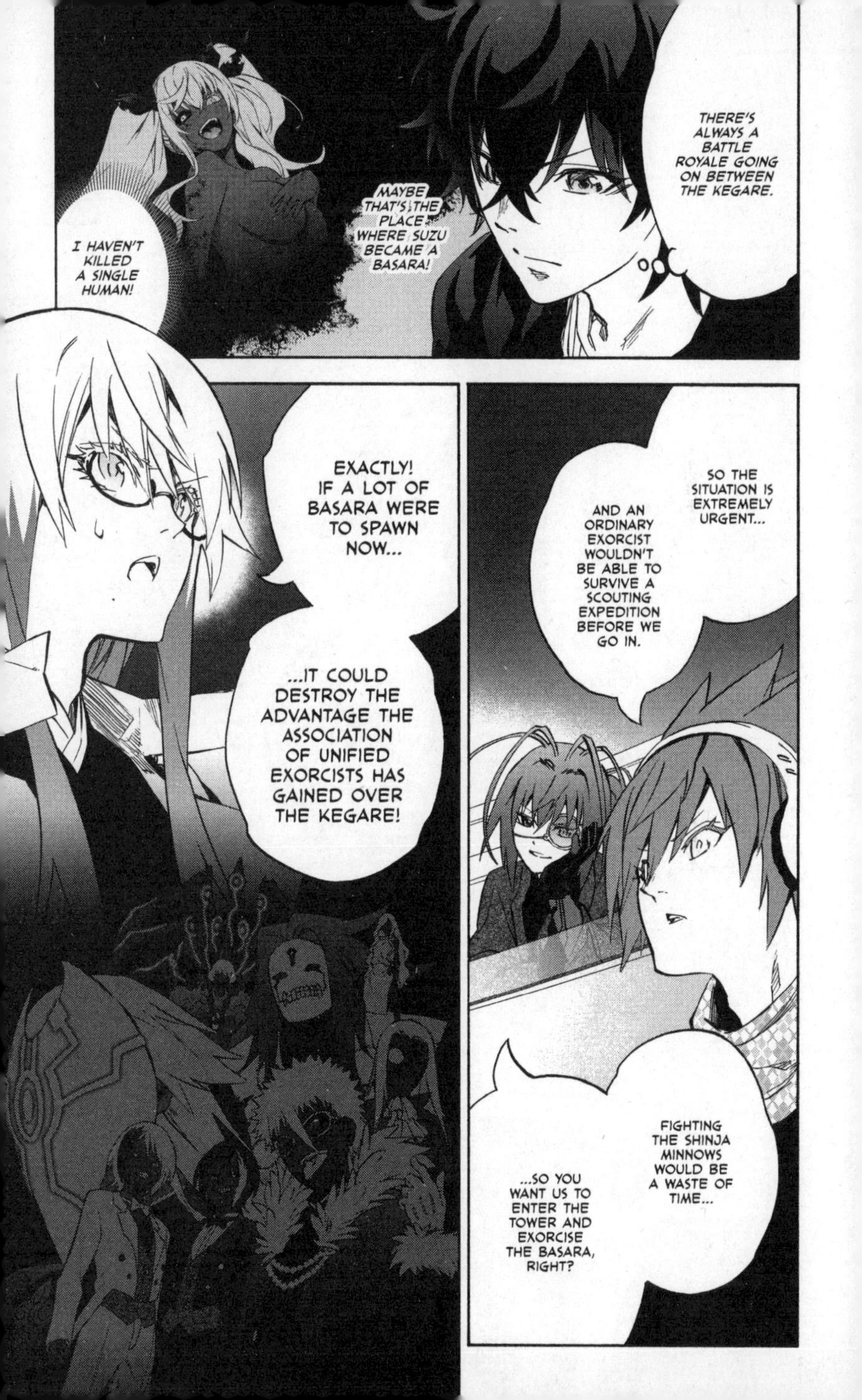
THERE'S ALWAYS A BATTLE ROYALE GOING ON BETWEEN THE KEGARE.
MAYBE THAT'S THE PLACE WHERE SUZU BECAME A BASARA!
I HAVEN'T KILLED A SINGLE HUMAN!
SO THE SITUATION IS EXTREMELY URGENT...
AND AN ORDINARY EXORCIST WOULDN'T BE ABLE TO SURVIVE A SCOUTING EXPEDITION BEFORE WE GO IN.
FIGHTING THE SHINJA MINNOWS WOULD BE A WASTE OF TIME...
...SO YOU WANT US TO ENTER THE TOWER AND EXORCISE THE BASARA, RIGHT?
EXACTLY! IF A LOT OF BASARA WERE TO SPAWN NOW...
...IT COULD DESTROY THE ADVANTAGE THE ASSOCIATION OF UNIFIED EXORCISTS HAS GAINED OVER THE KEGARE!

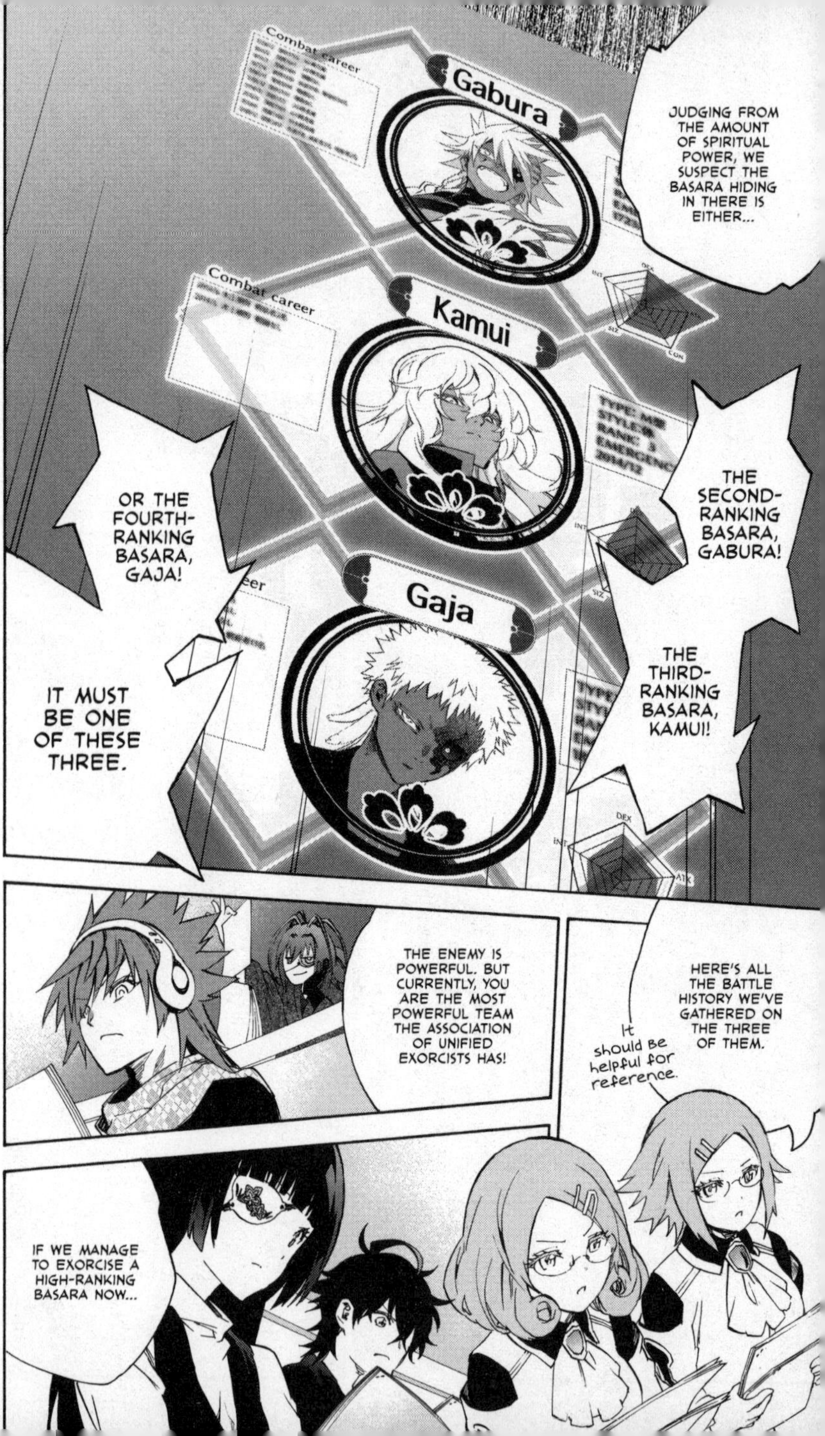
JUDGING FROM THE AMOUNT OF SPIRITUAL POWER, WE SUSPECT THE BASARA HIDING IN THERE IS EITHER...
Combat career
Gabura
Combat career
Kamui
Gaja
THE SECOND-RANKING BASARA, GABURA!
THE THIRD-RANKING BASARA, KAMUI!
OR THE FOURTH-RANKING BASARA, GAJA!
IT MUST BE ONE OF THESE THREE.
HERE'S ALL THE BATTLE HISTORY WE'VE GATHERED ON THE THREE OF THEM.
It should be helpful for reference.
THE ENEMY IS POWERFUL. BUT CURRENTLY, YOU ARE THE MOST POWERFUL TEAM THE ASSOCIATION OF UNIFIED EXORCISTS HAS!
IF WE MANAGE TO EXORCISE A HIGH-RANKING BASARA NOW...

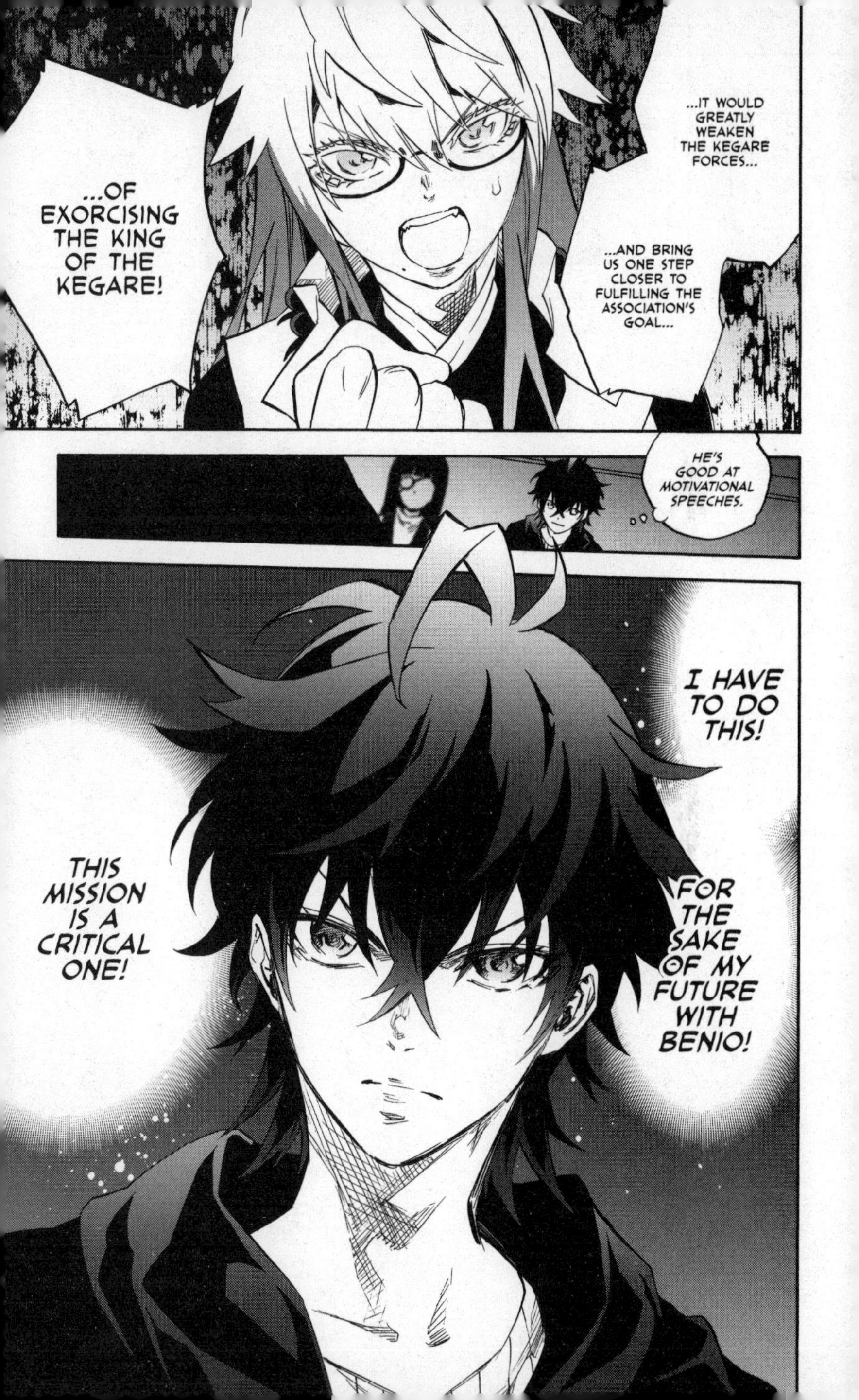
...OF EXORCISING THE KING OF THE KEGARE!
...IT WOULD GREATLY WEAKEN THE KEGARE FORCES...
...AND BRING US ONE STEP CLOSER TO FULFILLING THE ASSOCIATION'S GOAL...
HE'S GOOD AT MOTIVATIONAL SPEECHES.
I HAVE TO DO THIS!
THIS MISSION IS A CRITICAL ONE!
FOR THE SAKE OF MY FUTURE WITH BENIO!

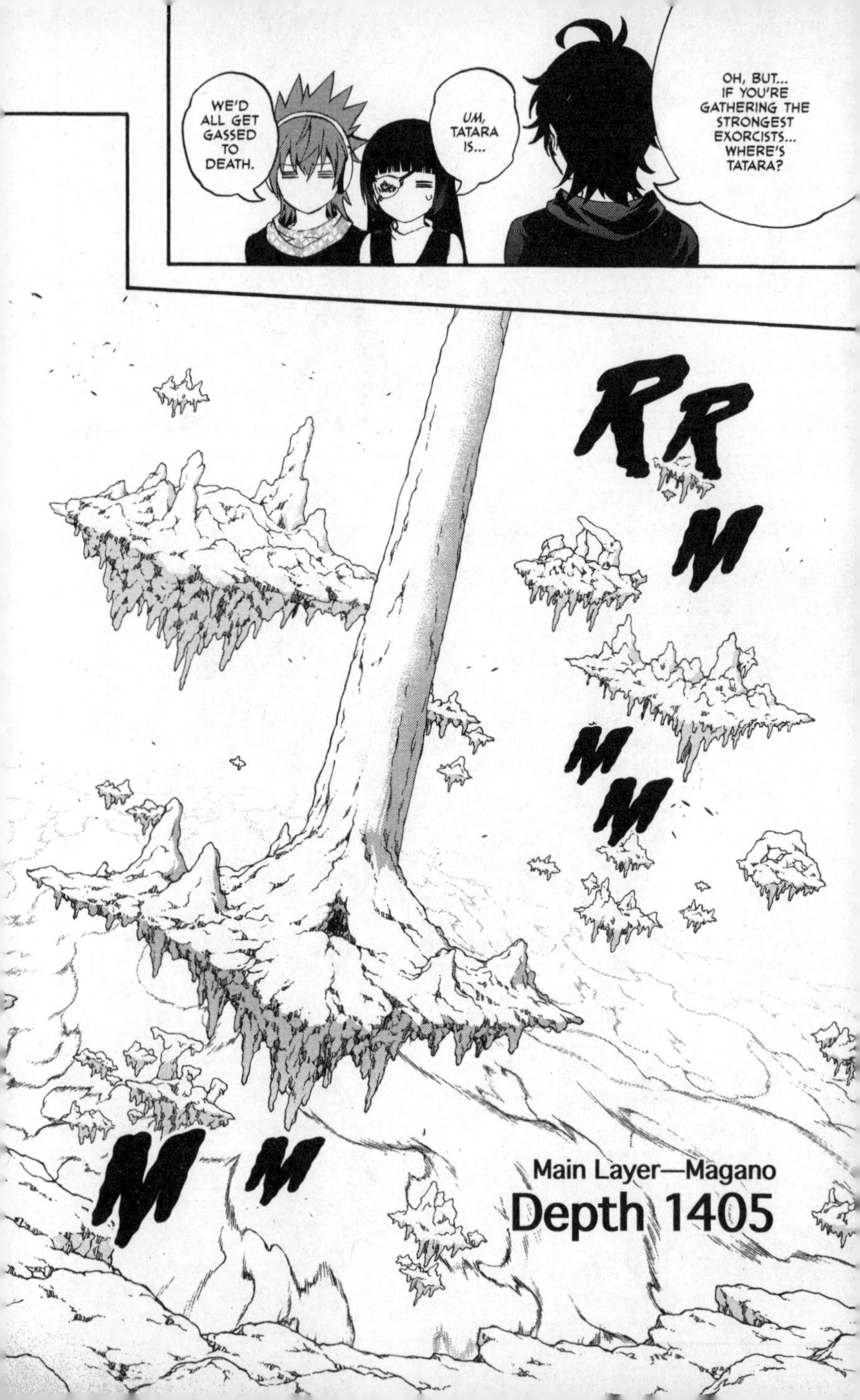
OH, BUT... IF YOU'RE GATHERING THE STRONGEST EXORCISTS... WHERE'S TATARA?
UM, TATARA IS...
WE'D ALL GET GASSED TO DEATH.
RRMMMM
MM
Main Layer—Magano
Depth 1405

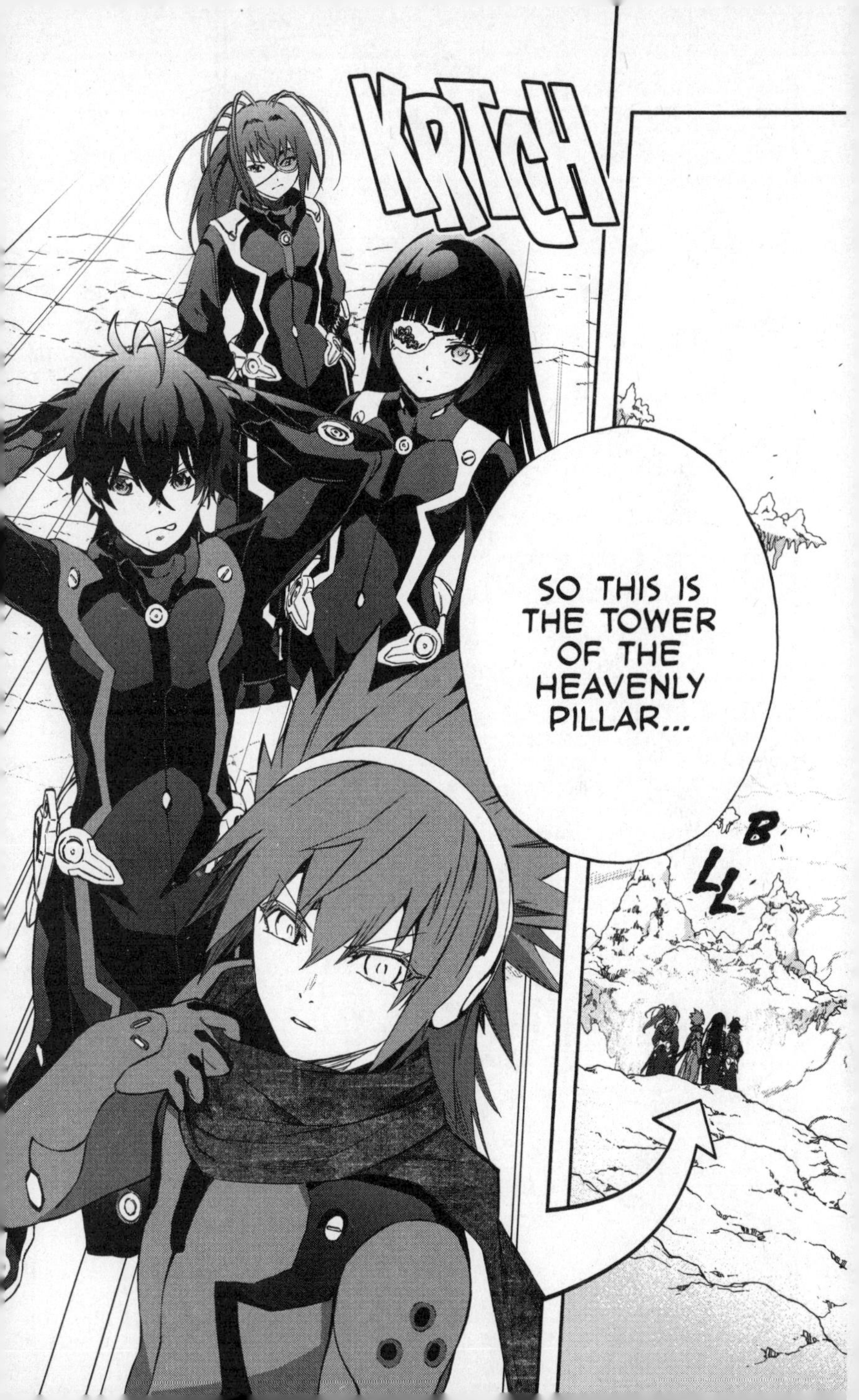
KRTCH
SO THIS IS THE TOWER OF THE HEAVENLY PILLAR...
BLL

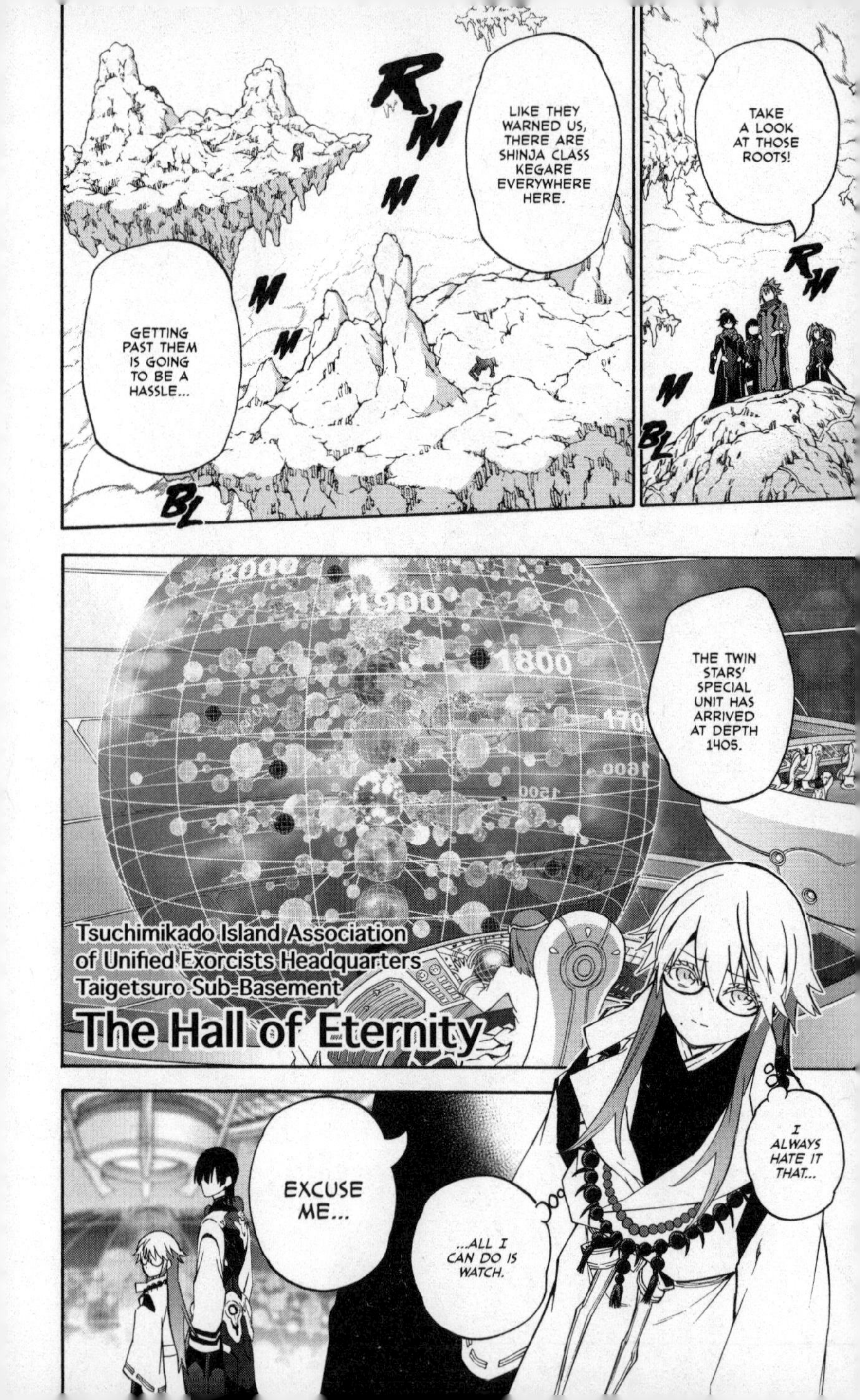
TAKE A LOOK AT THOSE ROOTS!
RMMBL
LIKE THEY WARNED US, THERE ARE SHINJA CLASS KEGARE EVERYWHERE HERE.
GETTING PAST THEM IS GOING TO BE A HASSLE...
RMMMMMBL
2000
1900
1800
Tsuchimikado Island Association of Unified Exorcists Headquarters Taigetsuro Sub-Basement
The Hall of Eternity
THE TWIN STARS' SPECIAL UNIT HAS ARRIVED AT DEPTH 1405.
I ALWAYS HATE IT THAT...
...ALL I CAN DO IS WATCH.
EXCUSE ME...

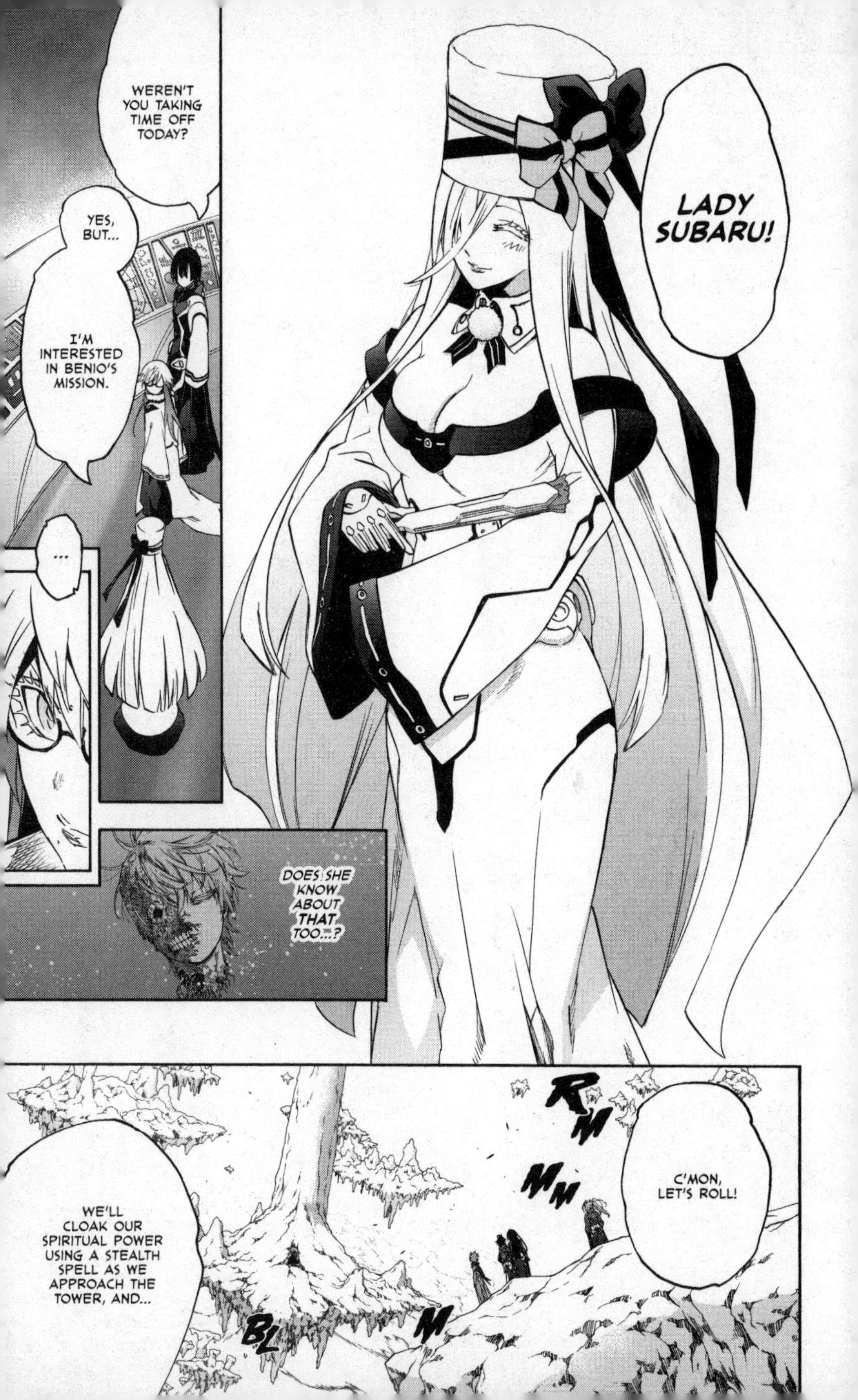
LADY SUBARU!
WEREN'T YOU TAKING TIME OFF TODAY?
YES, BUT...
I'M INTERESTED IN BENIO'S MISSION.
...
DOES SHE KNOW ABOUT THAT TOO...?
RMMM
C'MON, LET'S ROLL!
WE'LL CLOAK OUR SPIRITUAL POWER USING A STEALTH SPELL AS WE APPROACH THE TOWER, AND...
BLM

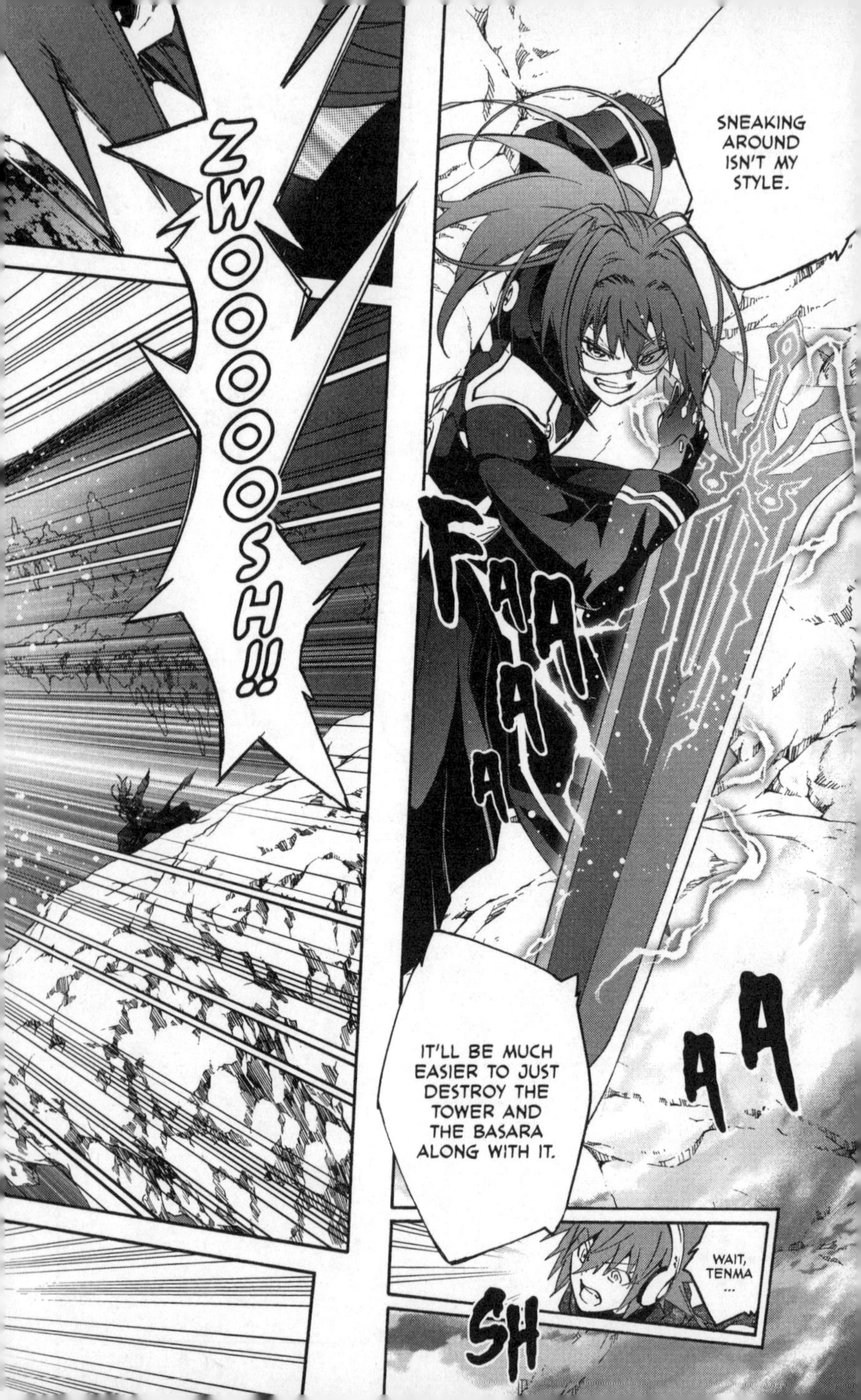
SNEAKING AROUND ISN'T MY STYLE.
FAAAAA
IT'LL BE MUCH EASIER TO JUST DESTROY THE TOWER AND THE BASARA ALONG WITH IT.
AA
WAIT, TENMA ...
SH
ZWOOOOOSH!!

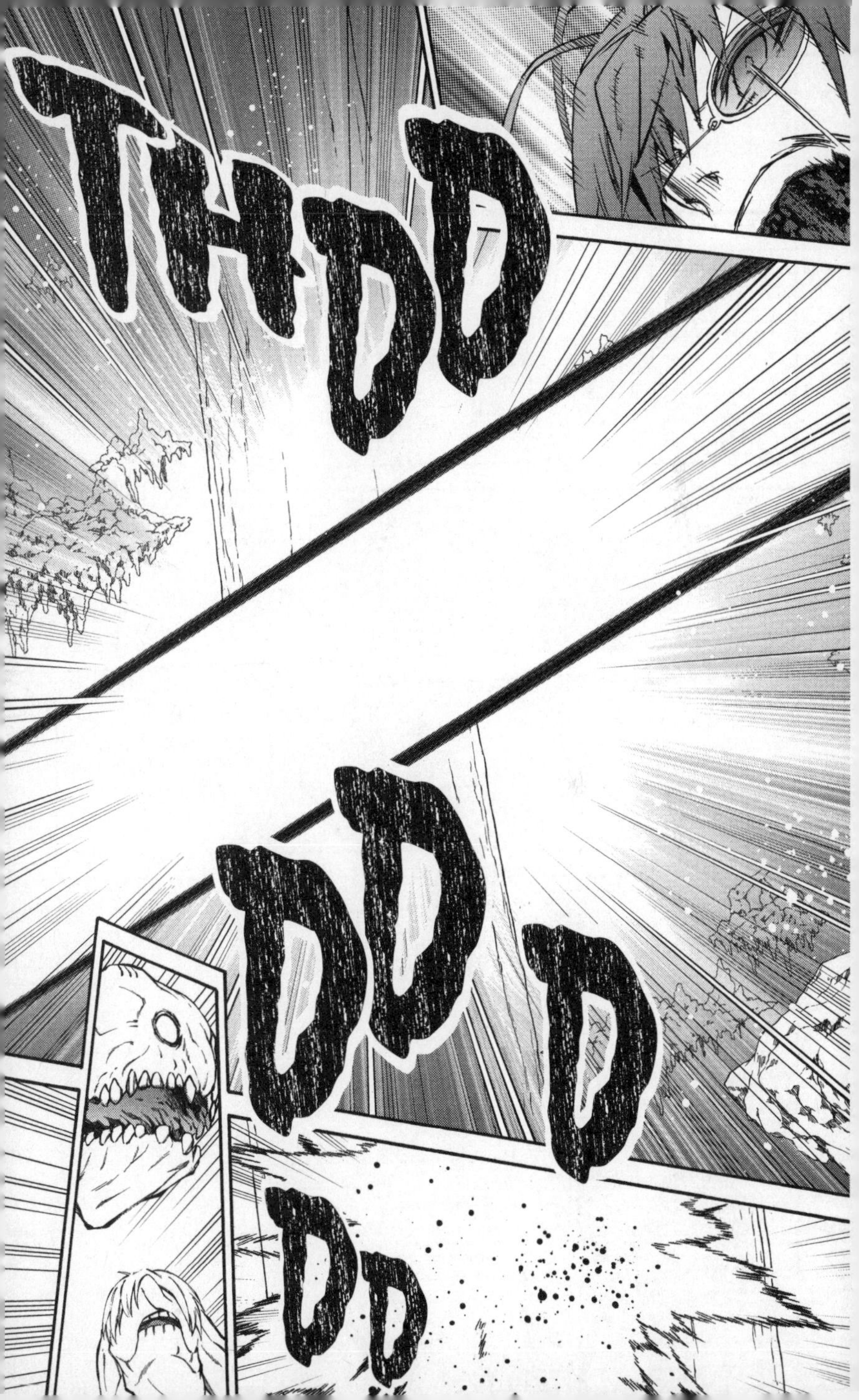

THDD
DDD
DDD

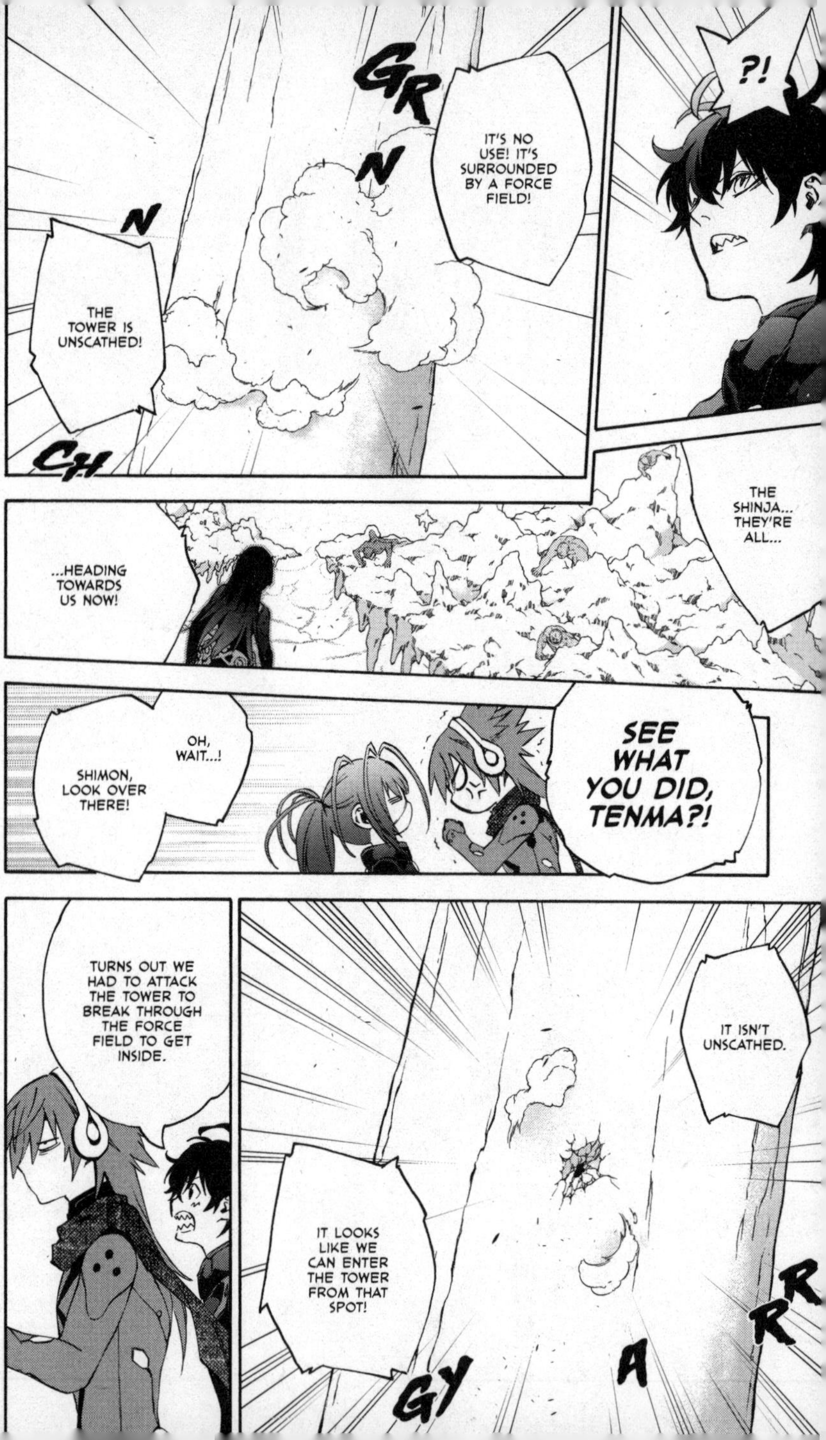
?!
GR
N
N
IT'S NO USE! IT'S SURROUNDED BY A FORCE FIELD!
THE TOWER IS UNSCATHED!
CH
THE SHINJA... THEY'RE ALL...
...HEADING TOWARDS US NOW!
SEE WHAT YOU DID, TENMA?!
OH, WAIT...!
SHIMON, LOOK OVER THERE!
IT ISN'T UNSCATHED.
RR
A
GY
IT LOOKS LIKE WE CAN ENTER THE TOWER FROM THAT SPOT!
TURNS OUT WE HAD TO ATTACK THE TOWER TO BREAK THROUGH THE FORCE FIELD TO GET INSIDE.

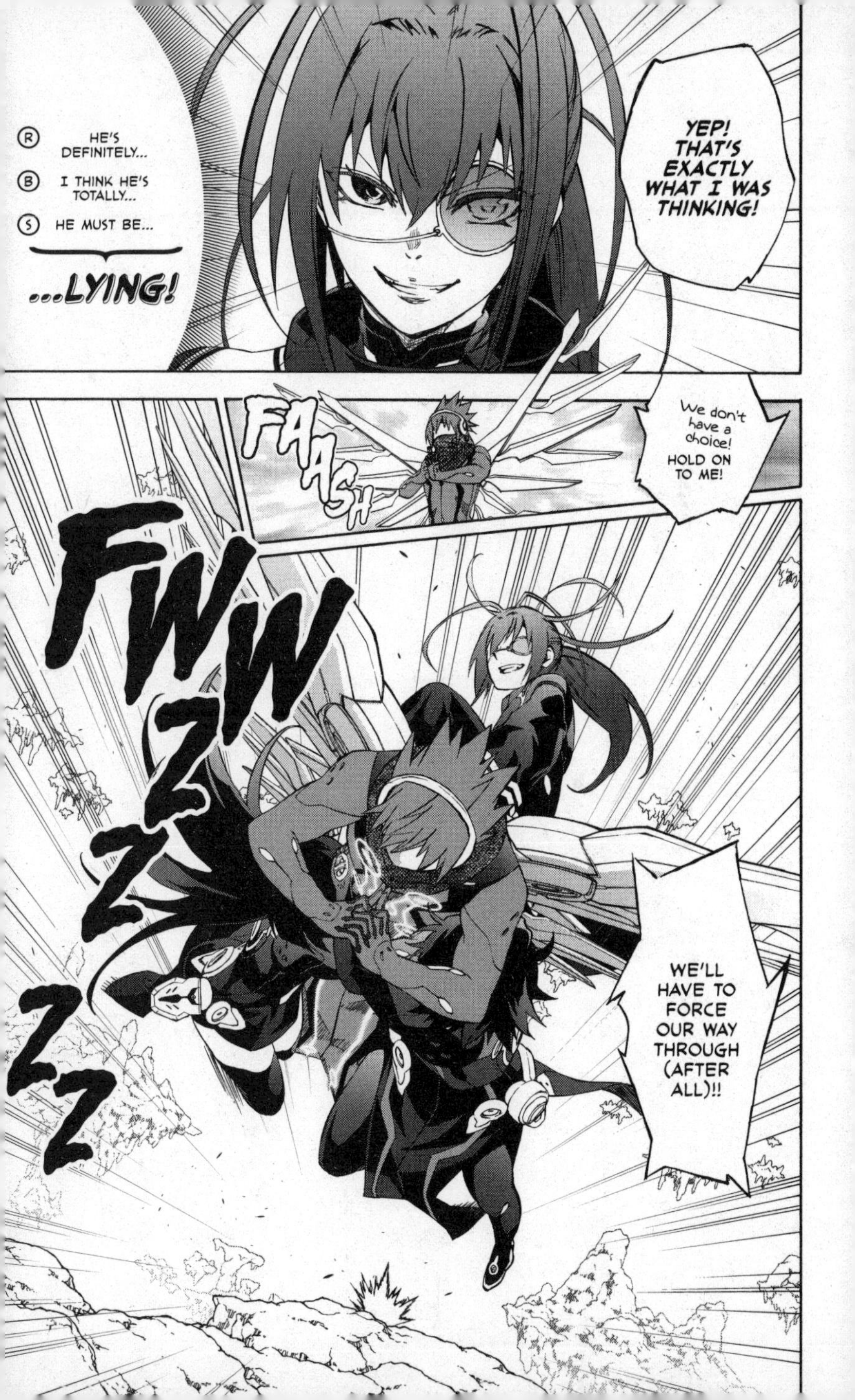
YEP! THAT'S EXACTLY WHAT I WAS THINKING!
Ⓡ HE'S DEFINITELY...
Ⓑ I THINK HE'S TOTALLY...
Ⓢ HE MUST BE...
...LYING!
We don't have a choice! HOLD ON TO ME!
FAAASH
WE'LL HAVE TO FORCE OUR WAY THROUGH (AFTER ALL)!!
FWWZZZZ

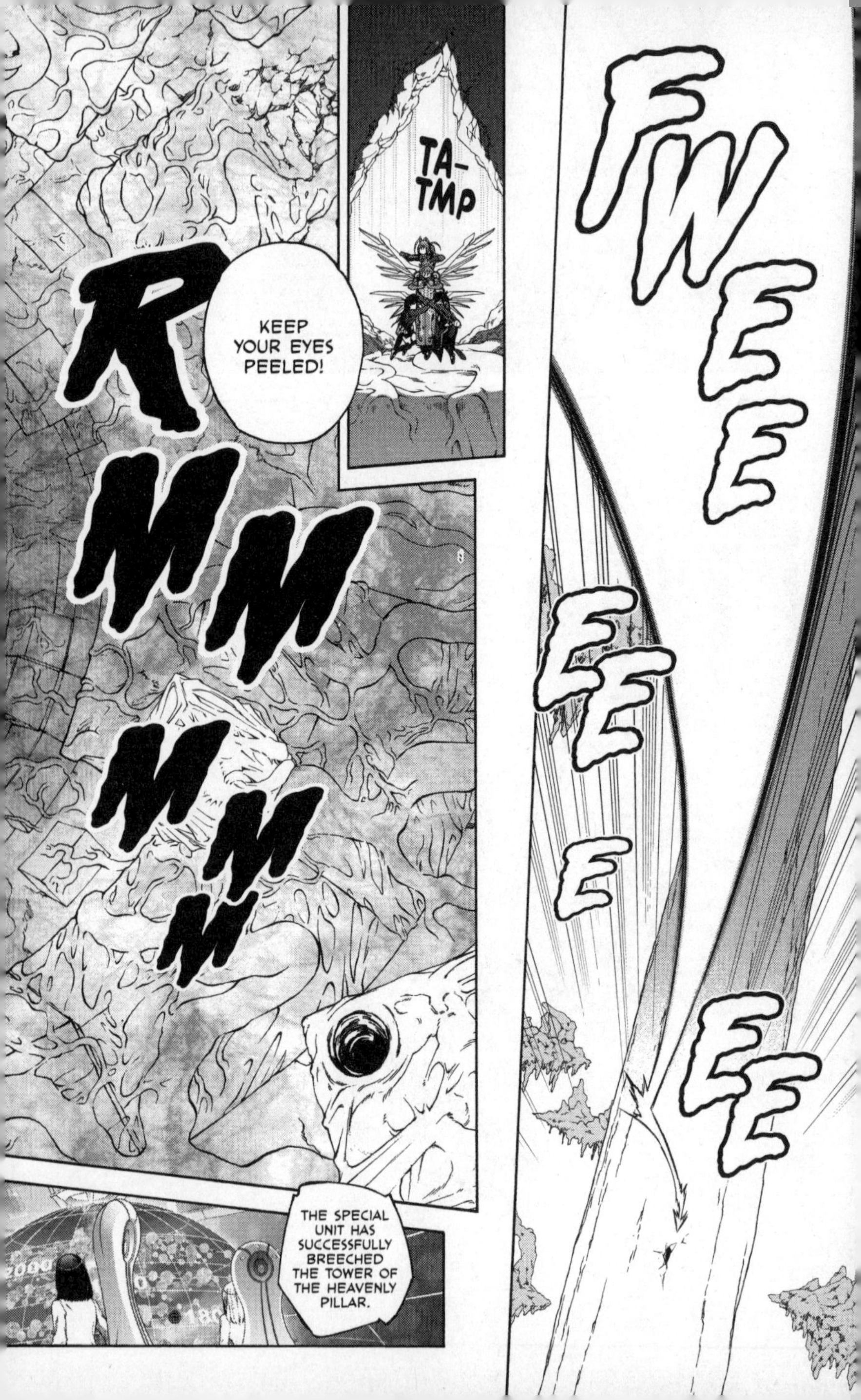
FWEEEEEEEEE
TA-TMP
KEEP YOUR EYES PEELED!
RMMMMMM
THE SPECIAL UNIT HAS SUCCESSFULLY BREECHED THE TOWER OF THE HEAVENLY PILLAR.

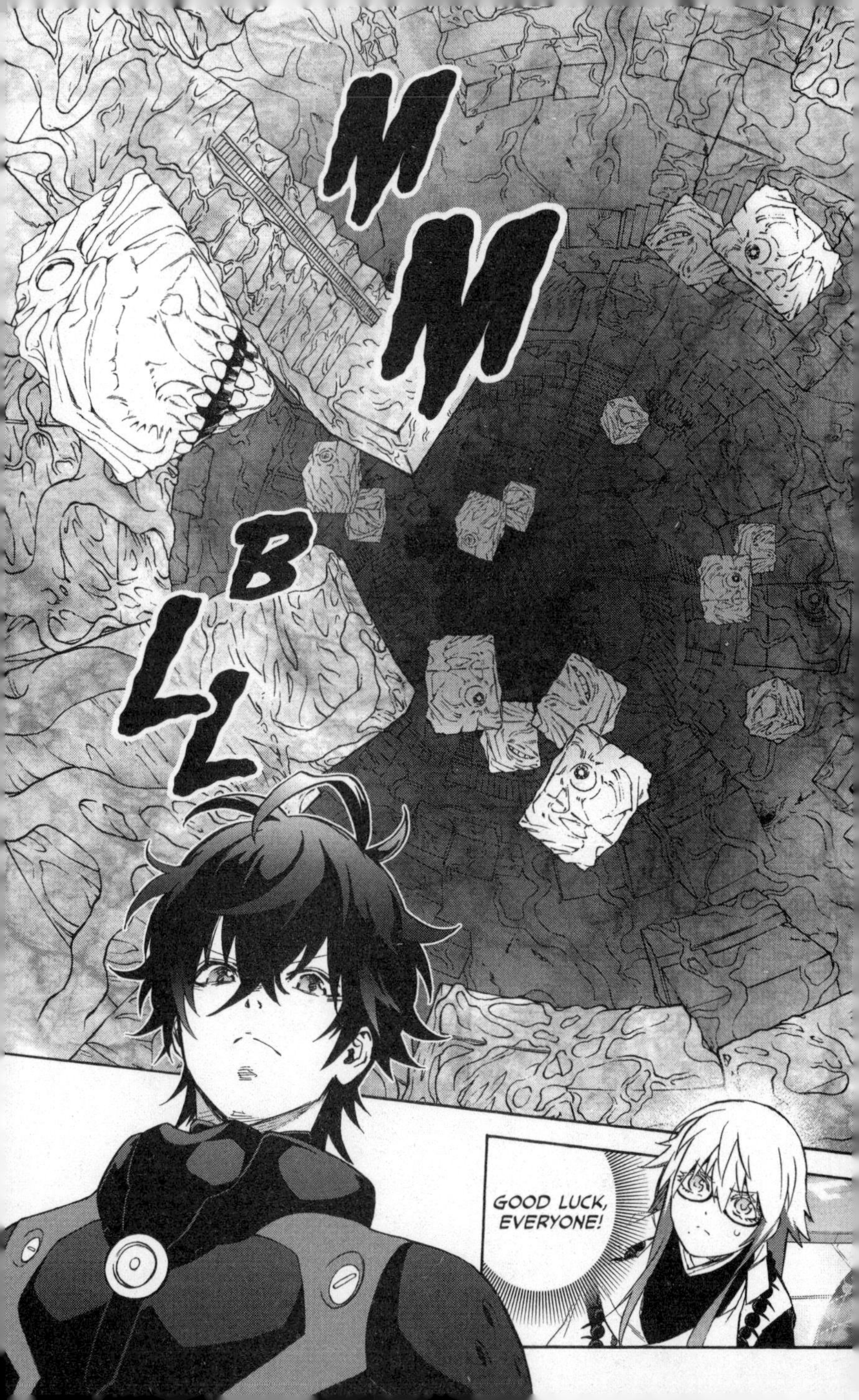
MMBLL
GOOD LUCK, EVERYONE!

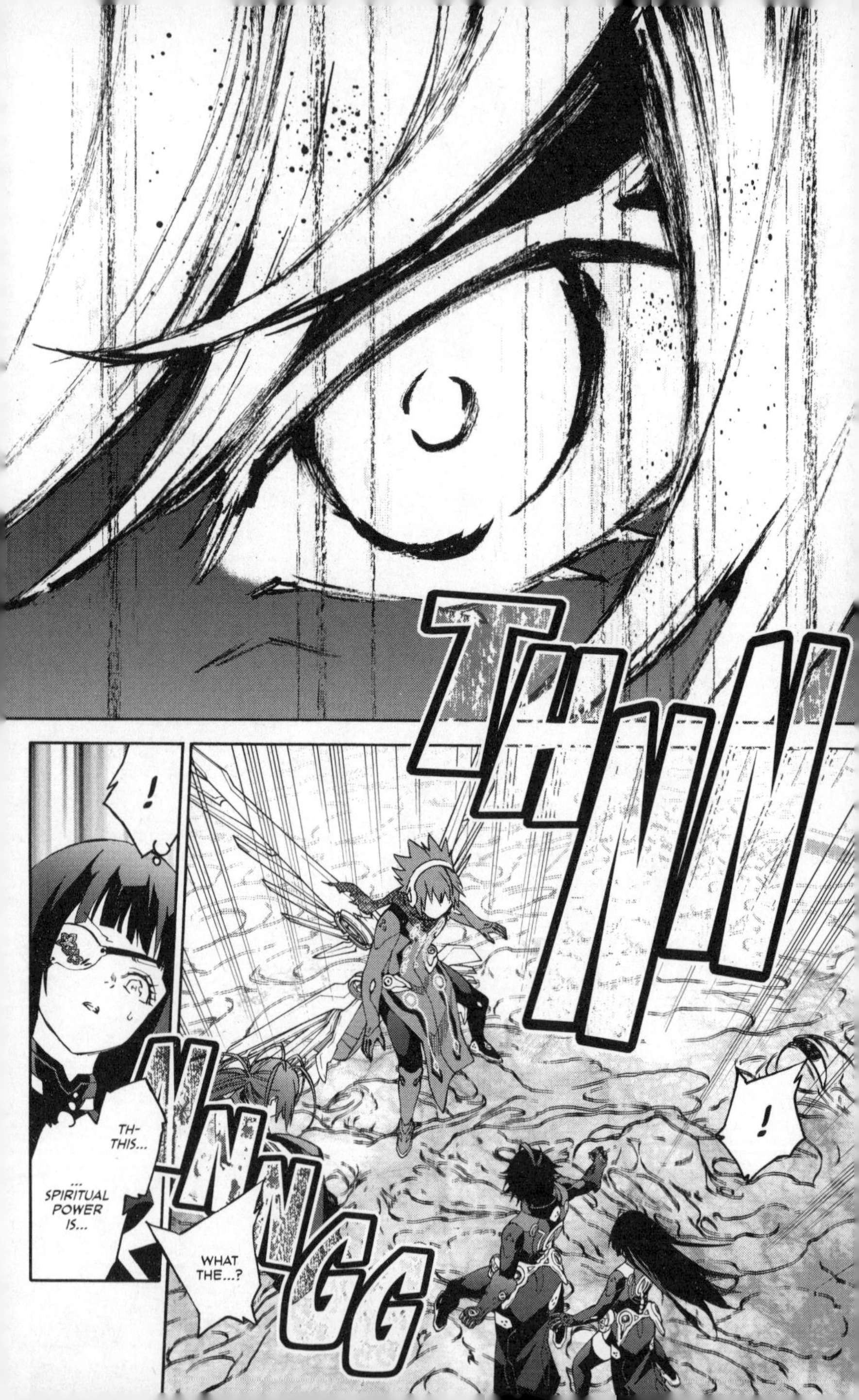
THNNNNNGG
!
WHAT THE...?
!
TH- THIS...
... SPIRITUAL POWER IS...

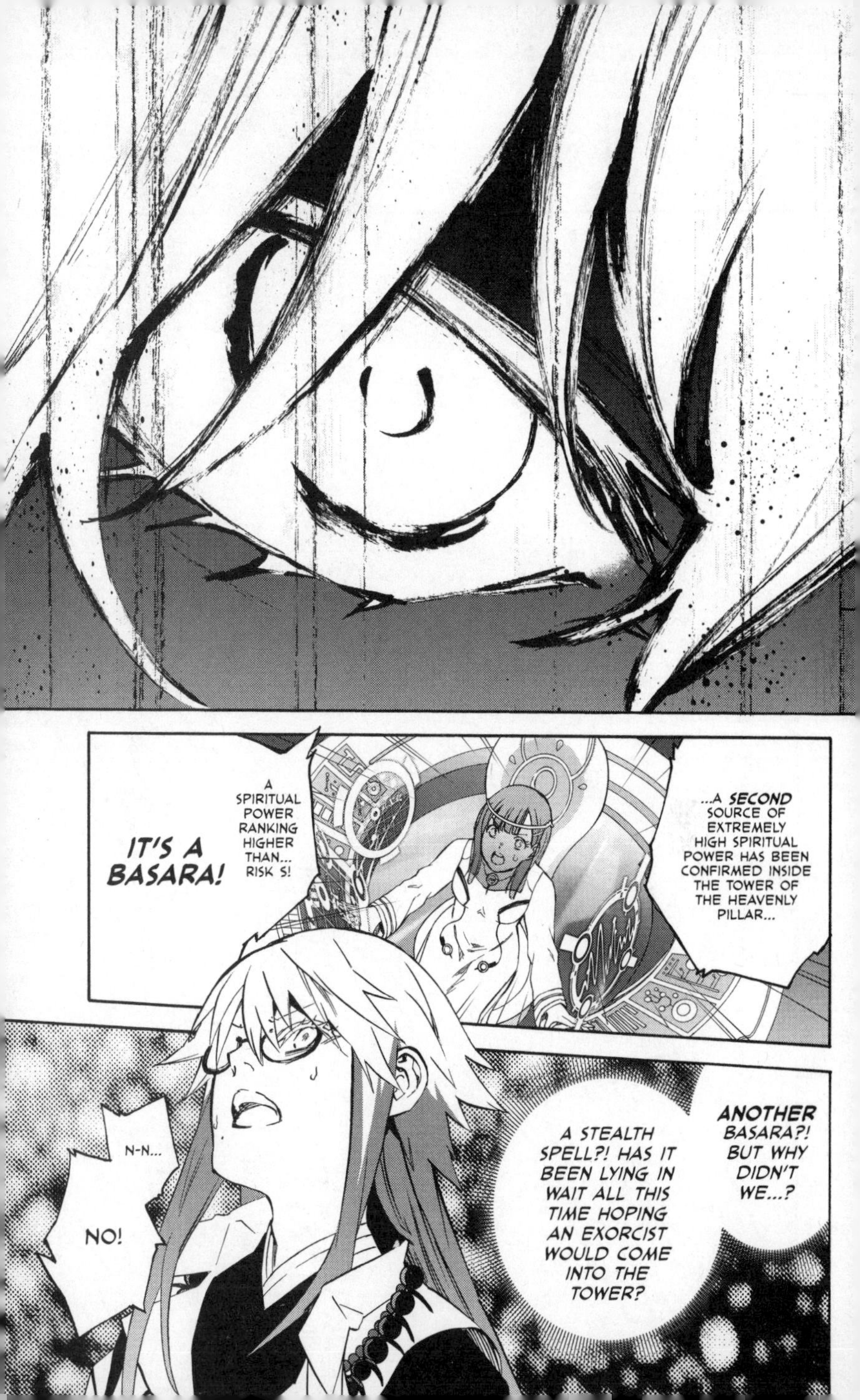
...A SECOND SOURCE OF EXTREMELY HIGH SPIRITUAL POWER HAS BEEN CONFIRMED INSIDE THE TOWER OF THE HEAVENLY PILLAR...
A SPIRITUAL POWER RANKING HIGHER THAN... RISK 5!
IT'S A BASARA!
ANOTHER BASARA?! BUT WHY DIDN'T WE...?
A STEALTH SPELL?! HAS IT BEEN LYING IN WAIT ALL THIS TIME HOPING AN EXORCIST WOULD COME INTO THE TOWER?
N-N...
NO!

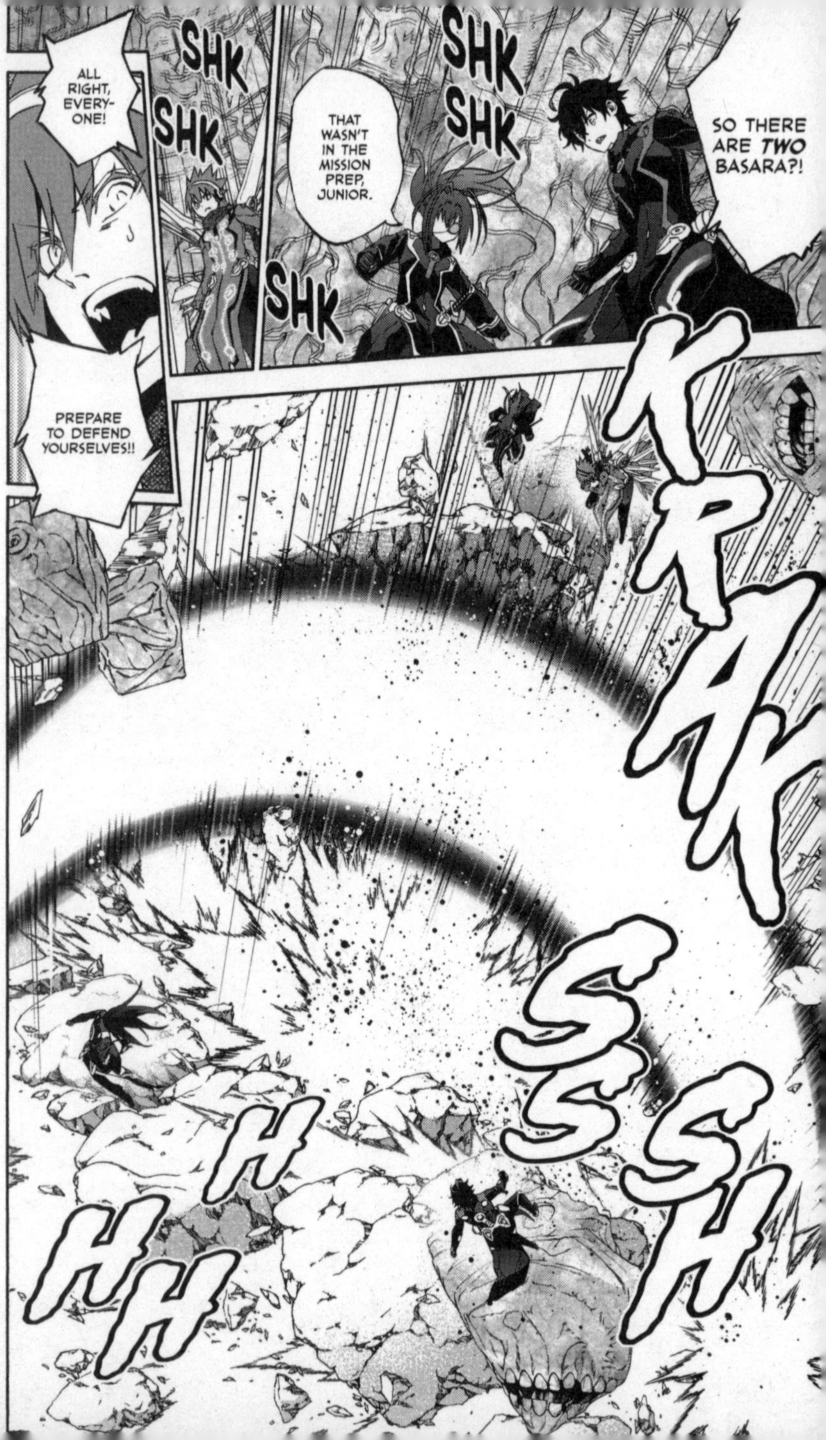
SO THERE ARE TWO BASARA?!
SHK SHK
THAT WASN'T IN THE MISSION PREP, JUNIOR.
SHK
SHK SHK
ALL RIGHT, EVERY-ONE!
PREPARE TO DEFEND YOURSELVES!!
KRAK
SSSHHHH

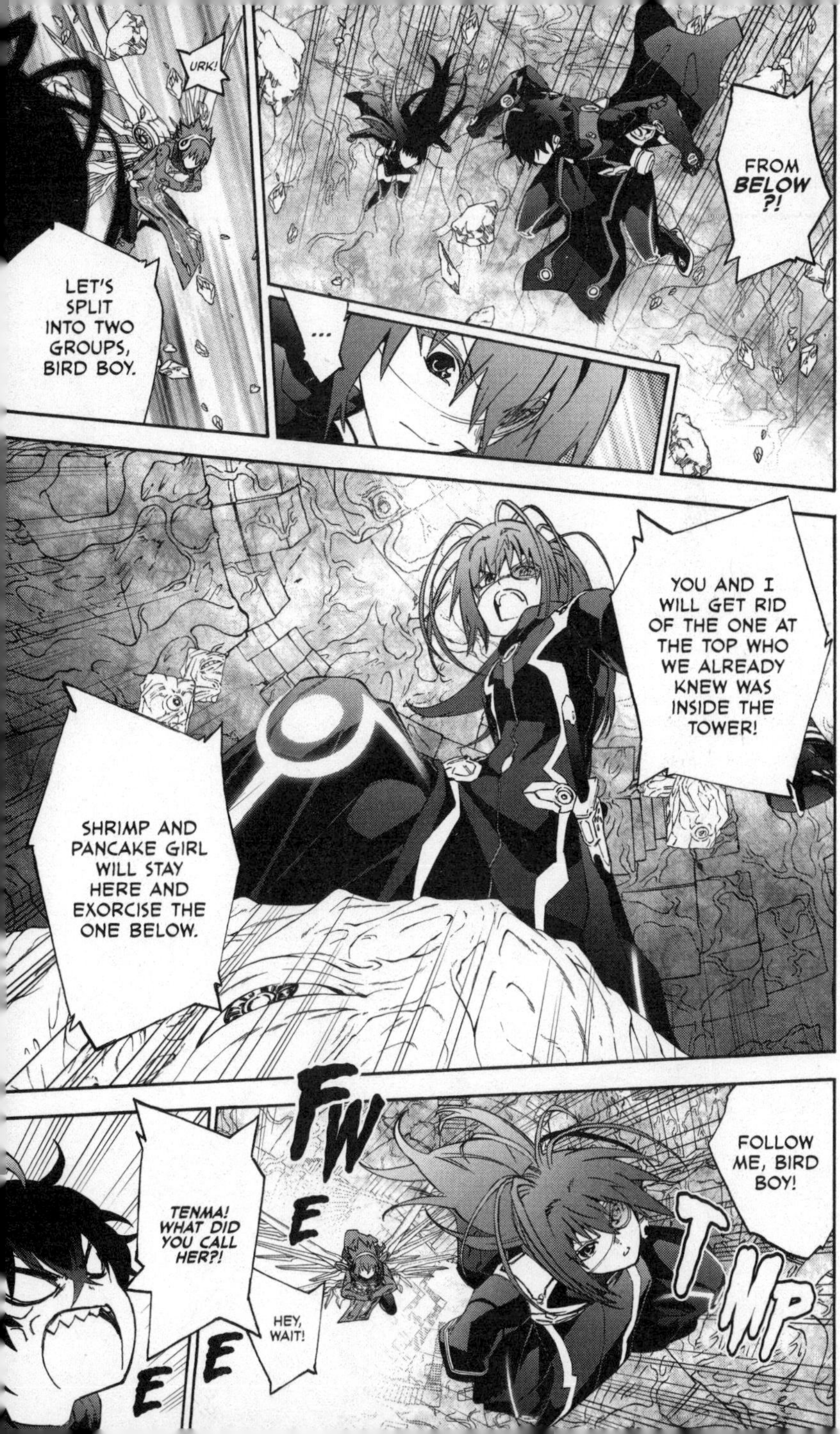
FROM BELOW?!
...
URK!
LET'S SPLIT INTO TWO GROUPS, BIRD BOY.
YOU AND I WILL GET RID OF THE ONE AT THE TOP WHO WE ALREADY KNEW WAS INSIDE THE TOWER!
SHRIMP AND PANCAKE GIRL WILL STAY HERE AND EXORCISE THE ONE BELOW.
FOLLOW ME, BIRD BOY!
TMP
FWE
HEY, WAIT!
TENMA! WHAT DID YOU CALL HER?!
EEE

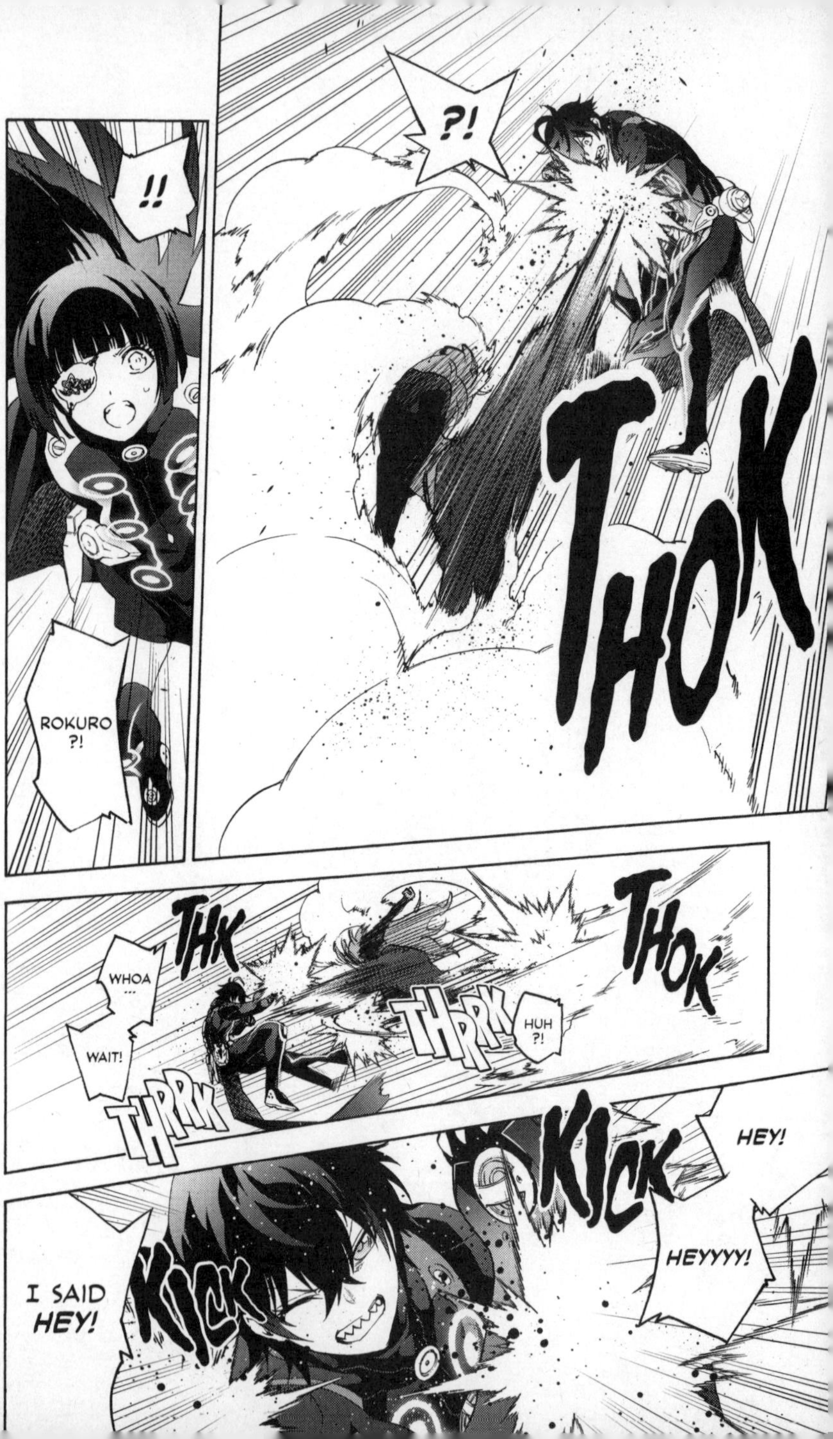
?!
THOK
!!
ROKURO ?!
THOK
HUH ?!
THRRK
THK
WHOA ...
WAIT!
THRRK
HEY!
KICK
HEYYYY!
KICK
I SAID HEY!

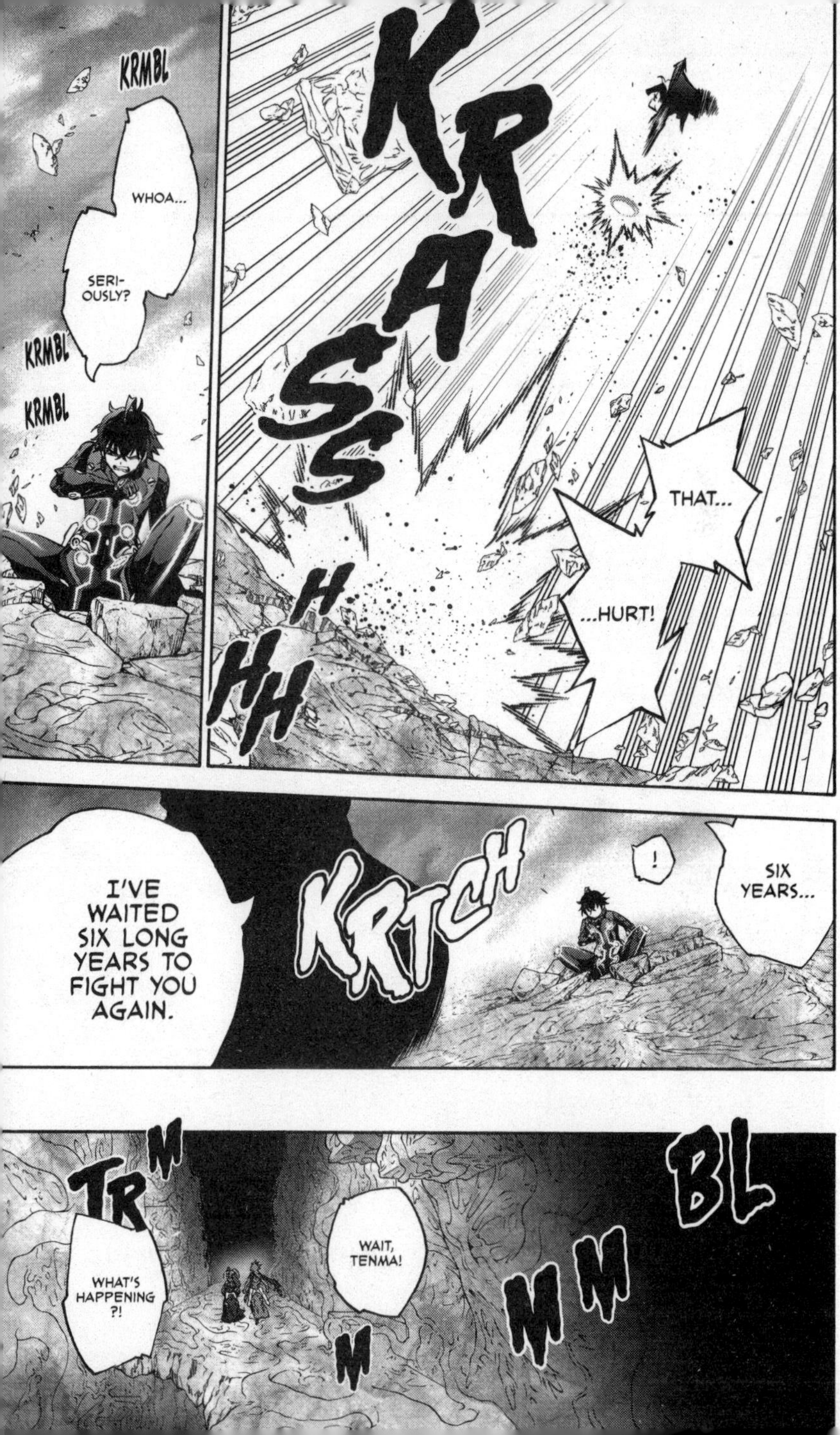
KRASSHHH
THAT...
...HURT!
KRMBL
WHOA...
SERI-OUSLY?
KRMBL
KRMBL
SIX YEARS...
!
KRTCH
I'VE WAITED SIX LONG YEARS TO FIGHT YOU AGAIN.
BL
M M M
M
WAIT, TENMA!
WHAT'S HAPPENING ?!
TRM

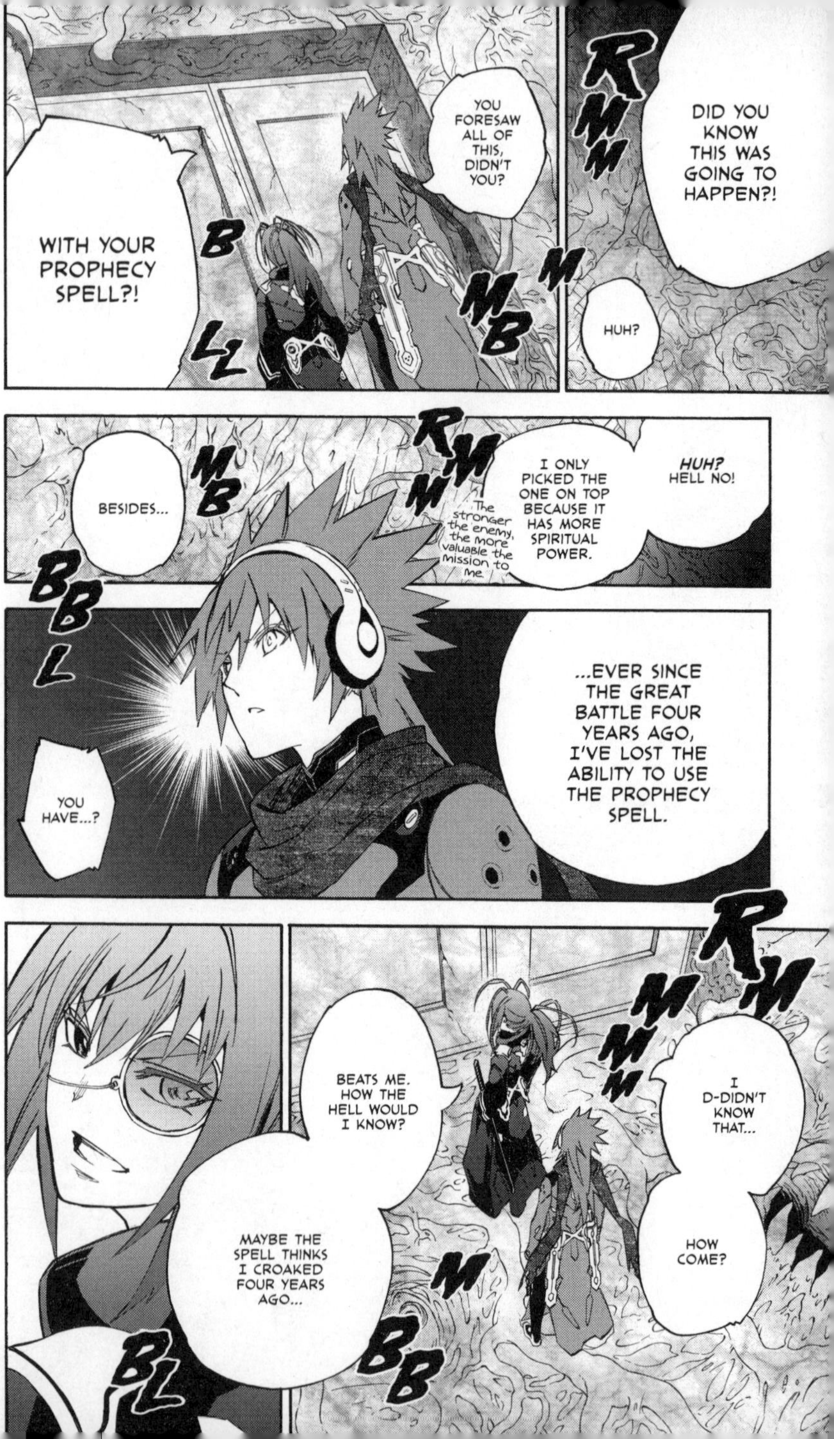
RMM
DID YOU KNOW THIS WAS GOING TO HAPPEN?!
HUH?
M
MB
YOU FORESAW ALL OF THIS, DIDN'T YOU?
B
WITH YOUR PROPHECY SPELL?!
LL
HUH? HELL NO!
I ONLY PICKED THE ONE ON TOP BECAUSE IT HAS MORE SPIRITUAL POWER.
RMM
The stronger the enemy, the more valuable the mission to me.
MB
BESIDES...
BBL
...EVER SINCE THE GREAT BATTLE FOUR YEARS AGO, I'VE LOST THE ABILITY TO USE THE PROPHECY SPELL.
YOU HAVE...?
RM
MMMM
I D-DIDN'T KNOW THAT...
HOW COME?
BEATS ME. HOW THE HELL WOULD I KNOW?
MAYBE THE SPELL THINKS I CROAKED FOUR YEARS AGO...
M
BB
BL

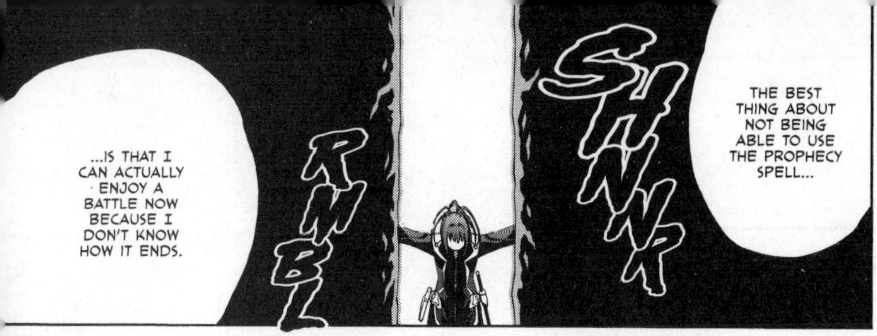
THE BEST THING ABOUT NOT BEING ABLE TO USE THE PROPHECY SPELL...
SHNNR
RMBL
...IS THAT I CAN ACTUALLY ENJOY A BATTLE NOW BECAUSE I DON'T KNOW HOW IT ENDS.

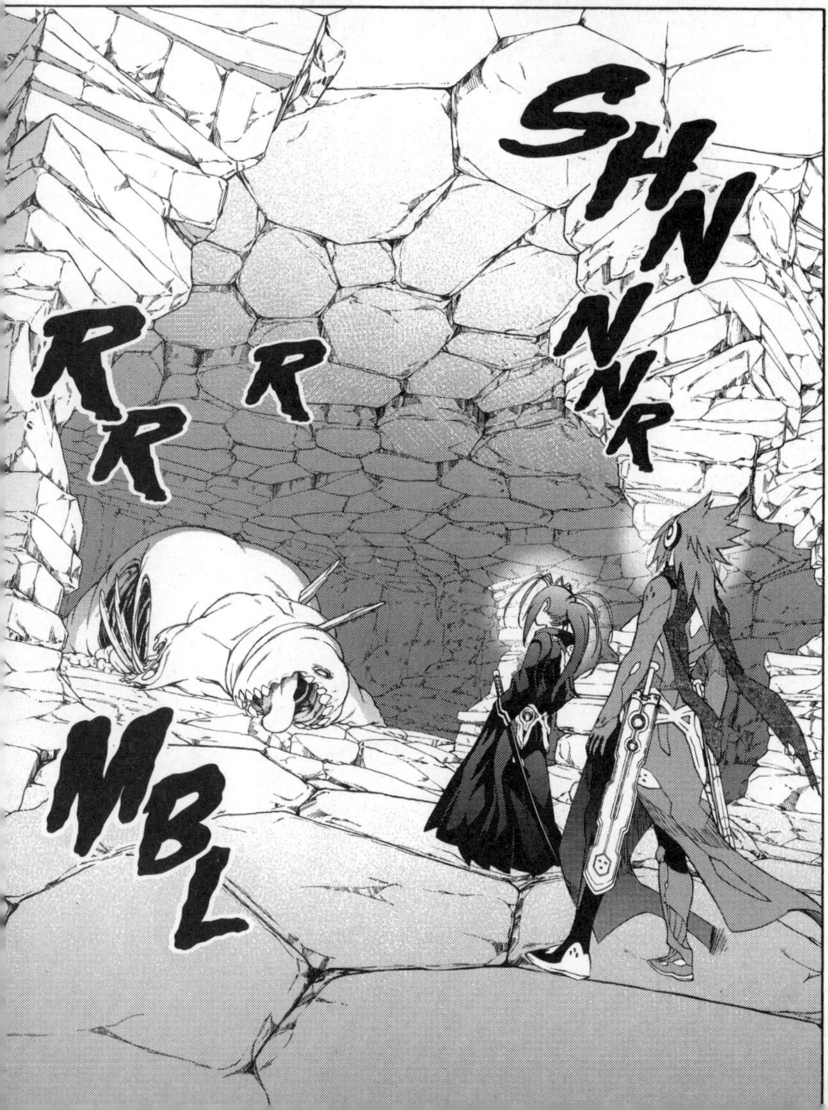
SHNNR
RRRMBL

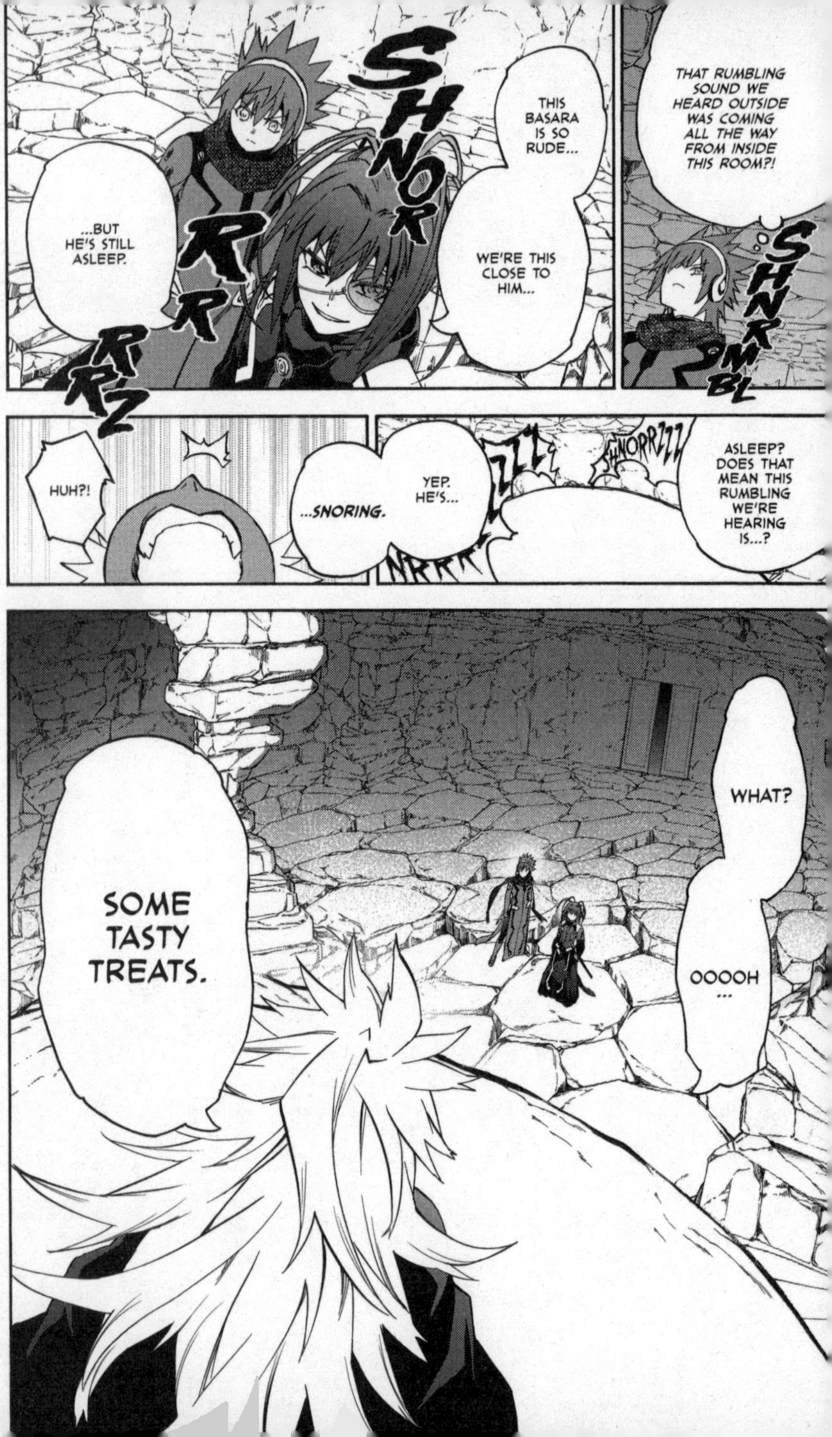

THAT RUMBLING SOUND WE HEARD OUTSIDE WAS COMING ALL THE WAY FROM INSIDE THIS ROOM?!
SHNRMBL
THIS BASARA IS SO RUDE...
WE'RE THIS CLOSE TO HIM...
SHNORRRRZ
...BUT HE'S STILL ASLEEP.
ASLEEP? DOES THAT MEAN THIS RUMBLING WE'RE HEARING IS...?
SHNORRZZZ
ZZZ
NRRR
YEP. HE'S...
...SNORING.
HUH?!
WHAT?
OOOOH ...
SOME TASTY TREATS.

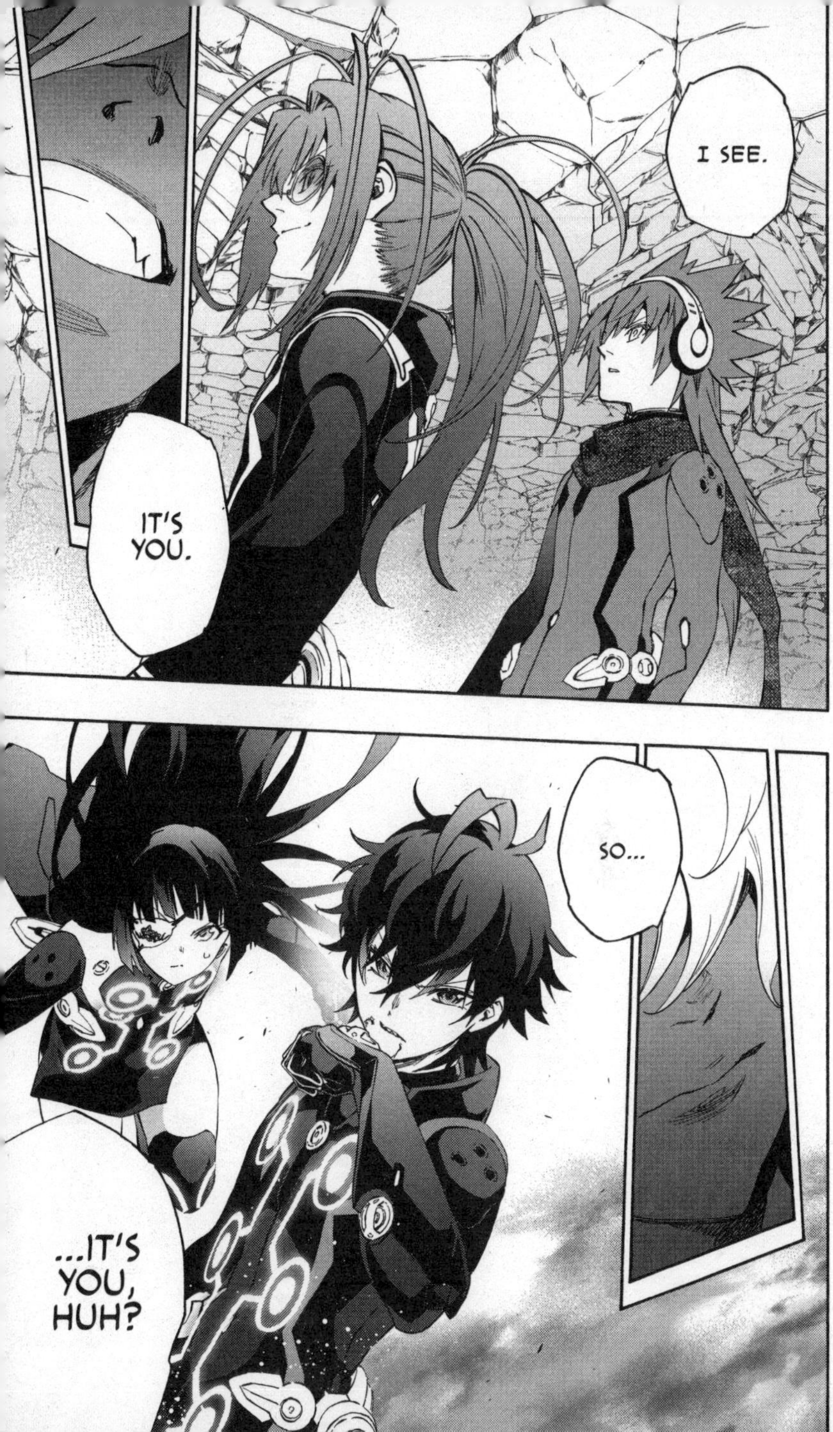
I SEE.
IT'S YOU.
SO...
...IT'S YOU, HUH?

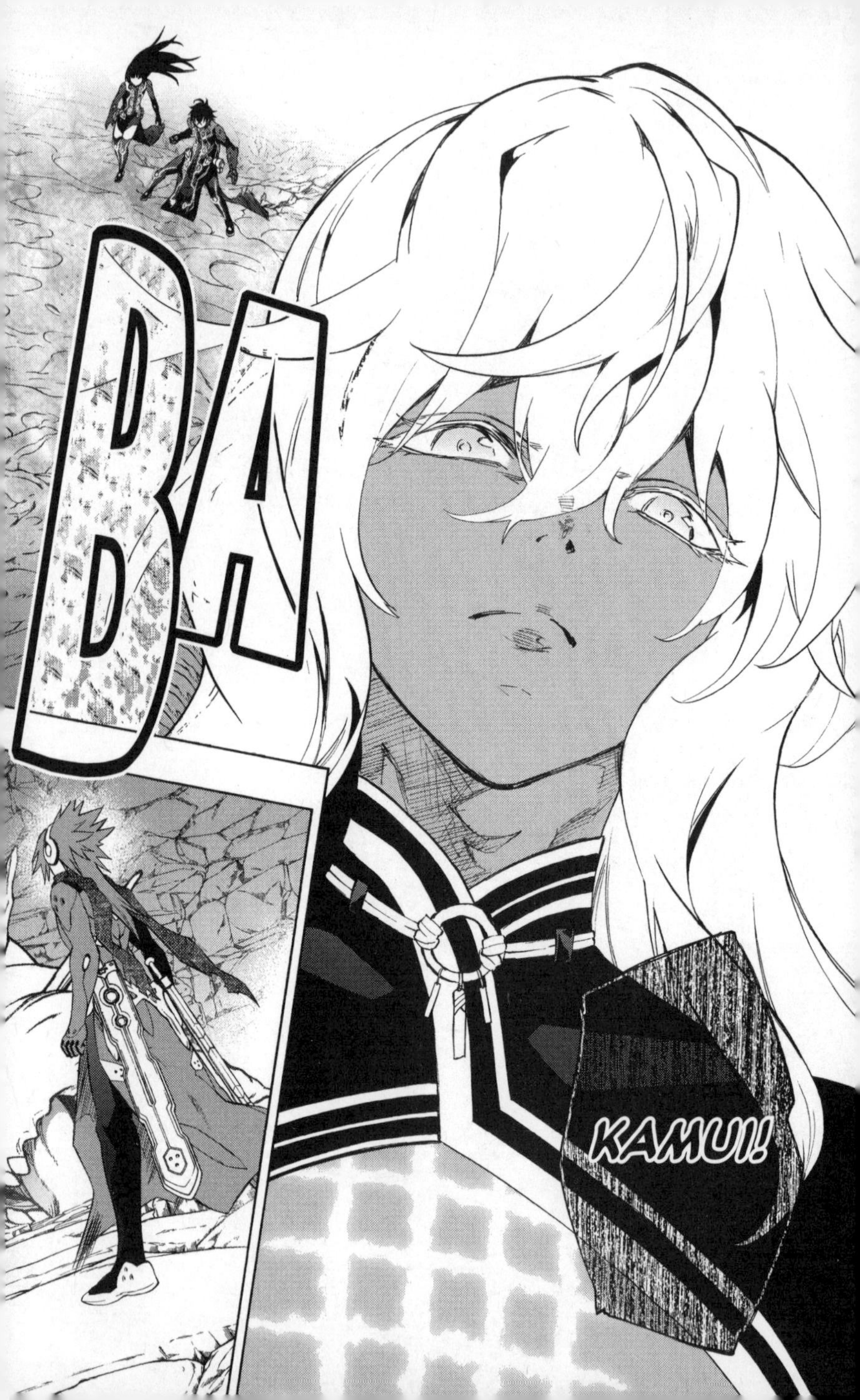
BA
DA
KAMUI!

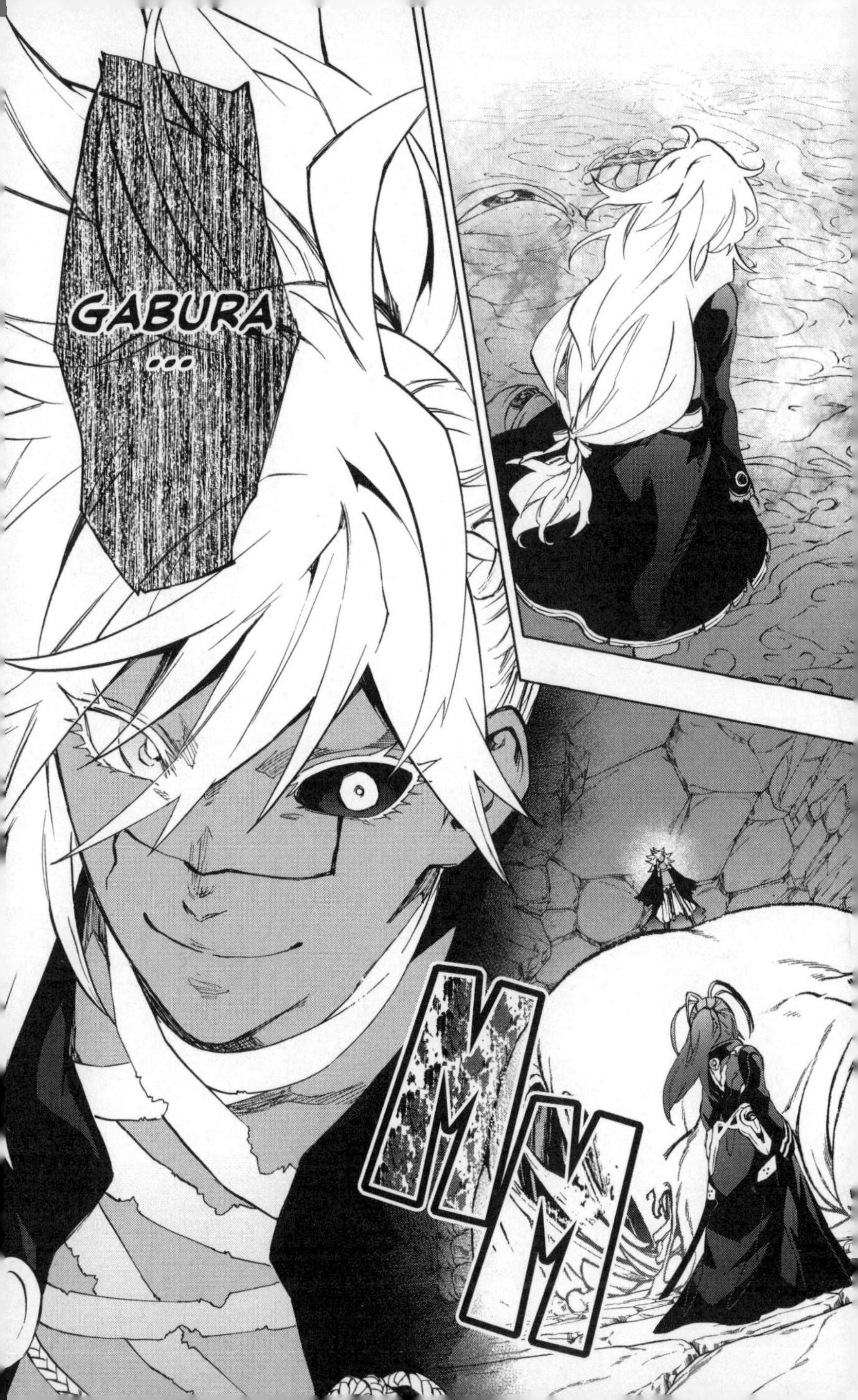
GABURA ...
MMM

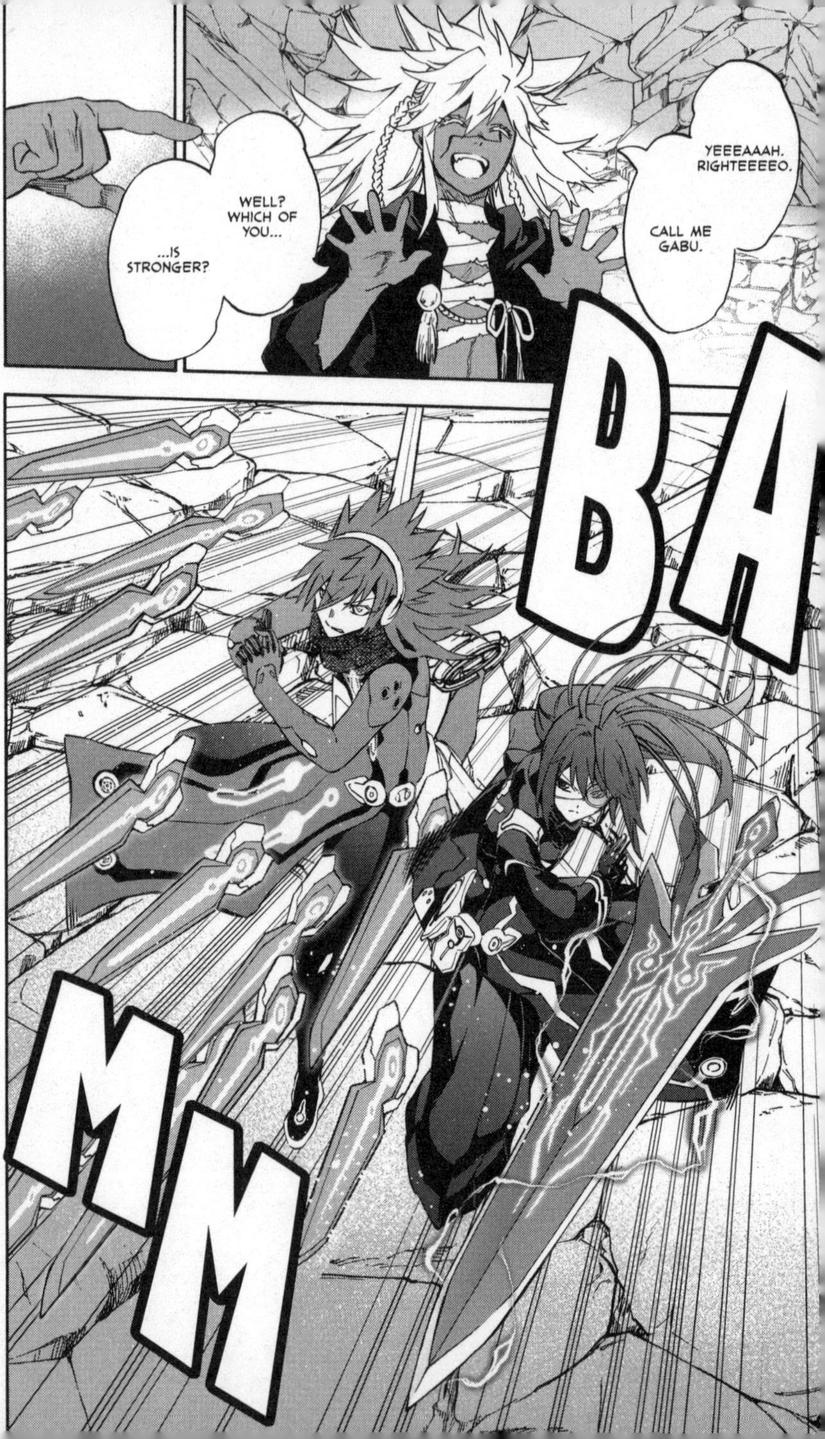
YEEEAAAH. RIGHTEEEEO.
CALL ME GABU.
WELL? WHICH OF YOU...
...IS STRONGER?
BA
MM

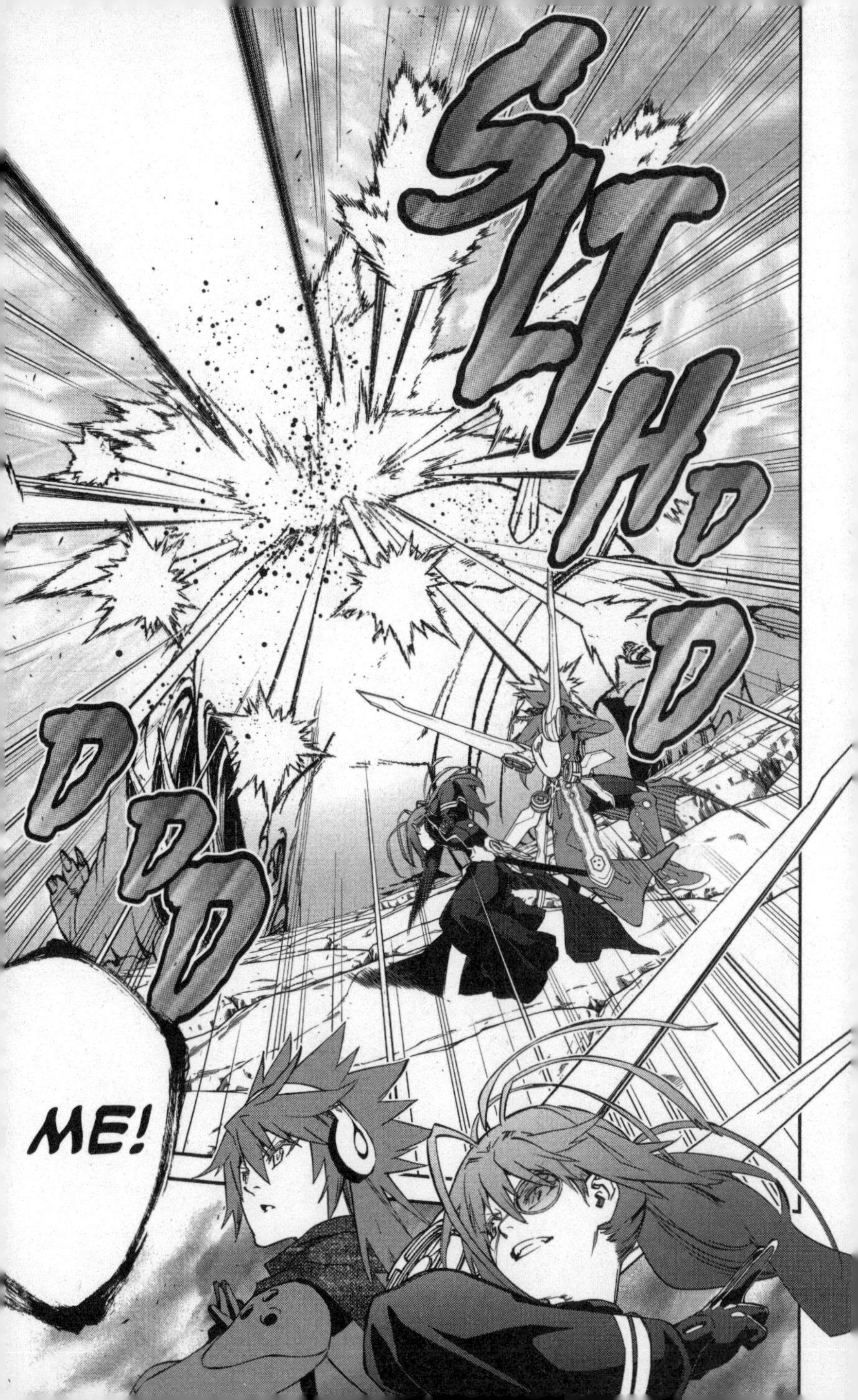
DDD
ME!

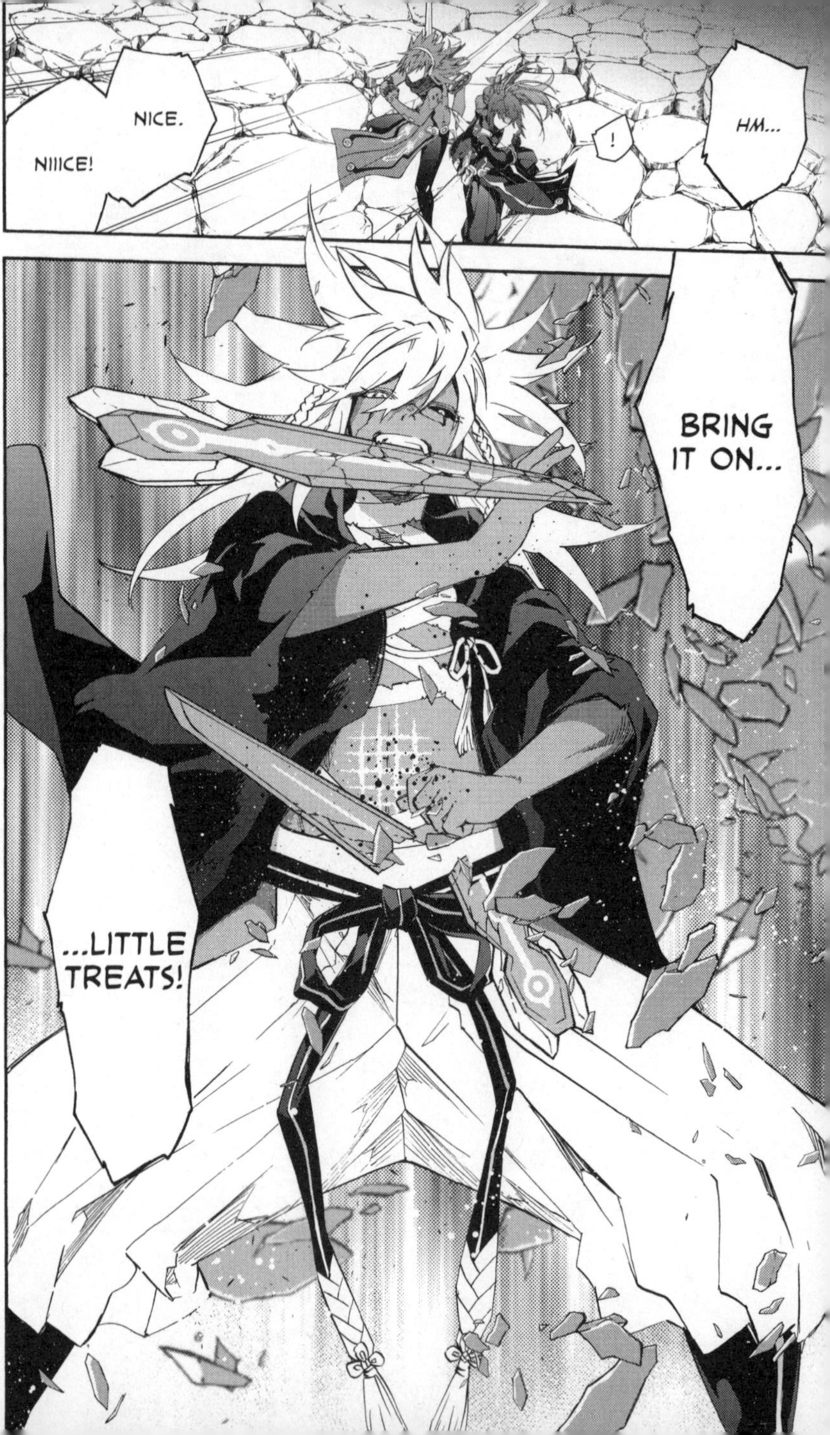
HM...
!
NICE.
NIIICE!
BRING IT ON...
...LITTLE TREATS!

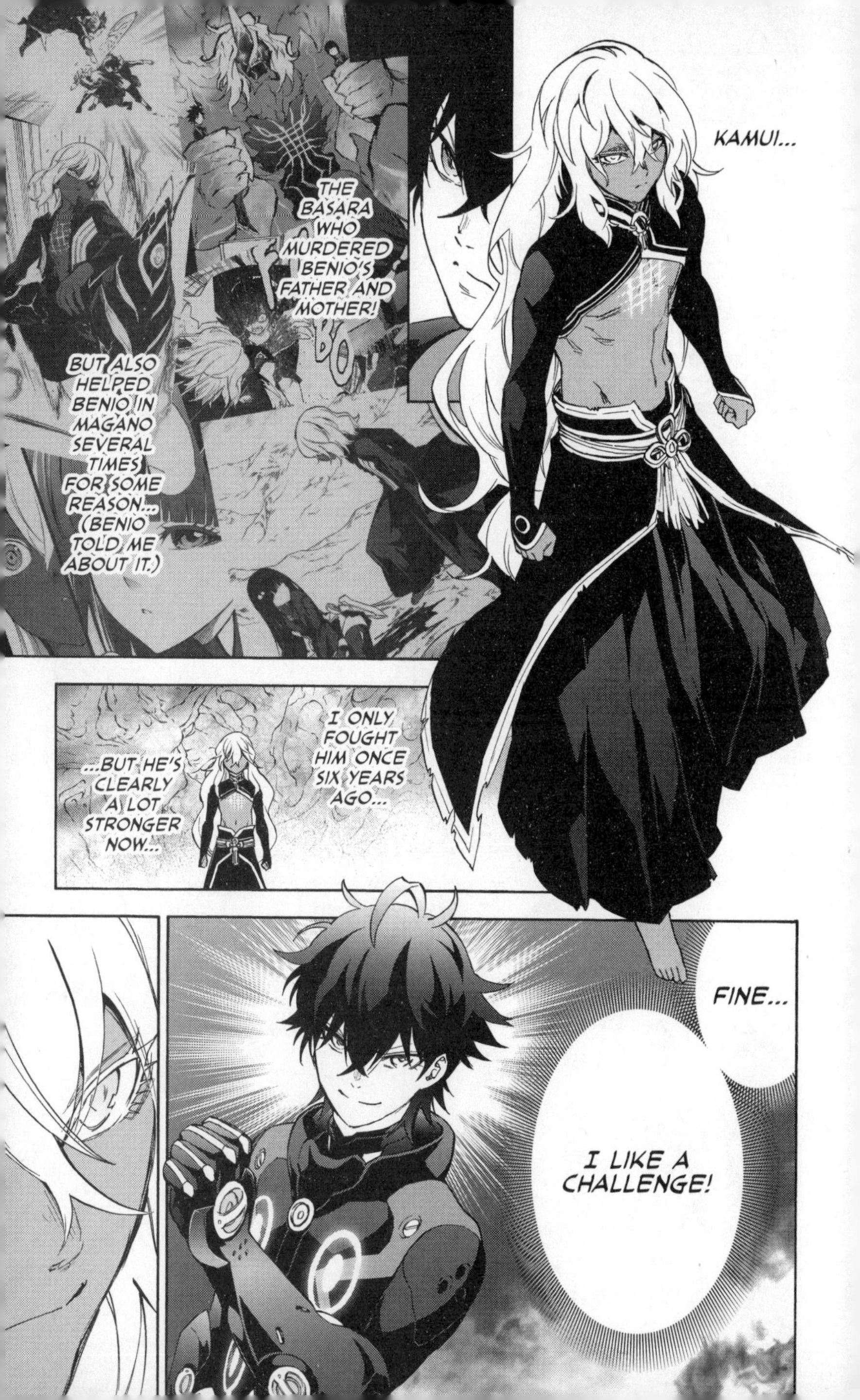
KAMUI...
THE BASARA WHO MURDERED BENIO'S FATHER AND MOTHER!
BUT ALSO HELPED BENIO IN MAGANO SEVERAL TIMES FOR SOME REASON... (BENIO TOLD ME ABOUT IT.)
I ONLY FOUGHT HIM ONCE SIX YEARS AGO...
...BUT HE'S CLEARLY A LOT STRONGER NOW...
FINE...
I LIKE A CHALLENGE!

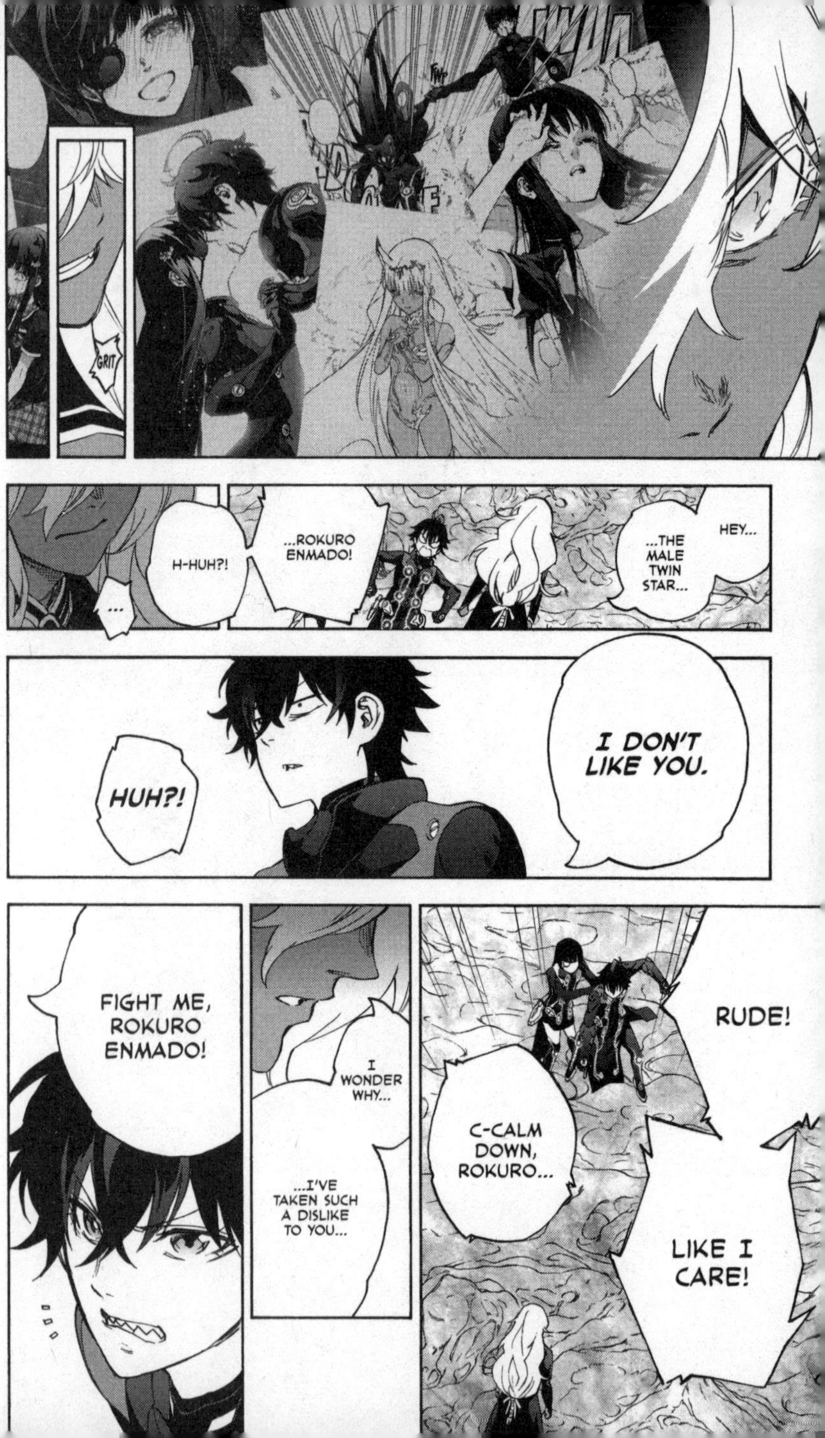
GRIT
HEY...
...THE MALE TWIN STAR...
...ROKURO ENMADO!
H-HUH?!
...
I DON'T LIKE YOU.
HUH?!
RUDE!
C-CALM DOWN, ROKURO...
LIKE I CARE!
I WONDER WHY...
...I'VE TAKEN SUCH A DISLIKE TO YOU...
FIGHT ME, ROKURO ENMADO!

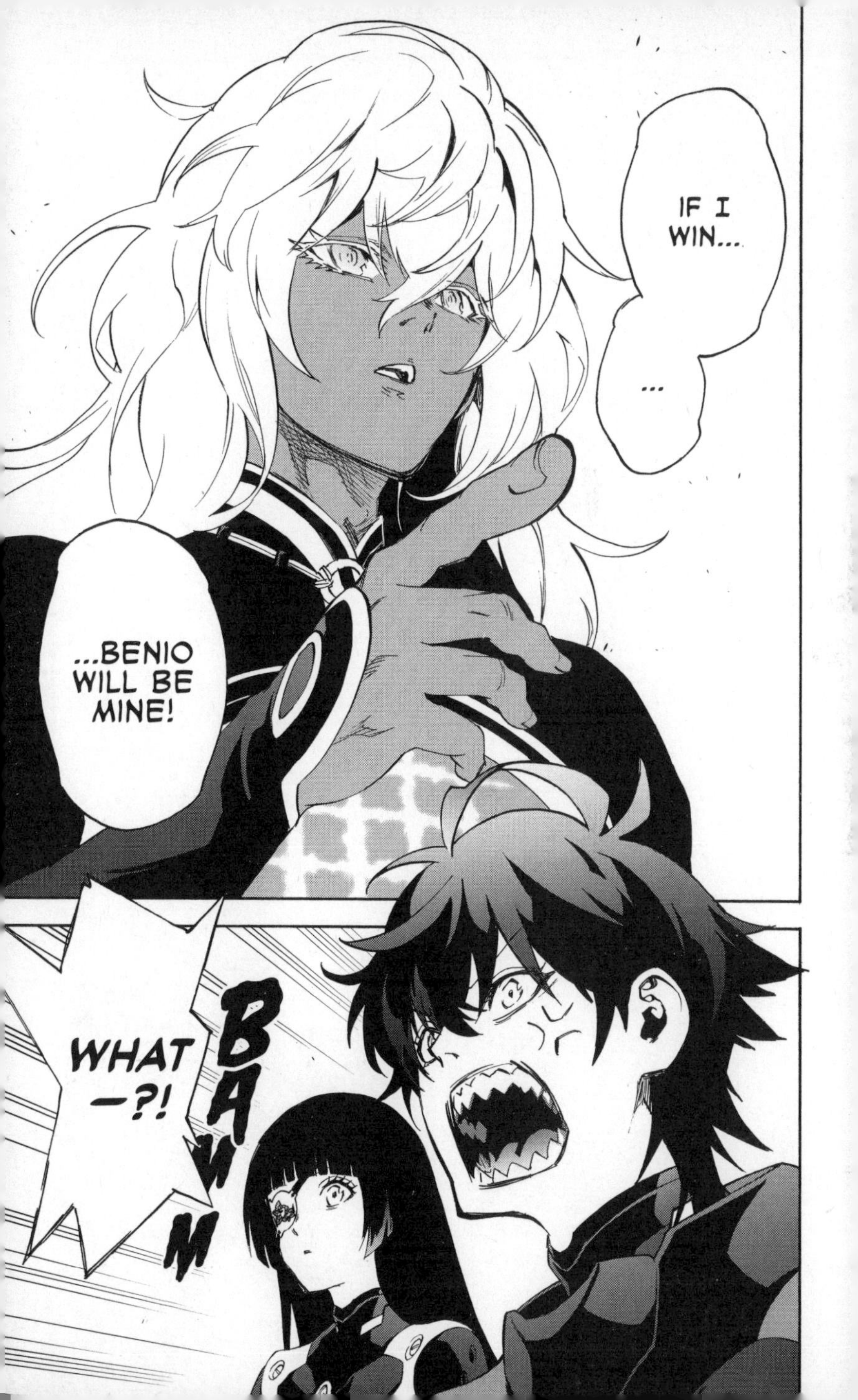
IF I WIN...
...
...BENIO WILL BE MINE!
BAMM
WHAT—?!

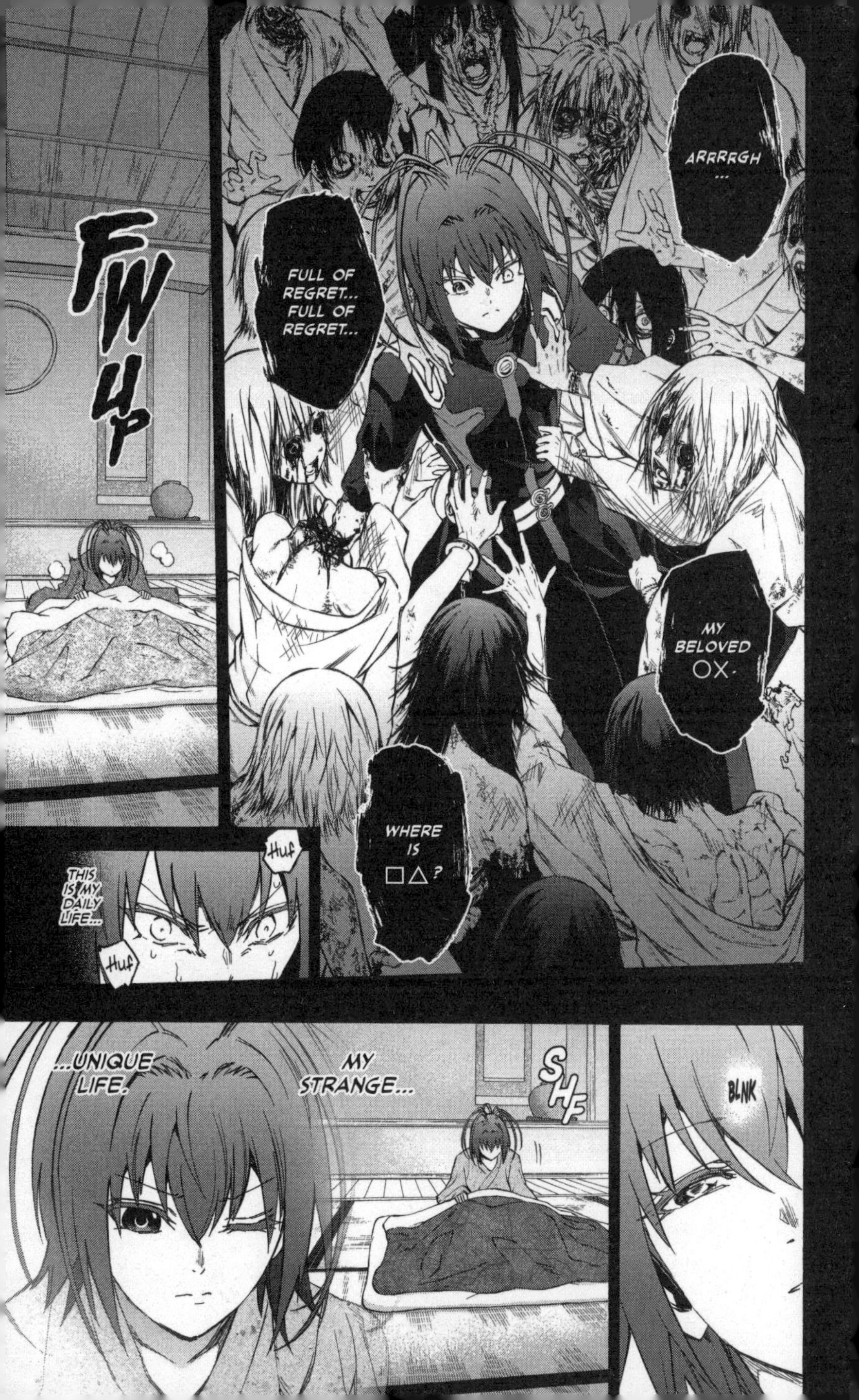
ARRRRGH ...
FULL OF REGRET... FULL OF REGRET...
MY BELOVED ○X.
WHERE IS □△?
FWUP
Huf
THIS IS MY DAILY LIFE...
Huf
BLNK
SHF
MY STRANGE...
...UNIQUE LIFE.

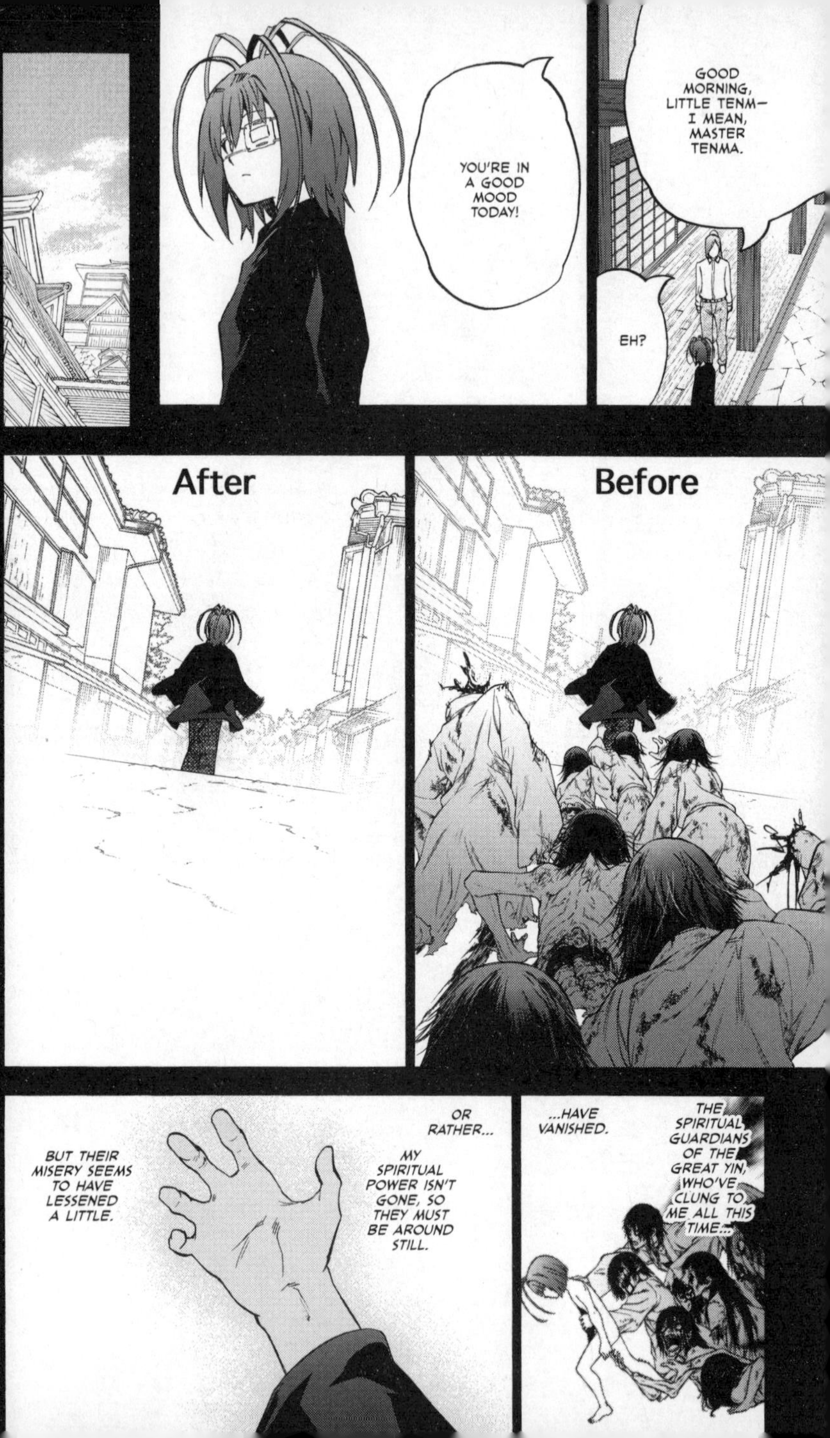
GOOD MORNING, LITTLE TENM— I MEAN, MASTER TENMA.
EH?
YOU'RE IN A GOOD MOOD TODAY!
Before
After
THE SPIRITUAL GUARDIANS OF THE GREAT YIN, WHO'VE CLUNG TO ME ALL THIS TIME...
...HAVE VANISHED.
OR RATHER...
MY SPIRITUAL POWER ISN'T GONE, SO THEY MUST BE AROUND STILL.
BUT THEIR MISERY SEEMS TO HAVE LESSENED A LITTLE.

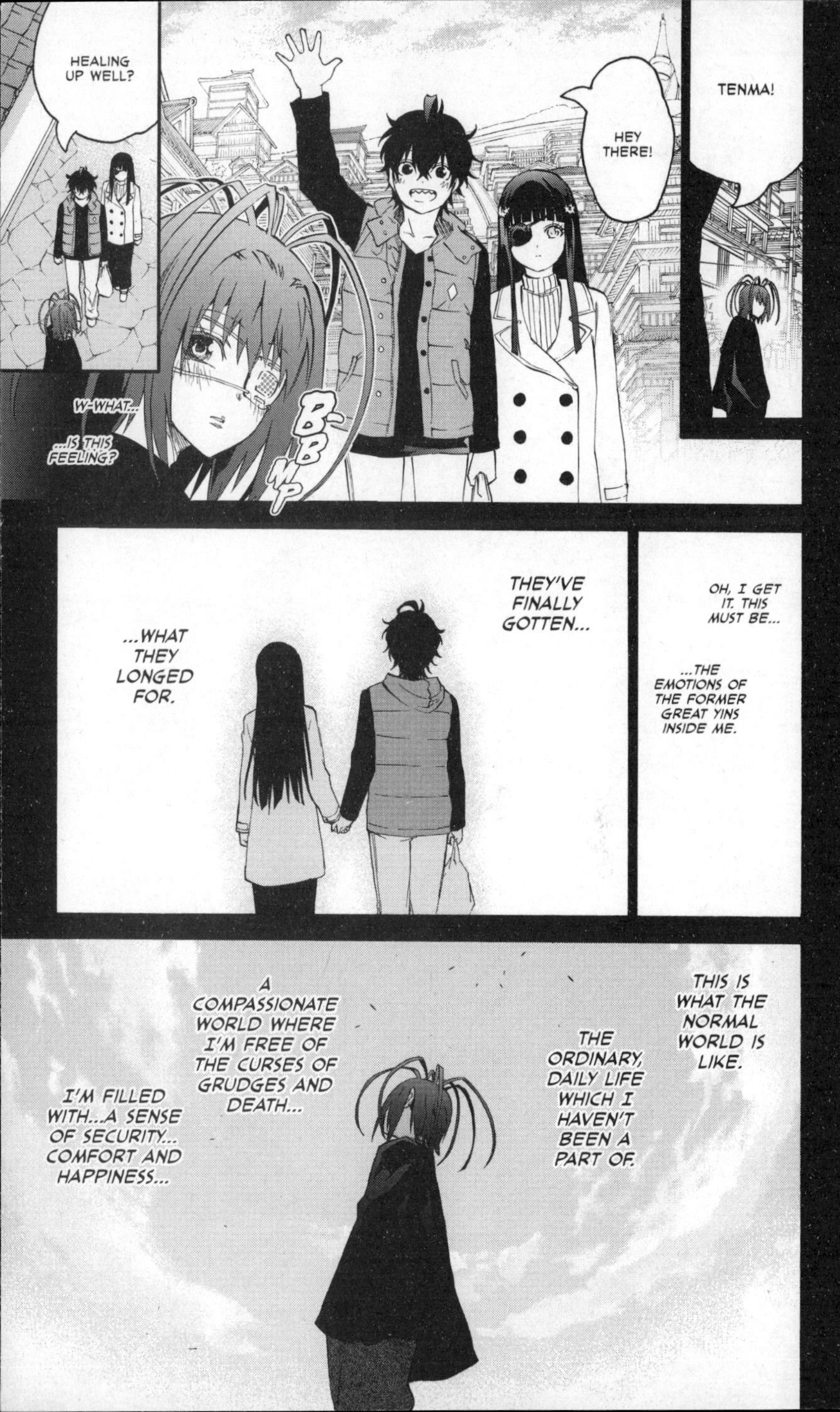
TENMA!
HEY THERE!
HEALING UP WELL?
B-BMP
W-WHAT...
...IS THIS FEELING?
OH, I GET IT. THIS MUST BE...
...THE EMOTIONS OF THE FORMER GREAT YINS INSIDE ME.
THEY'VE FINALLY GOTTEN...
...WHAT THEY LONGED FOR.
THIS IS WHAT THE NORMAL WORLD IS LIKE.
THE ORDINARY, DAILY LIFE WHICH I HAVEN'T BEEN A PART OF.
A COMPASSIONATE WORLD WHERE I'M FREE OF THE CURSES OF GRUDGES AND DEATH...
I'M FILLED WITH...A SENSE OF SECURITY... COMFORT AND HAPPINESS...

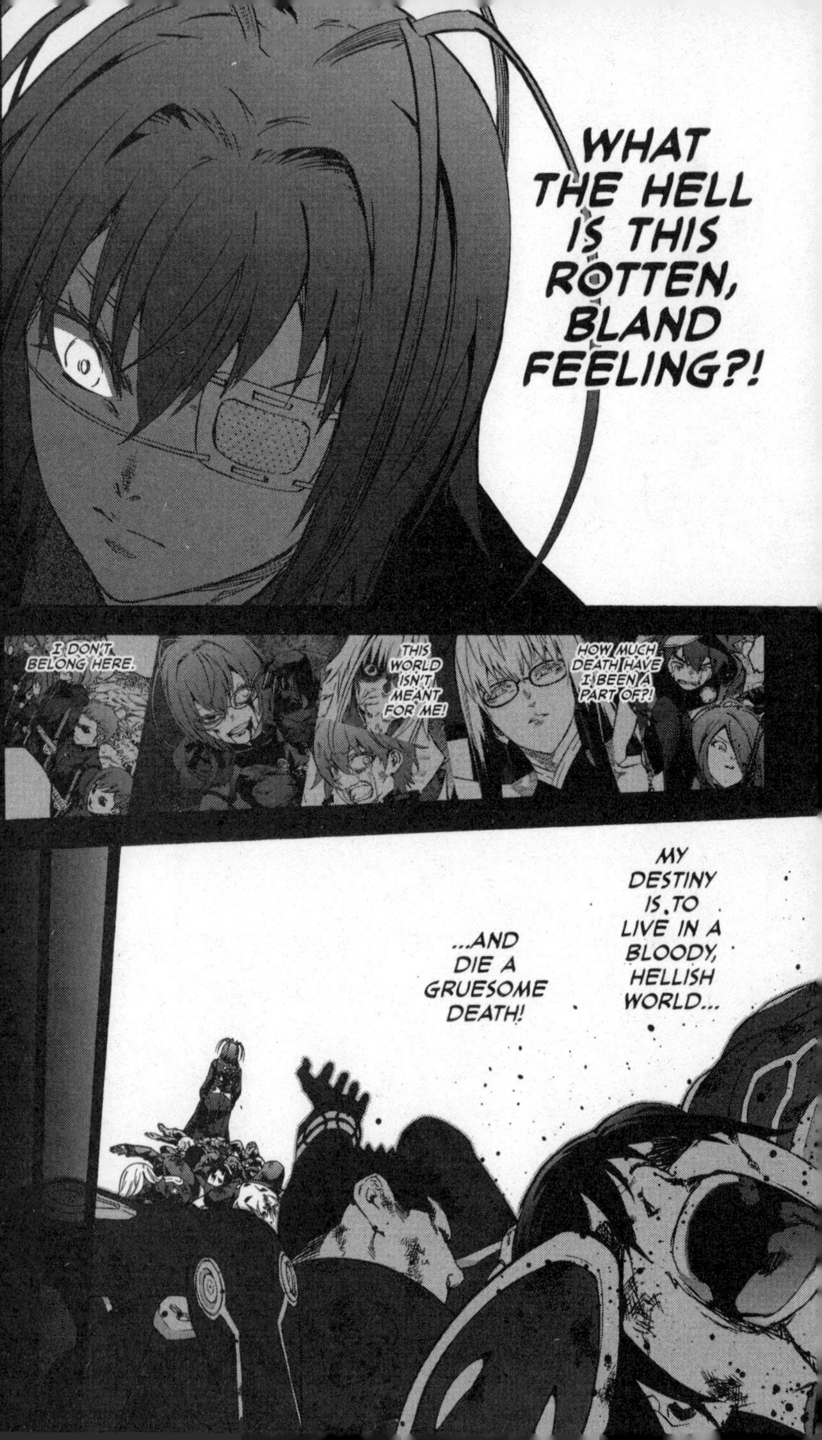
WHAT THE HELL IS THIS ROTTEN, BLAND FEELING?!
HOW MUCH DEATH HAVE I BEEN A PART OF?!
THIS WORLD ISN'T MEANT FOR ME!
I DON'T BELONG HERE.
MY DESTINY IS TO LIVE IN A BLOODY, HELLISH WORLD...
...AND DIE A GRUESOME DEATH!

#81: For Everyone (or Everything) You Care About

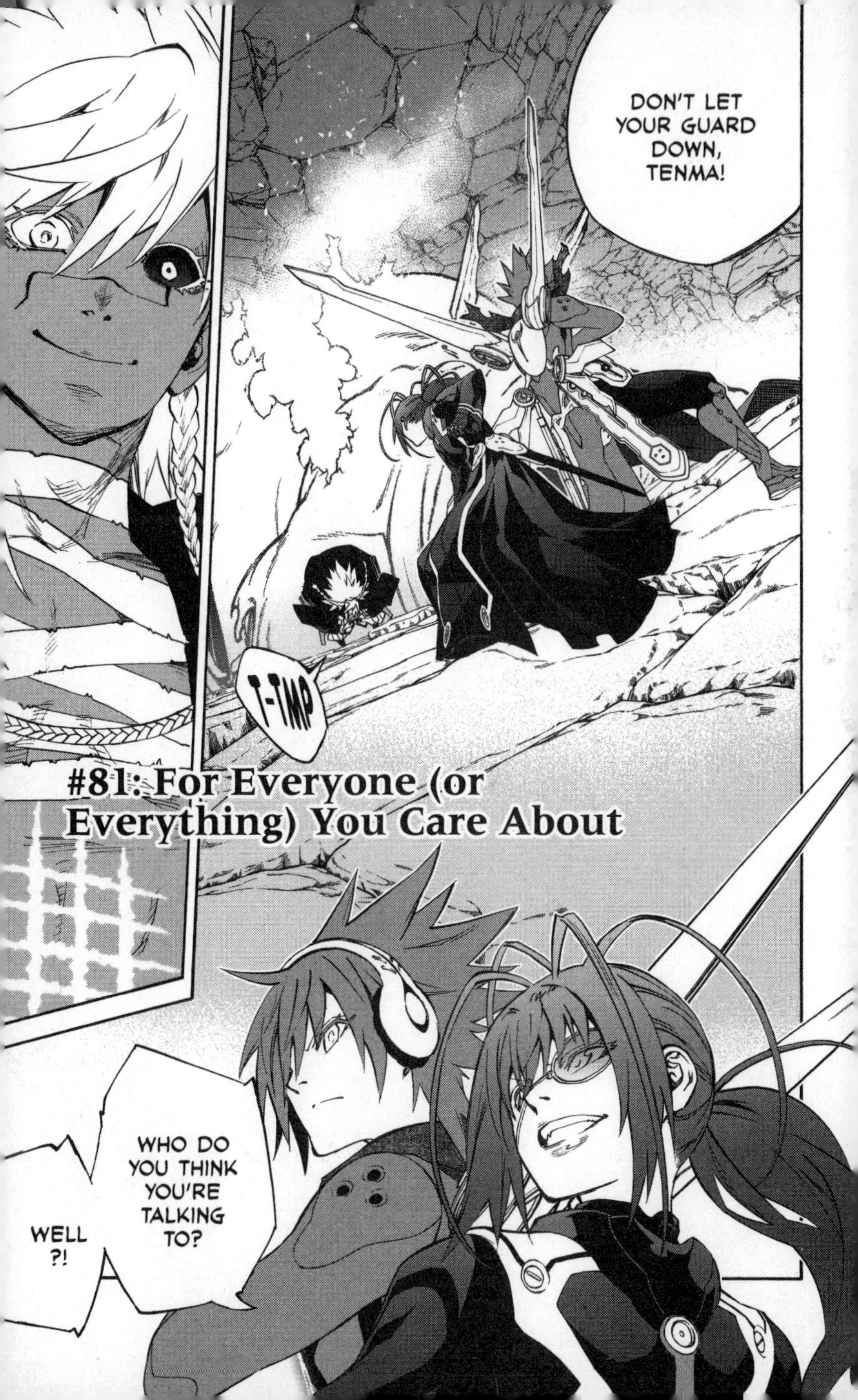
DON'T LET YOUR GUARD DOWN, TENMA!
T-TMP
#81: For Everyone (or Everything) You Care About
WHO DO YOU THINK YOU'RE TALKING TO?
WELL ?!

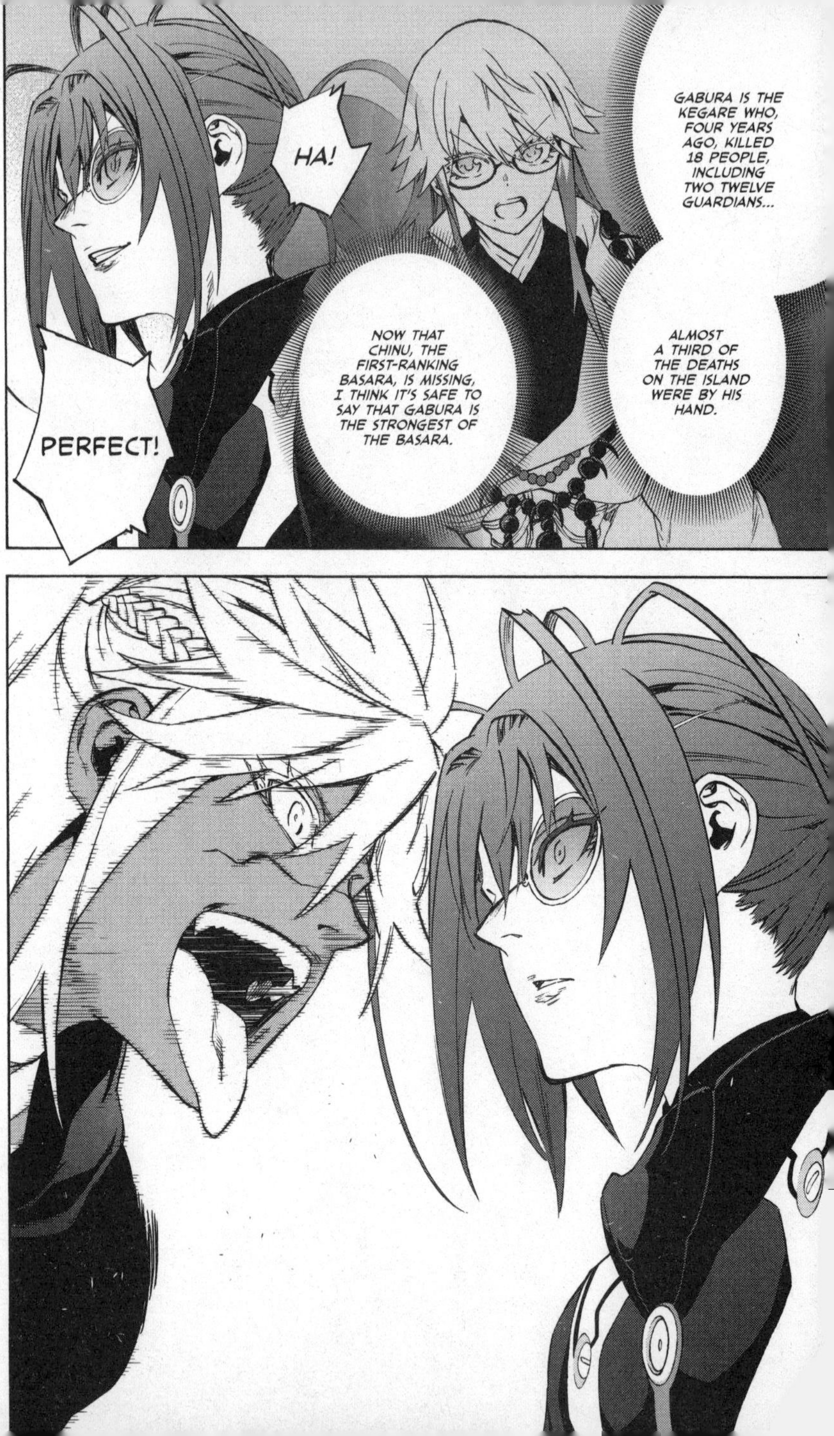
GABURA IS THE KEGARE WHO, FOUR YEARS AGO, KILLED 18 PEOPLE, INCLUDING TWO TWELVE GUARDIANS...
ALMOST A THIRD OF THE DEATHS ON THE ISLAND WERE BY HIS HAND.
NOW THAT CHINU, THE FIRST-RANKING BASARA, IS MISSING, I THINK IT'S SAFE TO SAY THAT GABURA IS THE STRONGEST OF THE BASARA.
HA!
PERFECT!

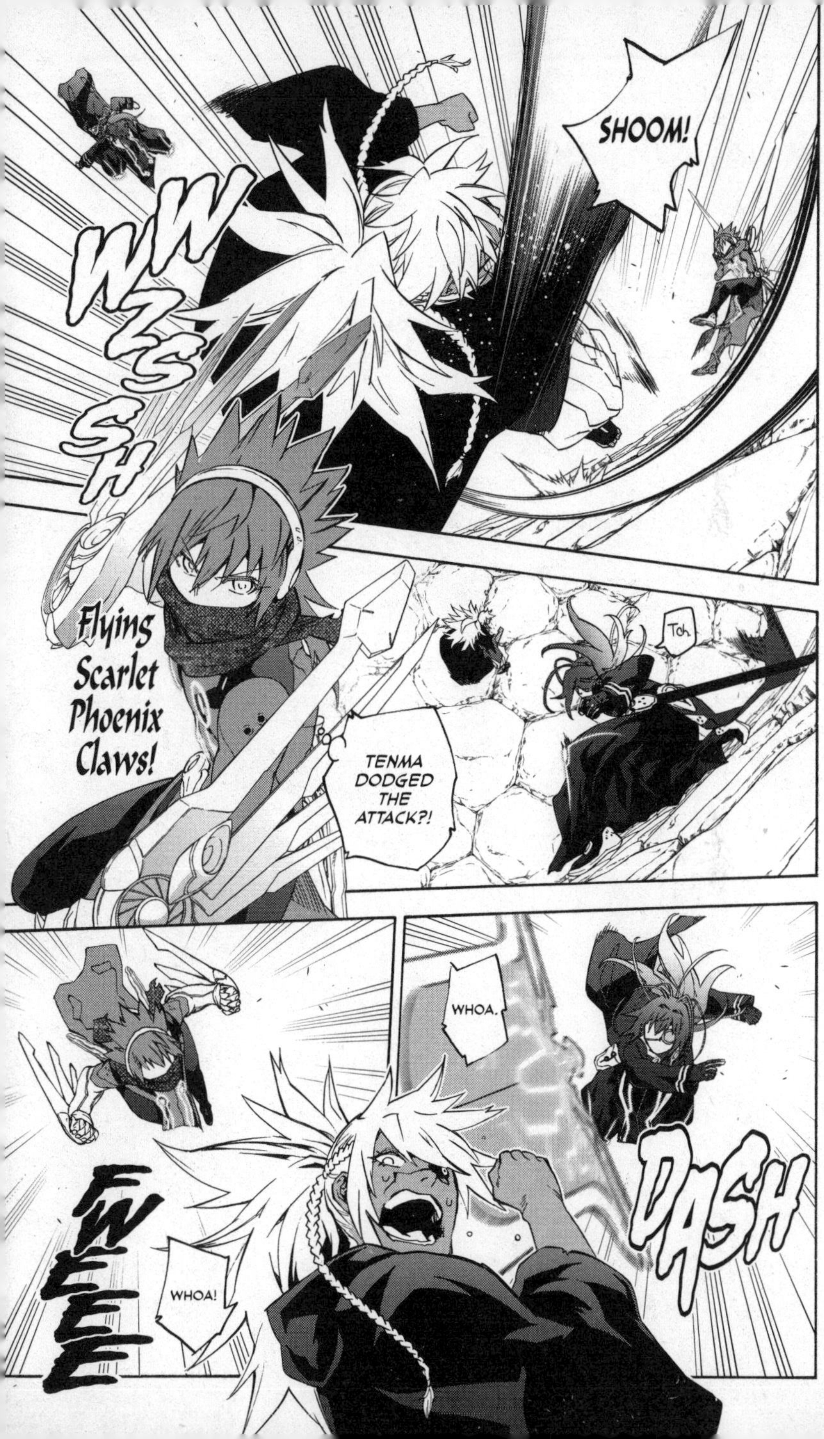
SHOOM!
WZSSH
Flying Scarlet Phoenix Claws!
Tch.
TENMA DODGED THE ATTACK?!
WHOA.
DASH
WHOA!
FWEEE

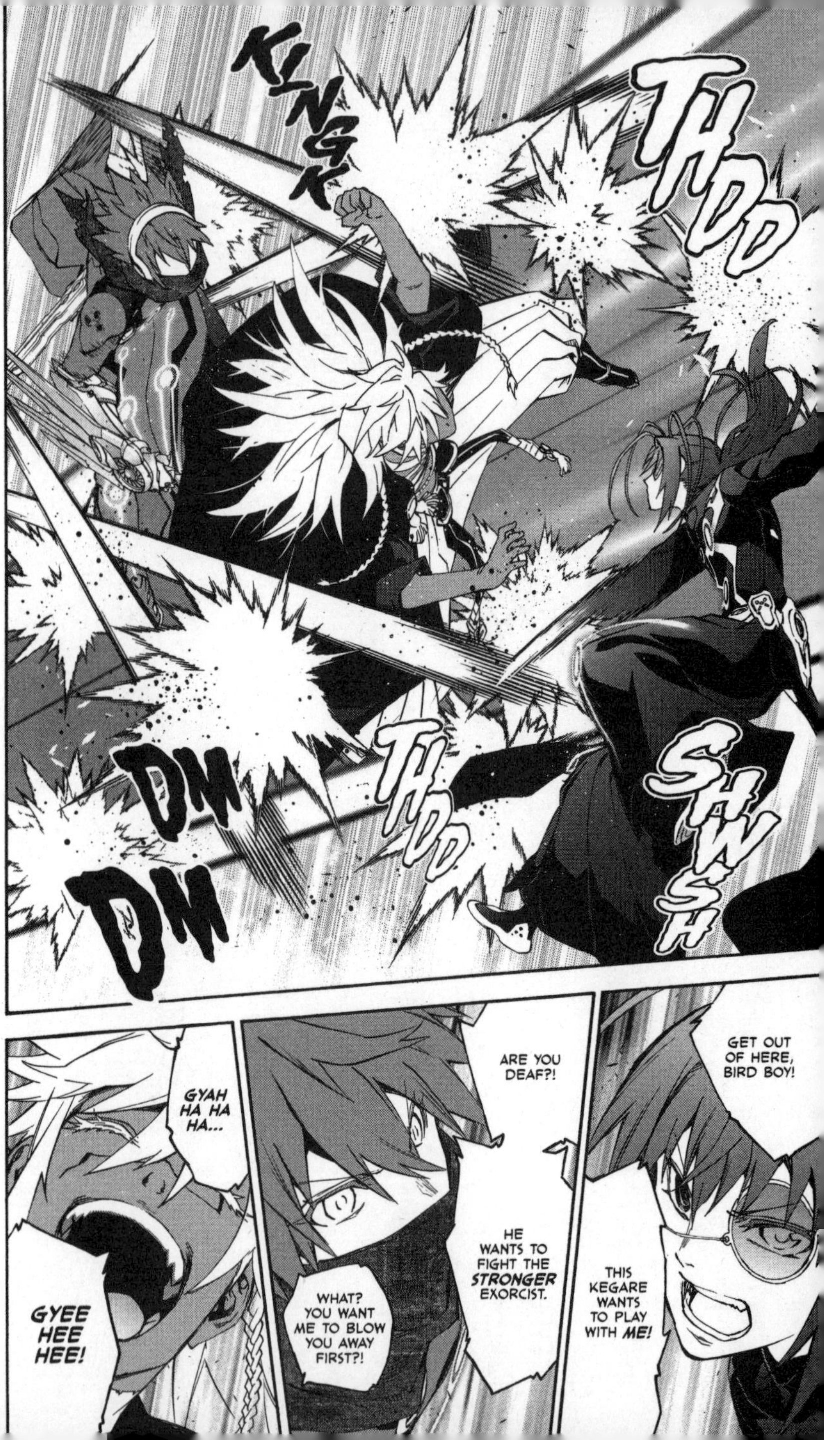
THOD
KLINGK
SHWSH
THOD
DM DM
GET OUT OF HERE, BIRD BOY!
THIS KEGARE WANTS TO PLAY WITH ME!
ARE YOU DEAF?!
HE WANTS TO FIGHT THE STRONGER EXORCIST.
WHAT? YOU WANT ME TO BLOW YOU AWAY FIRST?!
GYAH HA HA HA...
GYEE HEE HEE!

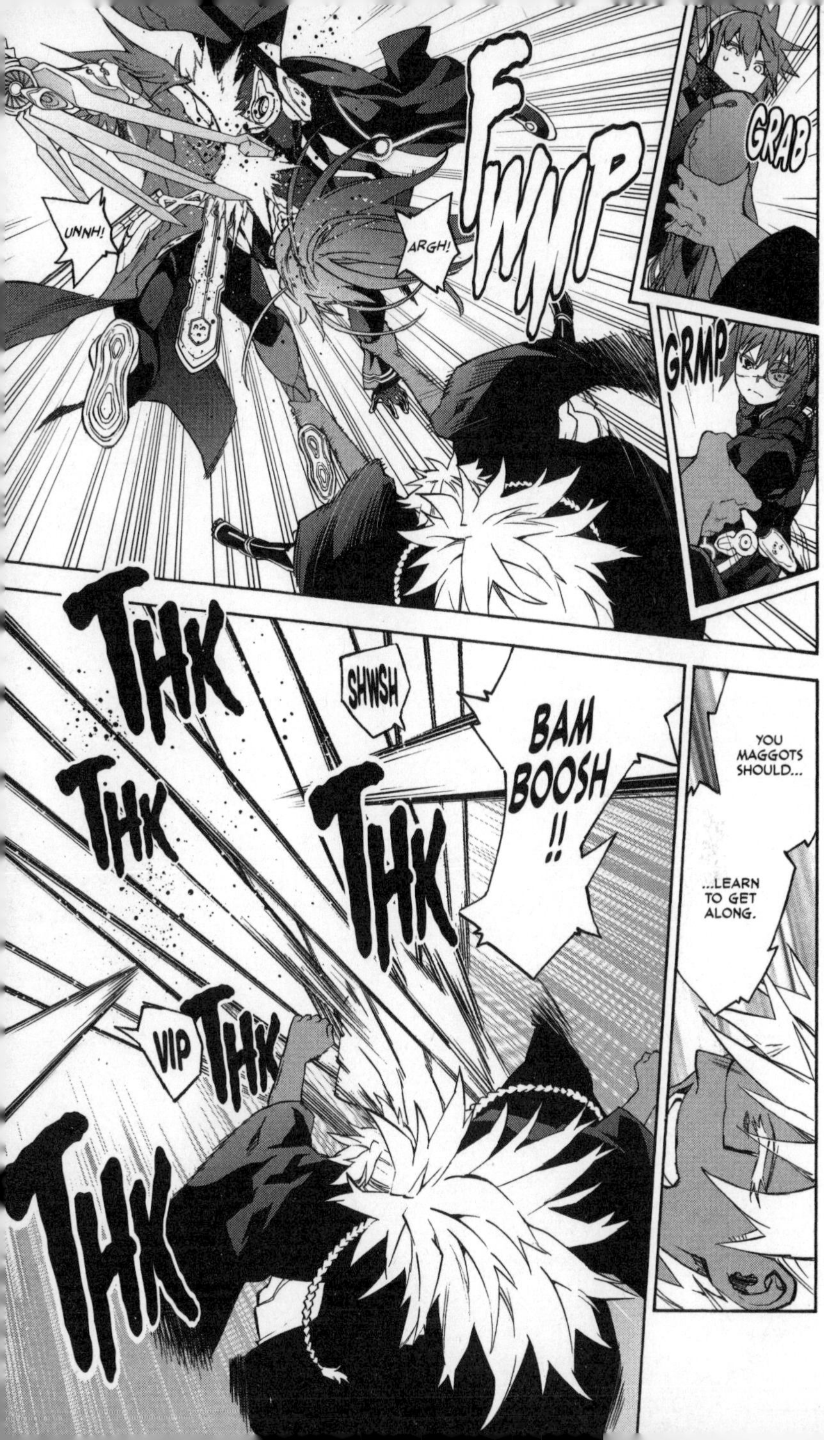
GRAB
GRMP
FWMP
ARGH!
UNNH!
YOU MAGGOTS SHOULD...
...LEARN TO GET ALONG.
BAM BOOSH !!
SHWSH
THK
THK
THK
THK
VIP
THK

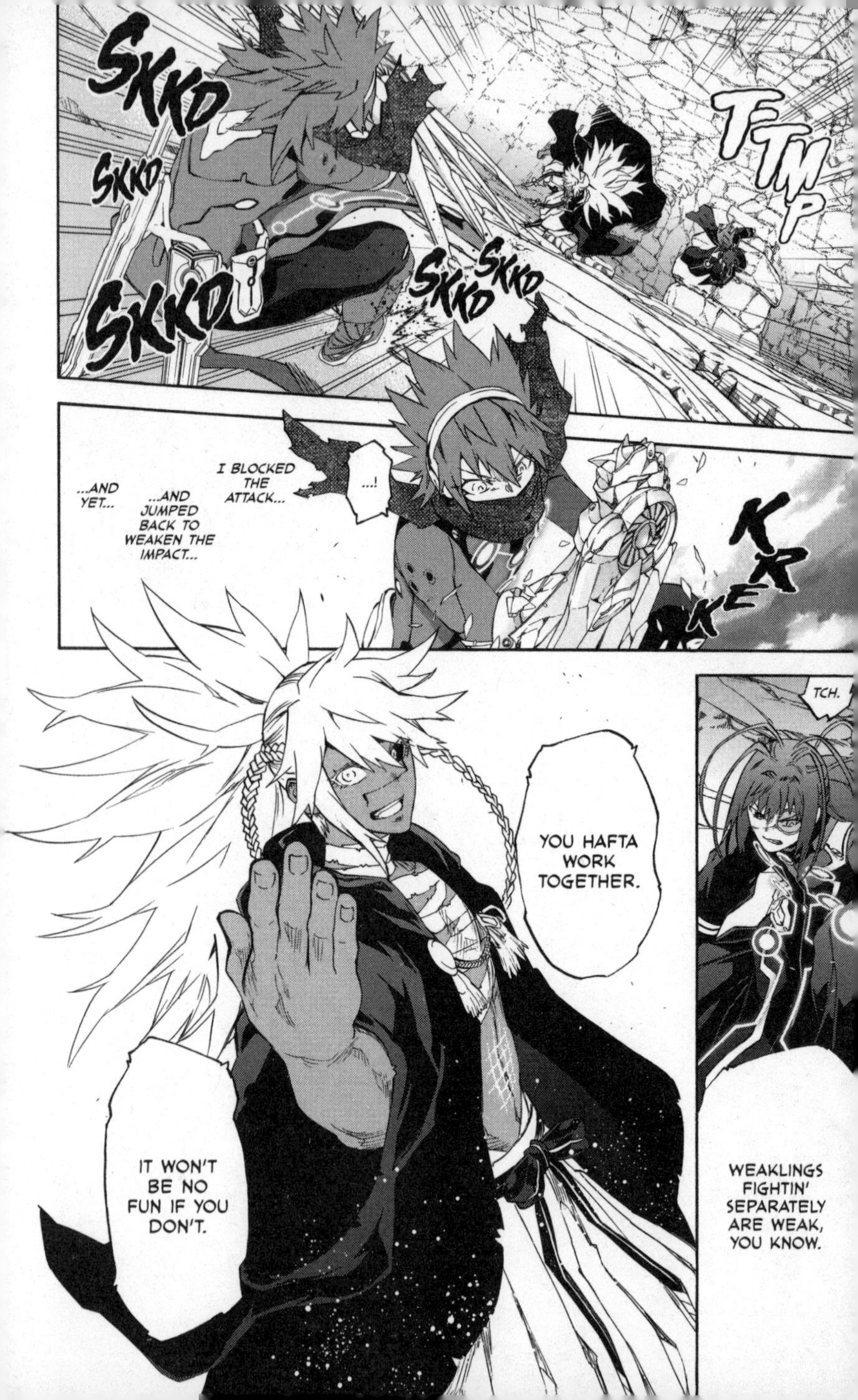
TTMP
SKKD
SKKD
SKKD
SKKD
SKKD
KREK
...!
I BLOCKED THE ATTACK...
...AND JUMPED BACK TO WEAKEN THE IMPACT...
...AND YET...
TCH.
WEAKLINGS FIGHTIN' SEPARATELY ARE WEAK, YOU KNOW.
YOU HAFTA WORK TOGETHER.
IT WON'T BE NO FUN IF YOU DON'T.

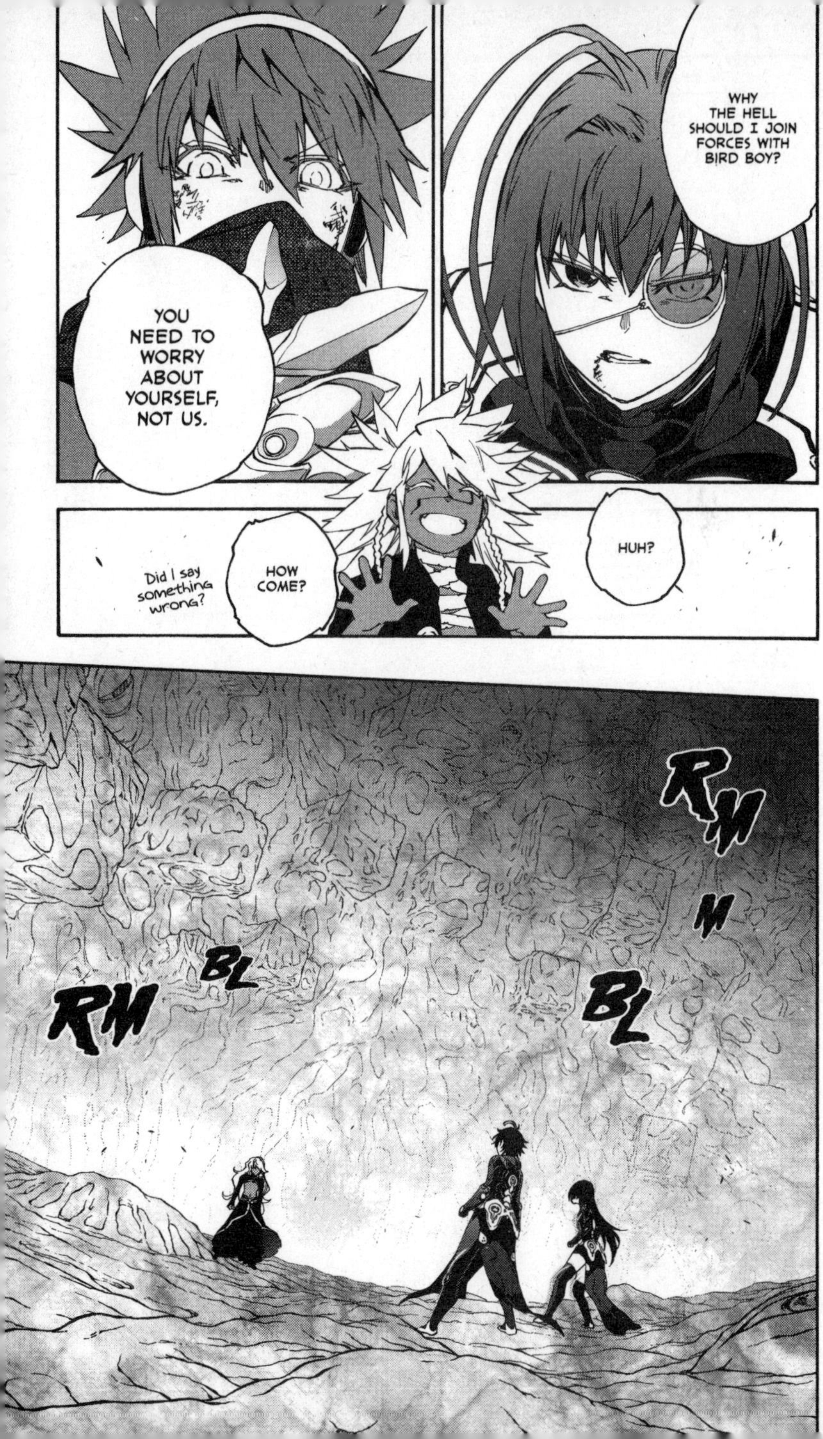
WHY THE HELL SHOULD I JOIN FORCES WITH BIRD BOY?
YOU NEED TO WORRY ABOUT YOURSELF, NOT US.
HUH?
HOW COME?
Did I say something wrong?
RMM
BL
BL
RM

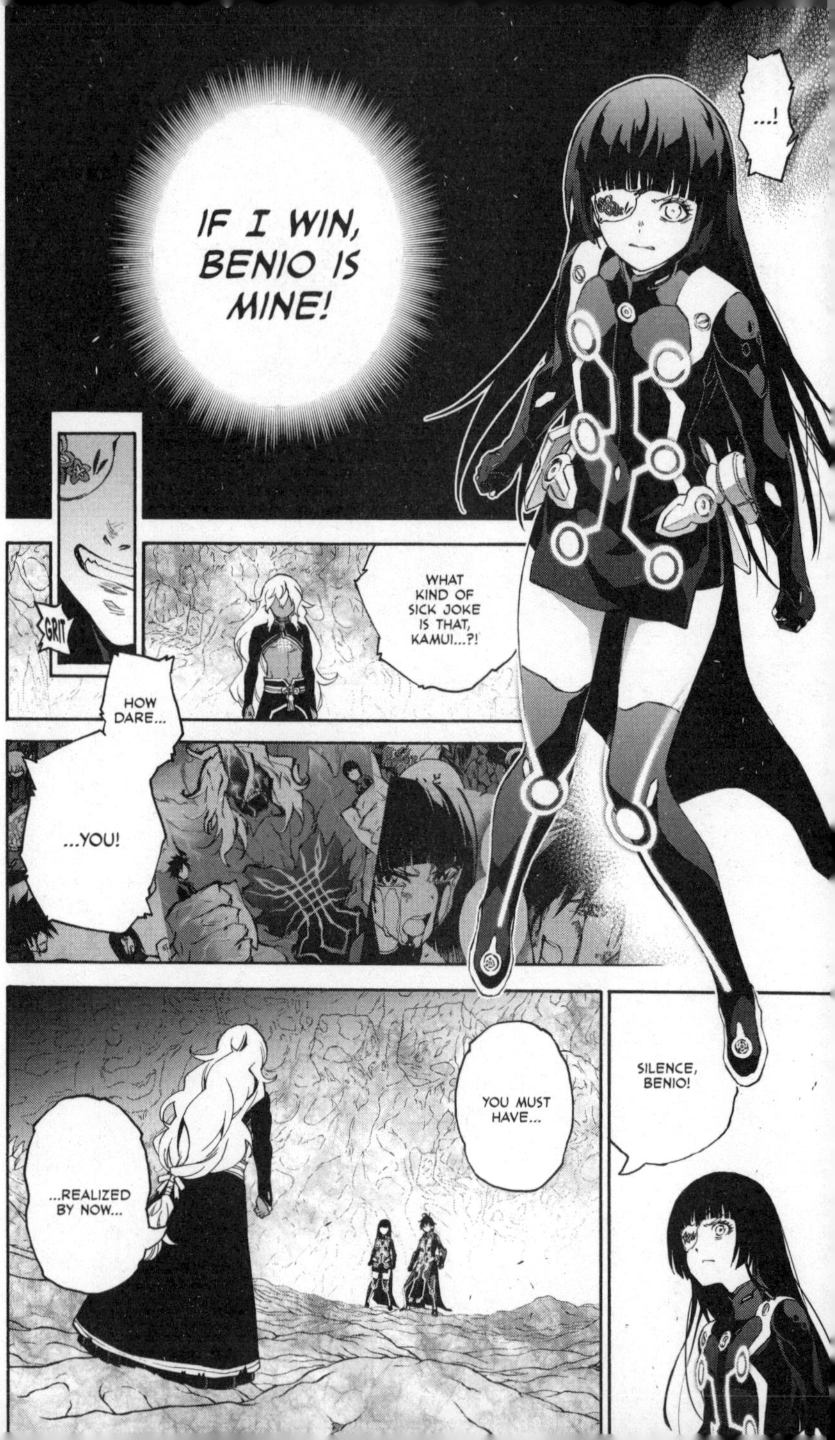
...!
IF I WIN, BENIO IS MINE!
WHAT KIND OF SICK JOKE IS THAT, KAMUI...?!
GRIT
HOW DARE...
...YOU!
SILENCE, BENIO!
YOU MUST HAVE...
...REALIZED BY NOW...

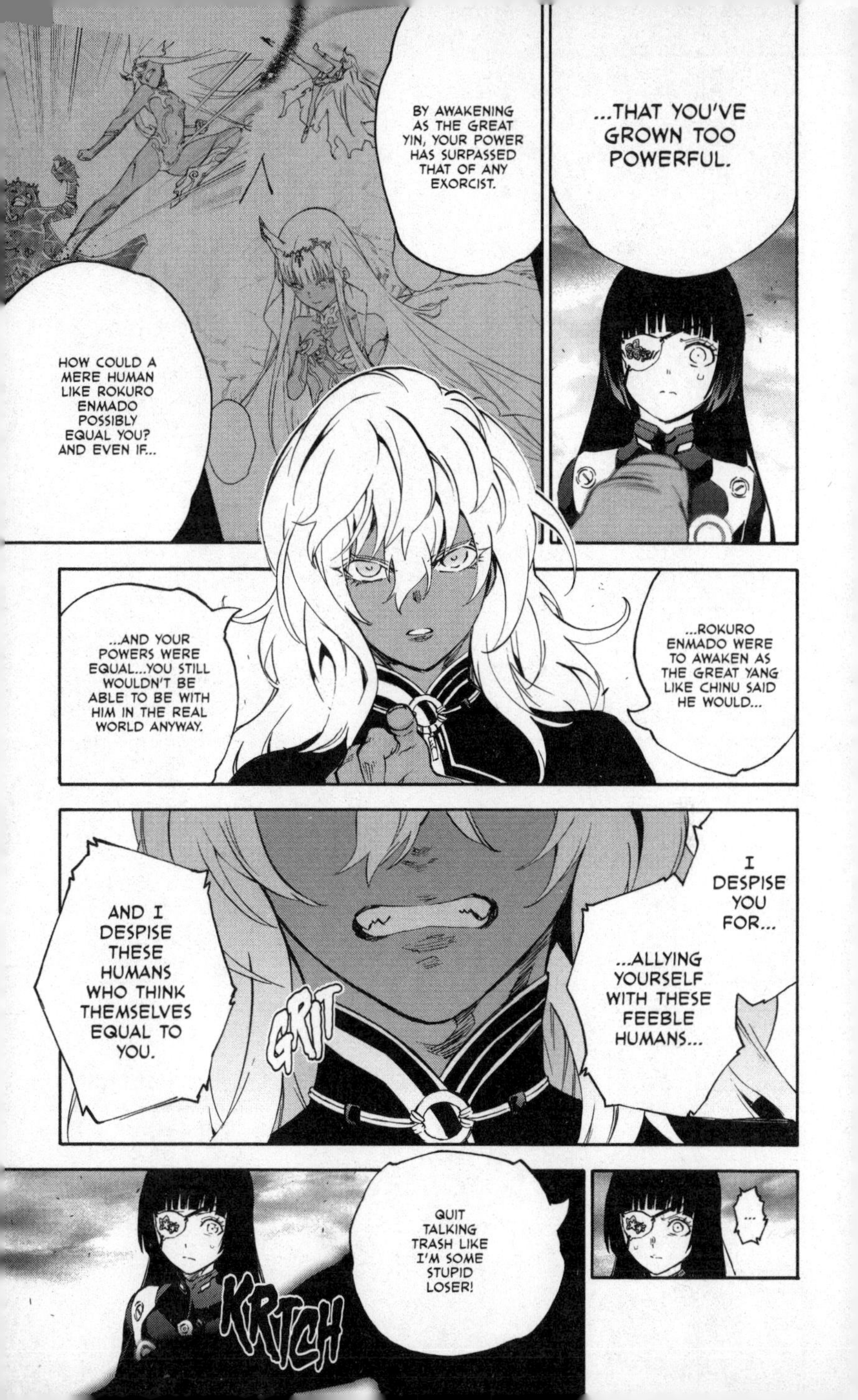
...THAT YOU'VE GROWN TOO POWERFUL.
BY AWAKENING AS THE GREAT YIN, YOUR POWER HAS SURPASSED THAT OF ANY EXORCIST.
HOW COULD A MERE HUMAN LIKE ROKURO ENMADO POSSIBLY EQUAL YOU? AND EVEN IF...
...ROKURO ENMADO WERE TO AWAKEN AS THE GREAT YANG LIKE CHINU SAID HE WOULD...
...AND YOUR POWERS WERE EQUAL...YOU STILL WOULDN'T BE ABLE TO BE WITH HIM IN THE REAL WORLD ANYWAY.
I DESPISE YOU FOR...
...ALLYING YOURSELF WITH THESE FEEBLE HUMANS...
AND I DESPISE THESE HUMANS WHO THINK THEMSELVES EQUAL TO YOU.
GRIT
....
QUIT TALKING TRASH LIKE I'M SOME STUPID LOSER!
KRTCH

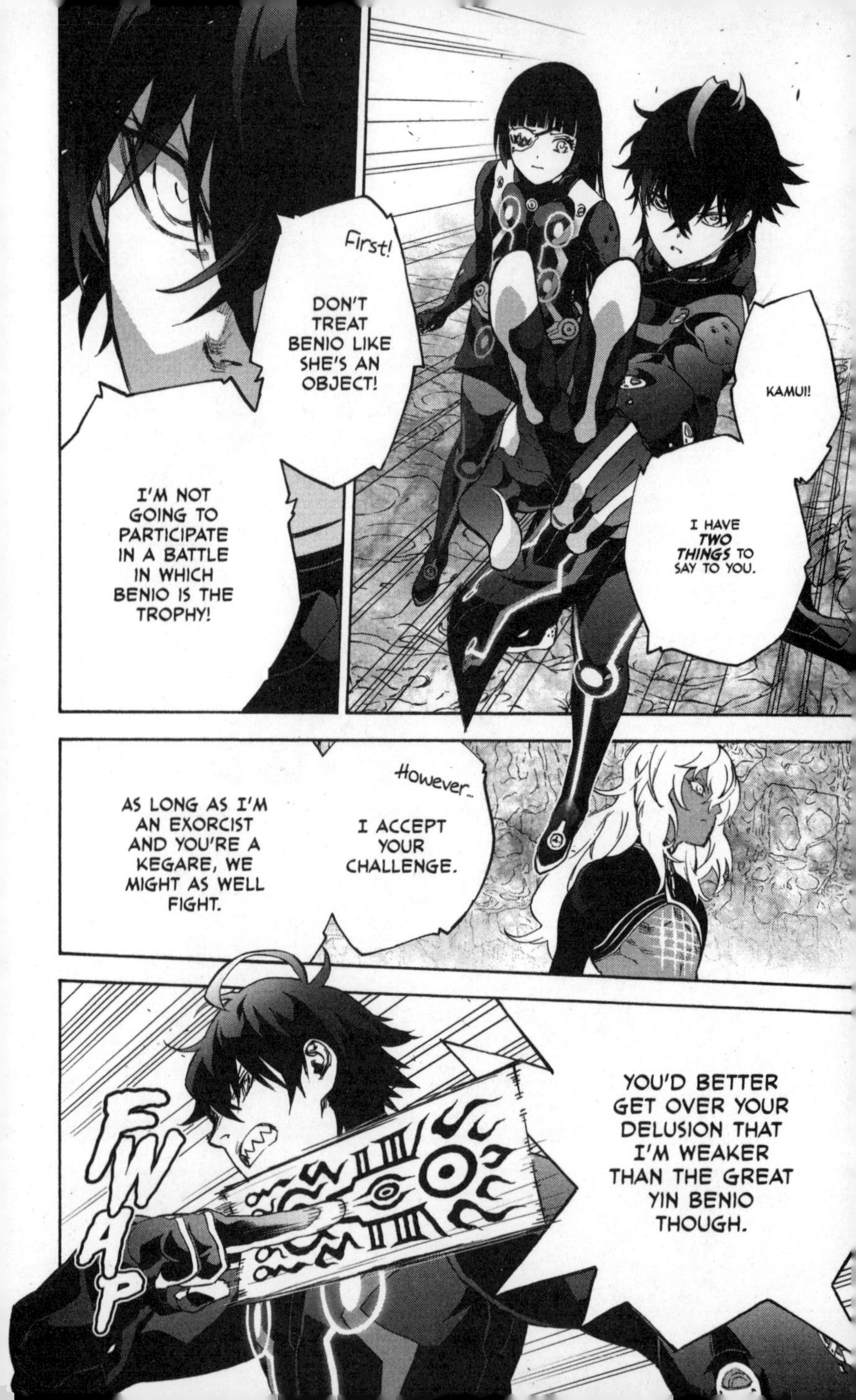
KAMUI!
I HAVE *TWO THINGS* TO SAY TO YOU.
First!
DON'T TREAT BENIO LIKE SHE'S AN OBJECT!
I'M NOT GOING TO PARTICIPATE IN A BATTLE IN WHICH BENIO IS THE TROPHY!
However...
I ACCEPT YOUR CHALLENGE.
AS LONG AS I'M AN EXORCIST AND YOU'RE A KEGARE, WE MIGHT AS WELL FIGHT.
YOU'D BETTER GET OVER YOUR DELUSION THAT I'M WEAKER THAN THE GREAT YIN BENIO THOUGH.
FWAP

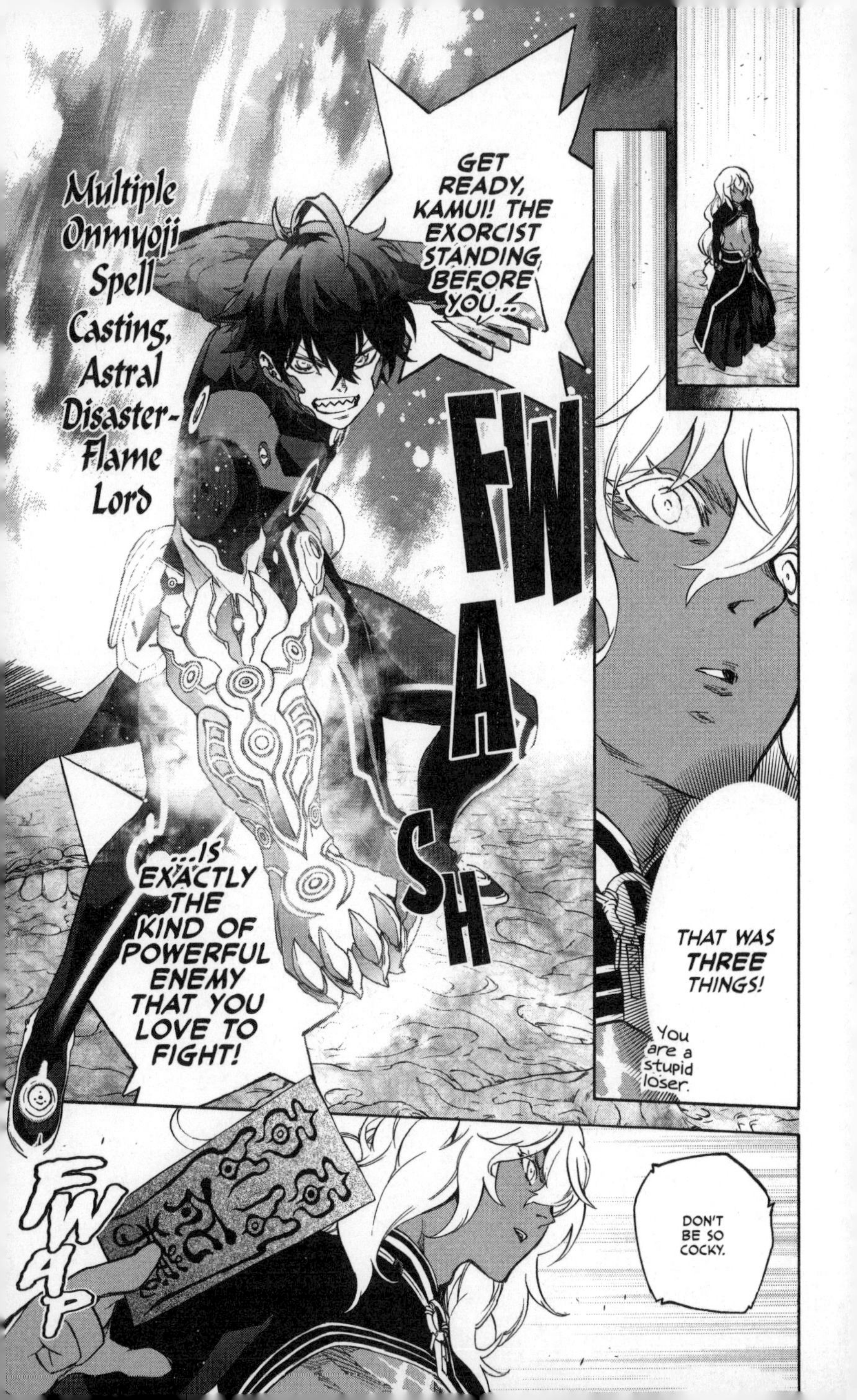
THAT WAS THREE THINGS!
You are a stupid loser.
GET READY, KAMUI! THE EXORCIST STANDING BEFORE YOU...
Multiple Onmyoji Spell Casting, Astral Disaster-Flame Lord
FWASH
...IS EXACTLY THE KIND OF POWERFUL ENEMY THAT YOU LOVE TO FIGHT!
DON'T BE SO COCKY.
FWAP

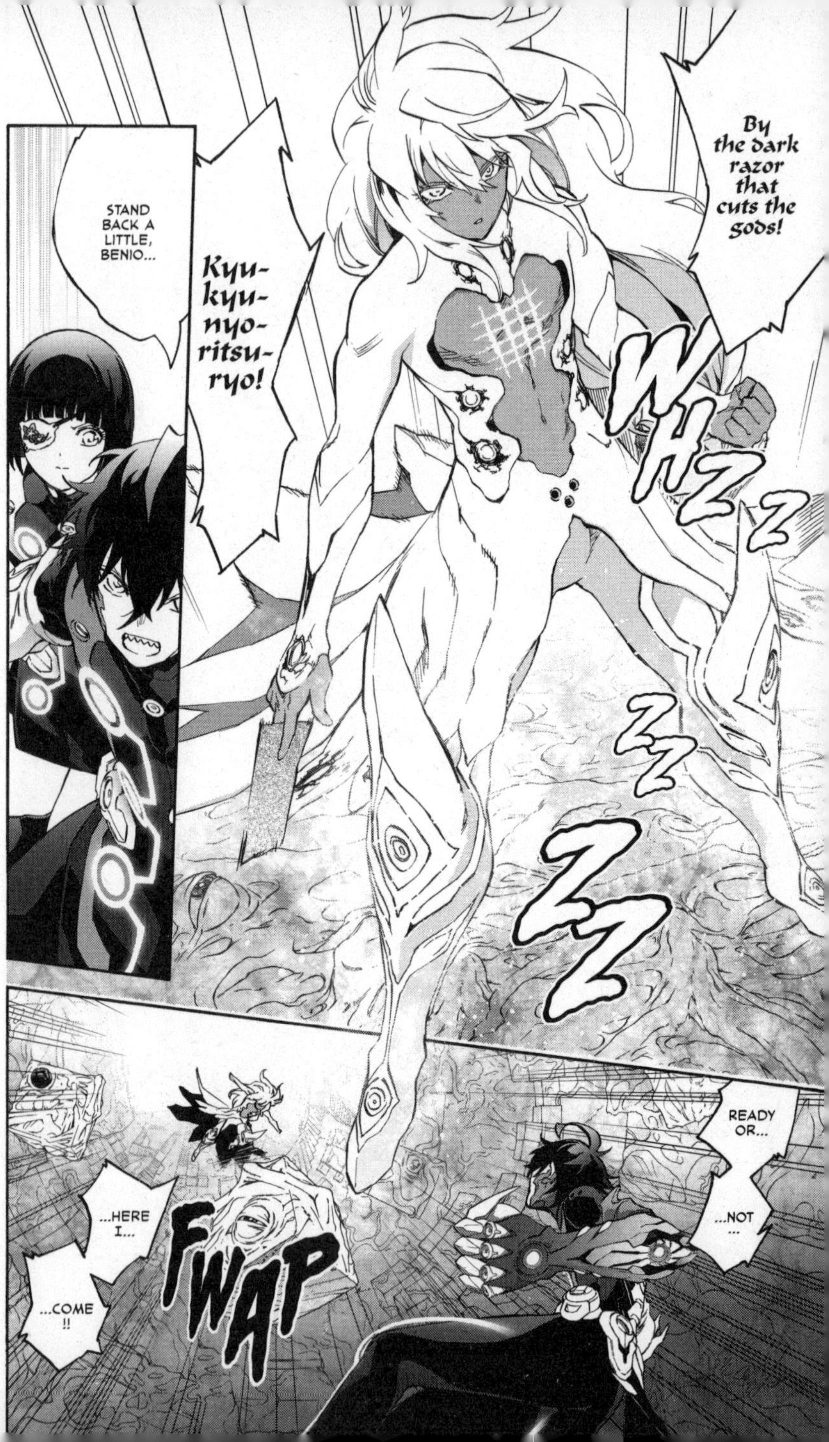
By the dark razor that cuts the gods!
WHZZZ
Kyu-kyu-nyo-ritsu-ryo!
STAND BACK A LITTLE, BENIO...
ZZZ
READY OR...
...NOT...
...HERE I...
...COME!!
FWAP

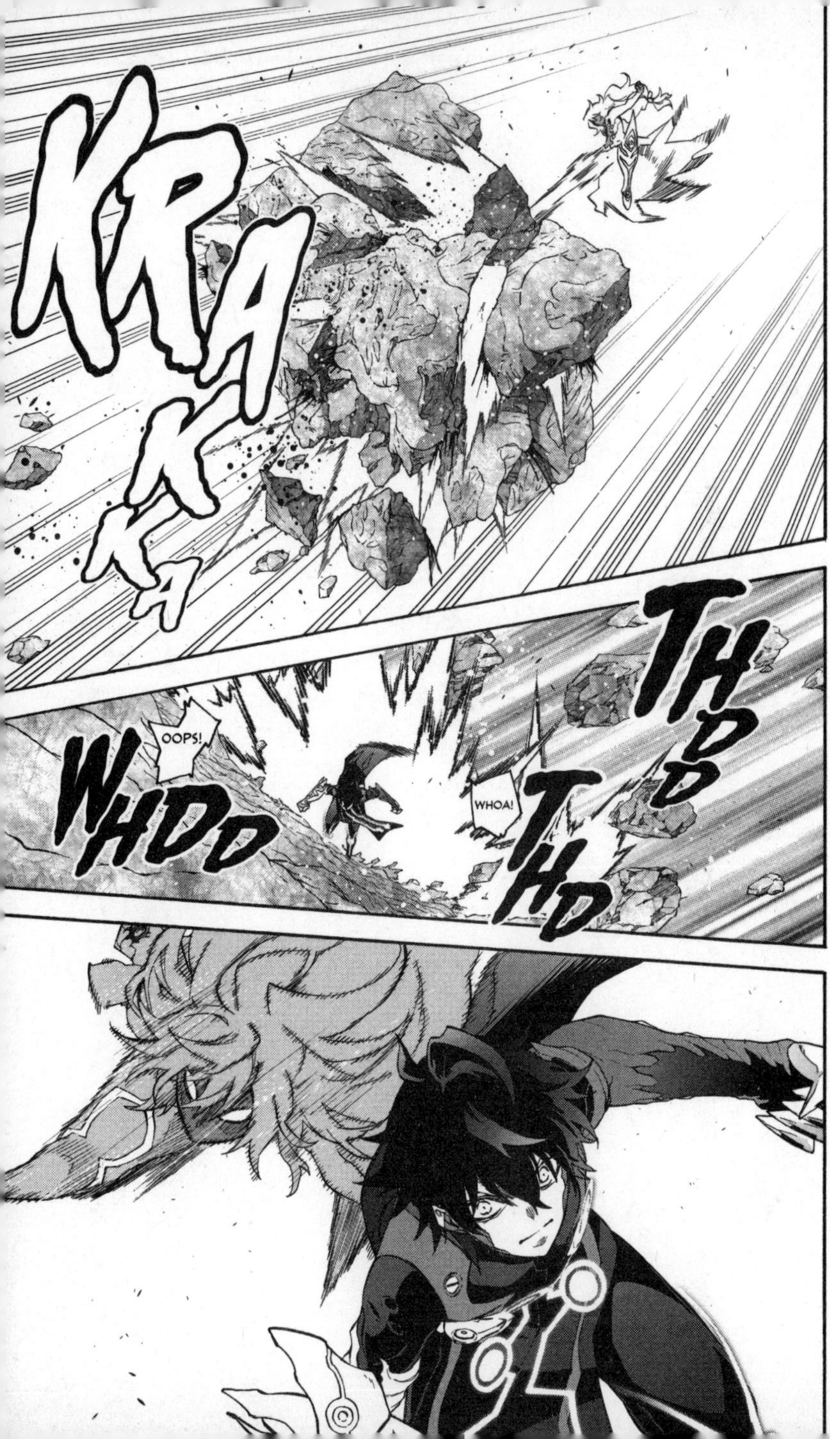
KRAKKA
THDD
WHOA!
THD
OOPS!
WHDD

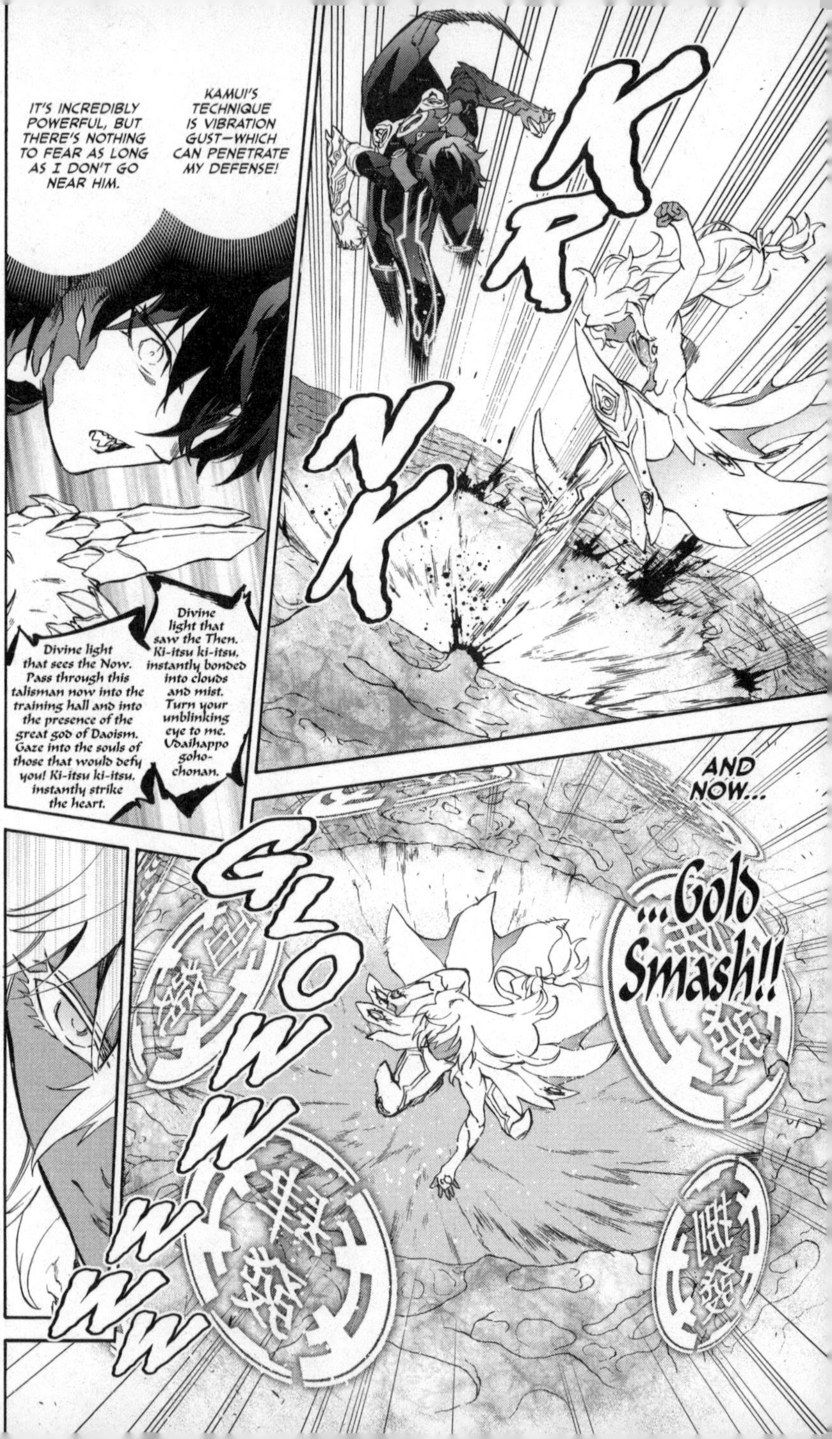
KRNK
KAMUI'S TECHNIQUE IS VIBRATION GUST—WHICH CAN PENETRATE MY DEFENSE!
IT'S INCREDIBLY POWERFUL, BUT THERE'S NOTHING TO FEAR AS LONG AS I DON'T GO NEAR HIM.
Divine light that saw the Then. Ki-itsu ki-itsu, instantly bonded into clouds and mist. Turn your unblinking eye to me. Udaihappo goho-chonan.
Divine light that sees the Now. Pass through this talisman now into the training hall and into the presence of the great god of Daoism. Gaze into the souls of those that would defy you! Ki-itsu ki-itsu, instantly strike the heart.
AND NOW...
...Gold Smash!!
GLOWWWWWW

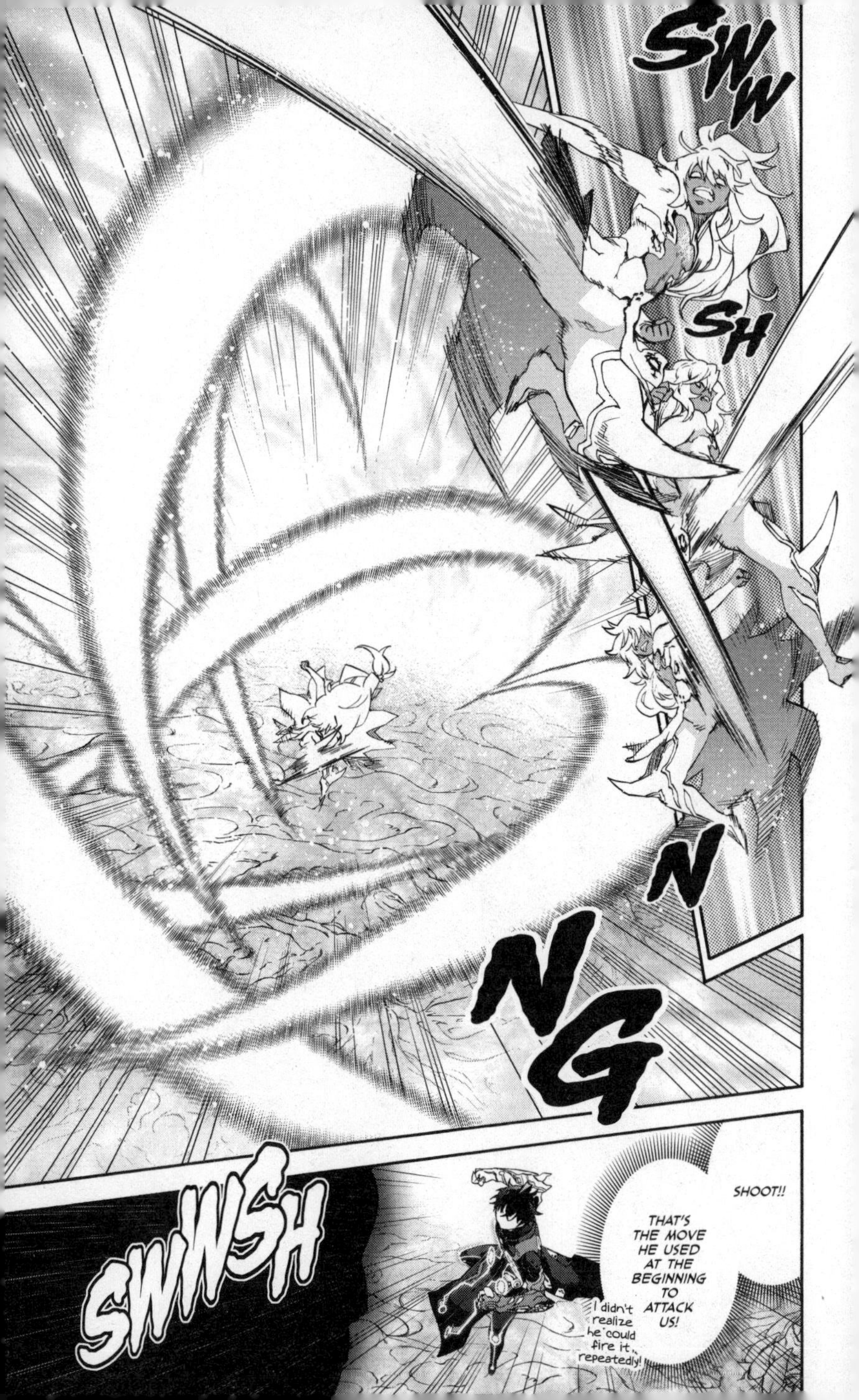
SWW
SH
N
NG
SHOOT!!
THAT'S THE MOVE HE USED AT THE BEGINNING TO ATTACK US!
I didn't realize he could fire it repeatedly!
SWNSH

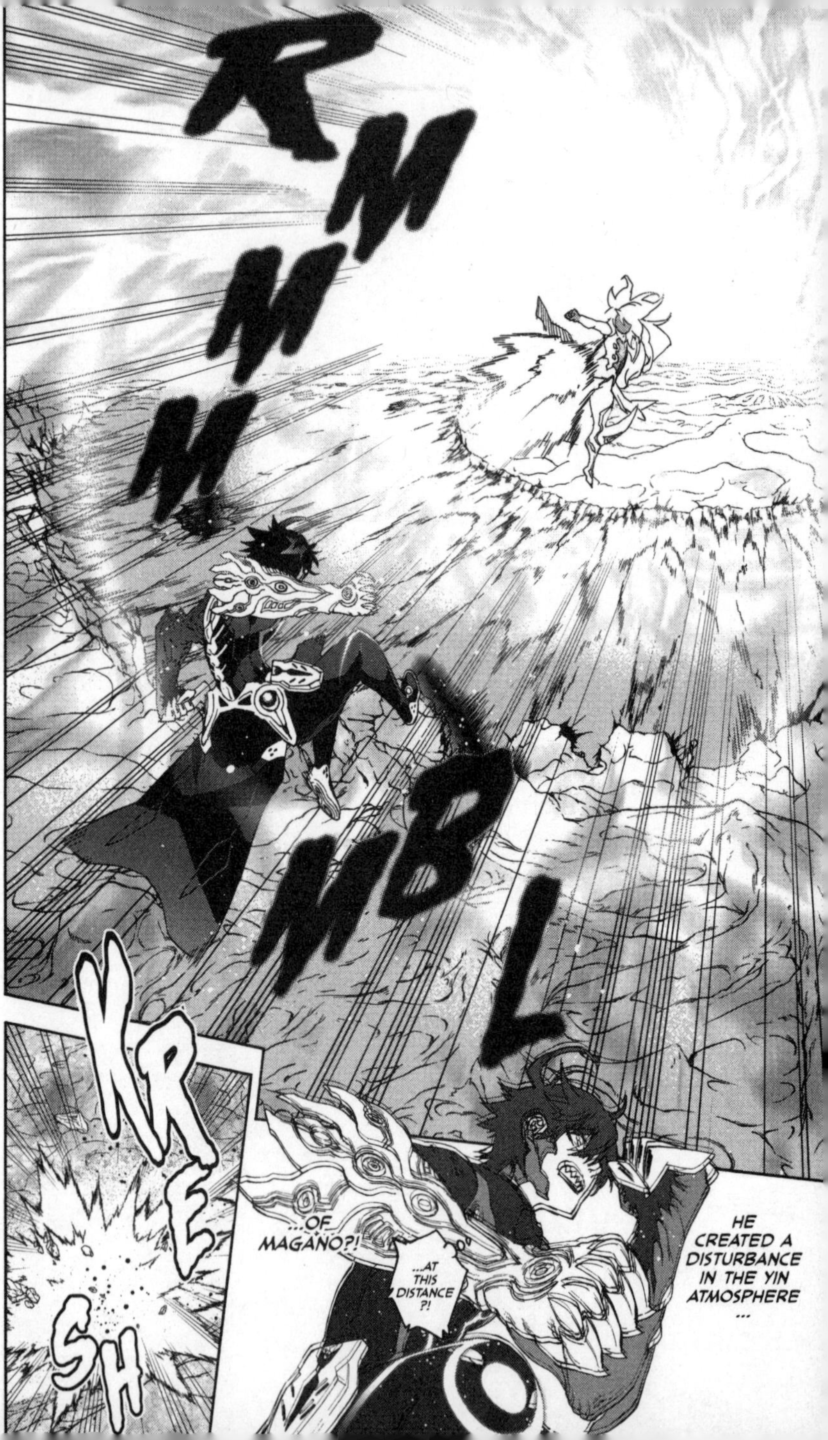

RMMMM
MBL
HE CREATED A DISTURBANCE IN THE YIN ATMOSPHERE ...
...AT THIS DISTANCE ?!
...OF MAGANO?!
KRE
SH

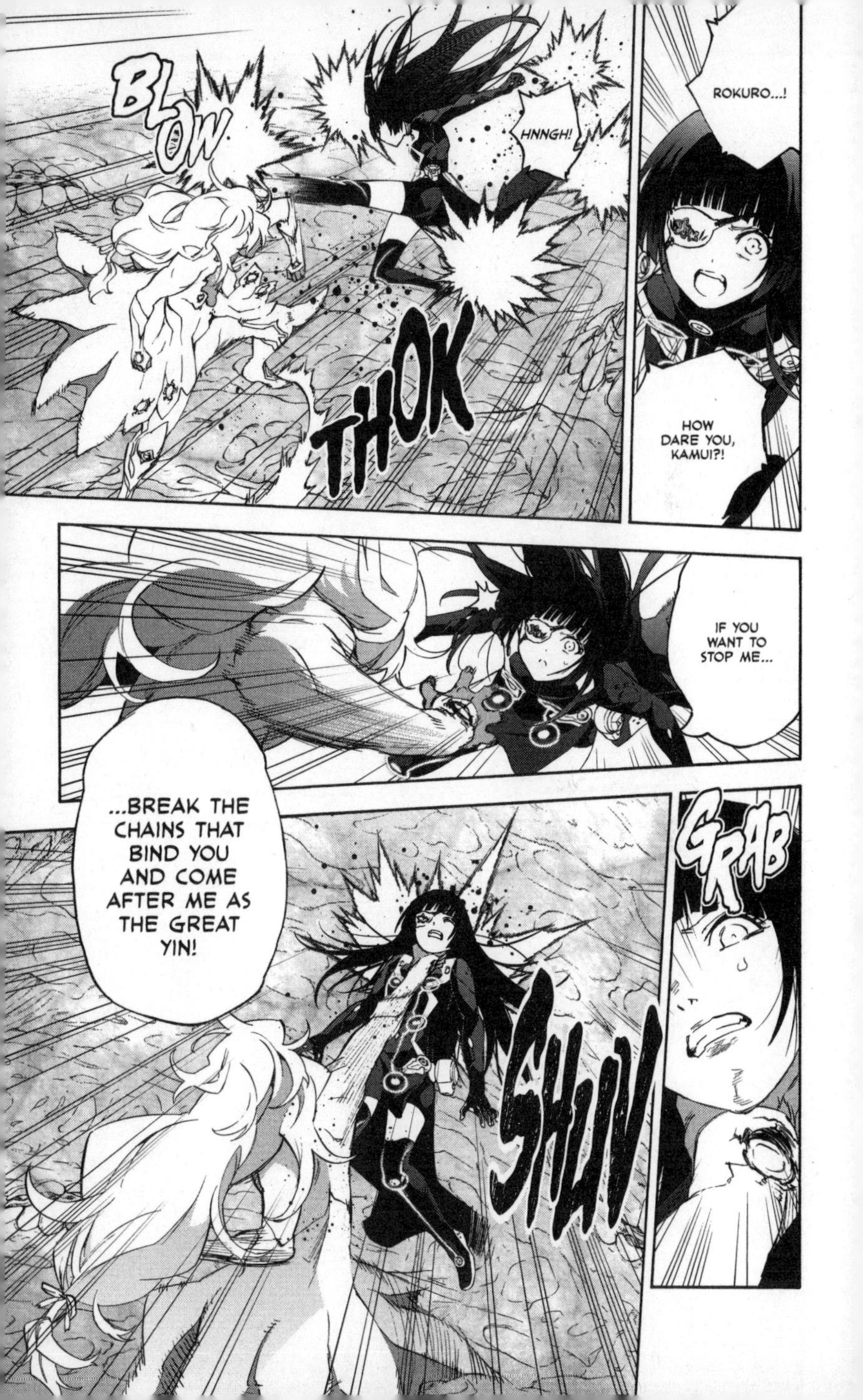
ROKURO...!
HOW DARE YOU, KAMUI?!
BLOW
HNNGH!
THOK
IF YOU WANT TO STOP ME...
GRAB
...BREAK THE CHAINS THAT BIND YOU AND COME AFTER ME AS THE GREAT YIN!
SHUN

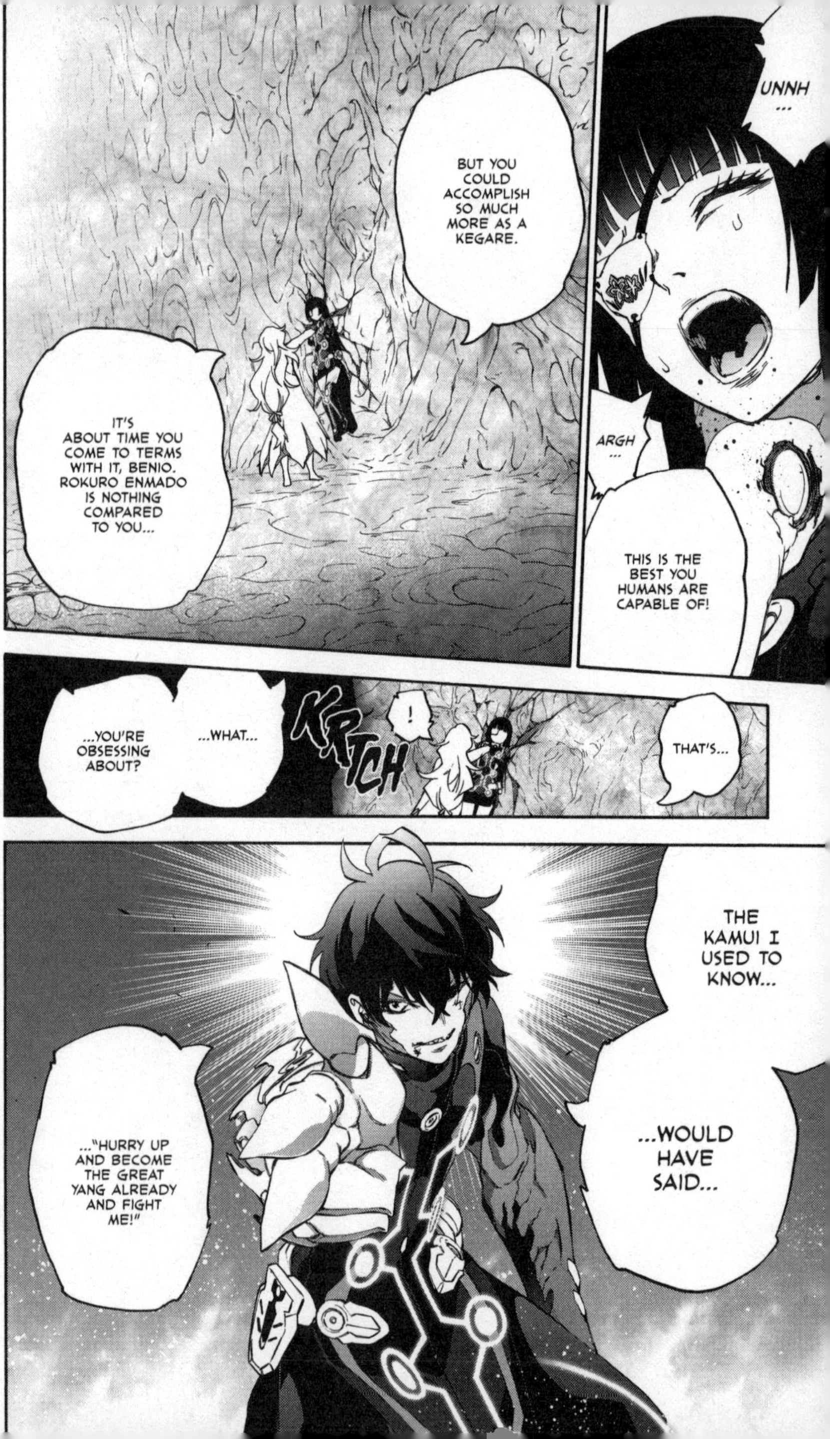
UNNH...
ARGH...
THIS IS THE BEST YOU HUMANS ARE CAPABLE OF!
BUT YOU COULD ACCOMPLISH SO MUCH MORE AS A KEGARE.
IT'S ABOUT TIME YOU COME TO TERMS WITH IT, BENIO. ROKURO ENMADO IS NOTHING COMPARED TO YOU...
THAT'S...
!
KRTCH
...WHAT...
...YOU'RE OBSESSING ABOUT?
THE KAMUI I USED TO KNOW...
...WOULD HAVE SAID...
..."HURRY UP AND BECOME THE GREAT YANG ALREADY AND FIGHT ME!"

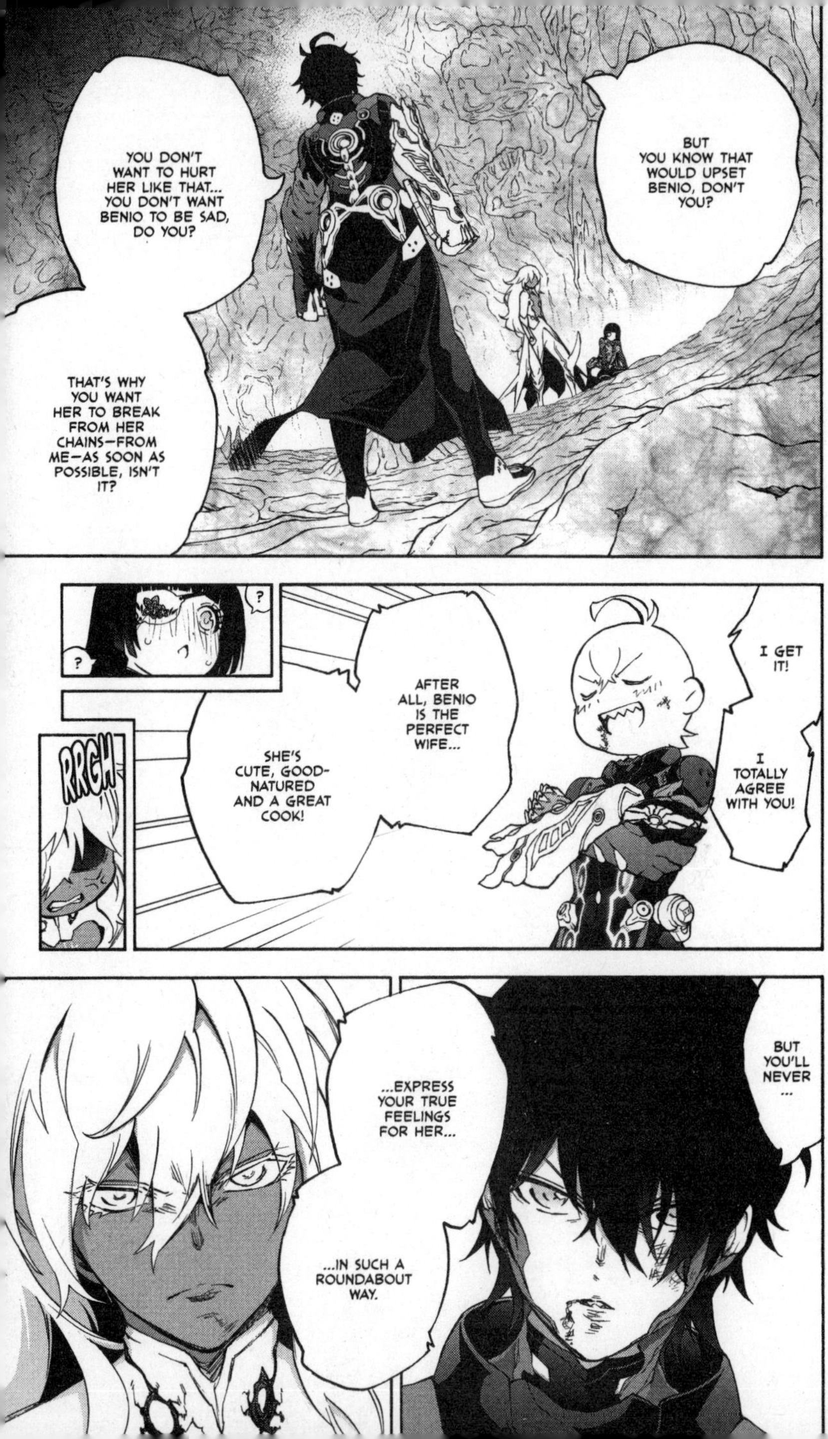
BUT YOU KNOW THAT WOULD UPSET BENIO, DON'T YOU?
YOU DON'T WANT TO HURT HER LIKE THAT... YOU DON'T WANT BENIO TO BE SAD, DO YOU?
THAT'S WHY YOU WANT HER TO BREAK FROM HER CHAINS—FROM ME—AS SOON AS POSSIBLE, ISN'T IT?
I GET IT!
I TOTALLY AGREE WITH YOU!
AFTER ALL, BENIO IS THE PERFECT WIFE...
SHE'S CUTE, GOOD-NATURED AND A GREAT COOK!
?
?
RRGH
BUT YOU'LL NEVER ...
...EXPRESS YOUR TRUE FEELINGS FOR HER...
...IN SUCH A ROUNDABOUT WAY.

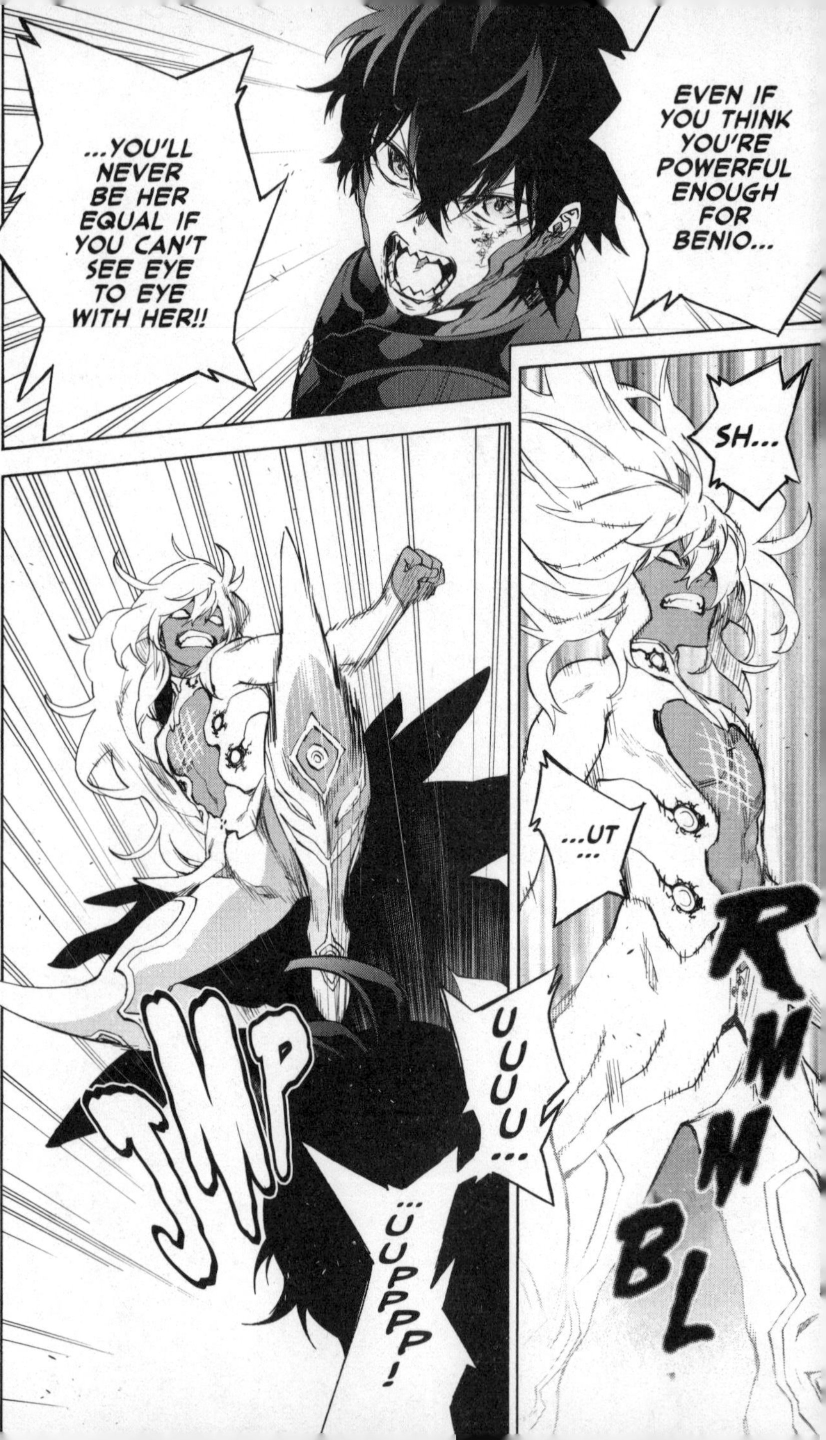
EVEN IF YOU THINK YOU'RE POWERFUL ENOUGH FOR BENIO...
...YOU'LL NEVER BE HER EQUAL IF YOU CAN'T SEE EYE TO EYE WITH HER!!
SH...
...UT ...
UUUU...
RMMBL
THMP
...ÜUPPPP!

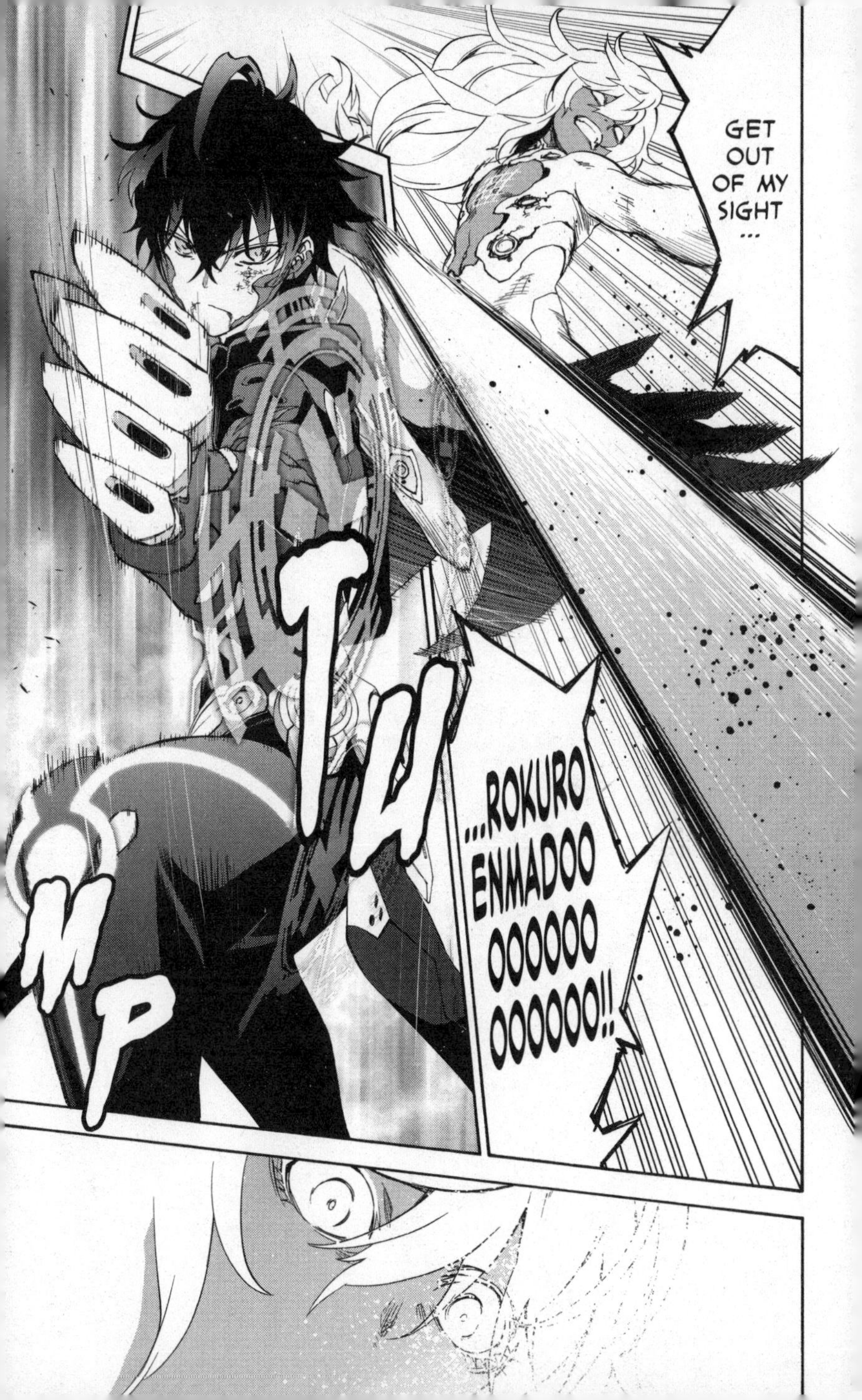
GET OUT OF MY SIGHT ...
...ROKURO ENMADOOOOOOOOOOOOO!!
JUMP

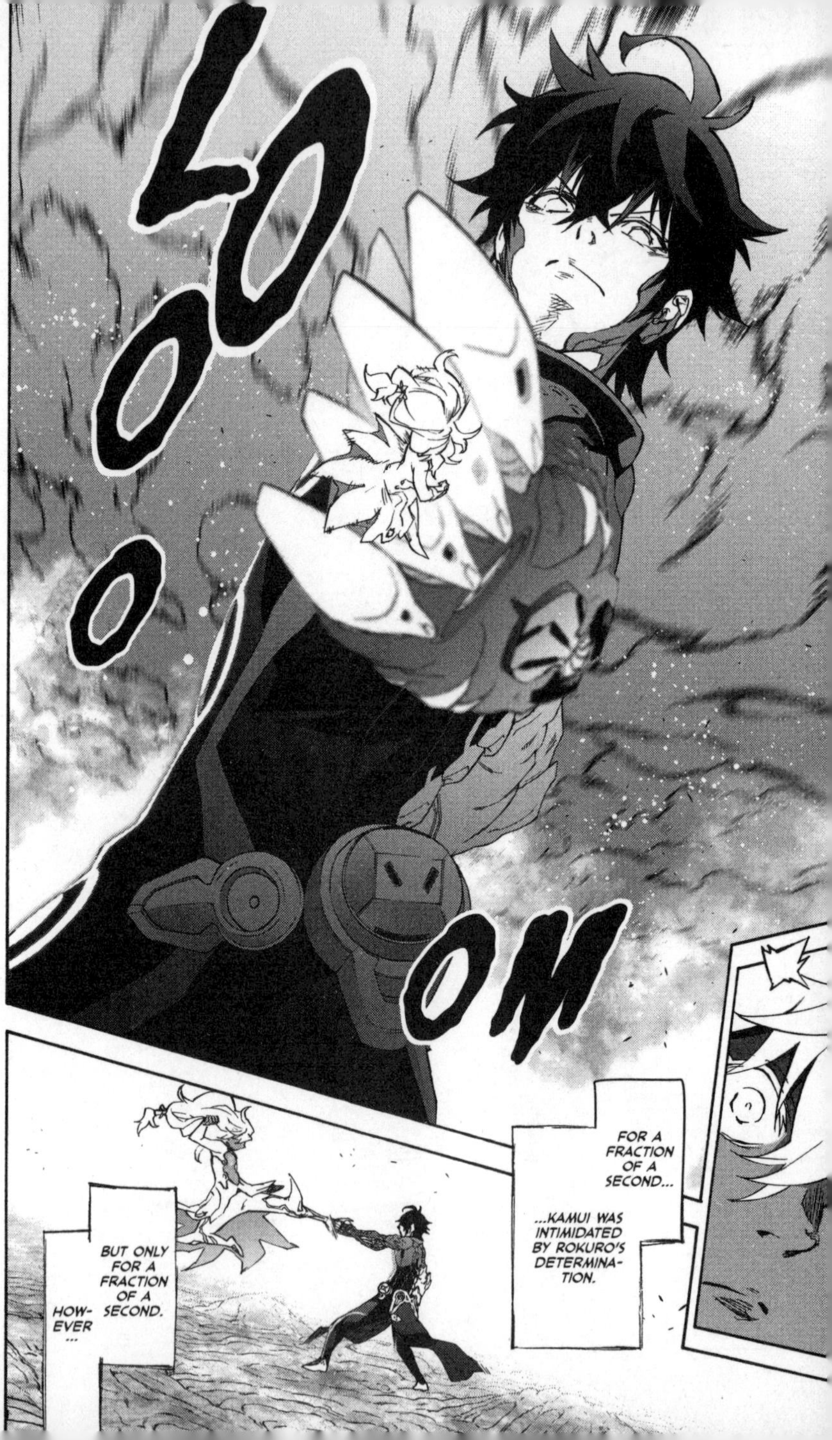
GOOOOM
FOR A FRACTION OF A SECOND...
...KAMUI WAS INTIMIDATED BY ROKURO'S DETERMINATION.
BUT ONLY FOR A FRACTION OF A SECOND.
HOWEVER...

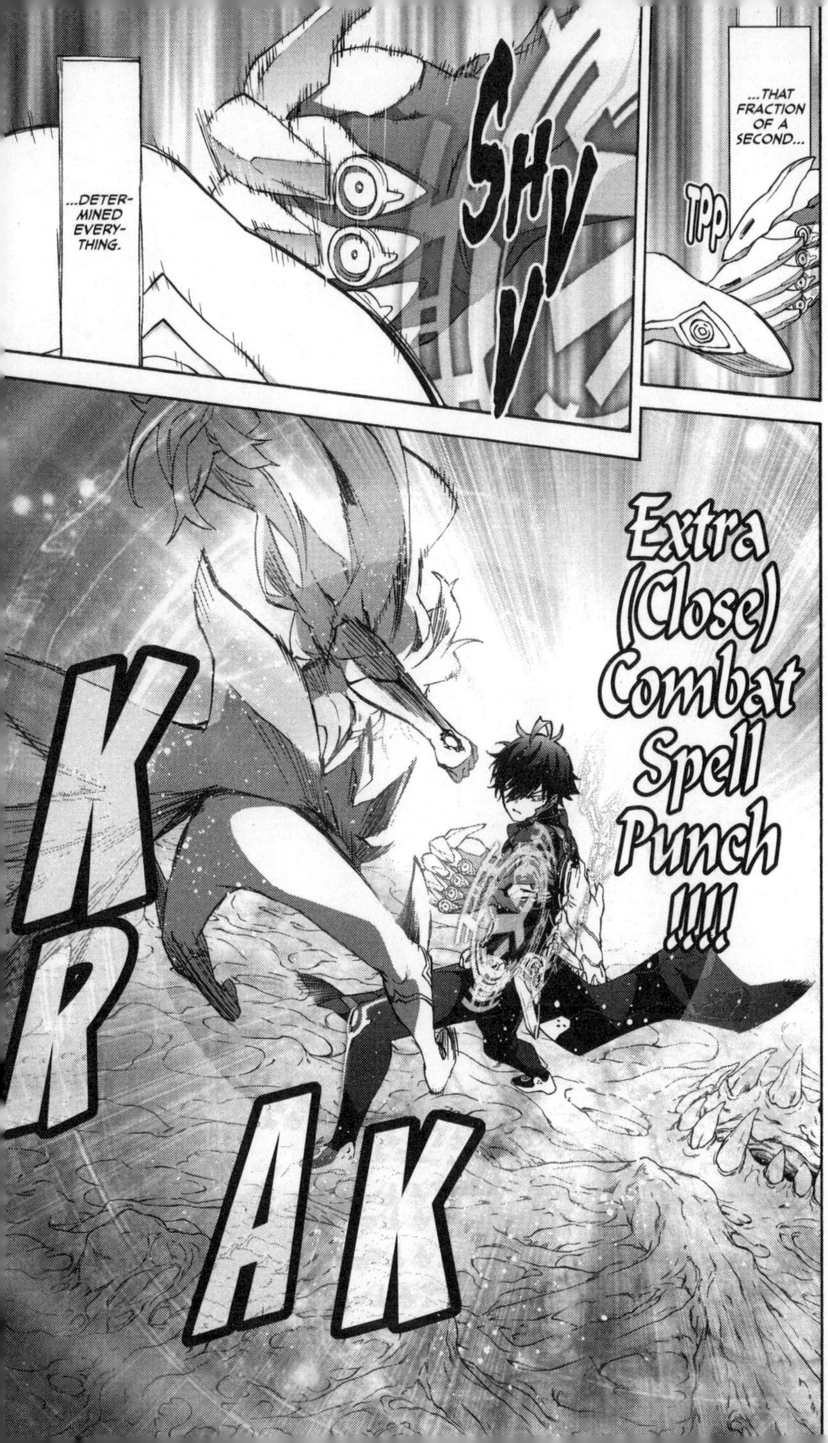
...THAT FRACTION OF A SECOND...
TPP
SHVV
...DETER-MINED EVERY-THING.
Extra (Close) Combat Spell Punch!!!!
KRAAK

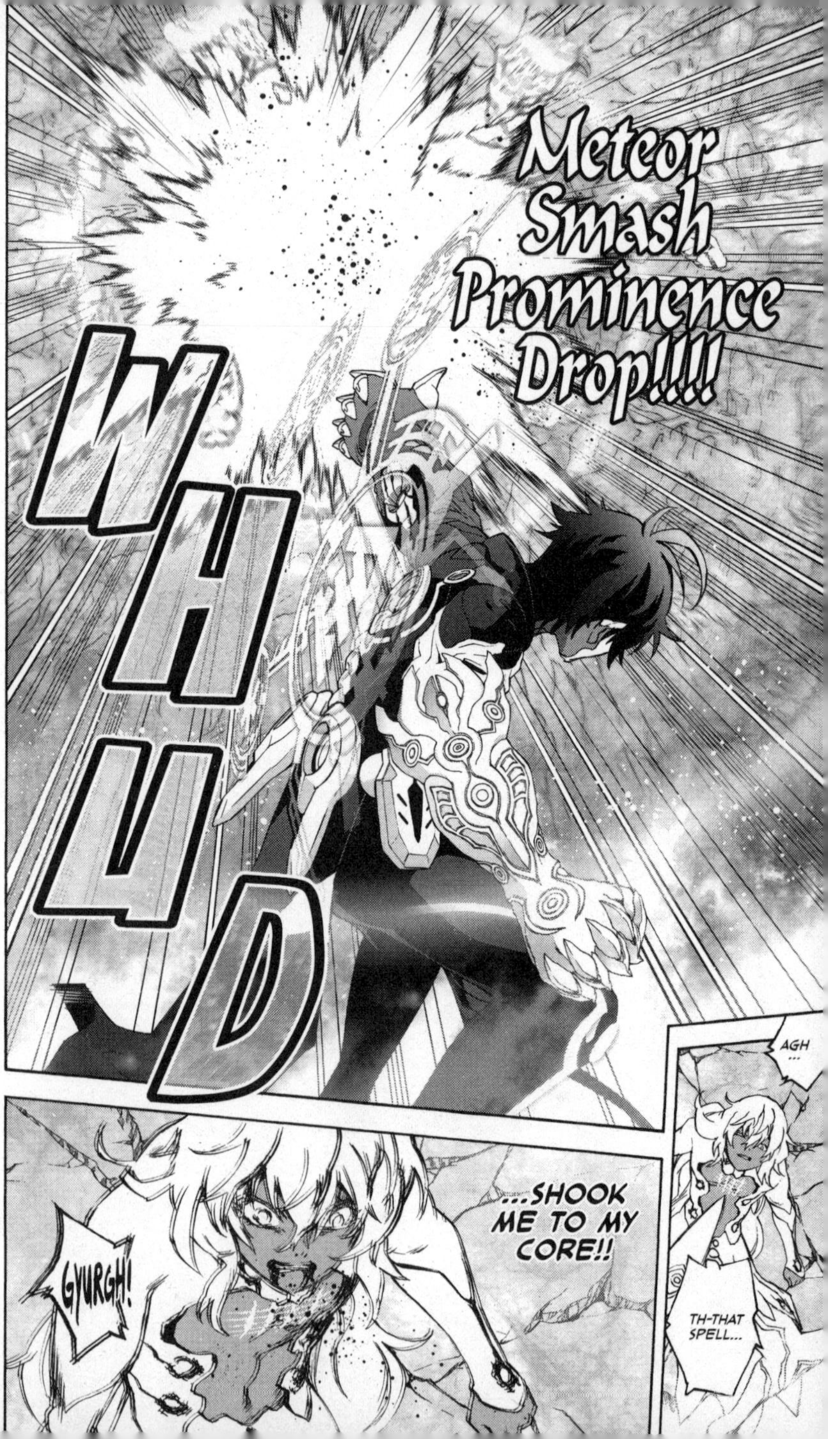
Meteor Smash Prominence Drop!!!!
WHUD
AGH ...
TH-THAT SPELL...
...SHOOK ME TO MY CORE!!
GYURGH!

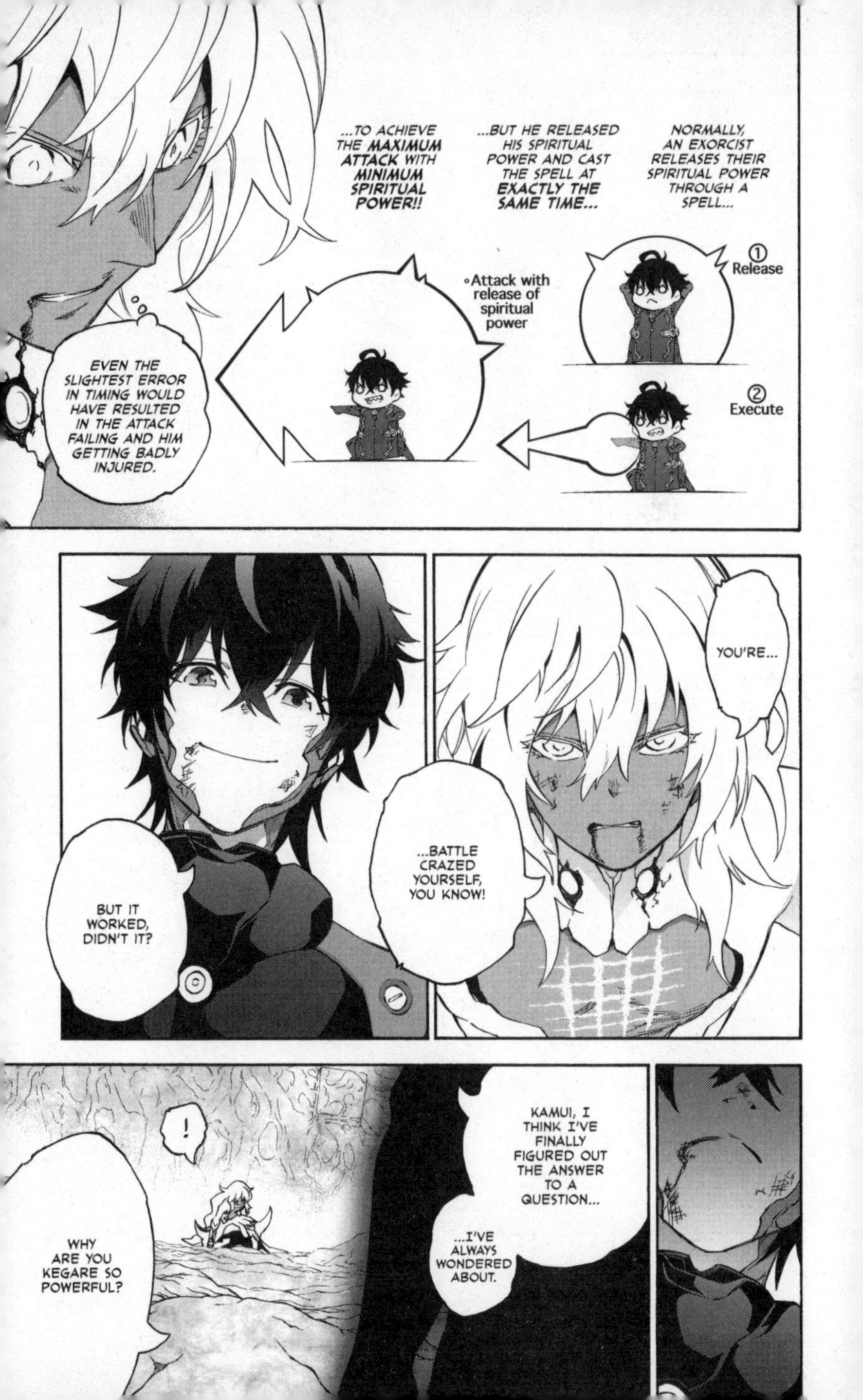
NORMALLY, AN EXORCIST RELEASES THEIR SPIRITUAL POWER THROUGH A SPELL...
...BUT HE RELEASED HIS SPIRITUAL POWER AND CAST THE SPELL AT EXACTLY THE SAME TIME...
...TO ACHIEVE THE MAXIMUM ATTACK WITH MINIMUM SPIRITUAL POWER!!
① Release
② Execute
∘Attack with release of spiritual power
EVEN THE SLIGHTEST ERROR IN TIMING WOULD HAVE RESULTED IN THE ATTACK FAILING AND HIM GETTING BADLY INJURED.
YOU'RE...
...BATTLE CRAZED YOURSELF, YOU KNOW!
BUT IT WORKED, DIDN'T IT?
KAMUI, I THINK I'VE FINALLY FIGURED OUT THE ANSWER TO A QUESTION...
...I'VE ALWAYS WONDERED ABOUT.
!
WHY ARE YOU KEGARE SO POWERFUL?

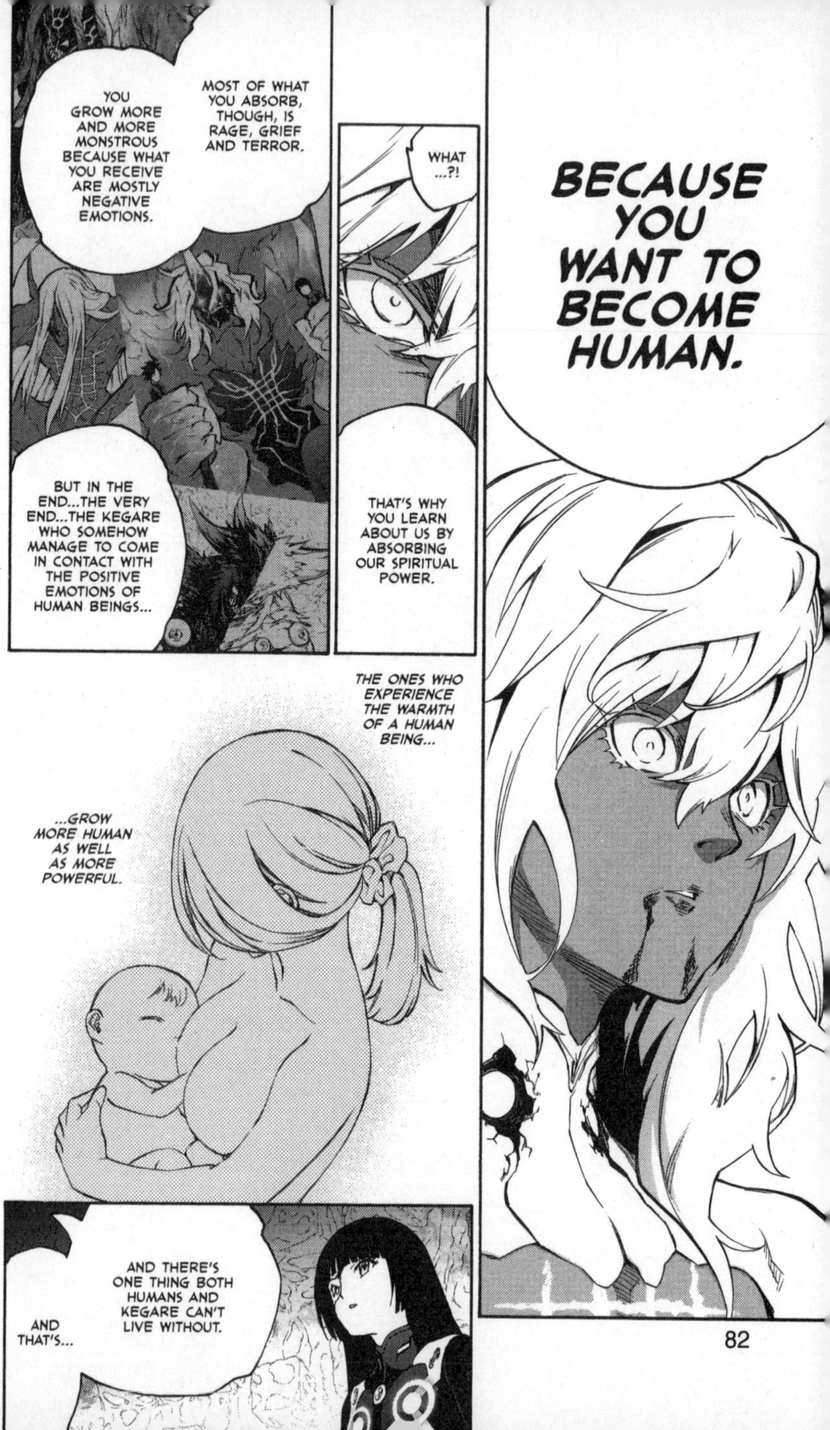
BECAUSE YOU WANT TO BECOME HUMAN.
WHAT ...?!
THAT'S WHY YOU LEARN ABOUT US BY ABSORBING OUR SPIRITUAL POWER.
MOST OF WHAT YOU ABSORB, THOUGH, IS RAGE, GRIEF AND TERROR.
YOU GROW MORE AND MORE MONSTROUS BECAUSE WHAT YOU RECEIVE ARE MOSTLY NEGATIVE EMOTIONS.
BUT IN THE END...THE VERY END...THE KEGARE WHO SOMEHOW MANAGE TO COME IN CONTACT WITH THE POSITIVE EMOTIONS OF HUMAN BEINGS...
THE ONES WHO EXPERIENCE THE WARMTH OF A HUMAN BEING...
...GROW MORE HUMAN AS WELL AS MORE POWERFUL.
AND THERE'S ONE THING BOTH HUMANS AND KEGARE CAN'T LIVE WITHOUT.
AND THAT'S...

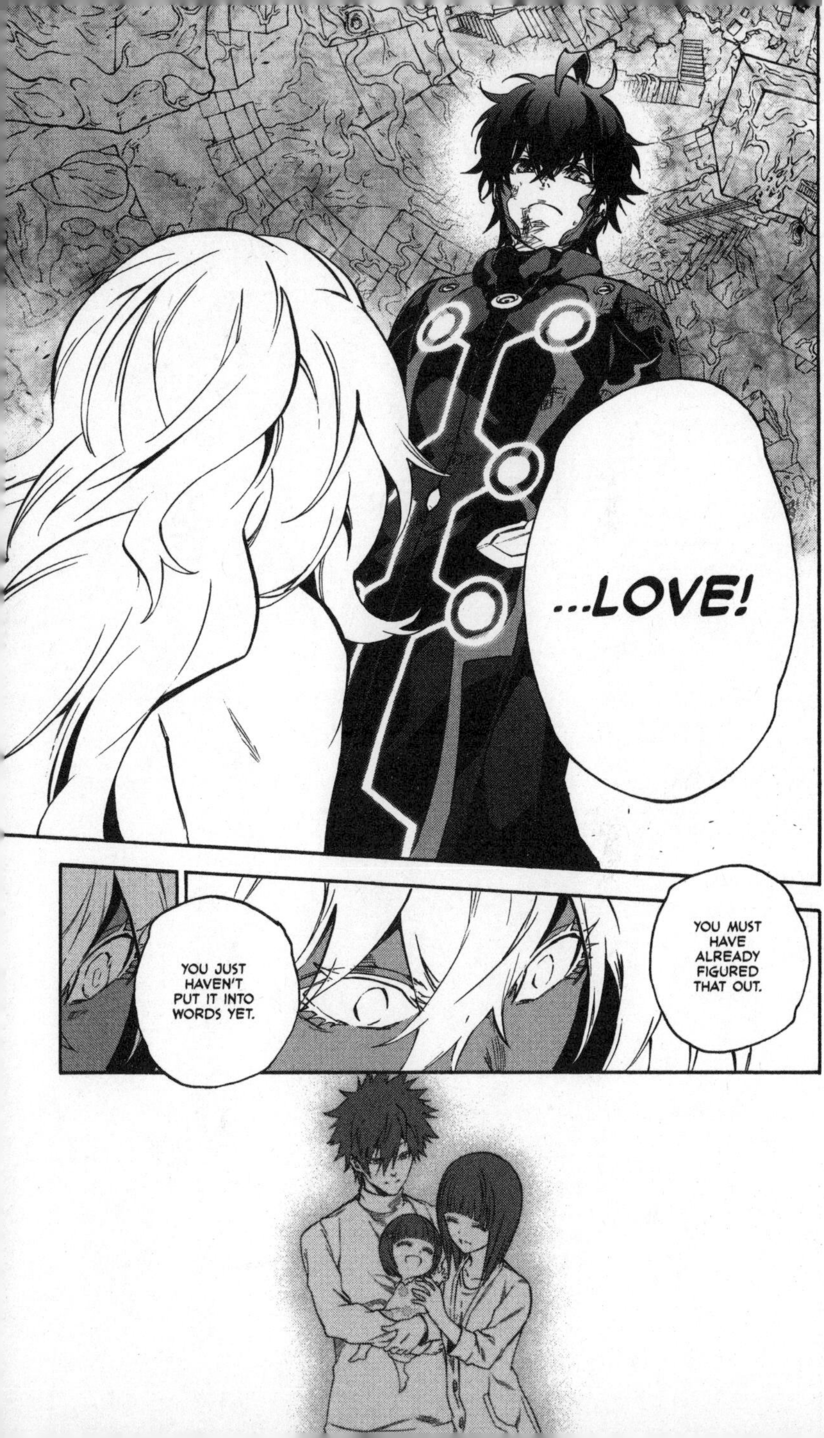
...LOVE!
YOU MUST HAVE ALREADY FIGURED THAT OUT.
YOU JUST HAVEN'T PUT IT INTO WORDS YET.

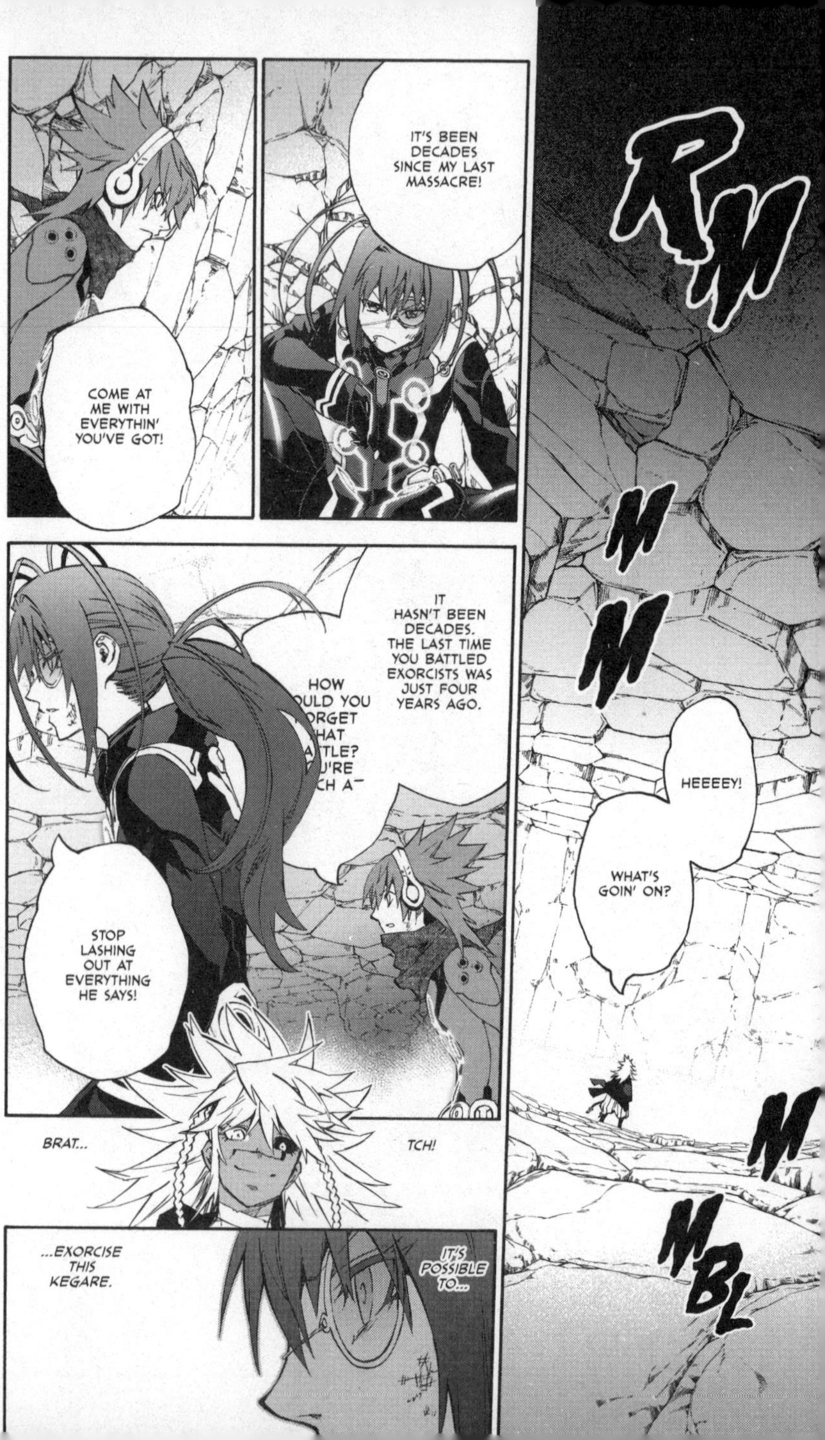
RM
M
M
HEEEEY!
WHAT'S GOIN' ON?
M
MBL
IT'S BEEN DECADES SINCE MY LAST MASSACRE!
COME AT ME WITH EVERYTHIN' YOU'VE GOT!
IT HASN'T BEEN DECADES. THE LAST TIME YOU BATTLED EXORCISTS WAS JUST FOUR YEARS AGO.
HOW OULD YOU ORGET HAT TTLE? U'RE CH A—
STOP LASHING OUT AT EVERYTHING HE SAYS!
TCH!
BRAT...
IT'S POSSIBLE TO...
...EXORCISE THIS KEGARE.

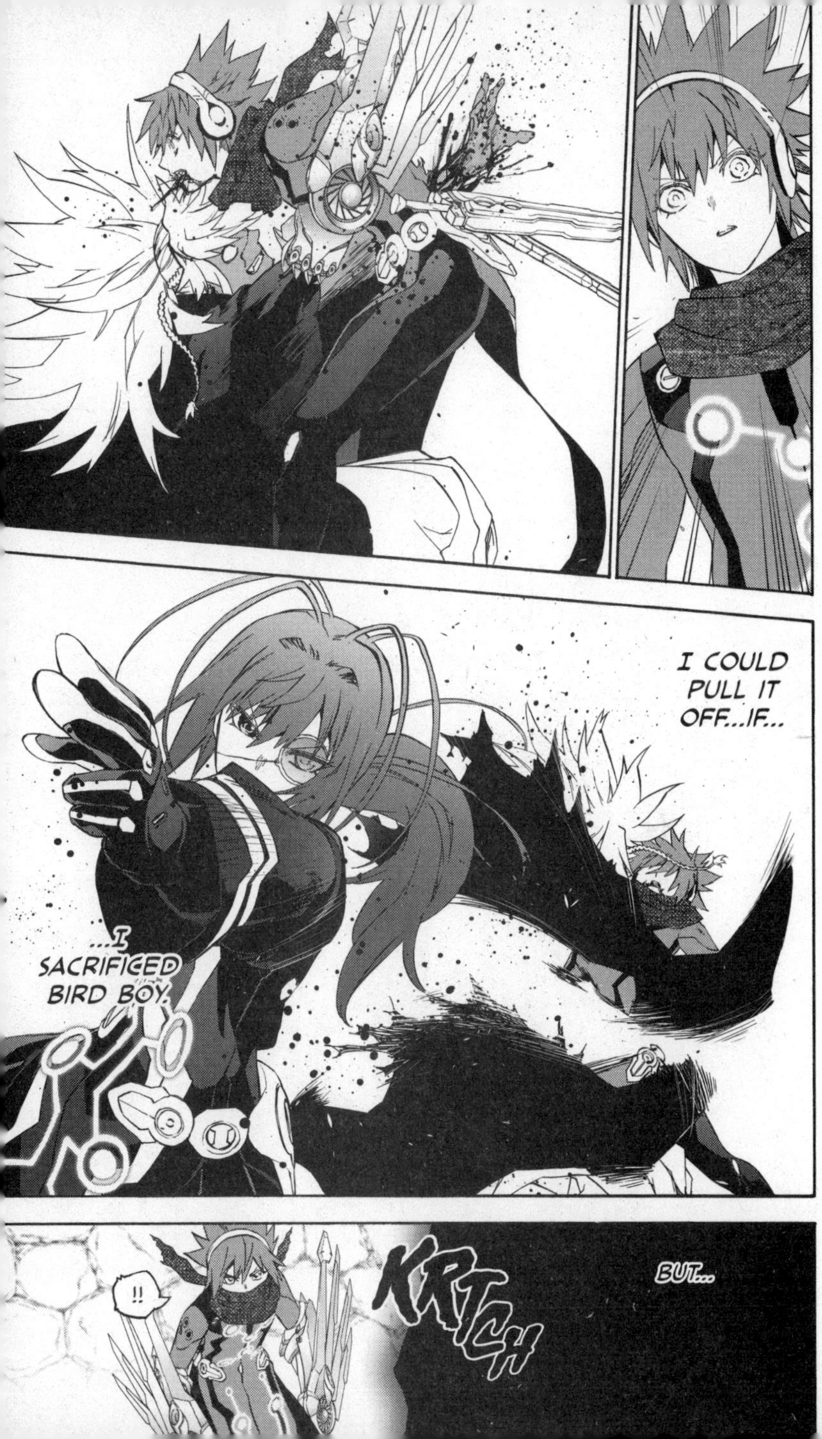
I COULD PULL IT OFF...IF...
...I SACRIFICED BIRD BOY.
BUT...
KRTCH
!!

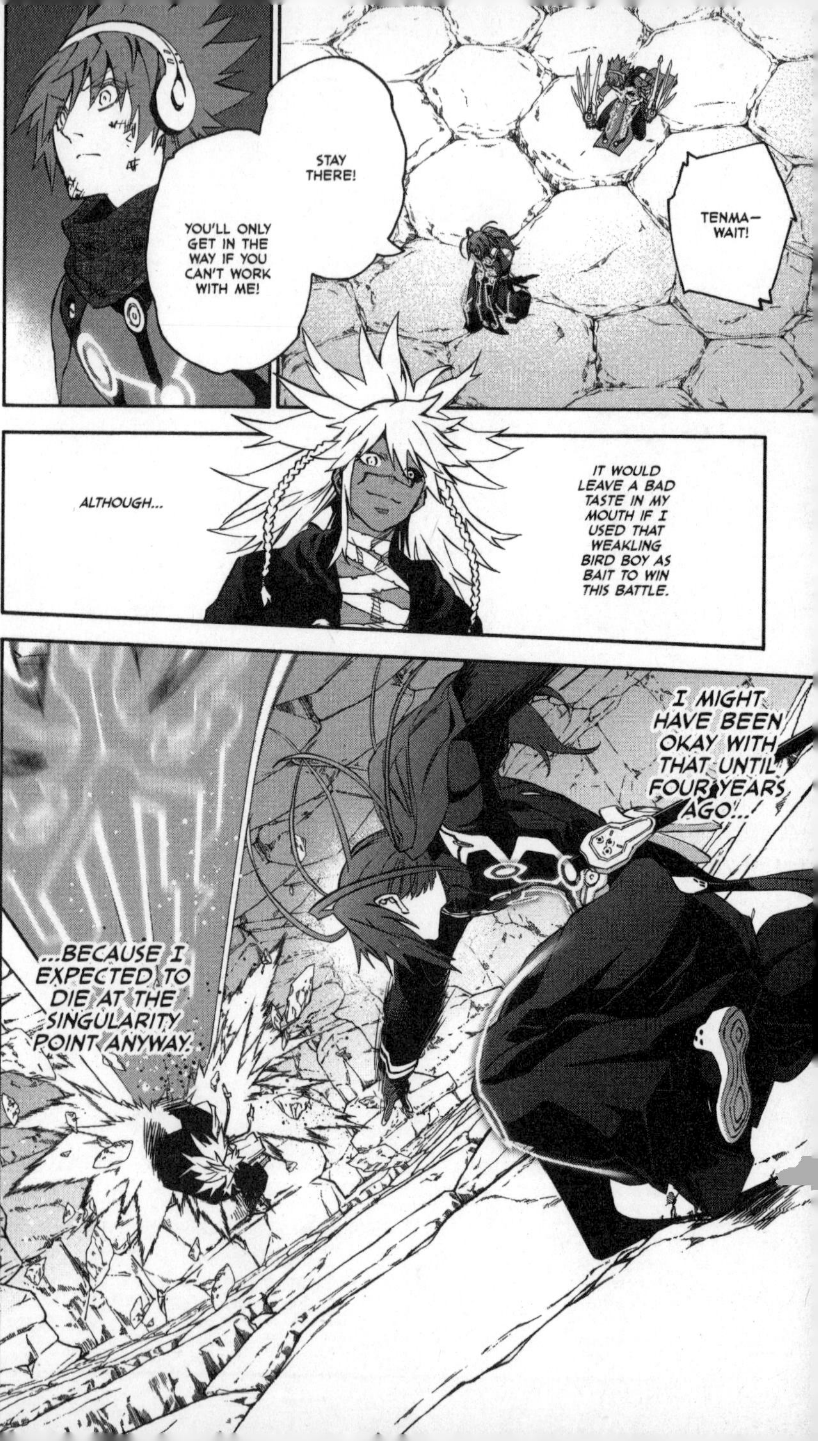
TENMA—WAIT!
STAY THERE!
YOU'LL ONLY GET IN THE WAY IF YOU CAN'T WORK WITH ME!
IT WOULD LEAVE A BAD TASTE IN MY MOUTH IF I USED THAT WEAKLING BIRD BOY AS BAIT TO WIN THIS BATTLE.
ALTHOUGH...
I MIGHT HAVE BEEN OKAY WITH THAT UNTIL FOUR YEARS AGO...
...BECAUSE I EXPECTED TO DIE AT THE SINGULARITY POINT ANYWAY.

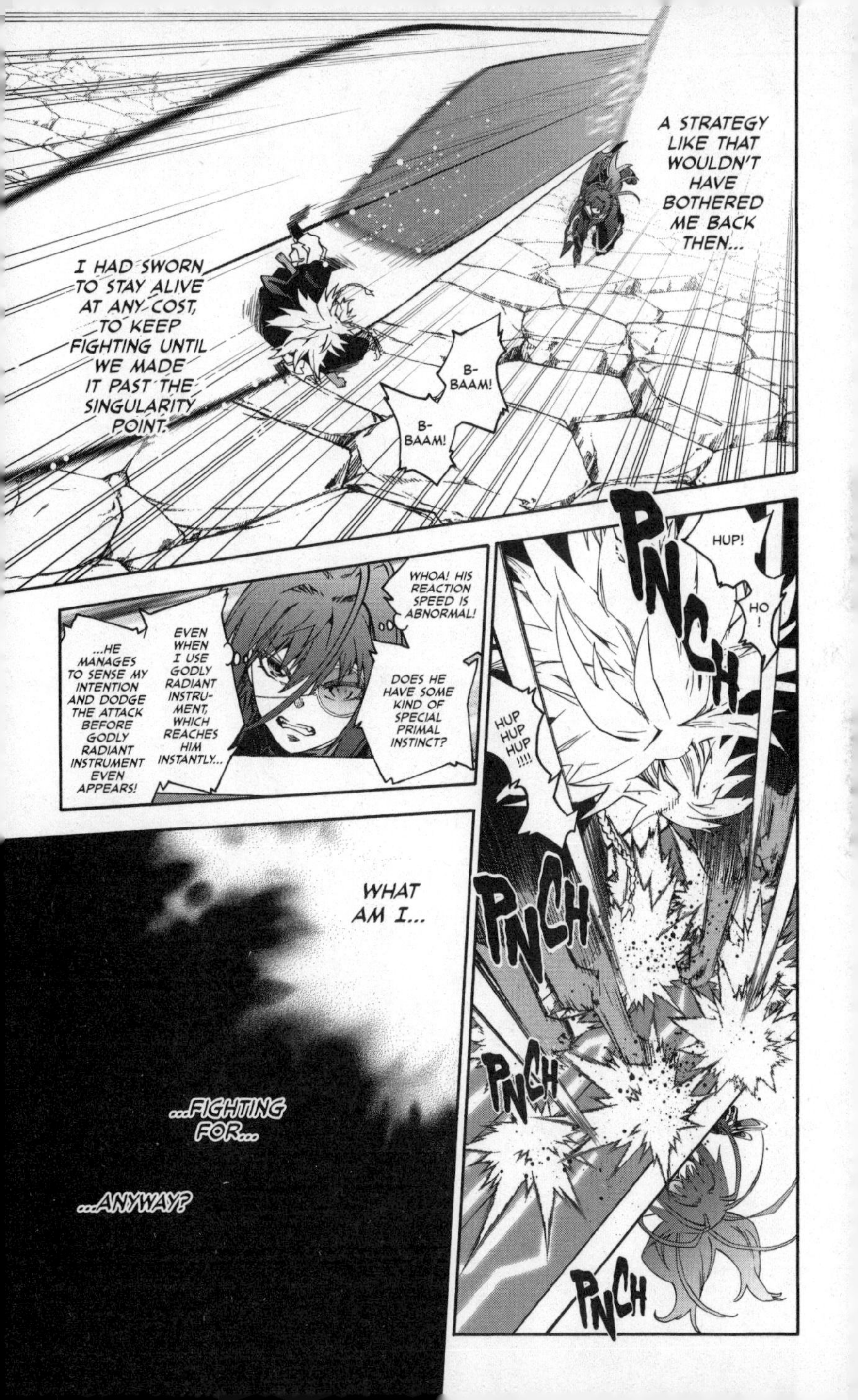
A STRATEGY LIKE THAT WOULDN'T HAVE BOTHERED ME BACK THEN...
B-BAAM!
B-BAAM!
I HAD SWORN TO STAY ALIVE AT ANY COST, TO KEEP FIGHTING UNTIL WE MADE IT PAST THE SINGULARITY POINT.
PINCH
HUP!
HO!
HUP HUP HUP!!!!
PINCH
PINCH
PINCH
WHOA! HIS REACTION SPEED IS ABNORMAL!
DOES HE HAVE SOME KIND OF SPECIAL PRIMAL INSTINCT?
EVEN WHEN I USE GODLY RADIANT INSTRUMENT, WHICH REACHES HIM INSTANTLY...
...HE MANAGES TO SENSE MY INTENTION AND DODGE THE ATTACK BEFORE GODLY RADIANT INSTRUMENT EVEN APPEARS!
WHAT AM I...
...FIGHTING FOR...
...ANYWAY?

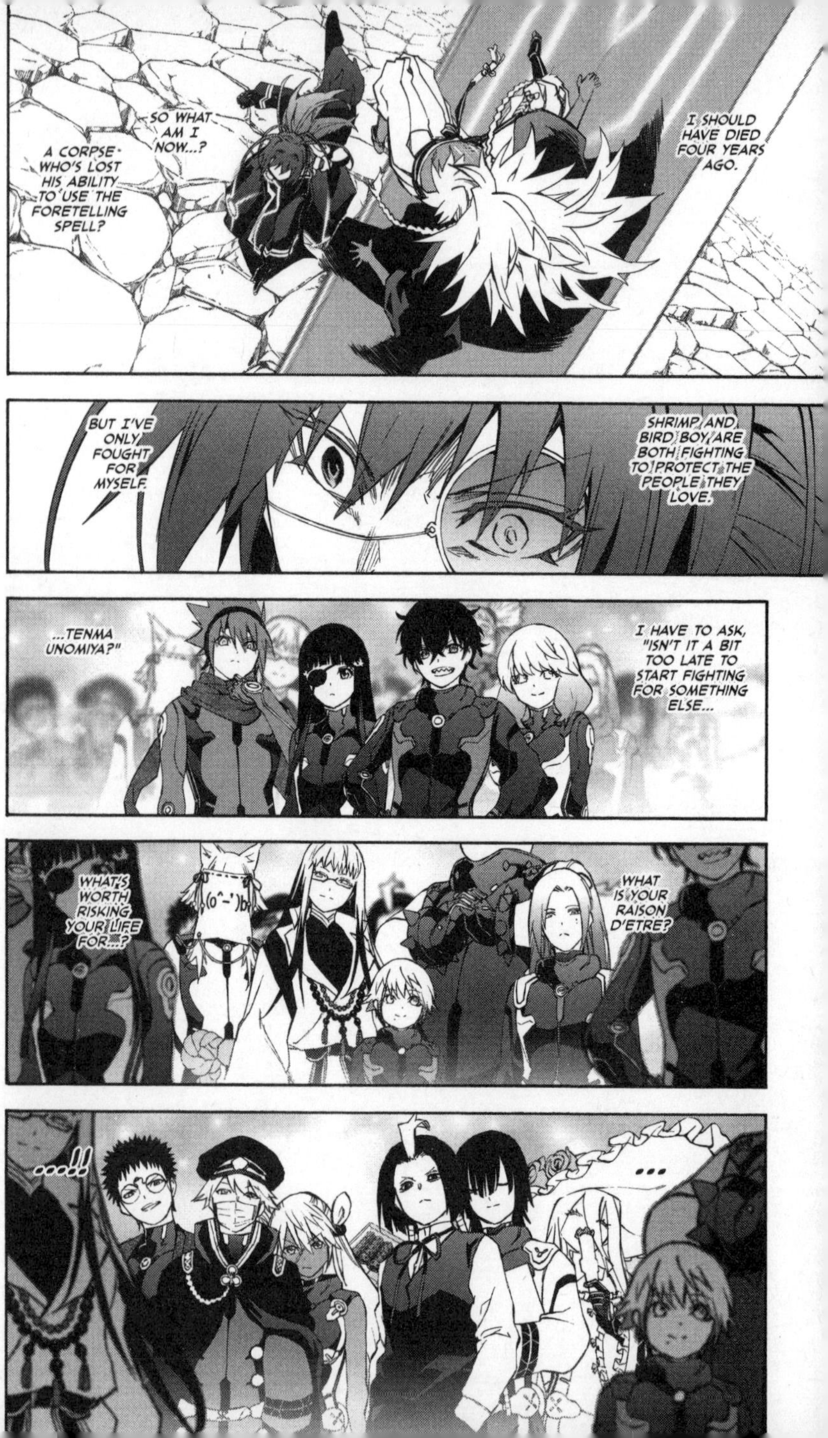
I SHOULD HAVE DIED FOUR YEARS AGO.
SO WHAT AM I NOW...?
A CORPSE WHO'S LOST HIS ABILITY TO USE THE FORETELLING SPELL?
SHRIMP AND BIRD BOY ARE BOTH FIGHTING TO PROTECT THE PEOPLE THEY LOVE.
BUT I'VE ONLY FOUGHT FOR MYSELF.
I HAVE TO ASK, "ISN'T IT A BIT TOO LATE TO START FIGHTING FOR SOMETHING ELSE...
...TENMA UNOMIYA?"
WHAT IS YOUR RAISON D'ETRE?
(o^-')b
WHAT'S WORTH RISKING YOUR LIFE FOR...?
...
...!!

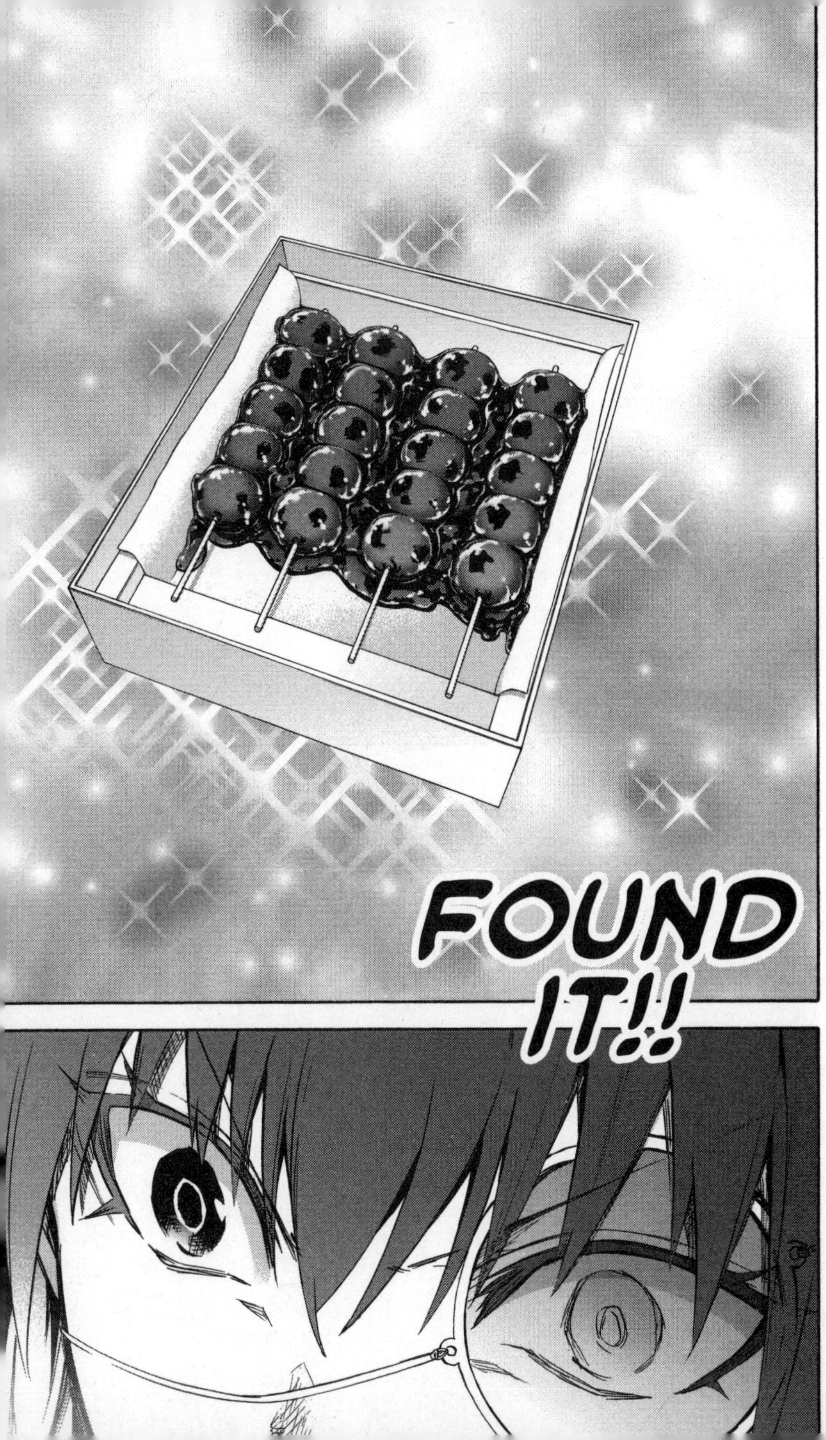
FOUND IT!!

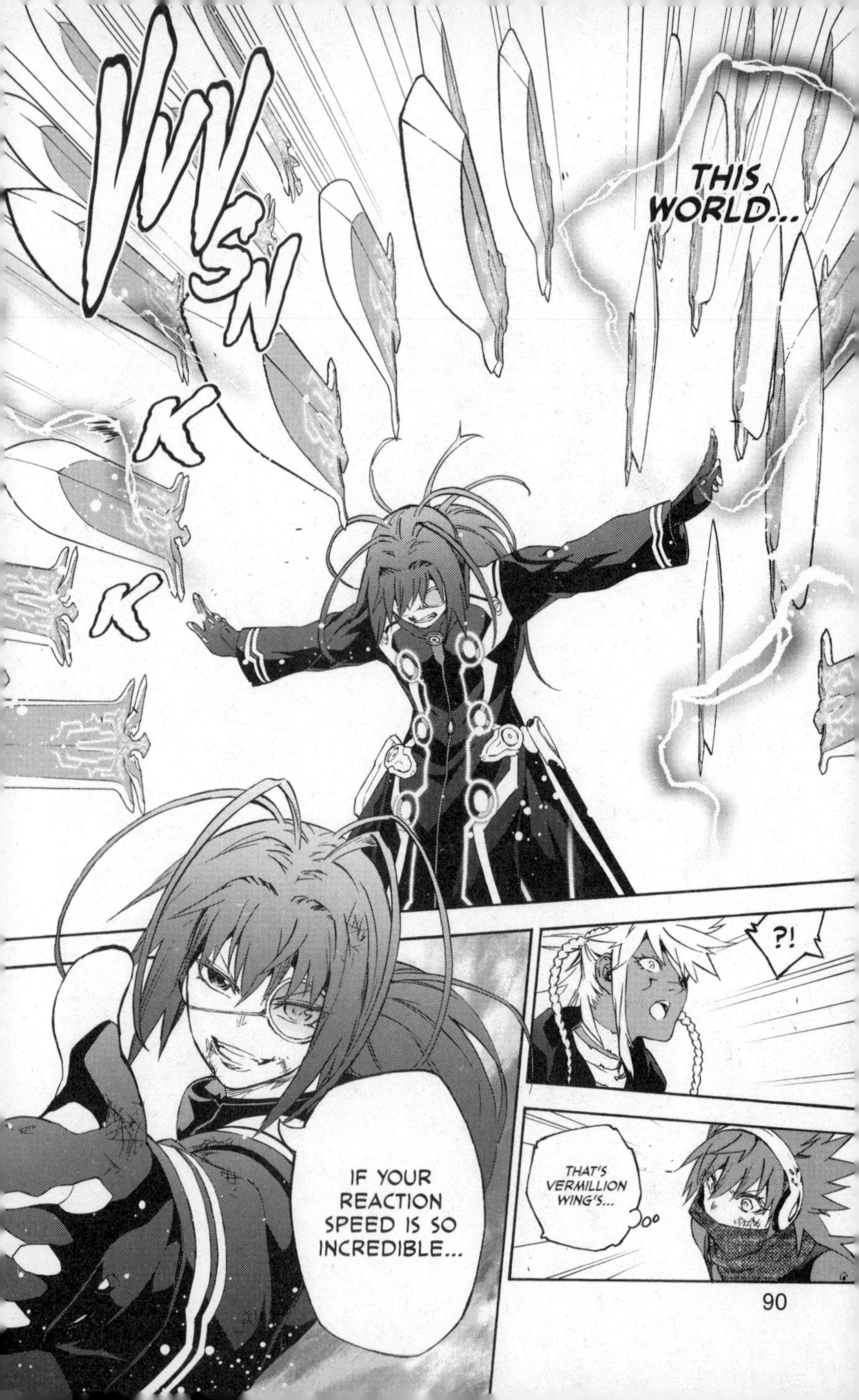
THIS WORLD...
VWSN
K
K
?!
THAT'S VERMILLION WING'S...
IF YOUR REACTION SPEED IS SO INCREDIBLE...

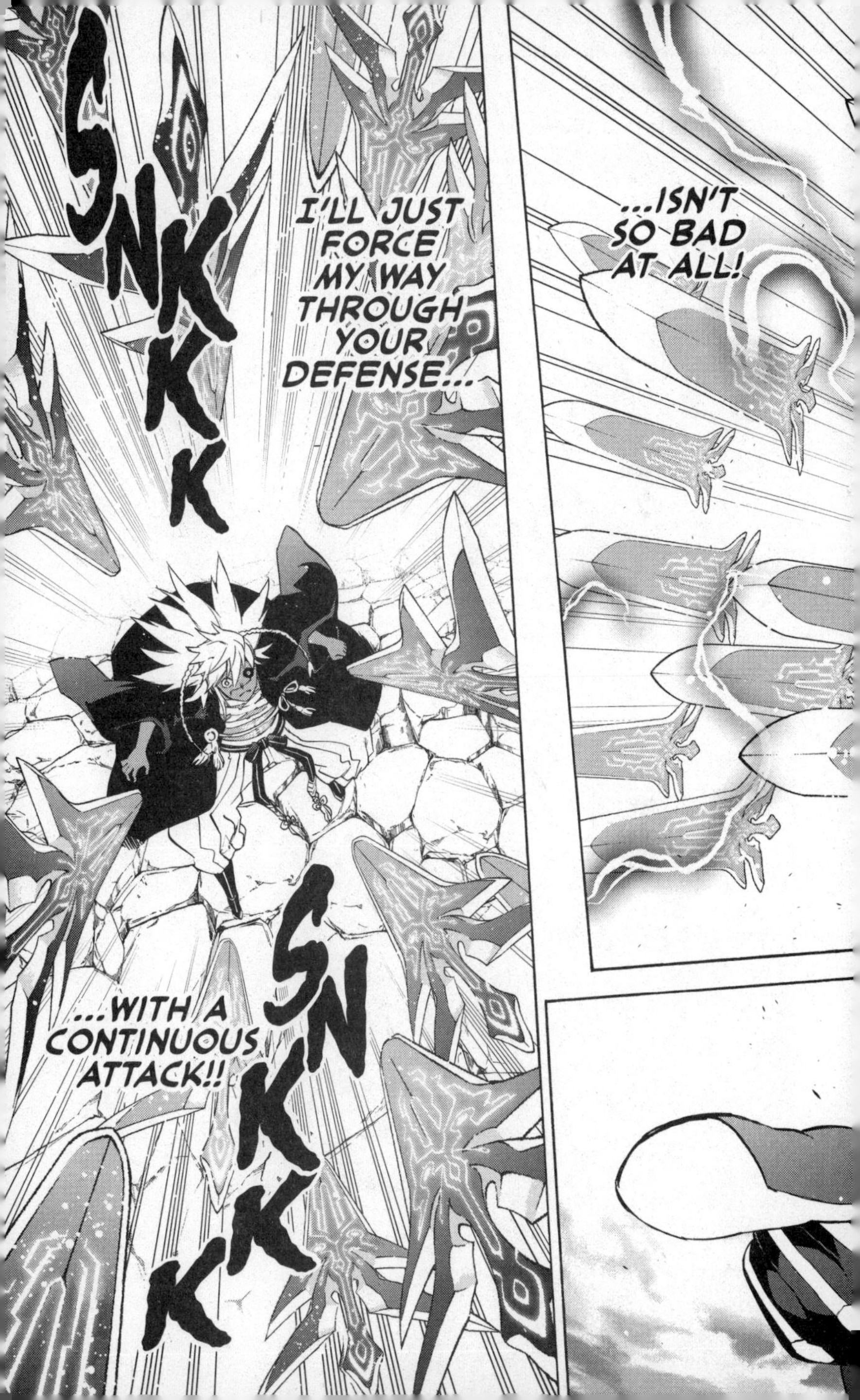
...ISN'T SO BAD AT ALL!
SNK K K
I'LL JUST FORCE MY WAY THROUGH YOUR DEFENSE...
SNK K K K
...WITH A CONTINUOUS ATTACK!!

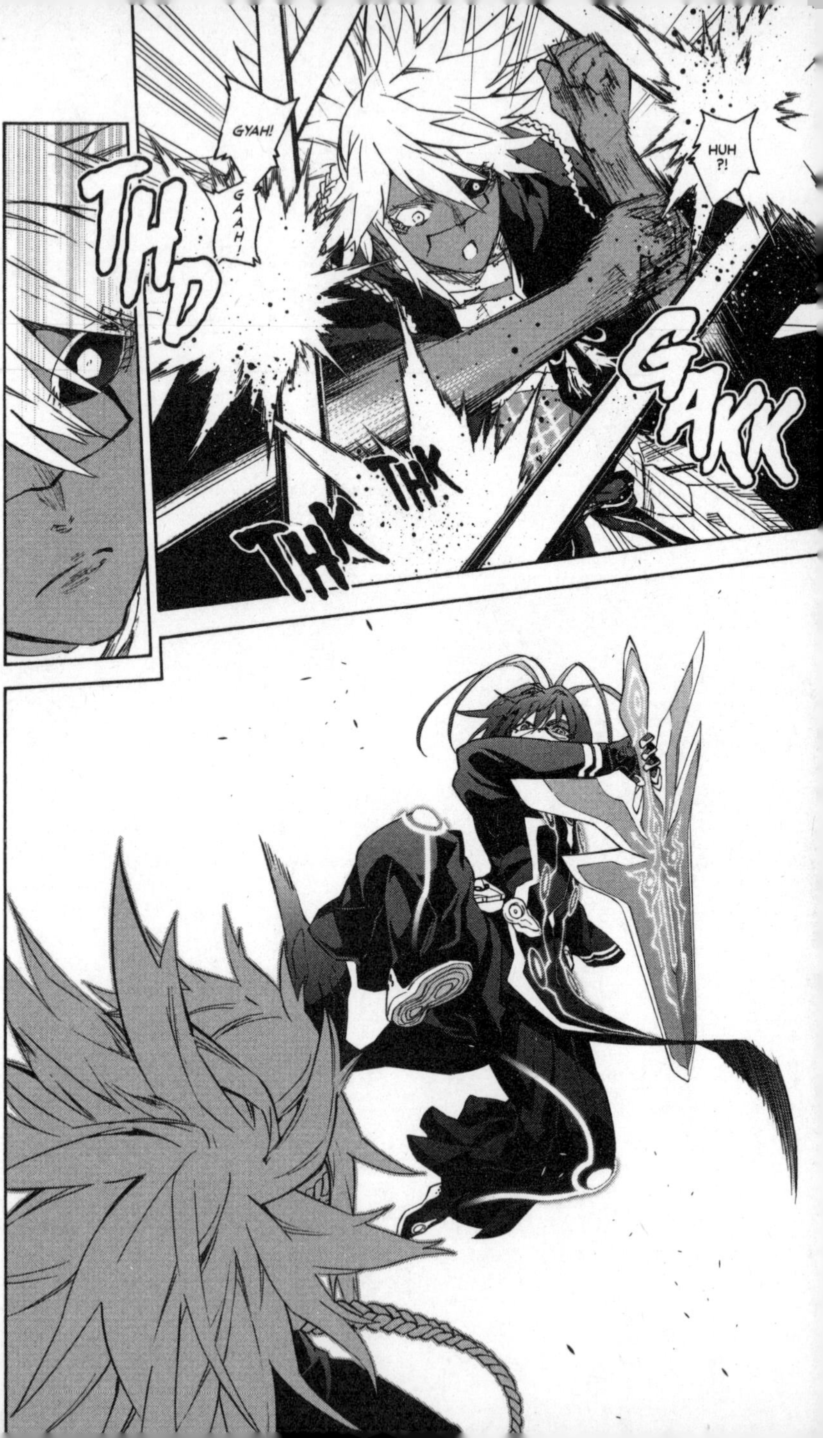
HUH ?!
GAKK
GYAH!
GAAH!
THD
THK
THK

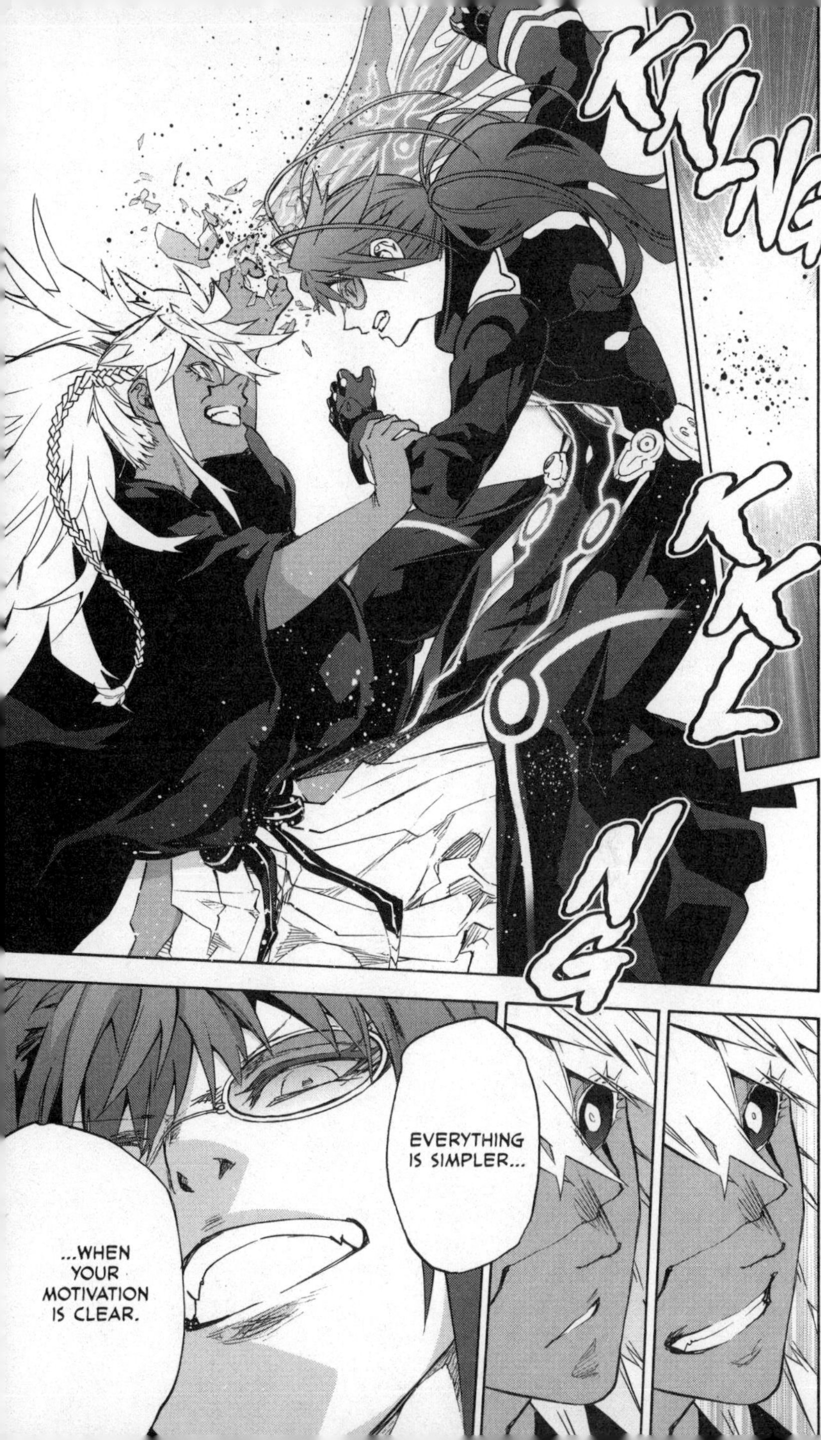
KKLNG
KKLNG
EVERYTHING IS SIMPLER...
...WHEN YOUR MOTIVATION IS CLEAR.

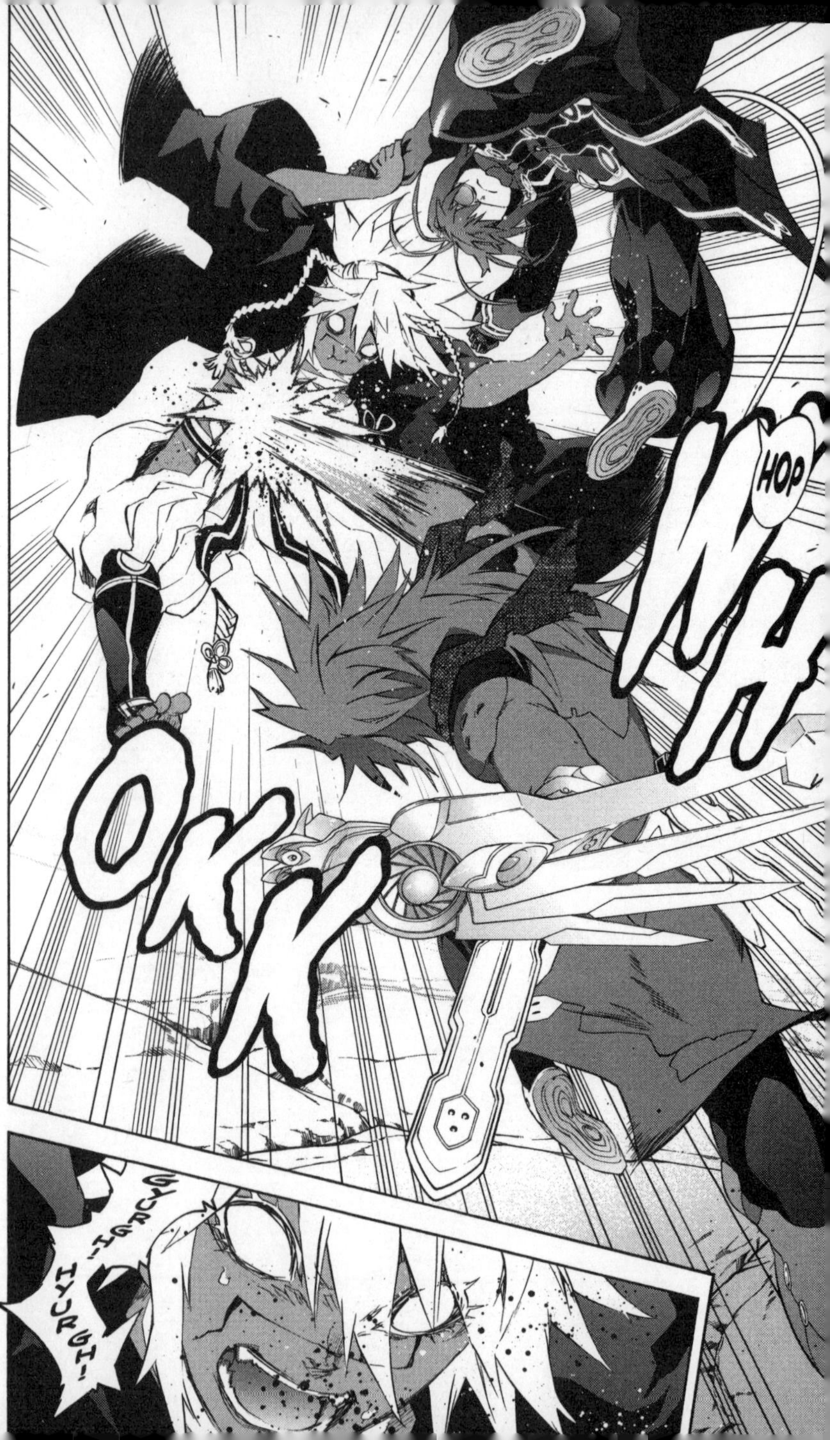
HOP
WH
OKK
GYURGH!
HYURGH!

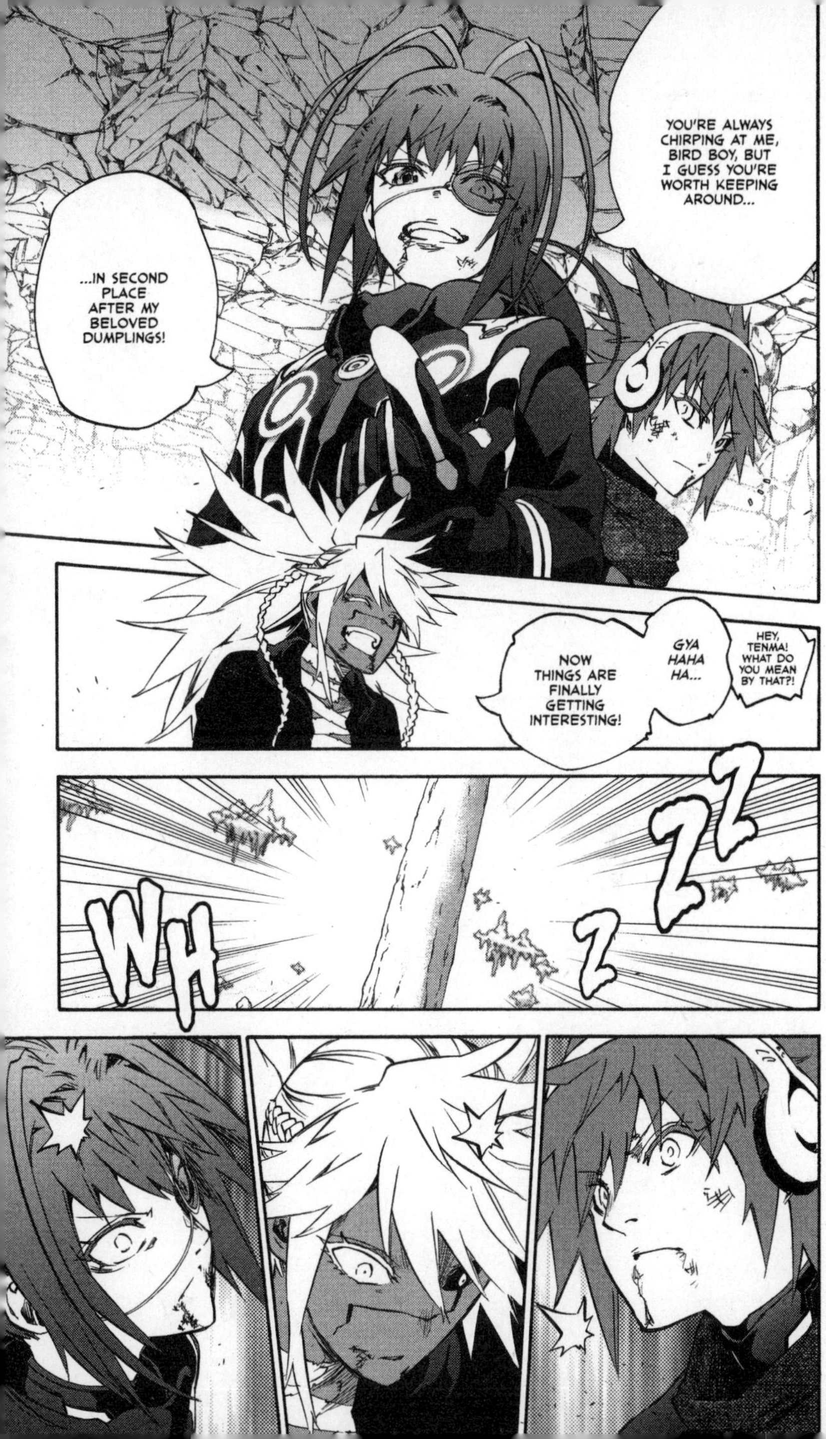
YOU'RE ALWAYS CHIRPING AT ME, BIRD BOY, BUT I GUESS YOU'RE WORTH KEEPING AROUND...
...IN SECOND PLACE AFTER MY BELOVED DUMPLINGS!
HEY, TENMA! WHAT DO YOU MEAN BY THAT?!
GYA HAHA HA...
NOW THINGS ARE FINALLY GETTING INTERESTING!
WHZZZ

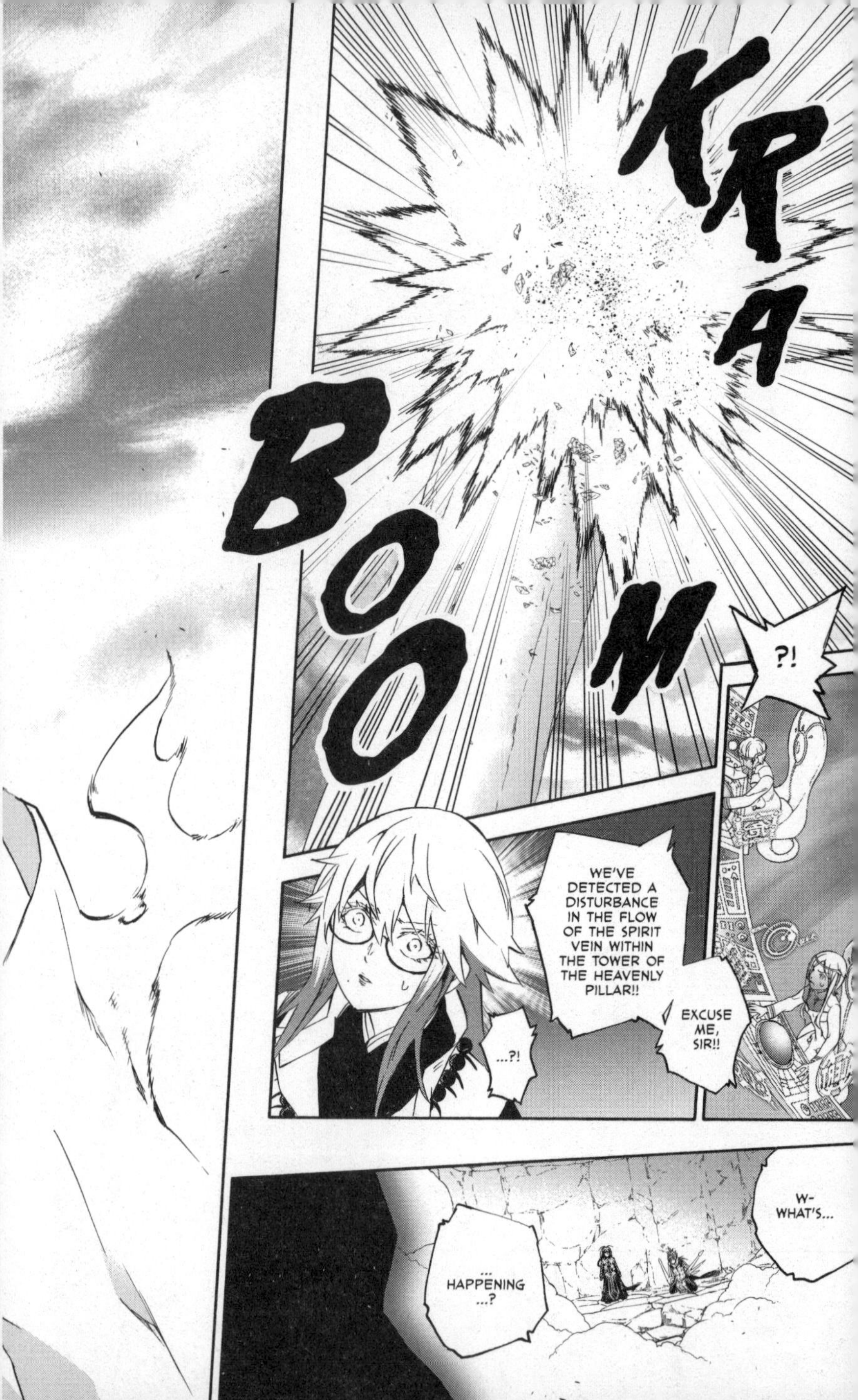
KRA BOOM
?!
EXCUSE ME, SIR!!
WE'VE DETECTED A DISTURBANCE IN THE FLOW OF THE SPIRIT VEIN WITHIN THE TOWER OF THE HEAVENLY PILLAR!!
...?!
W-WHAT'S...
...HAPPENING...?

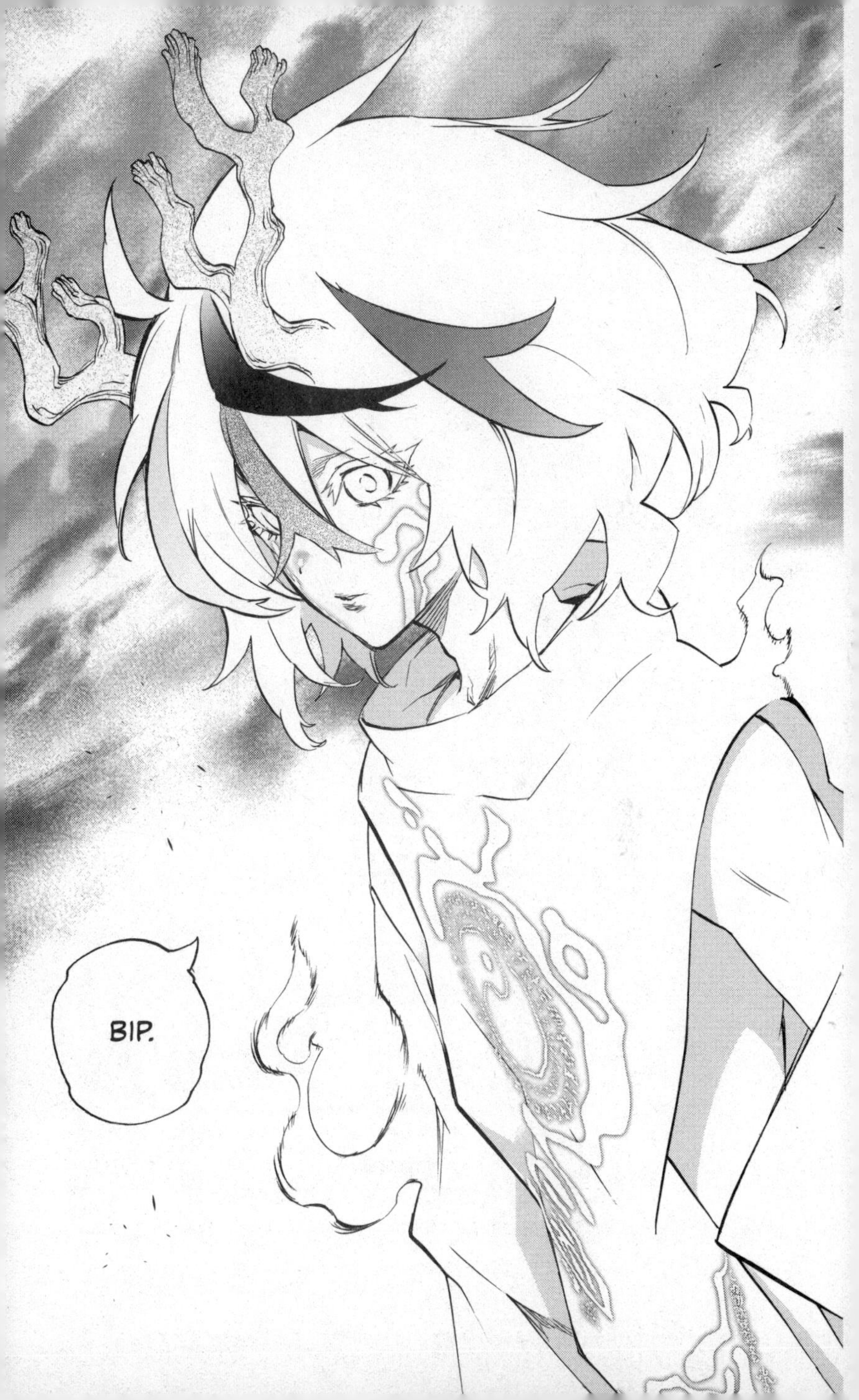
BIP.

QQnyoritsuryo!

Twin Star Exorcists

ONMYOJI

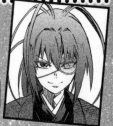

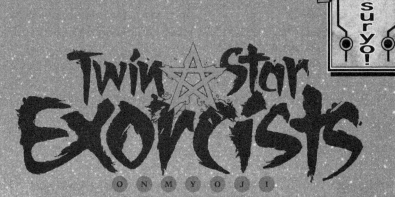

Question Corner

Q A question to Sukeno Sensei. If Tenma had a younger sister, what would she be like? (From Rena Nakamura)

A A physically frail character with little energy for herself or her family.

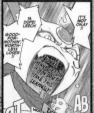

Q The members of the Adashino Family don't speak with a dialect, so why dos Kinako speak with a Kansai dialect? (From YURINUKI0524)

A I haven't had a chance to write about it in the main story, but Kinako had a big brother and sister named Yomogi and Azuki. They spoke with a Kyoto dialect, and he picked it up from them.

IT'S NOT OKAY !!
YA DOPE! LEECH!
GOOD-FOR-NOTHIN', WORTH-LESS LOSER !!
YOU'RE GONNA GET IT IF YOU DON'T TAKE THIS SERIOUSLY!
AB
DOPE
CT

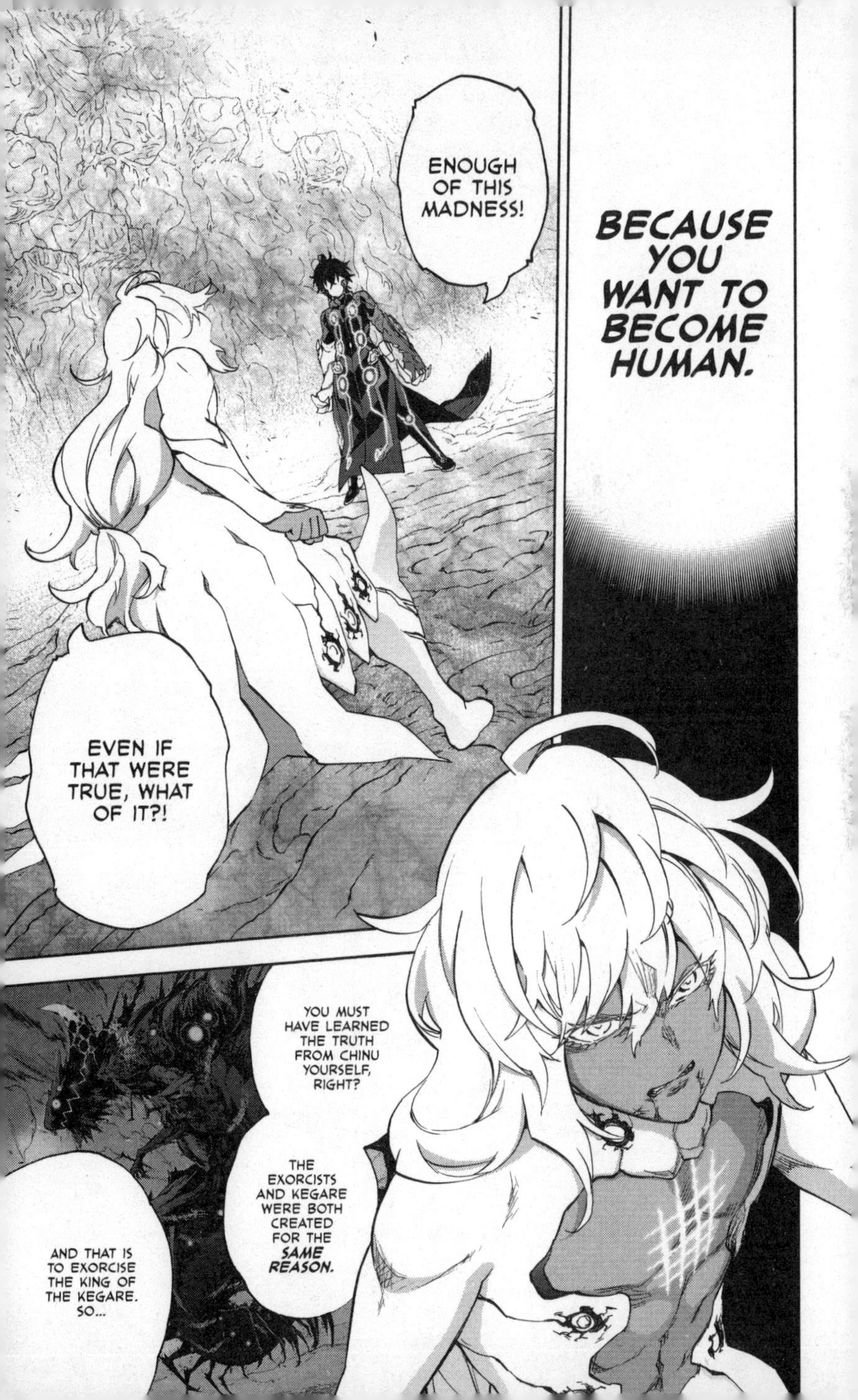
BECAUSE YOU WANT TO BECOME HUMAN.
ENOUGH OF THIS MADNESS!
EVEN IF THAT WERE TRUE, WHAT OF IT?!
YOU MUST HAVE LEARNED THE TRUTH FROM CHINU YOURSELF, RIGHT?
THE EXORCISTS AND KEGARE WERE BOTH CREATED FOR THE SAME REASON.
AND THAT IS TO EXORCISE THE KING OF THE KEGARE. SO...

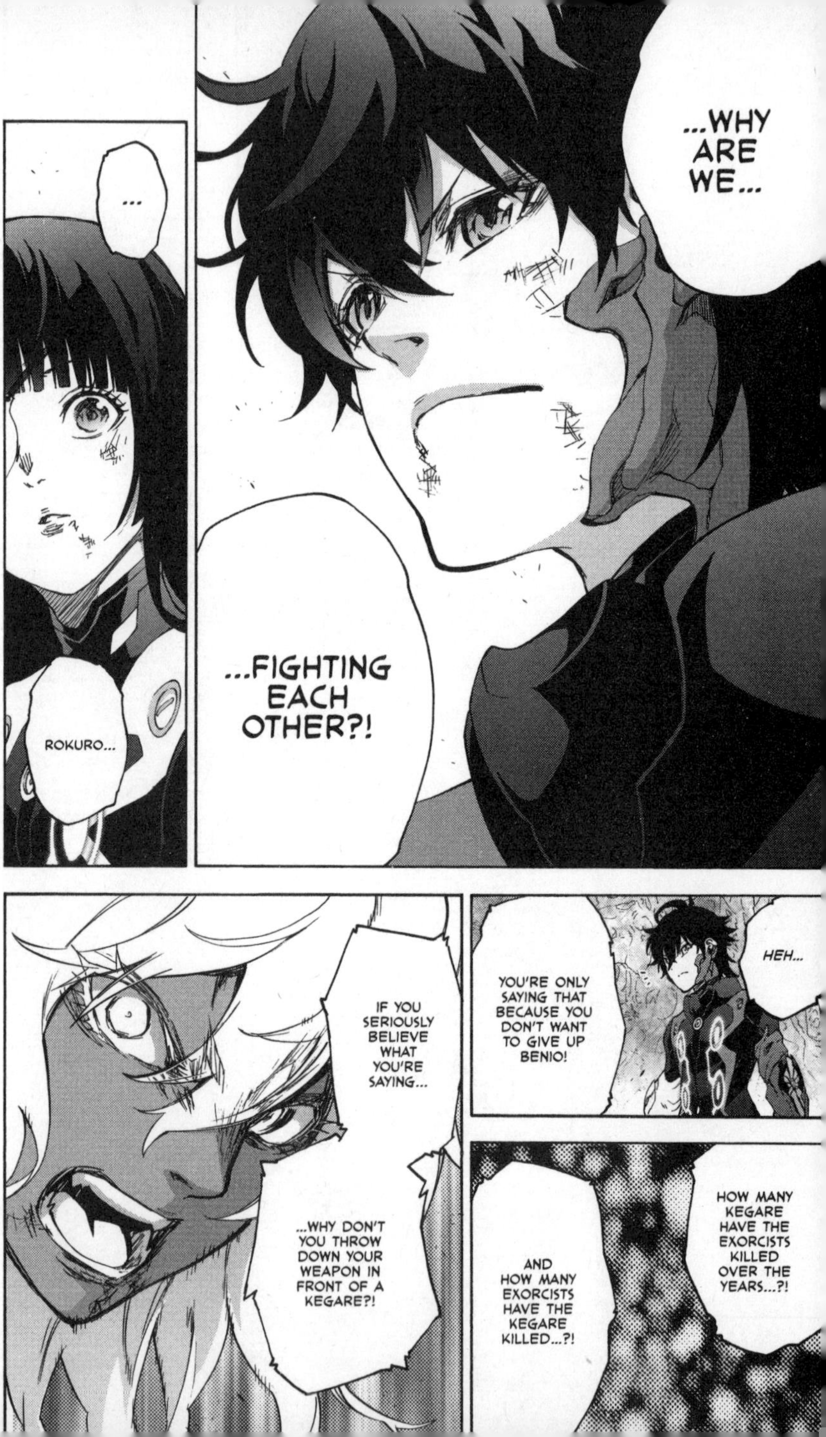
...WHY ARE WE...
...FIGHTING EACH OTHER?!
...
ROKURO...
HEH...
YOU'RE ONLY SAYING THAT BECAUSE YOU DON'T WANT TO GIVE UP BENIO!
HOW MANY KEGARE HAVE THE EXORCISTS KILLED OVER THE YEARS...?!
AND HOW MANY EXORCISTS HAVE THE KEGARE KILLED...?!
IF YOU SERIOUSLY BELIEVE WHAT YOU'RE SAYING...
...WHY DON'T YOU THROW DOWN YOUR WEAPON IN FRONT OF A KEGARE?!

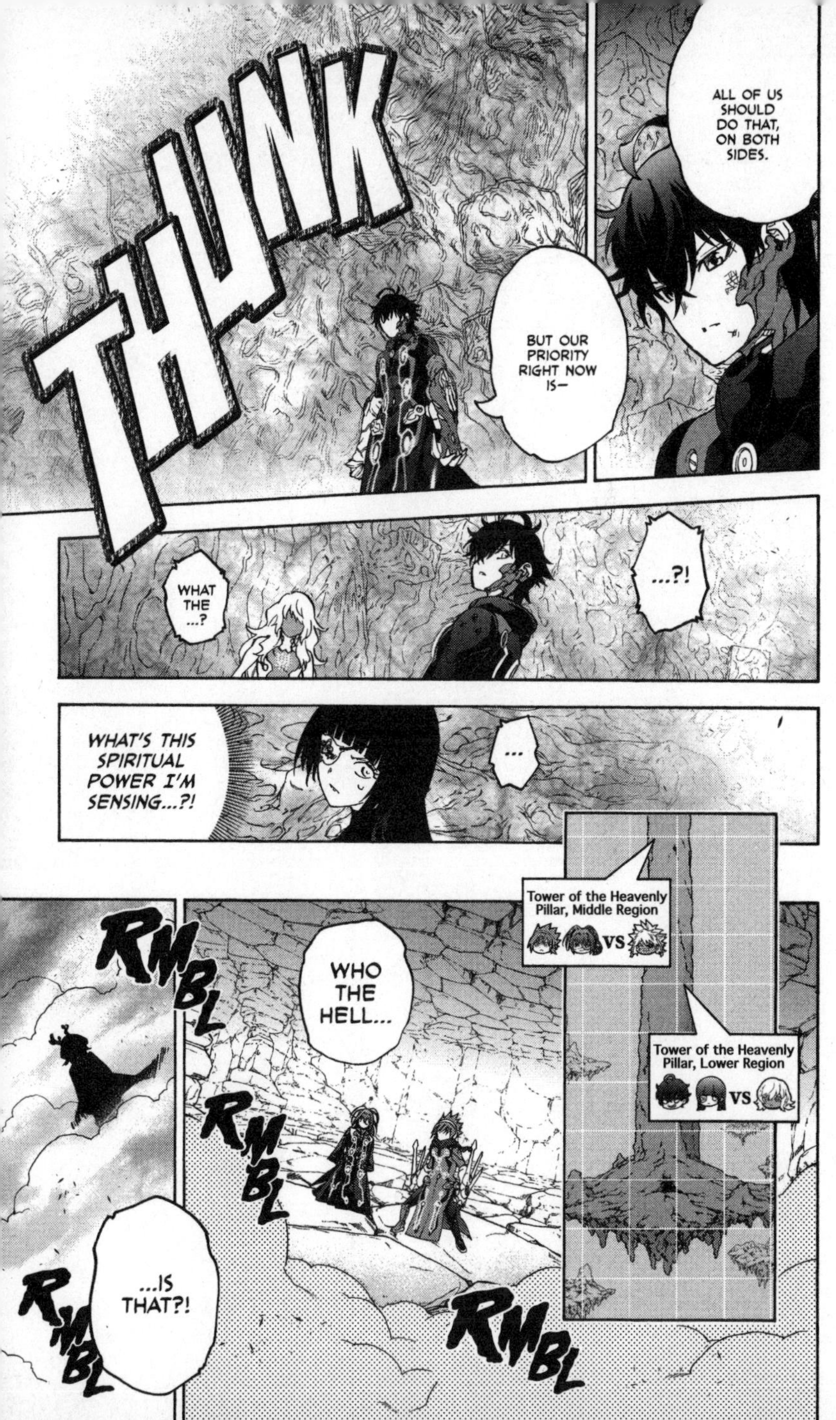
ALL OF US SHOULD DO THAT, ON BOTH SIDES.
BUT OUR PRIORITY RIGHT NOW IS—
THUNK
...?!
WHAT THE ...?
...
WHAT'S THIS SPIRITUAL POWER I'M SENSING...?!
Tower of the Heavenly Pillar, Middle Region
VS
Tower of the Heavenly Pillar, Lower Region
VS
WHO THE HELL...
RMBL
RMBL
RMBL
RMBL
...IS THAT?!
RMBL

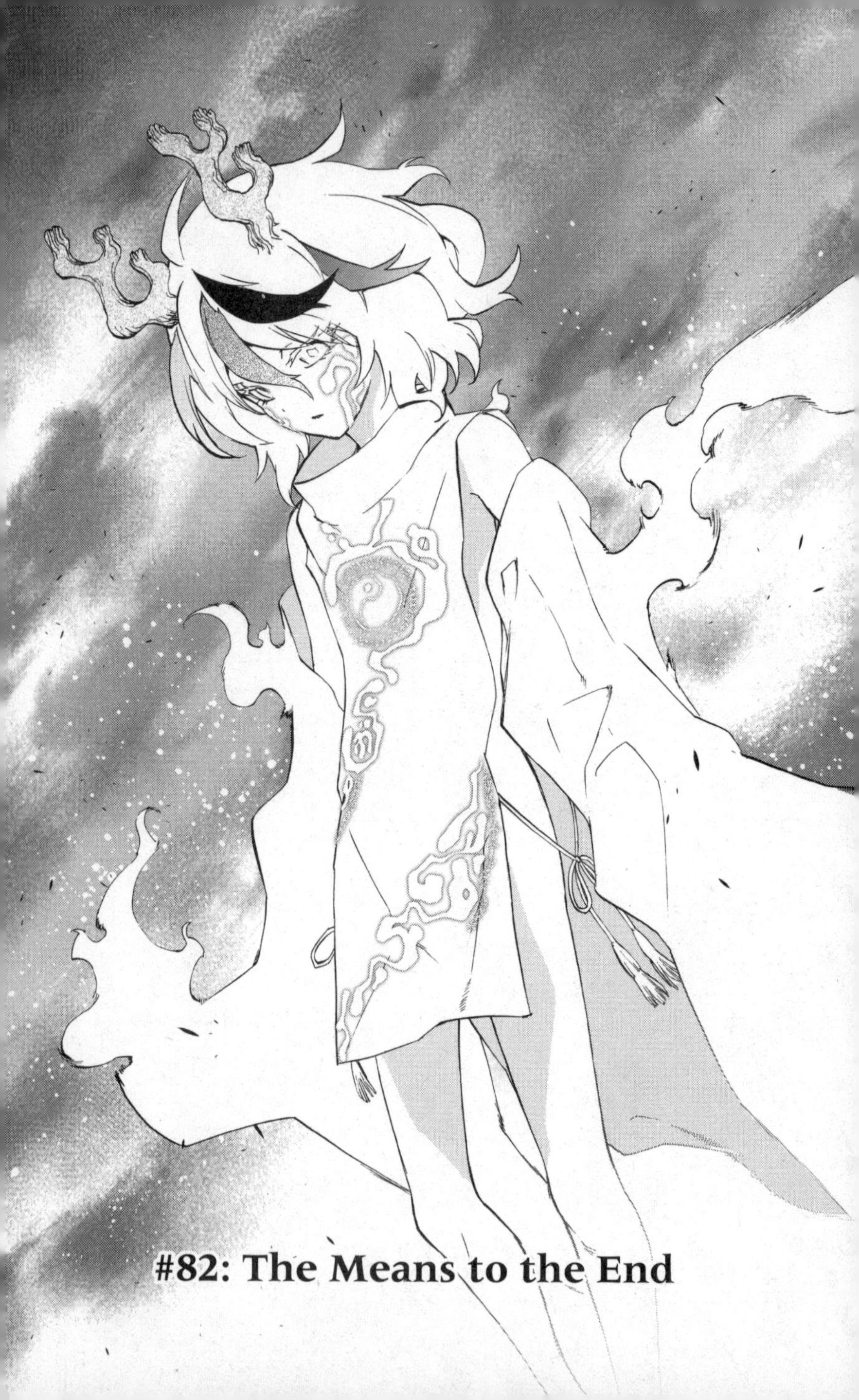

#82: The Means to the End

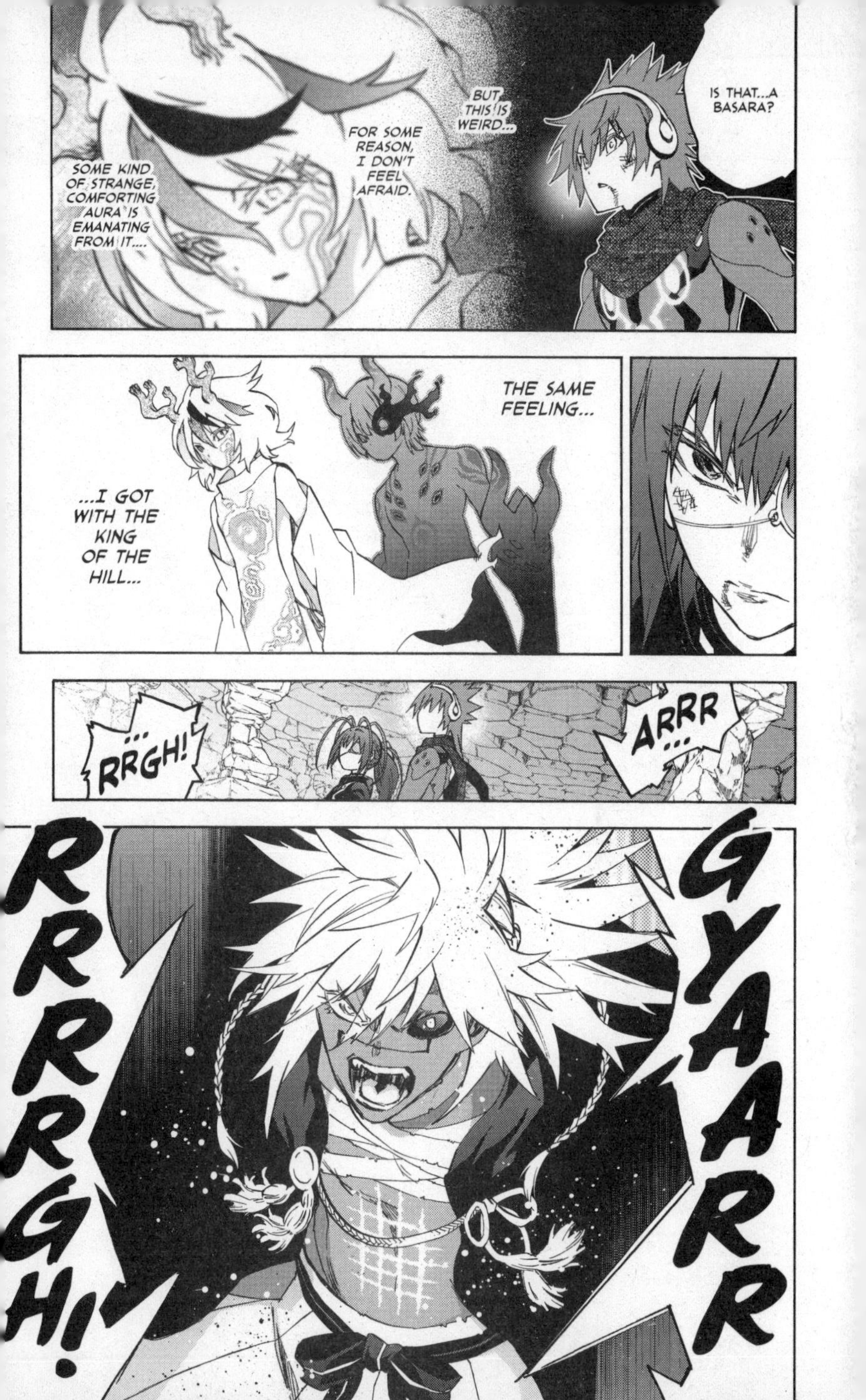
IS THAT...A BASARA?
BUT THIS IS WEIRD...
FOR SOME REASON, I DON'T FEEL AFRAID.
SOME KIND OF STRANGE, COMFORTING AURA IS EMANATING FROM IT....
THE SAME FEELING...
...I GOT WITH THE KING OF THE HILL...
ARRR...
...RRGH!
GYAARR
RRRRGH!

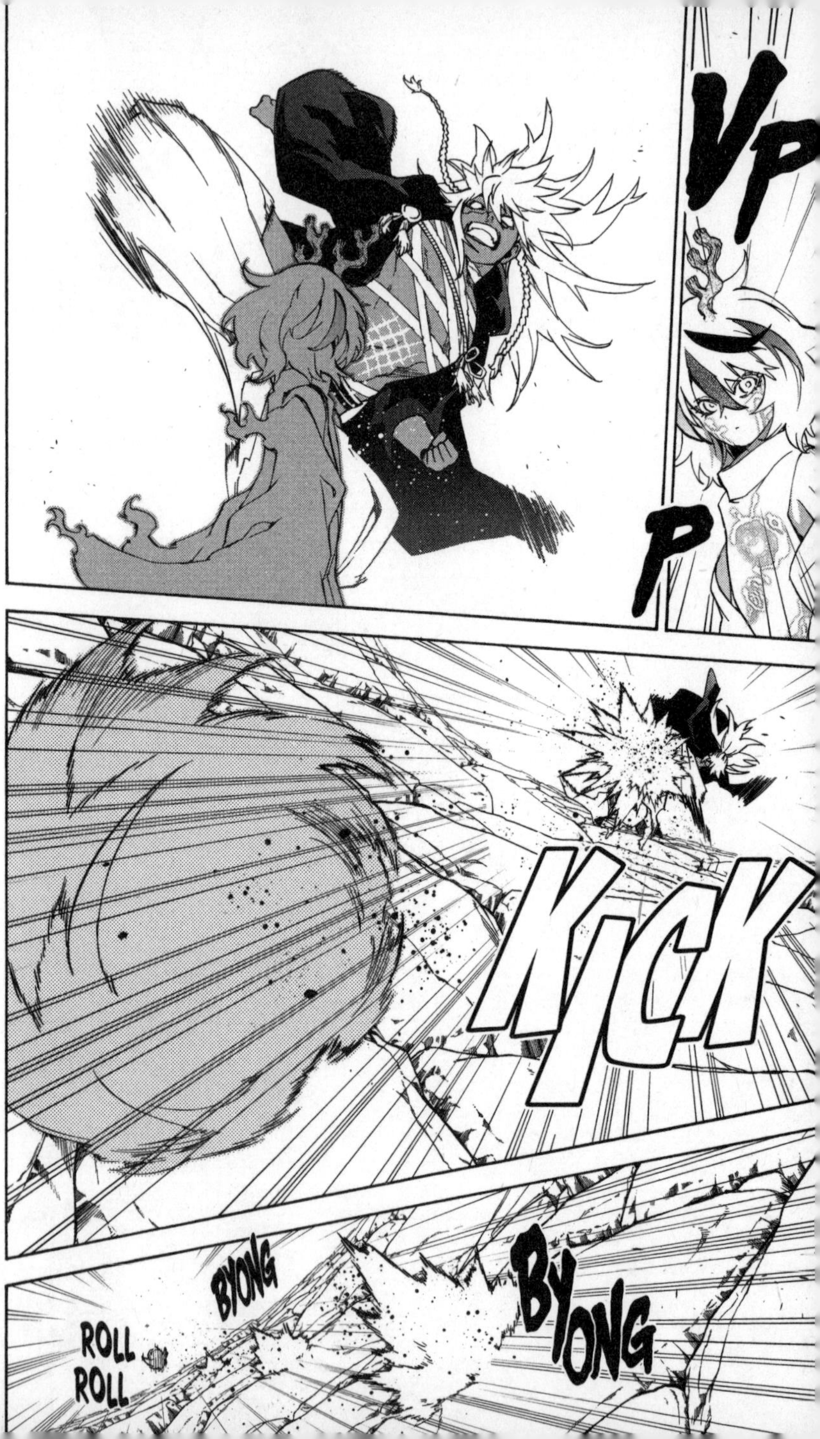
VP
P
KICK
BYONG
BYONG
ROLL
ROLL

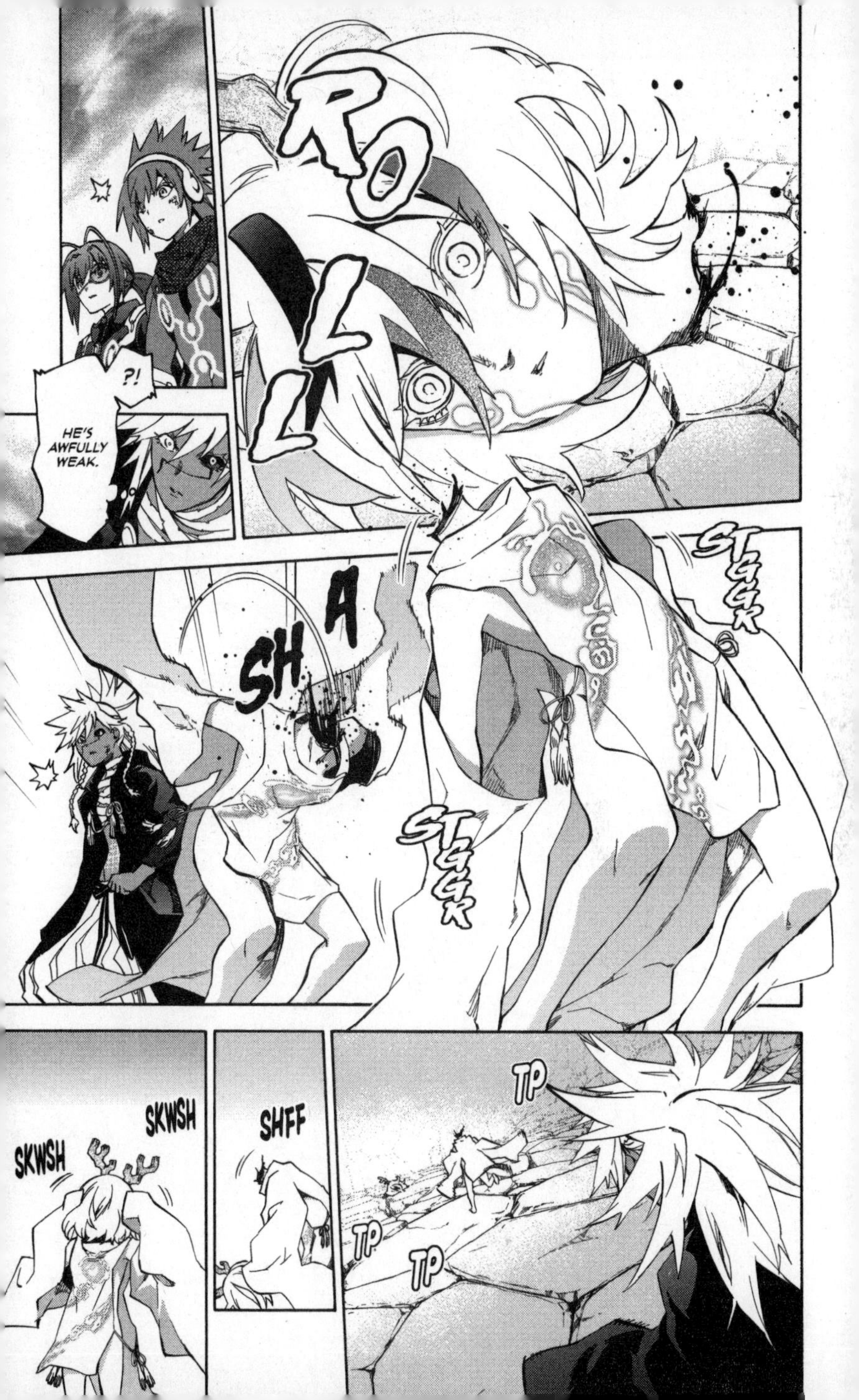

ROLL
?!
HE'S AWFULLY WEAK.
STGGR
SHA
STGGR
TP
TP
TP
SHFF
SKWSH
SKWSH

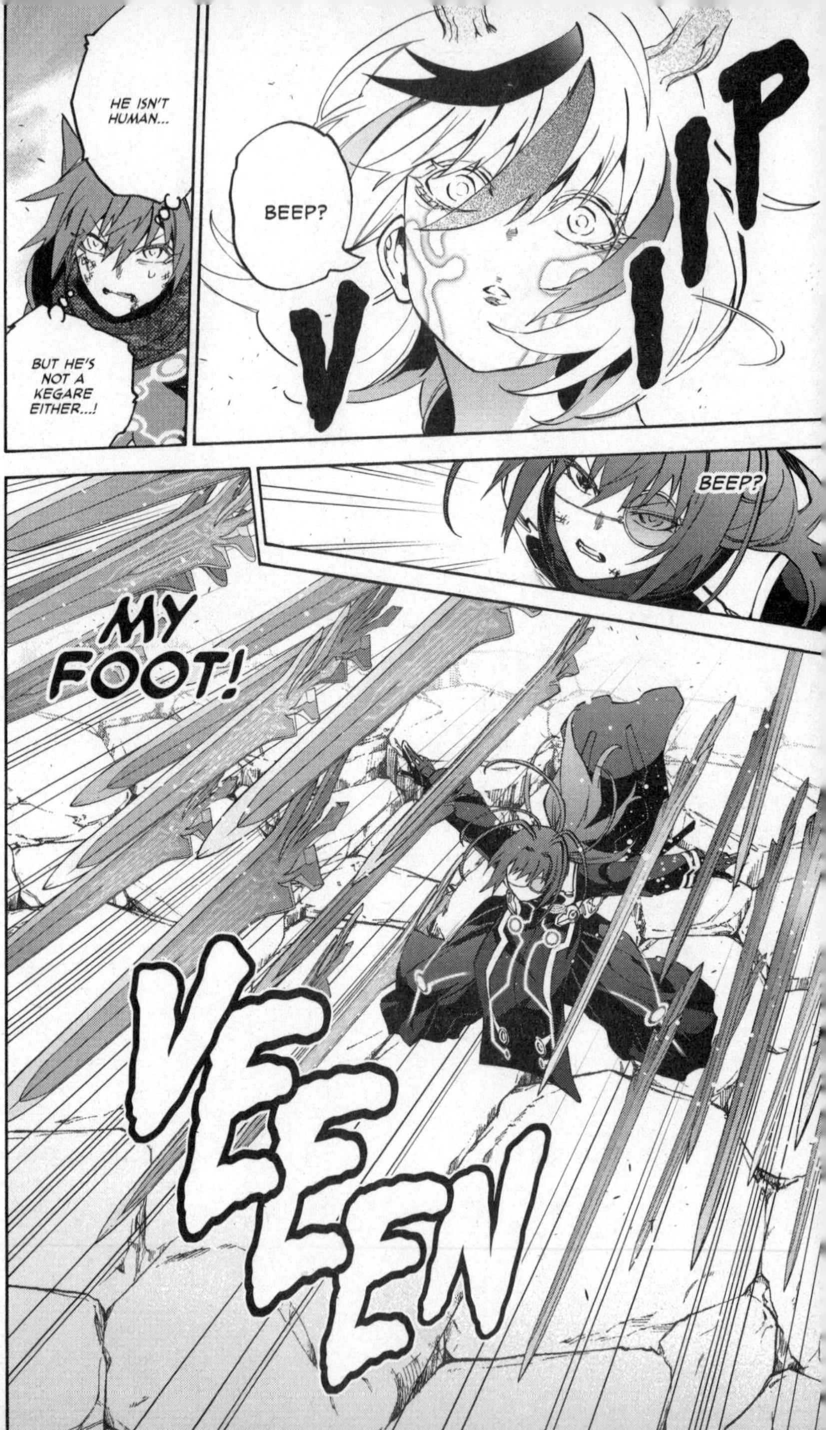
VIIP
BEEP?
HE ISN'T HUMAN...
BUT HE'S NOT A KEGARE EITHER...!
BEEP?
MY FOOT!
VEEEN

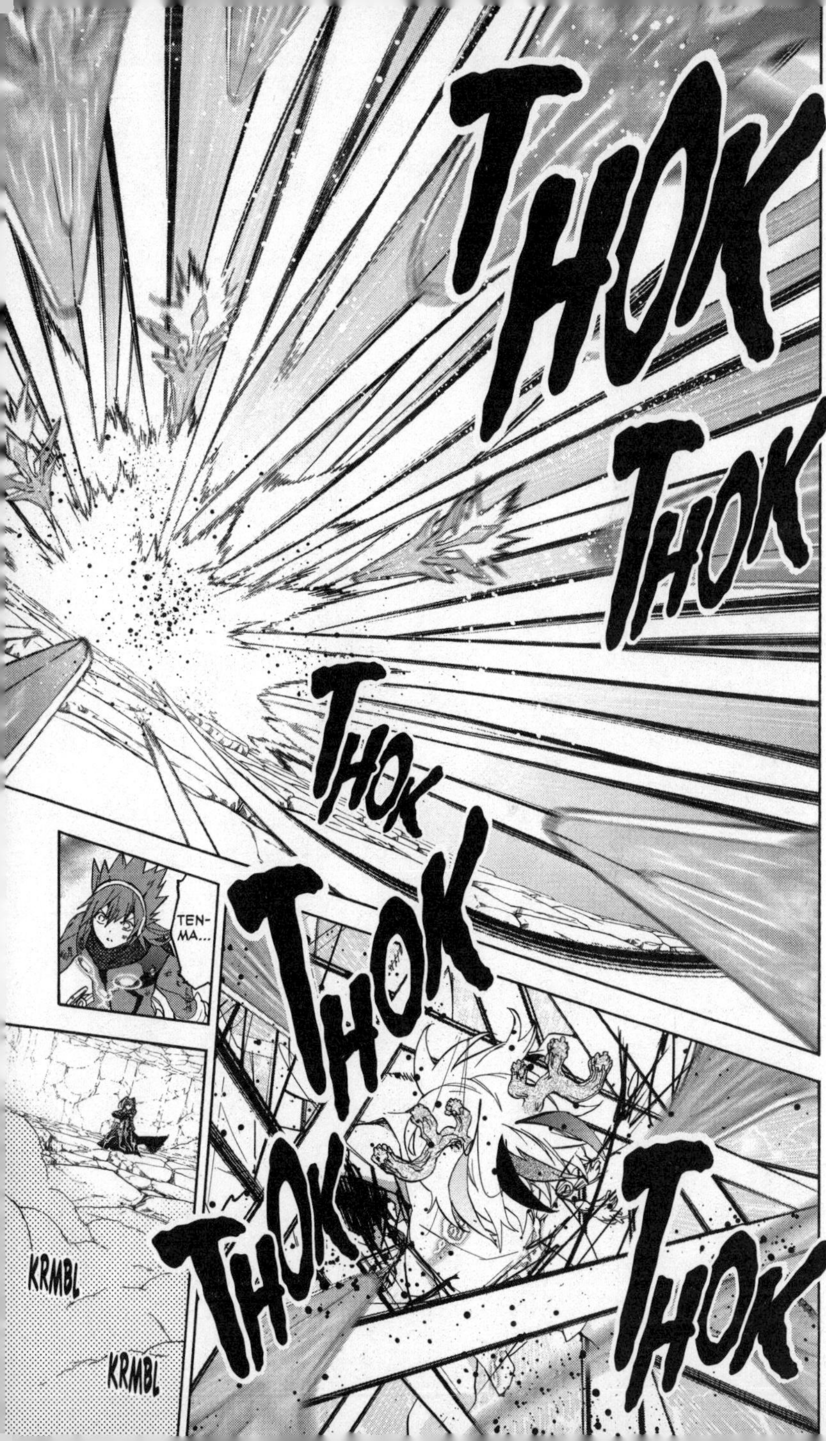
THOK
THOK
THOK
THOK
THOK
THOK
TEN-MA...
KRMBL
KRMBL

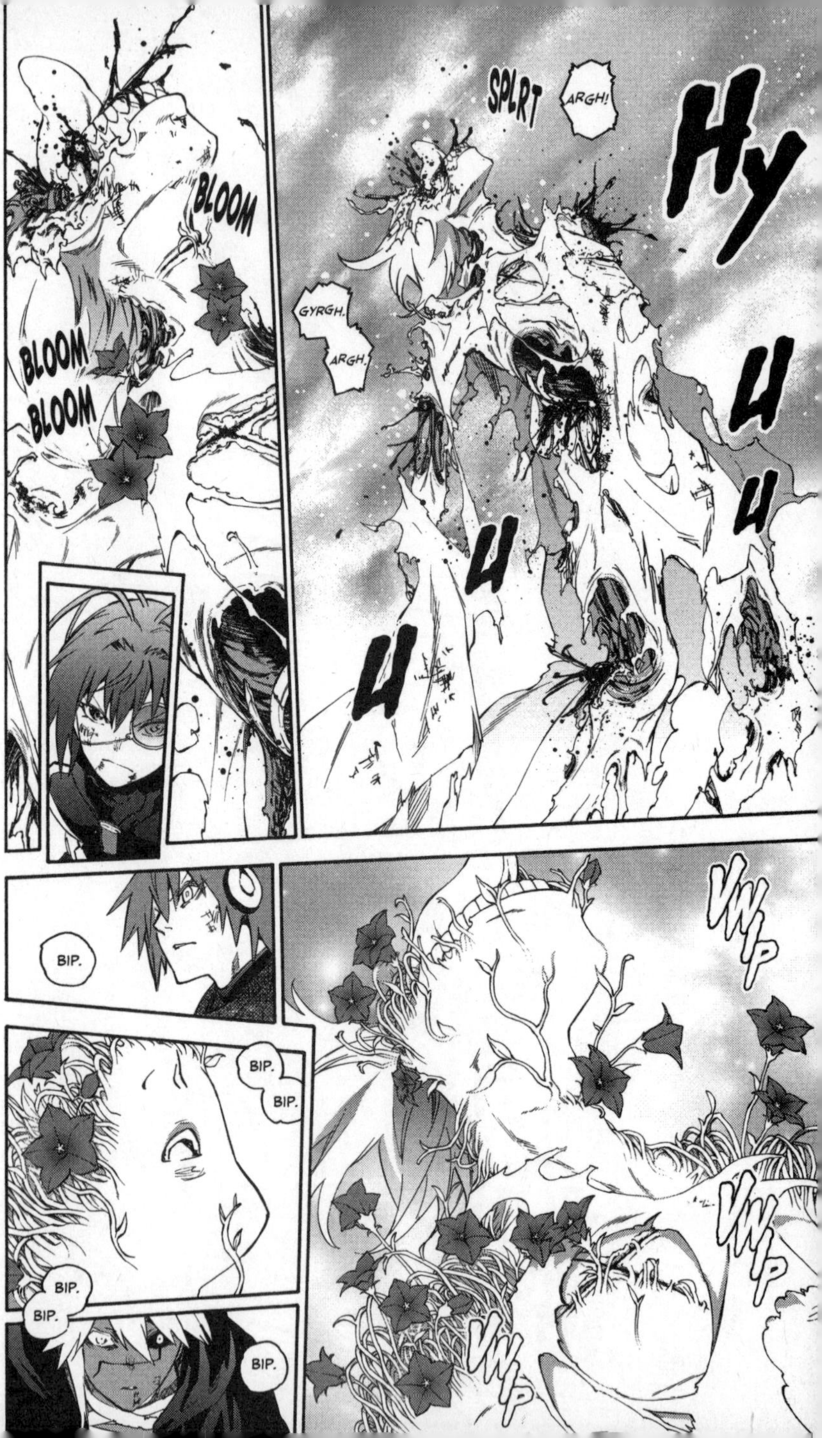
ARGH!
SPLRT
Hyuuuu
GYRGH.
ARGH.
BLOOM
BLOOM
BLOOM
VWIP
VWIP
VWIP
BIP.
BIP.
BIP.
BIP.
BIP.
BIP.

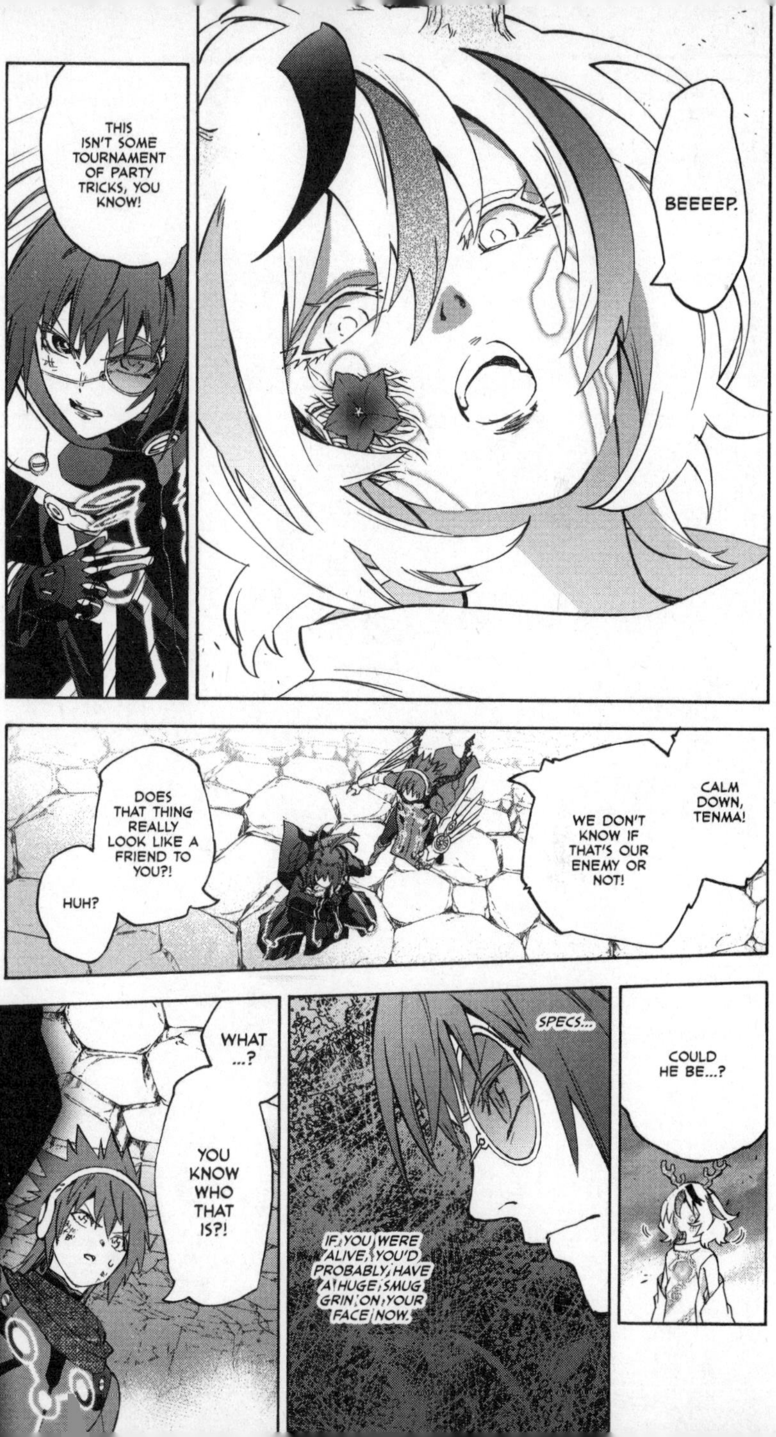
BEEEEP.
THIS ISN'T SOME TOURNAMENT OF PARTY TRICKS, YOU KNOW!
CALM DOWN, TENMA!
WE DON'T KNOW IF THAT'S OUR ENEMY OR NOT!
DOES THAT THING REALLY LOOK LIKE A FRIEND TO YOU?!
HUH?
COULD HE BE...?
SPECS...
IF YOU WERE ALIVE, YOU'D PROBABLY HAVE A HUGE SMUG GRIN ON YOUR FACE NOW.
WHAT ...?
YOU KNOW WHO THAT IS?!

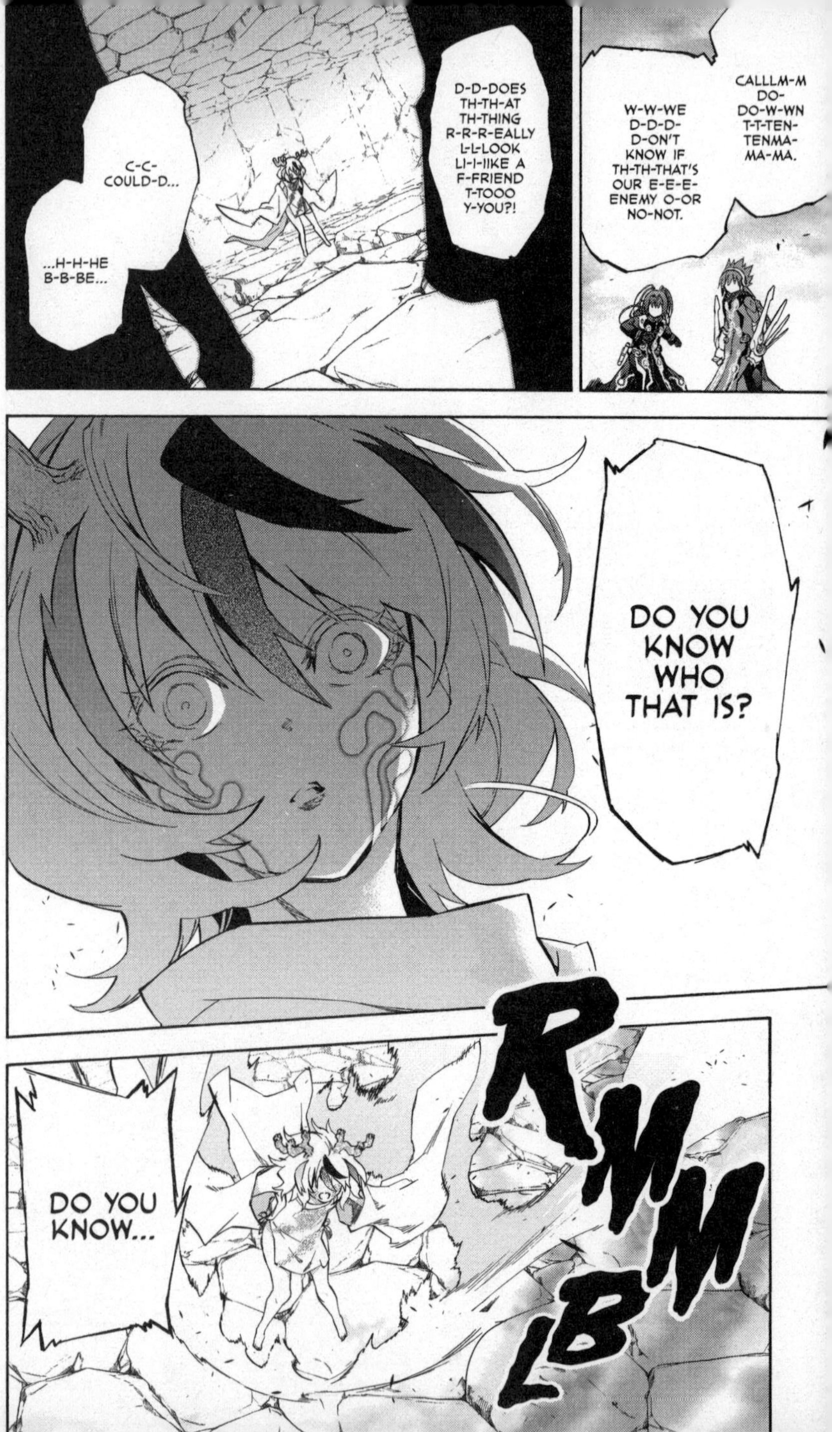
CALLLM-M DO- DO-W-WN T-T-TEN- TENMA- MA-MA.
W-W-WE D-D-D- D-ON'T KNOW IF TH-TH-THAT'S OUR E-E-E- ENEMY O-OR NO-NOT.
D-D-DOES TH-TH-AT TH-THING R-R-R-EALLY L-L-LOOK LI-I-IIKE A F-FRIEND T-TOOO Y-YOU?!
C-C- COULD-D...
...H-H-HE B-B-BE...
DO YOU KNOW WHO THAT IS?
RMMBL
DO YOU KNOW...

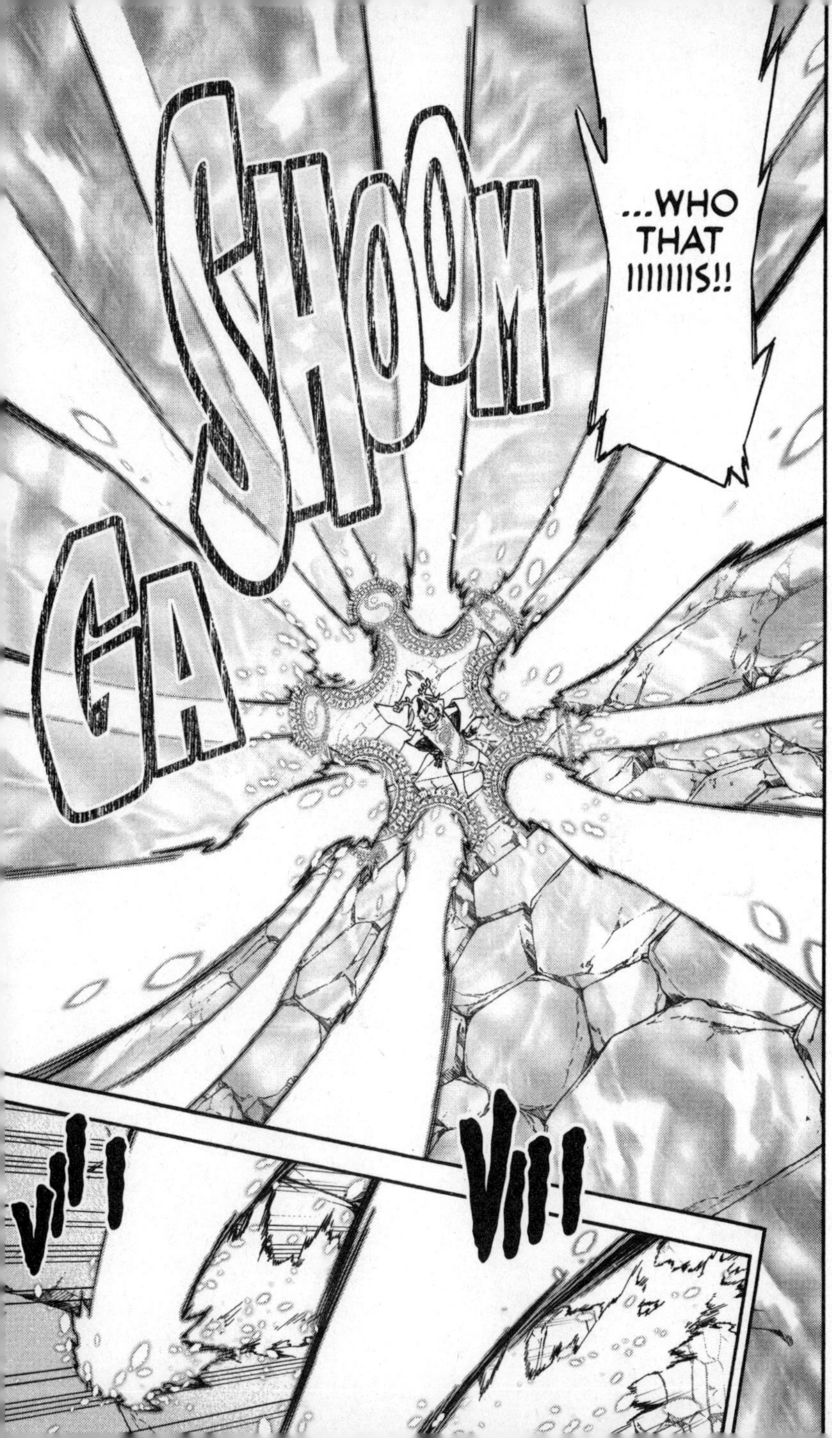
...WHO THAT IIIIIIIS!!
SHOOM
GA
VIII
VIII

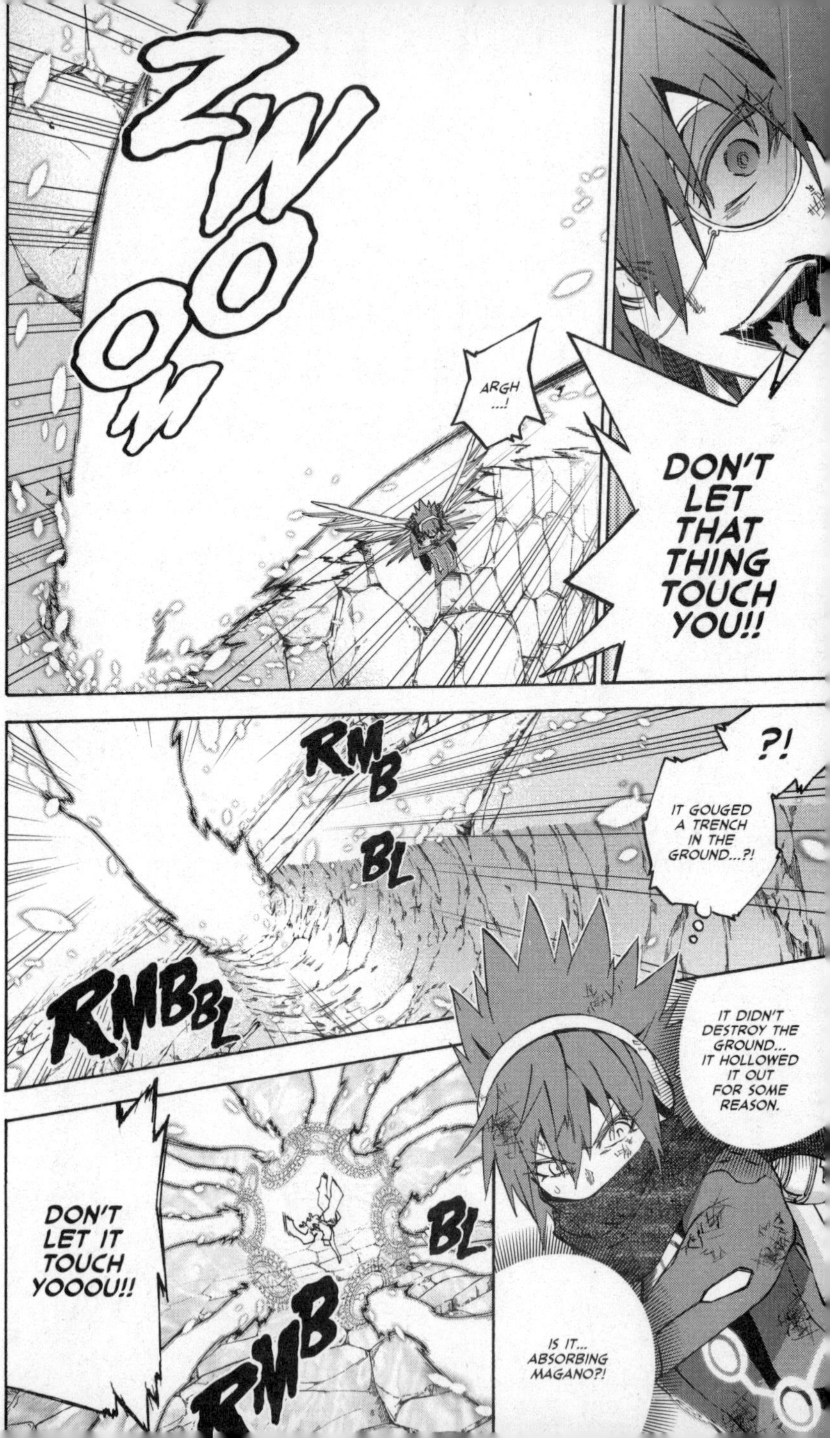

ZWOOOOM
DON'T LET THAT THING TOUCH YOU!!
ARGH ...!
?!
IT GOUGED A TRENCH IN THE GROUND...?!
RMB
BL
RMBBL
IT DIDN'T DESTROY THE GROUND... IT HOLLOWED IT OUT FOR SOME REASON.
IS IT... ABSORBING MAGANO?!
BL
RMB
DON'T LET IT TOUCH YOOOU!!

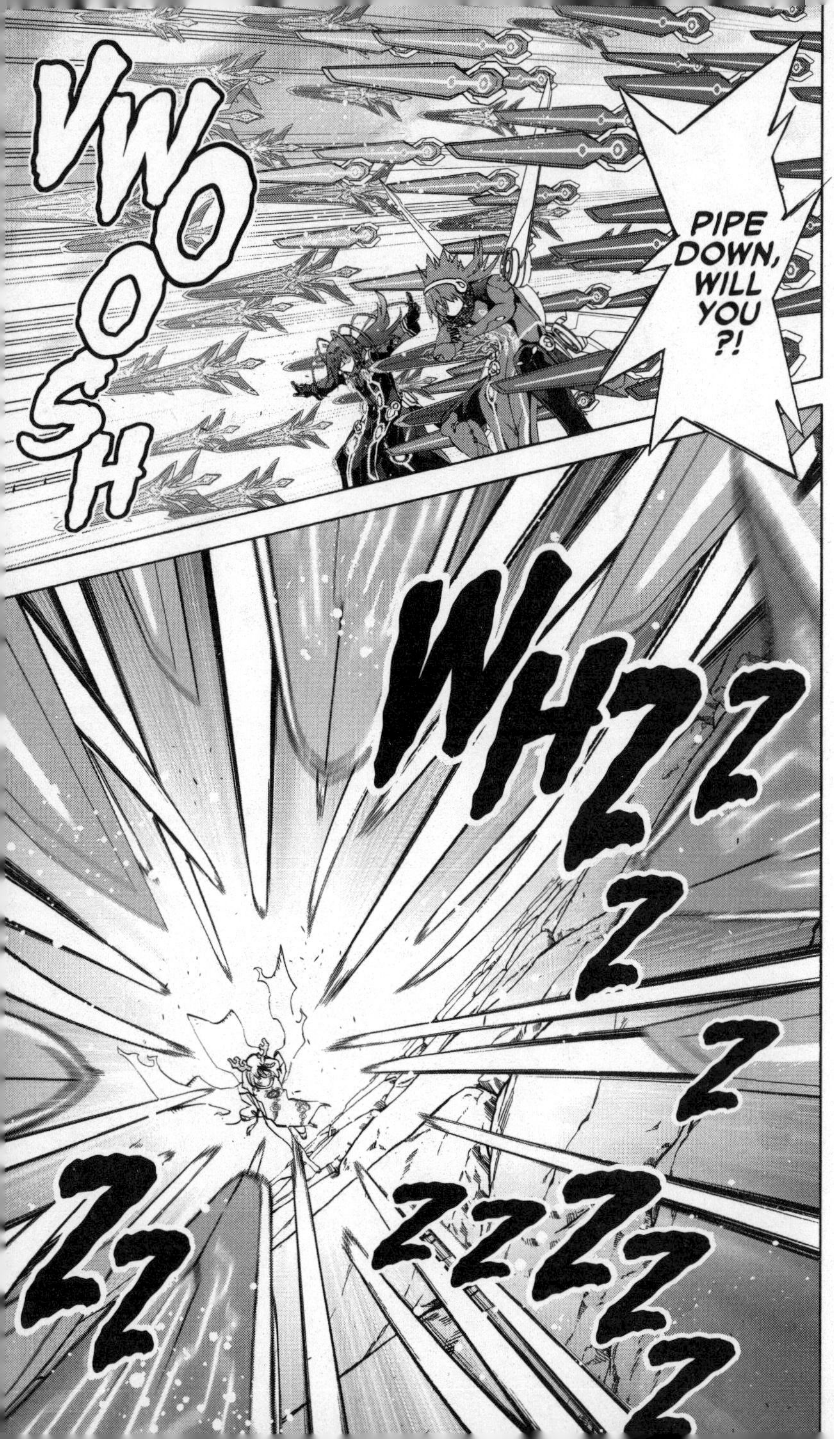
PIPE DOWN, WILL YOU?!
VWOOSH
WHZZZZZ
ZZ
ZZZZZZ

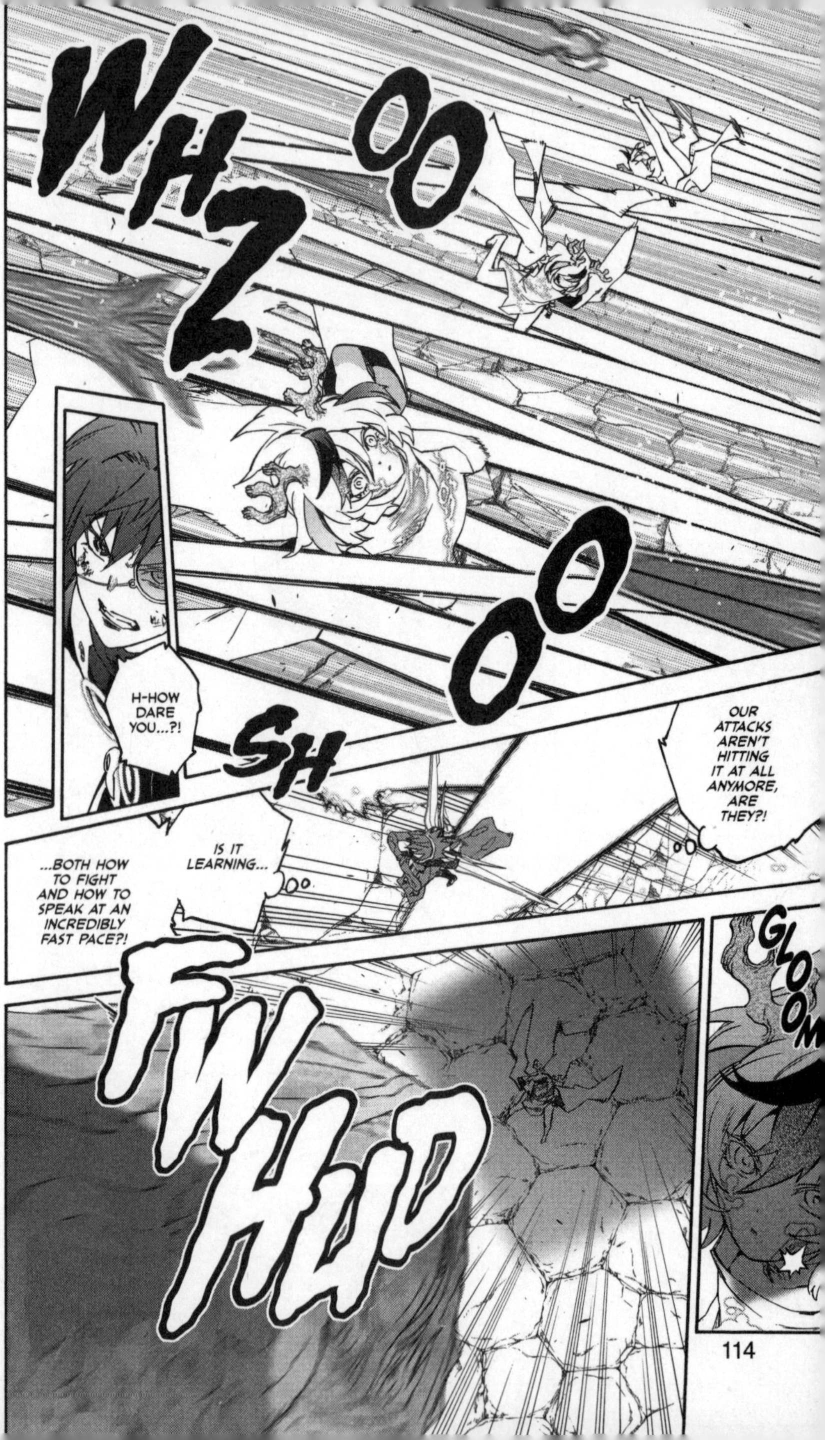
WHOOZ
OOO
H-HOW DARE YOU...?!
SH
OUR ATTACKS AREN'T HITTING IT AT ALL ANYMORE, ARE THEY?!
IS IT LEARNING...
...BOTH HOW TO FIGHT AND HOW TO SPEAK AT AN INCREDIBLY FAST PACE?!
GLOOM
FWHUD

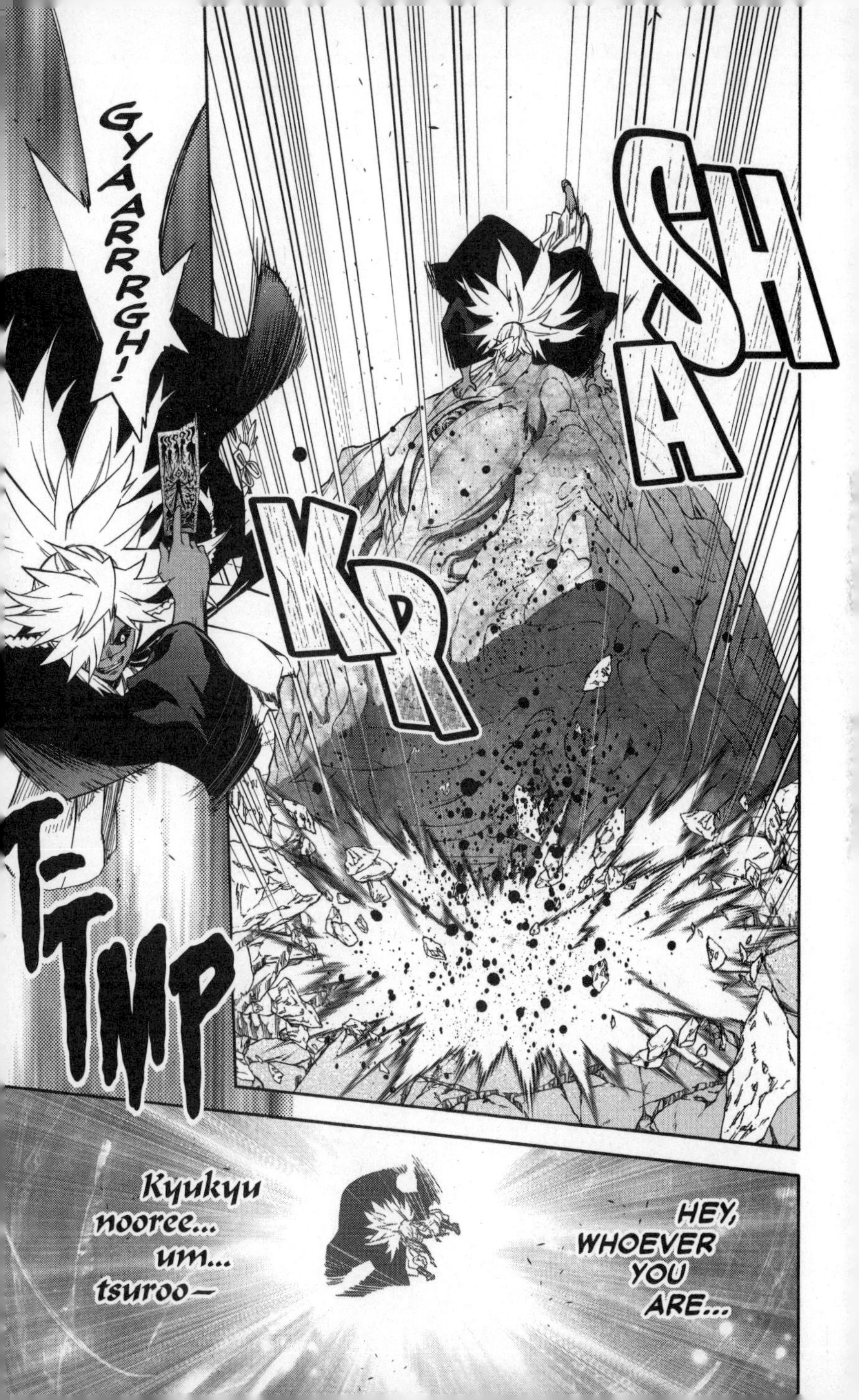
SHA
KR
GYAARRGH!
T-TMP
HEY, WHOEVER YOU ARE...
Kyukyu nooree... um... tsuroo—

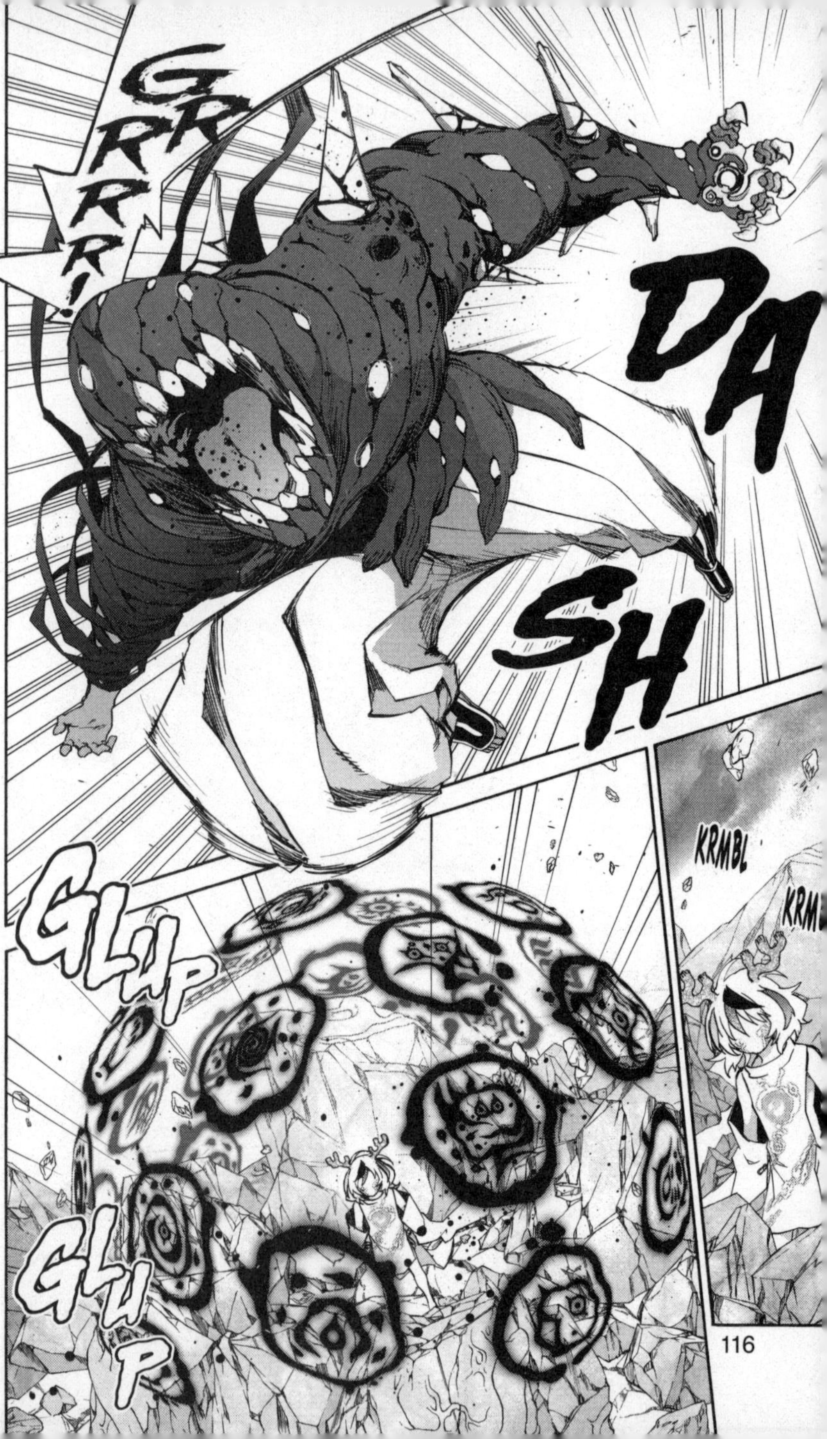
DASH
GRRRR!
KRMBL
KRM
GLUP
GLUP

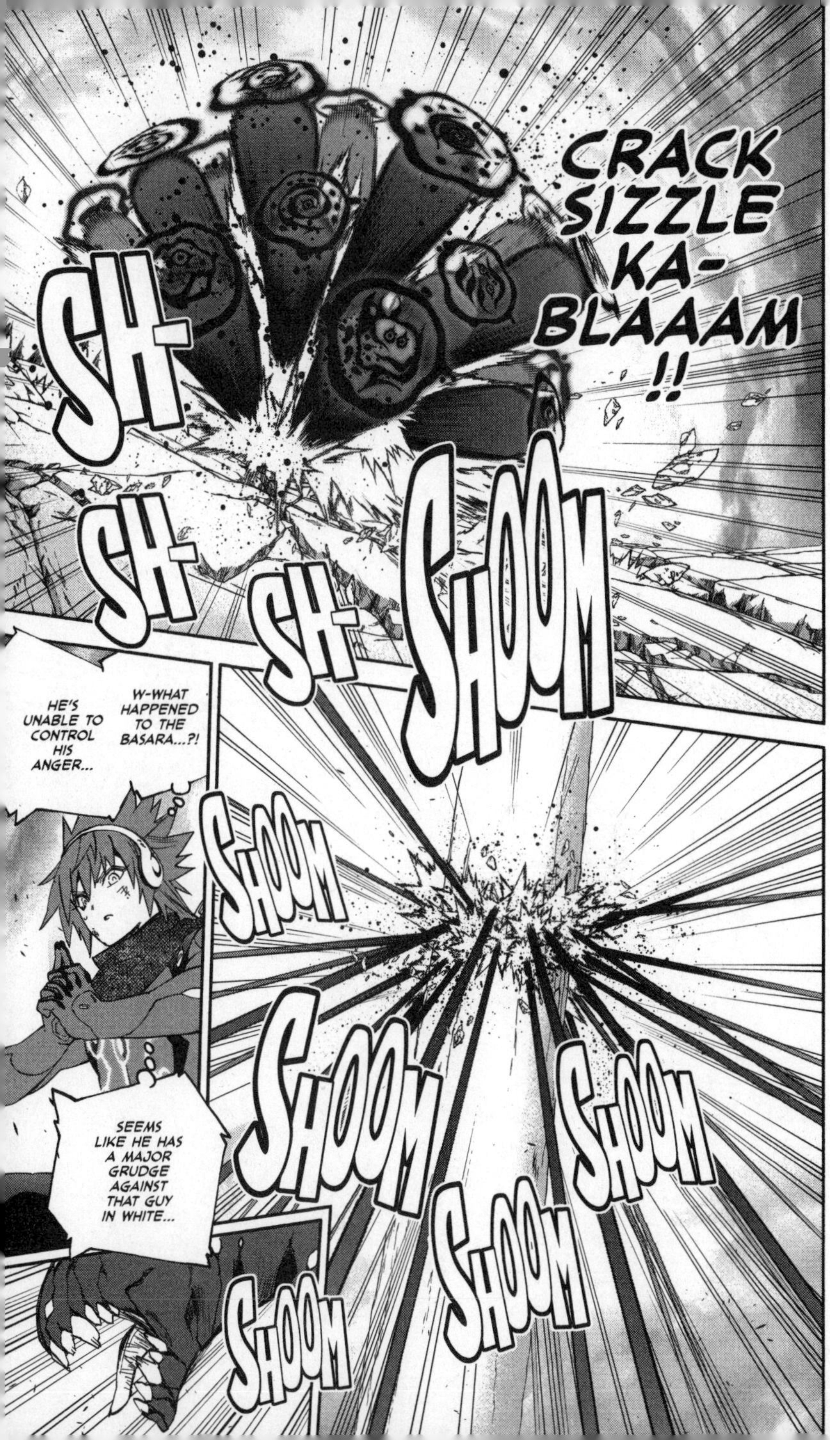
CRACK SIZZLE KA-BLAAAM!!
SH- SH- SH- SHOOM
SHOOM
SHOOM
SHOOM
SHOOM
SHOOM
SHOOM
W-WHAT HAPPENED TO THE BASARA...?!
HE'S UNABLE TO CONTROL HIS ANGER...
SEEMS LIKE HE HAS A MAJOR GRUDGE AGAINST THAT GUY IN WHITE...

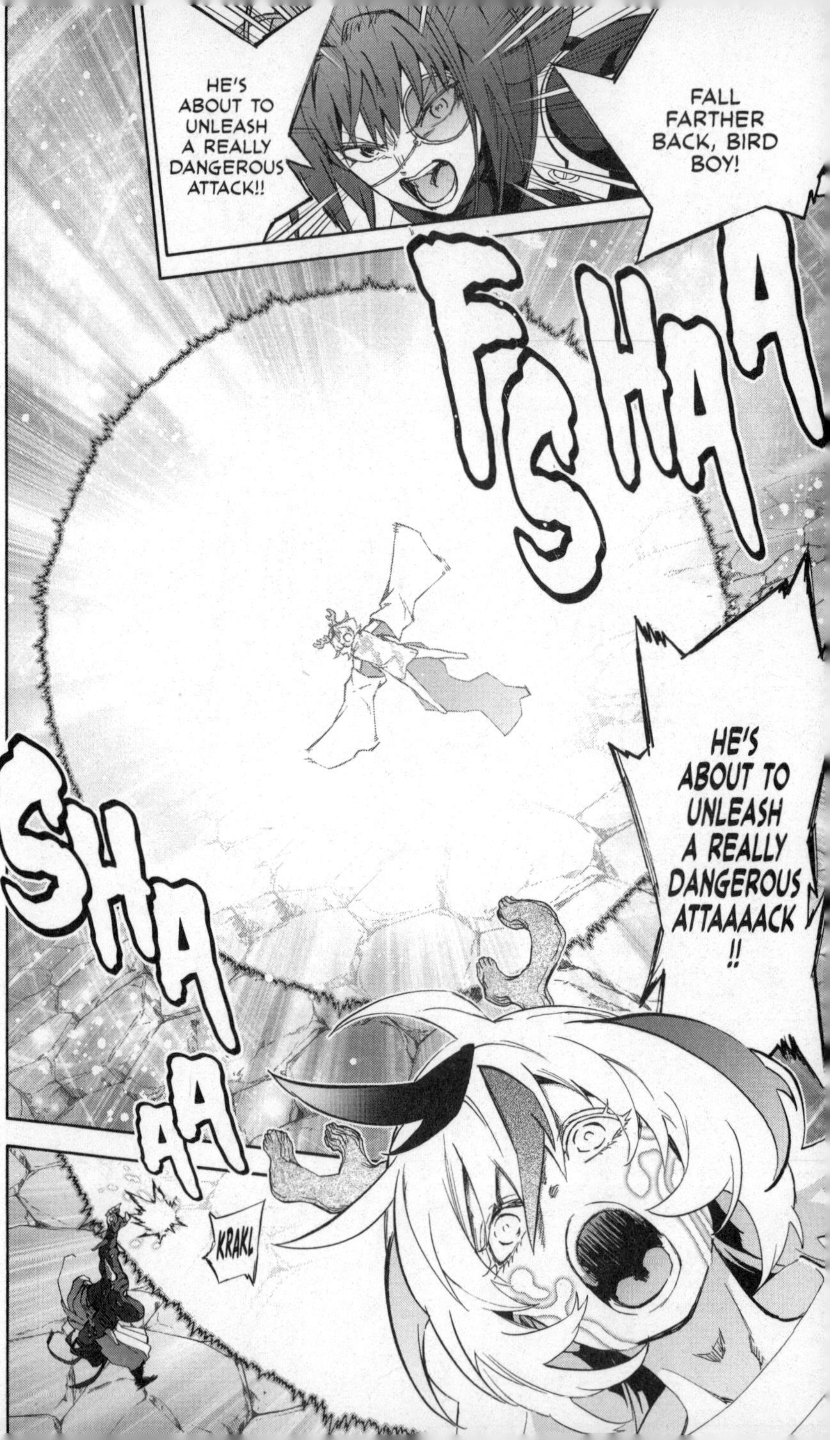
FALL FARTHER BACK, BIRD BOY!
HE'S ABOUT TO UNLEASH A REALLY DANGEROUS ATTACK!!
FSHAA
HE'S ABOUT TO UNLEASH A REALLY DANGEROUS ATTAAAACK!!
SHAAA
KRAKL

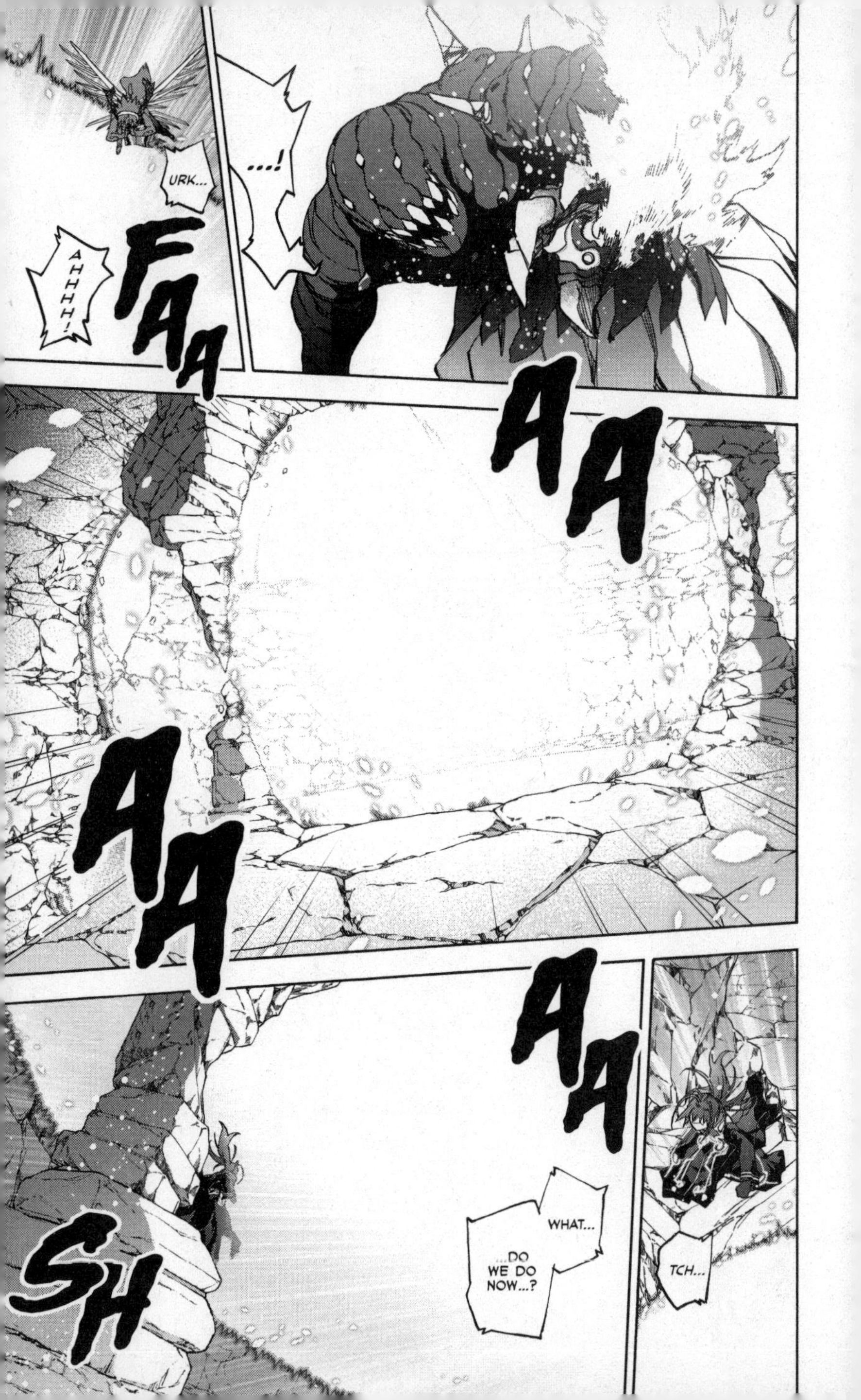
...!
URK...
AHHHH!
FAAAAAAAA
TCH...
WHAT...
...DO WE DO NOW...?
SH

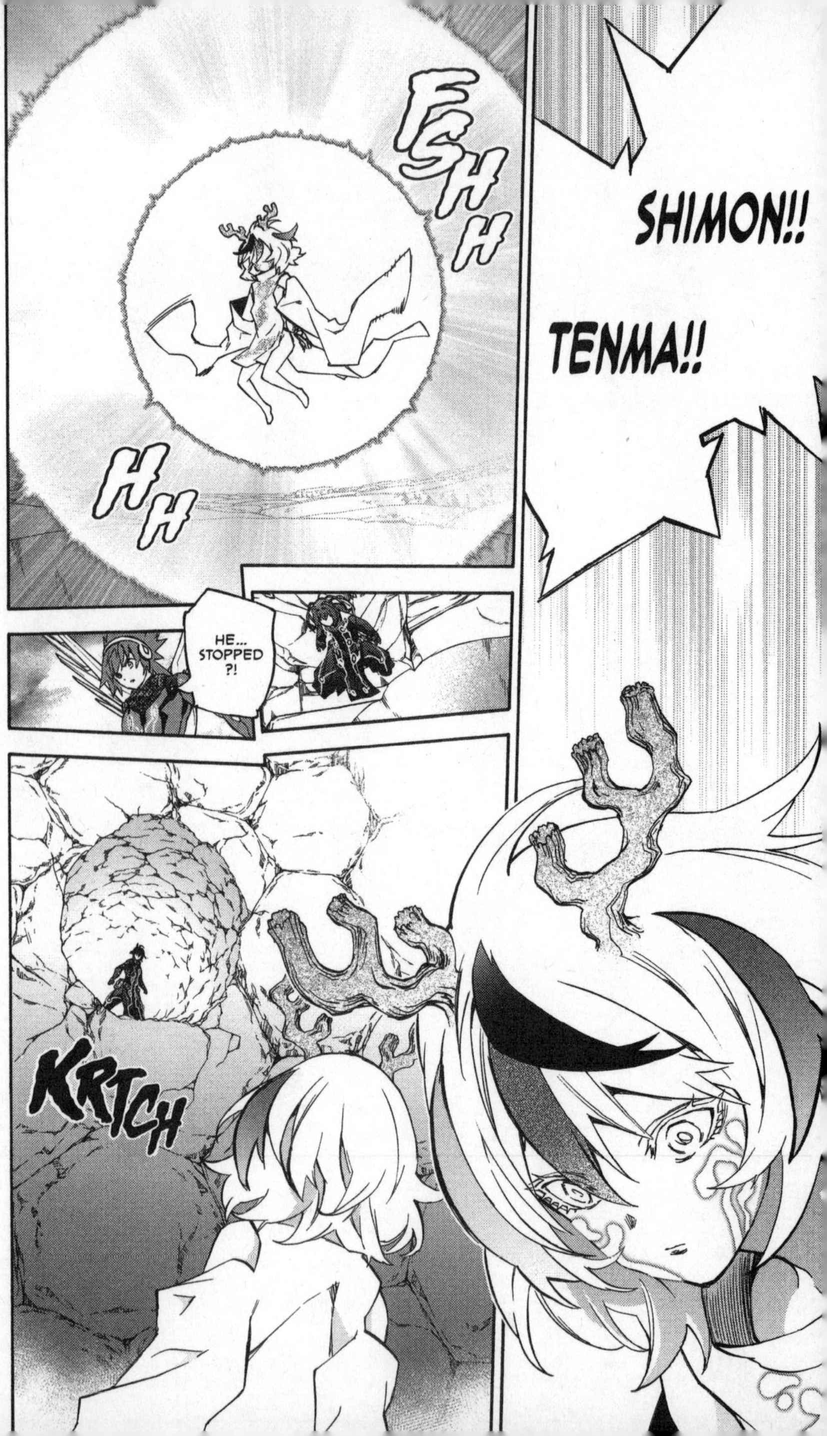
SHIMON!!
TENMA!!
FSHHHH
HE... STOPPED?!
KRTCH

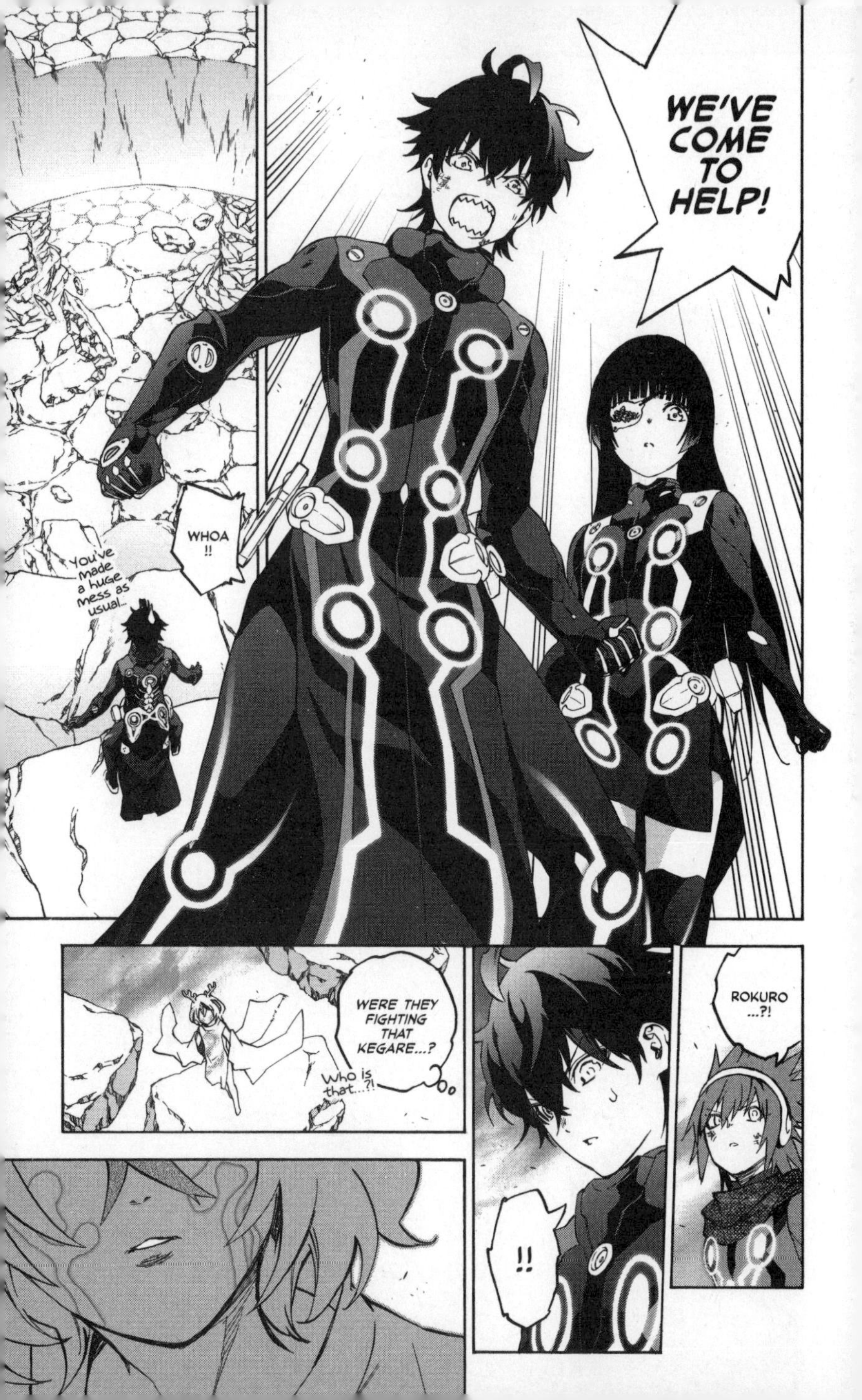
WE'VE COME TO HELP!
WHOA !!
You've made a huge mess as usual...
ROKURO ...?!
WERE THEY FIGHTING THAT KEGARE...?
Who is that...?!
!!

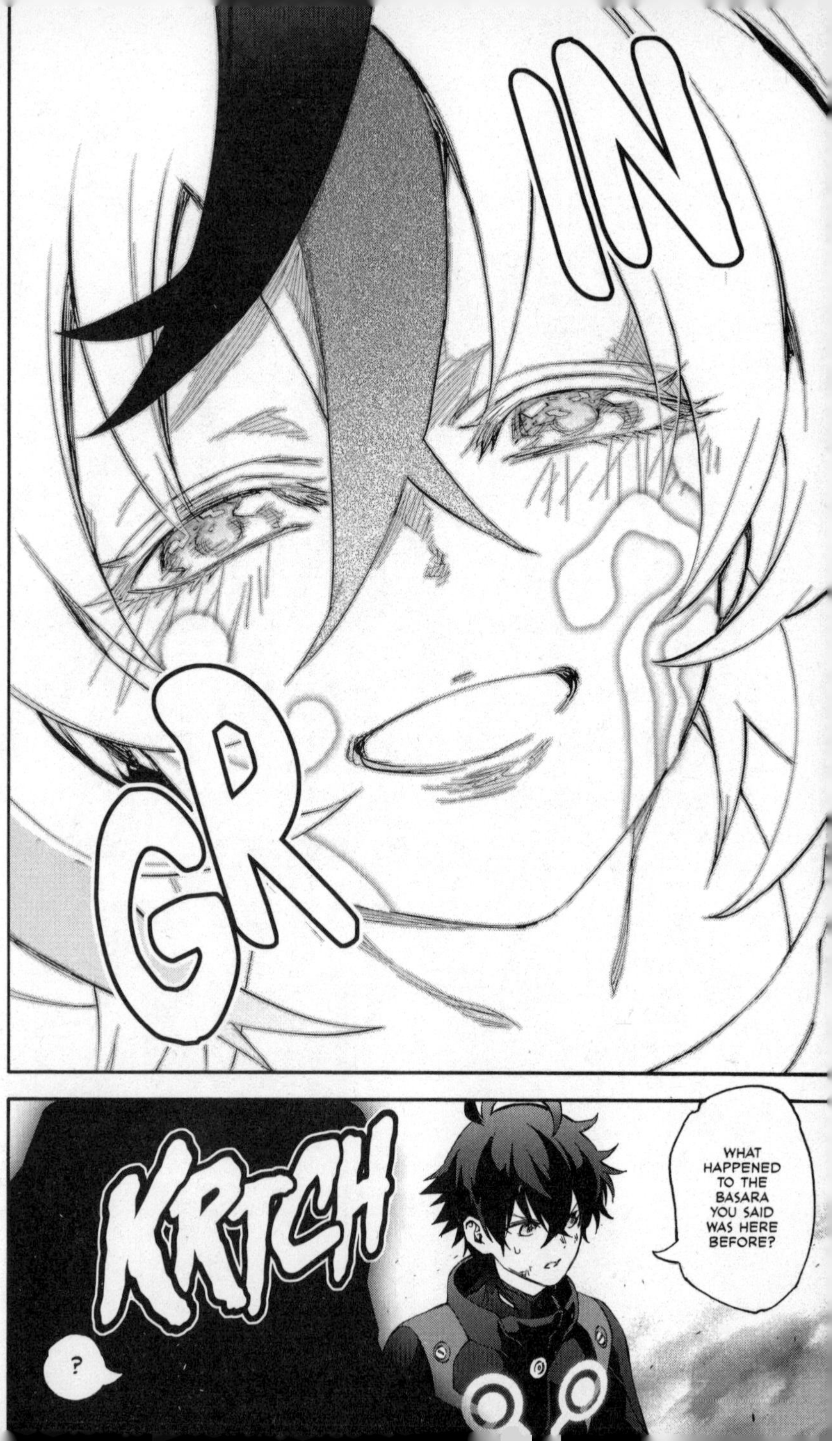
GR
IN
WHAT HAPPENED TO THE BASARA YOU SAID WAS HERE BEFORE?
KRTCH
?

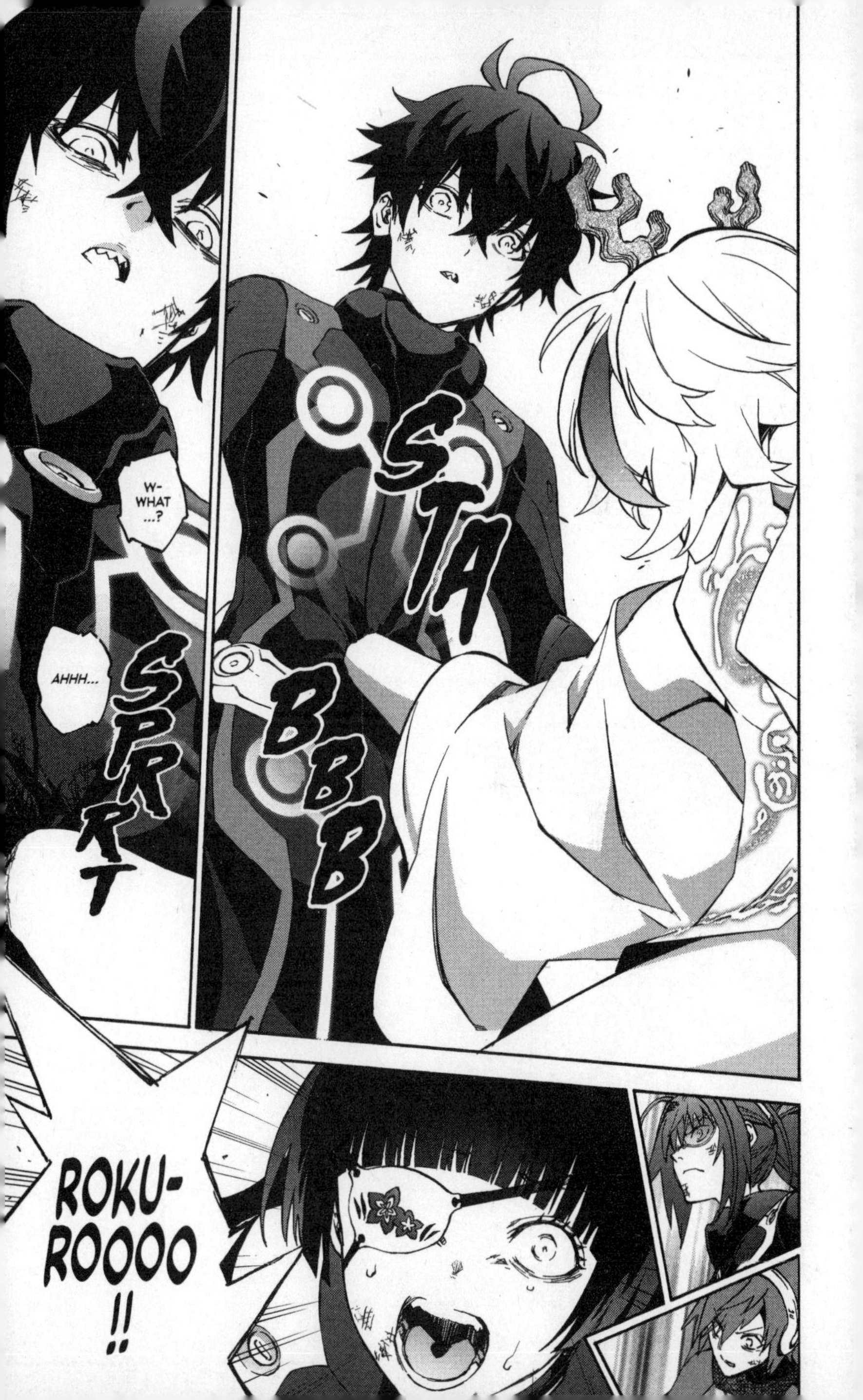
STABBB
W-WHAT ...?
AHHH...
SPRRT
ROKU-ROOOO!!

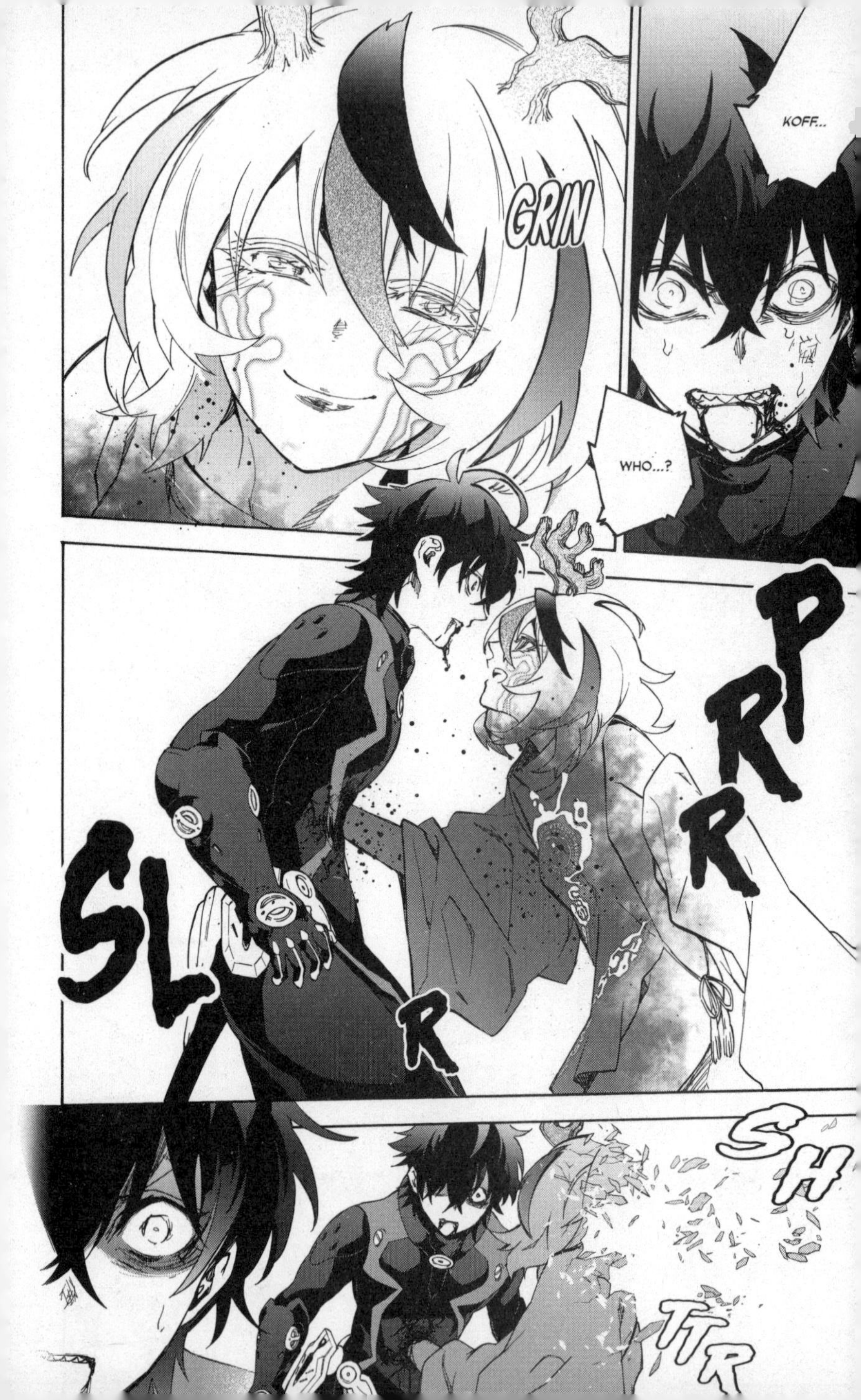
KOFF...
WHO...?
GRIN
PRRR
SLR
R
SH
TTR

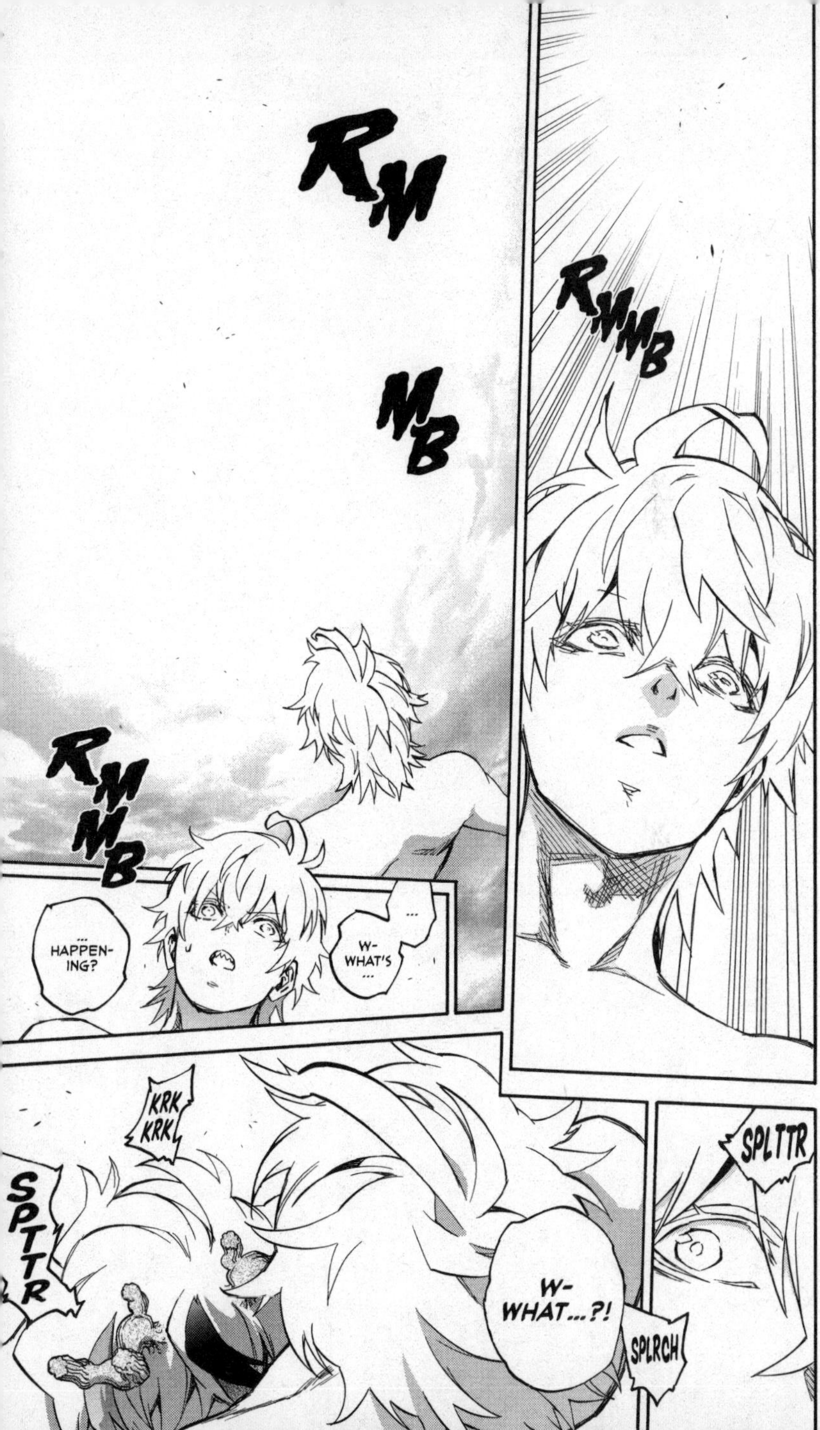
RMMB
RM
MB
RMMB
... W- WHAT'S ...
... HAPPENING?
SPLTTR
SPLRCH
KRK KRK
SPTTR
W- WHAT...?!

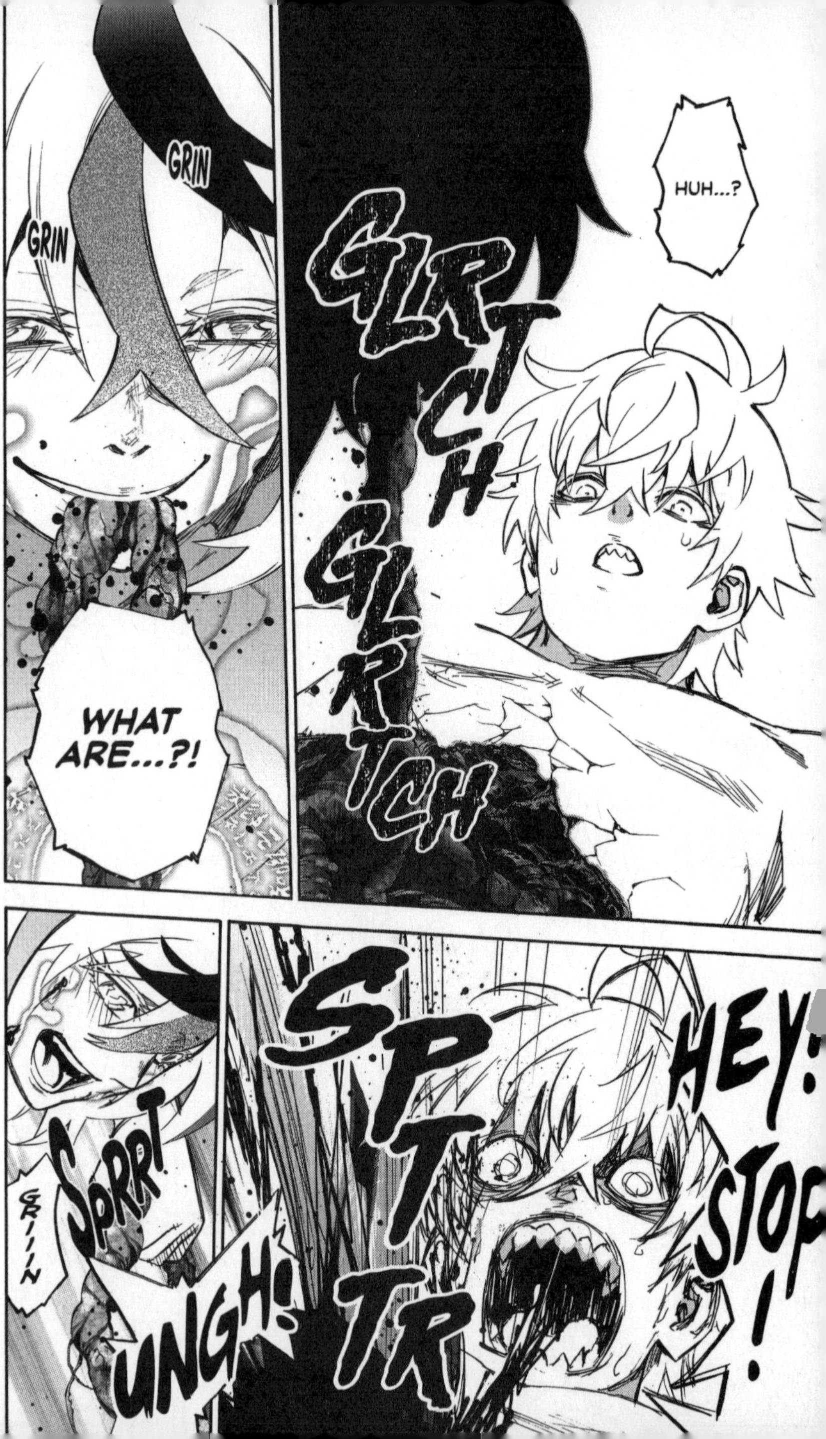
HUH...?
GLRTCH
GLRTCH
GRIN
GRIN
WHAT ARE...?!
HEY! STOP!
SPTTR
SPRRT
GRIIIN
UNGH!

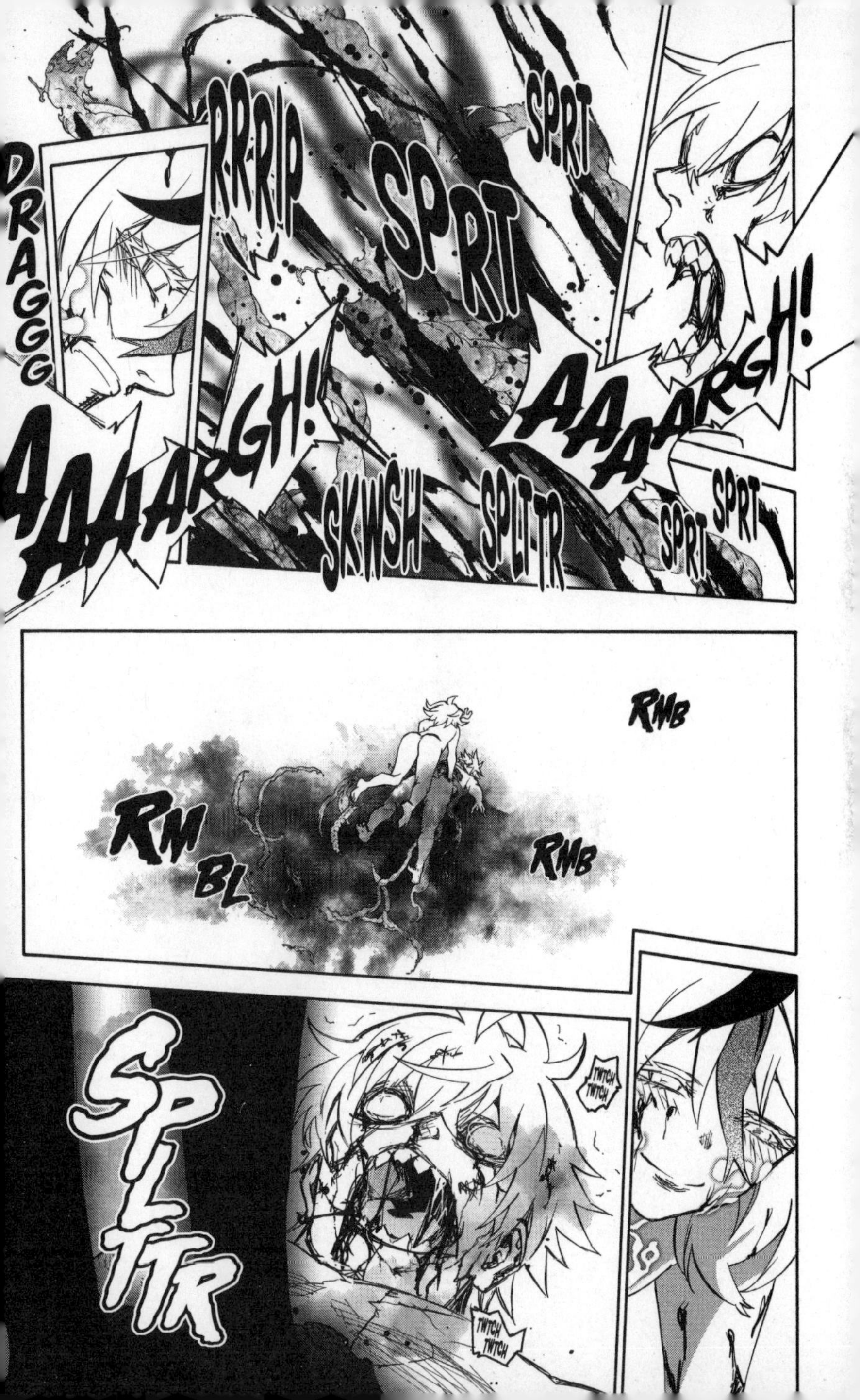
SPRT
SPRT
SPRT
AAAARGH!
R-R-RIP
DRAGGG
SPRT
SPLT-T-R
SKWSH
AAAARGH!
RMB
RMB
RMBL
TWITCH TWITCH
SPLTTR
TWITCH TWITCH

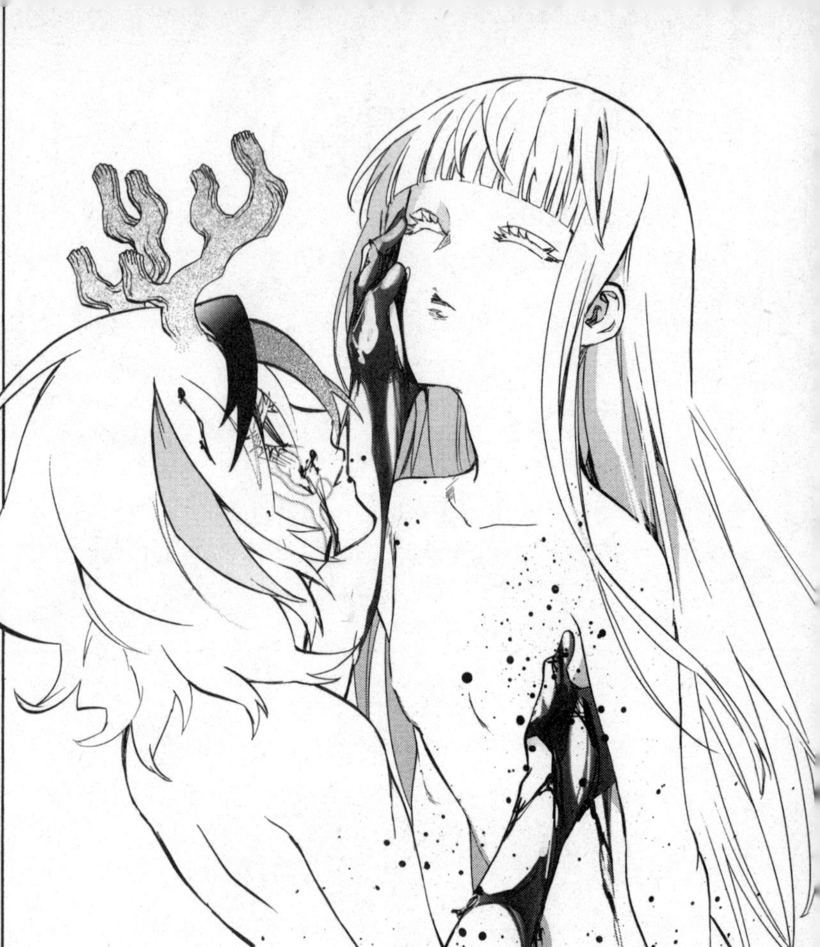

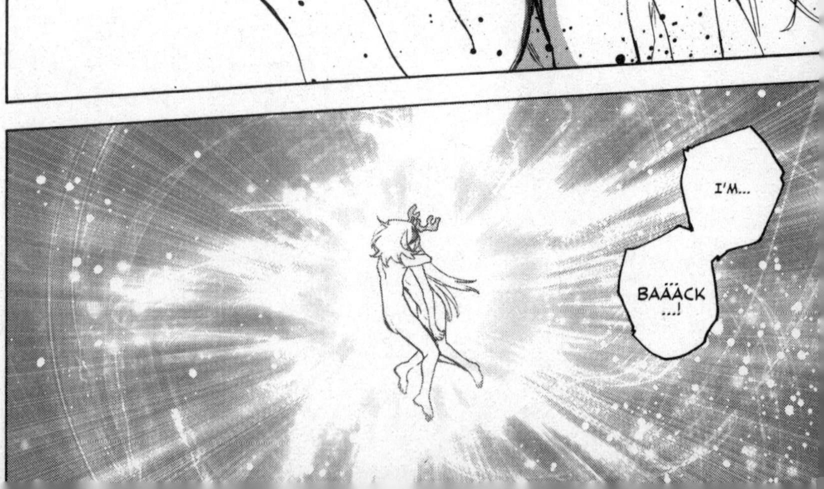
I'M...
...BAÄÄCK ...!

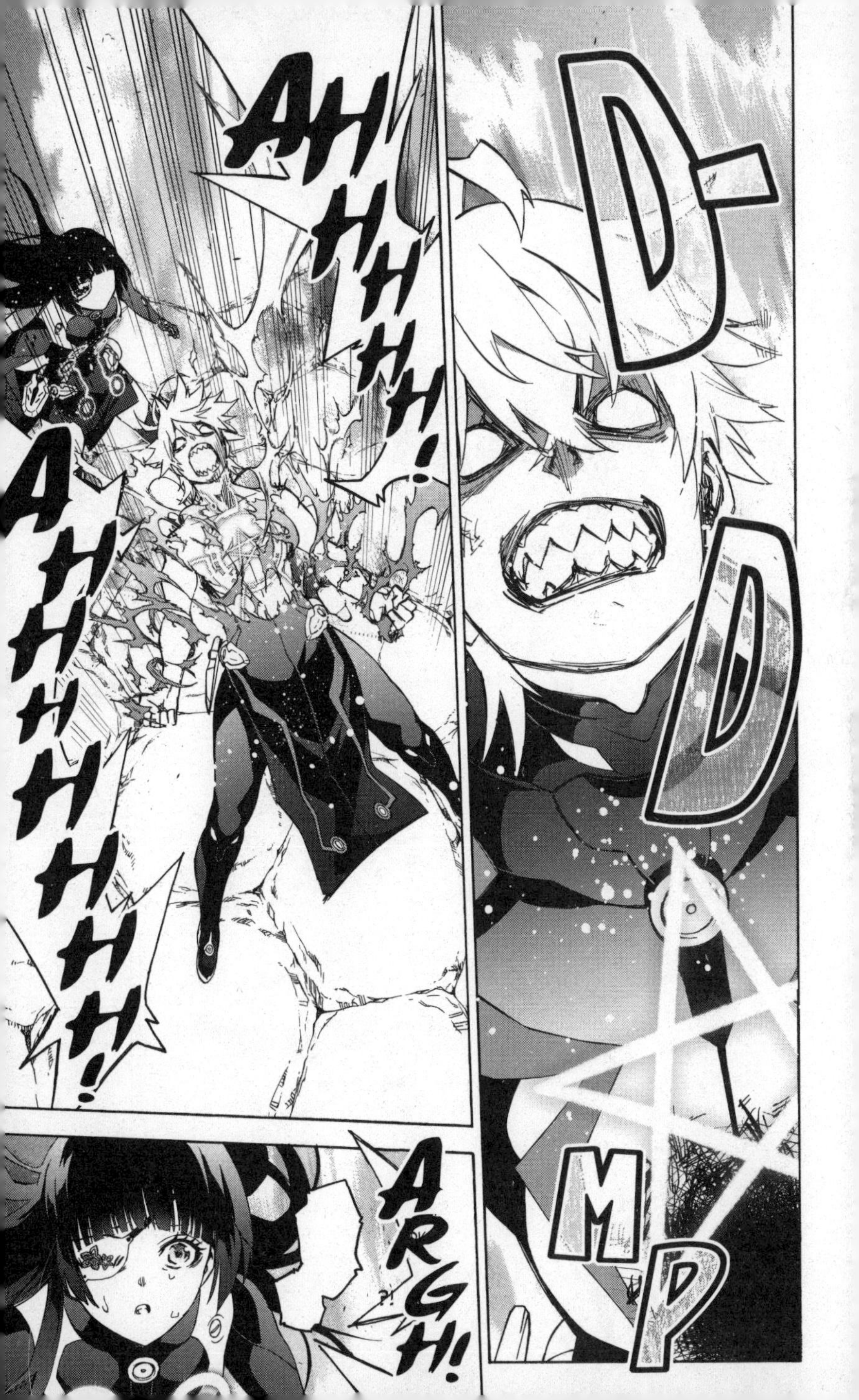

D-D
MP
AHHHHH!
AHHHHHHHHHH!
ARGH!
?!

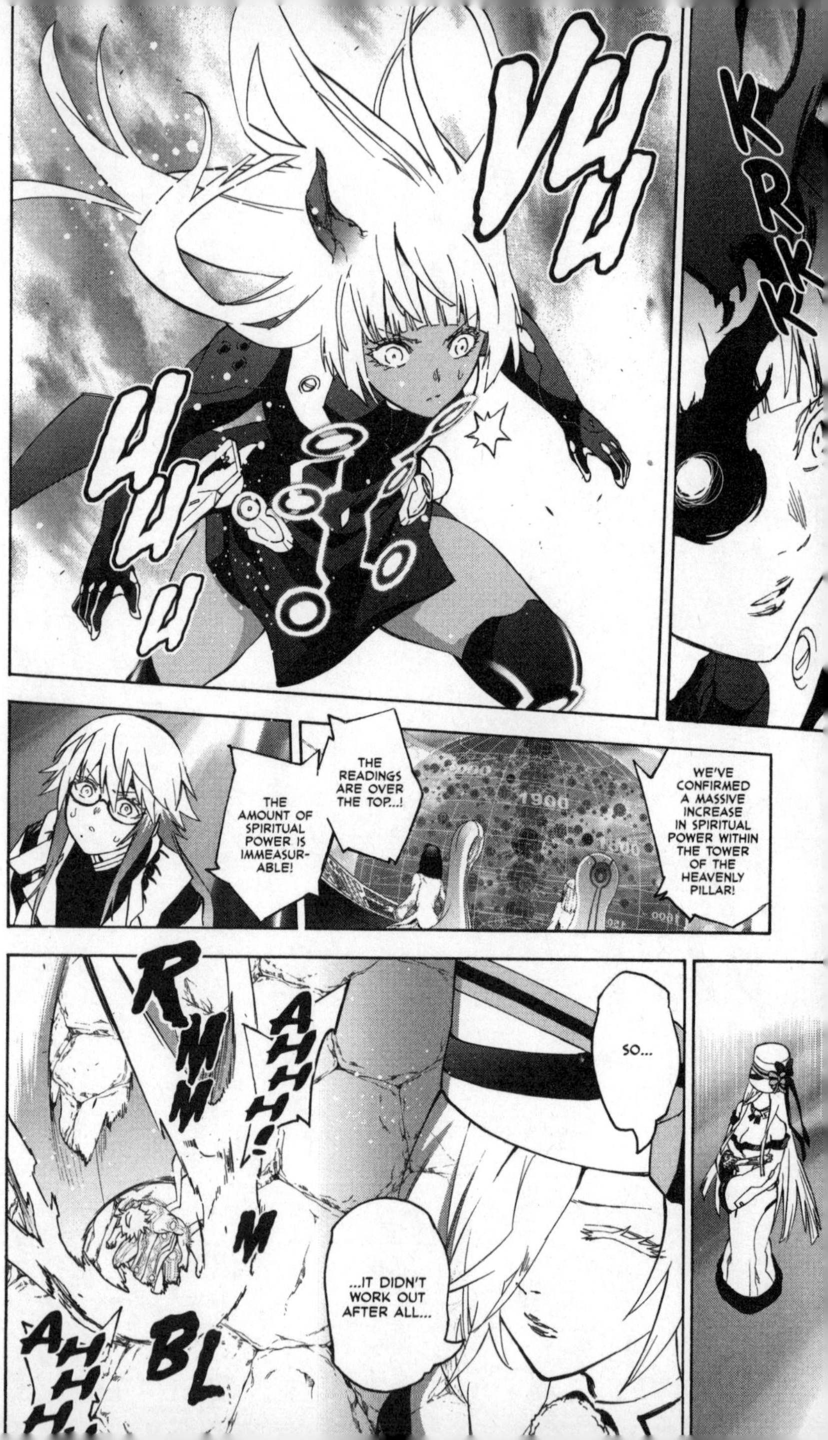
KRKKK
WE'VE CONFIRMED A MASSIVE INCREASE IN SPIRITUAL POWER WITHIN THE TOWER OF THE HEAVENLY PILLAR!
THE READINGS ARE OVER THE TOP...!
THE AMOUNT OF SPIRITUAL POWER IS IMMEASURABLE!
SO...
AHHH!!
RMMM
M
...IT DIDN'T WORK OUT AFTER ALL...
BL
AHHHH

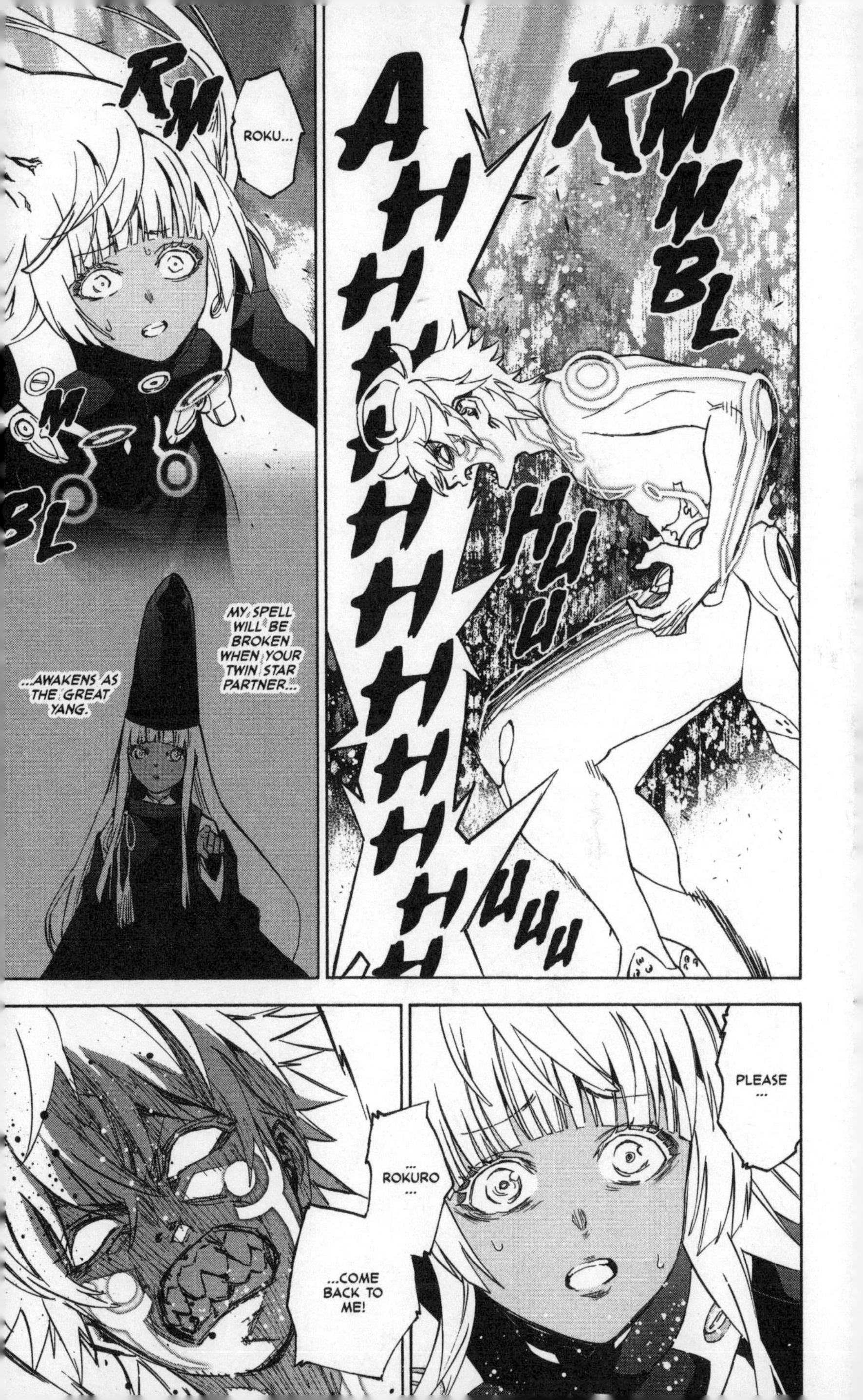
RMMBL
AHHHHHHHHHHH
HUUUUUU
RM
ROKU...
MBL
MY SPELL WILL BE BROKEN WHEN YOUR TWIN STAR PARTNER...
...AWAKENS AS THE GREAT YANG.
PLEASE...
...ROKURO...
...COME BACK TO ME!

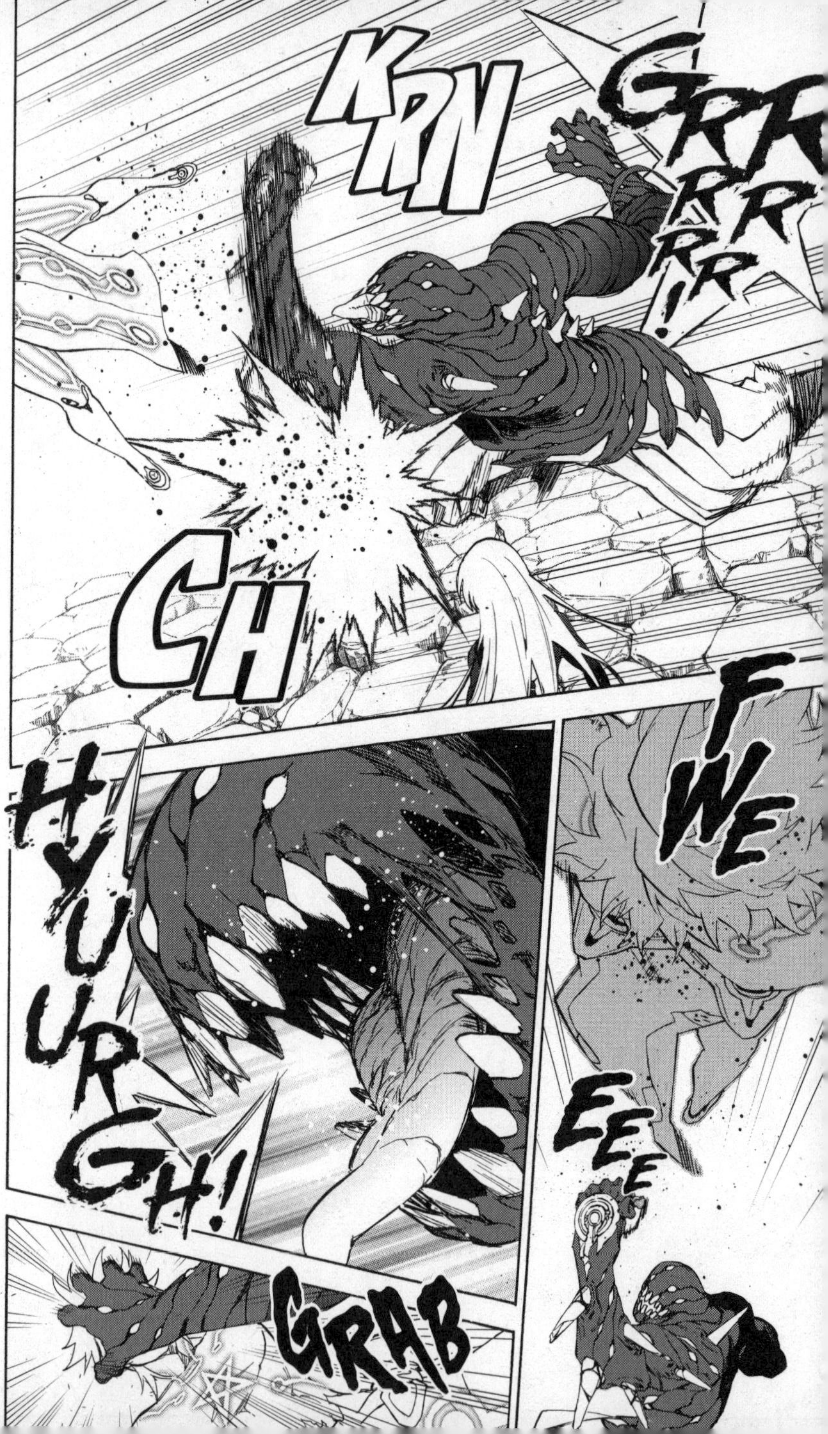
GRRRRRRR!
KRN
CH
FWE
HYUURGH!
EEEE
GRAB

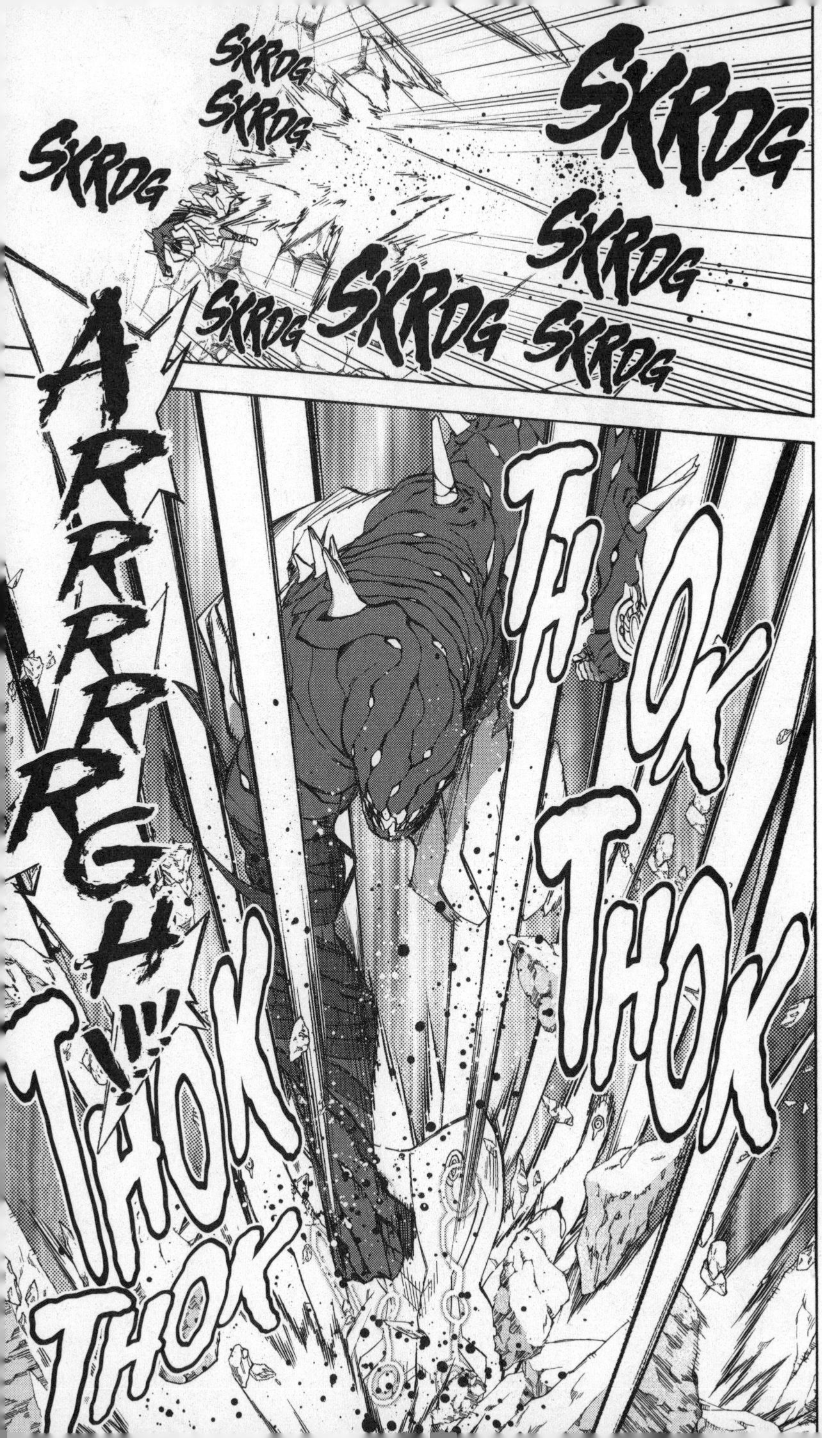
SKRDG
SKRDG
SKRDG
SKRDG
SKRDG
SKRDG
SKRDG
SKRDG
ARRRRRGH!!
THOK
THOK
THOK
THOK

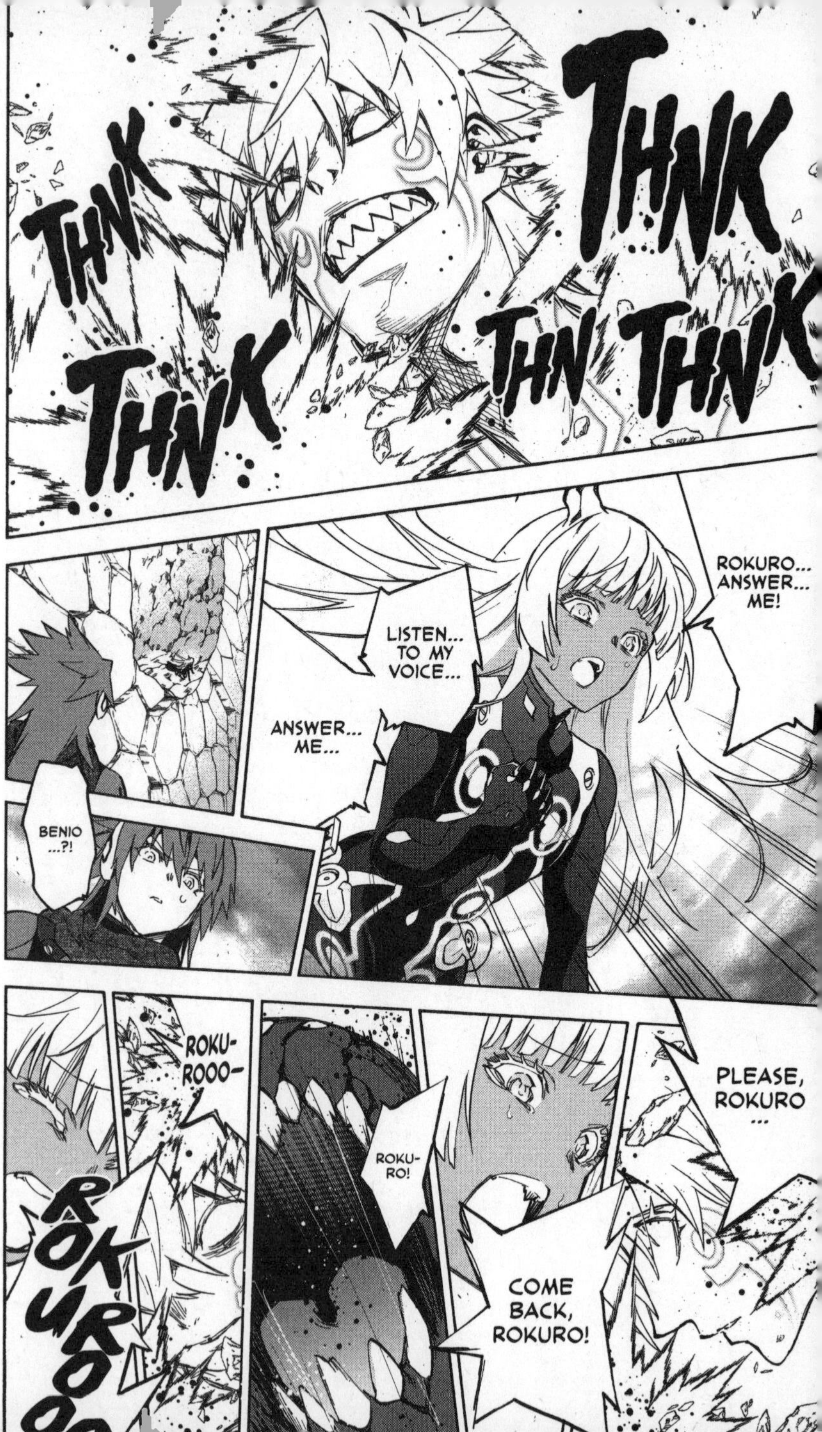
THNK
THN THNK
THNK
THNK
ROKURO... ANSWER... ME!
LISTEN... TO MY VOICE...
ANSWER... ME...
BENIO ...?!
PLEASE, ROKURO ...
COME BACK, ROKURO!
ROKU-RO!
ROKU-ROOO-
ROKUROOO

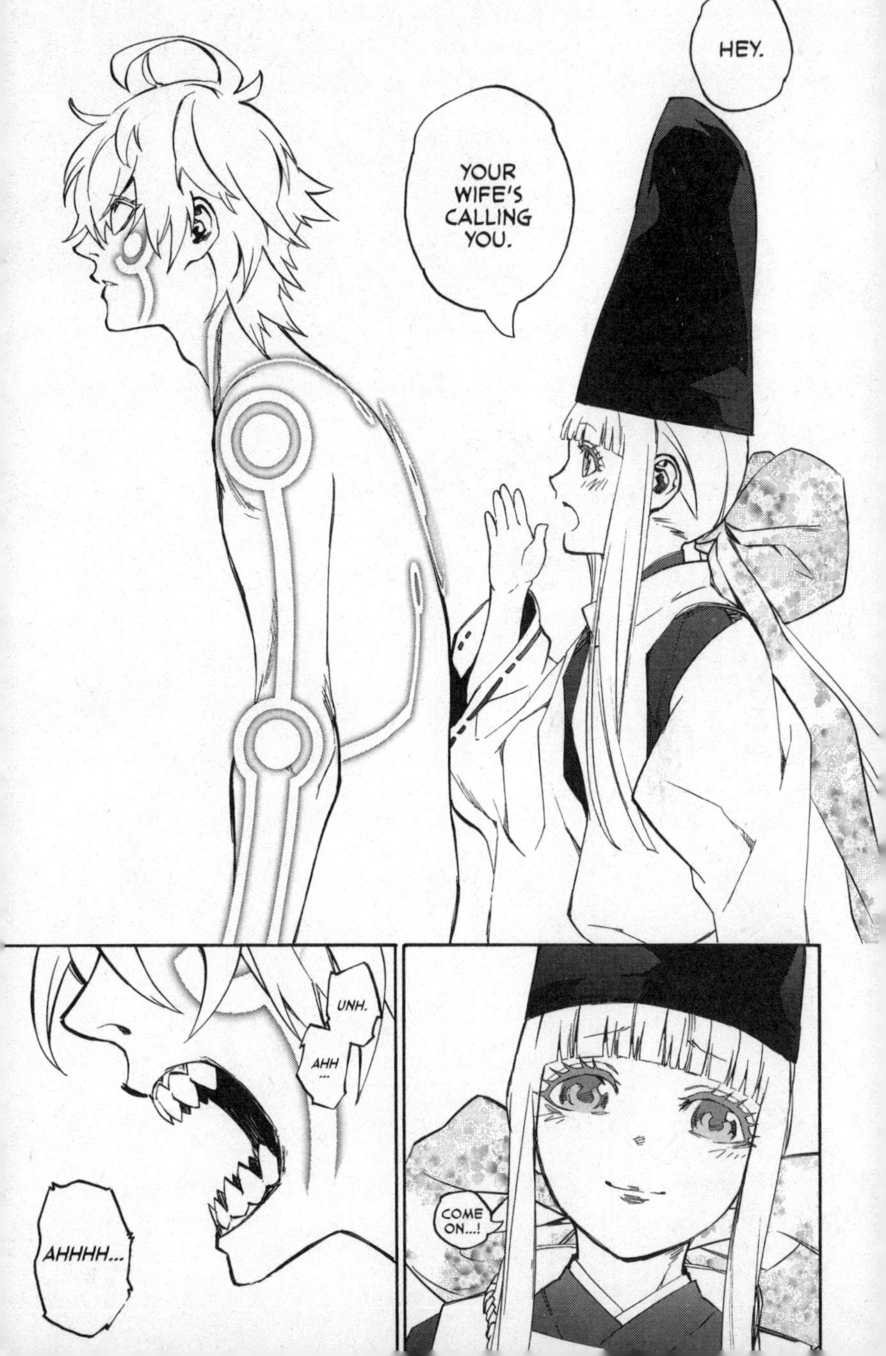
HEY.
YOUR WIFE'S CALLING YOU.
COME ON...!
UNH.
AHH...
AHHHH...

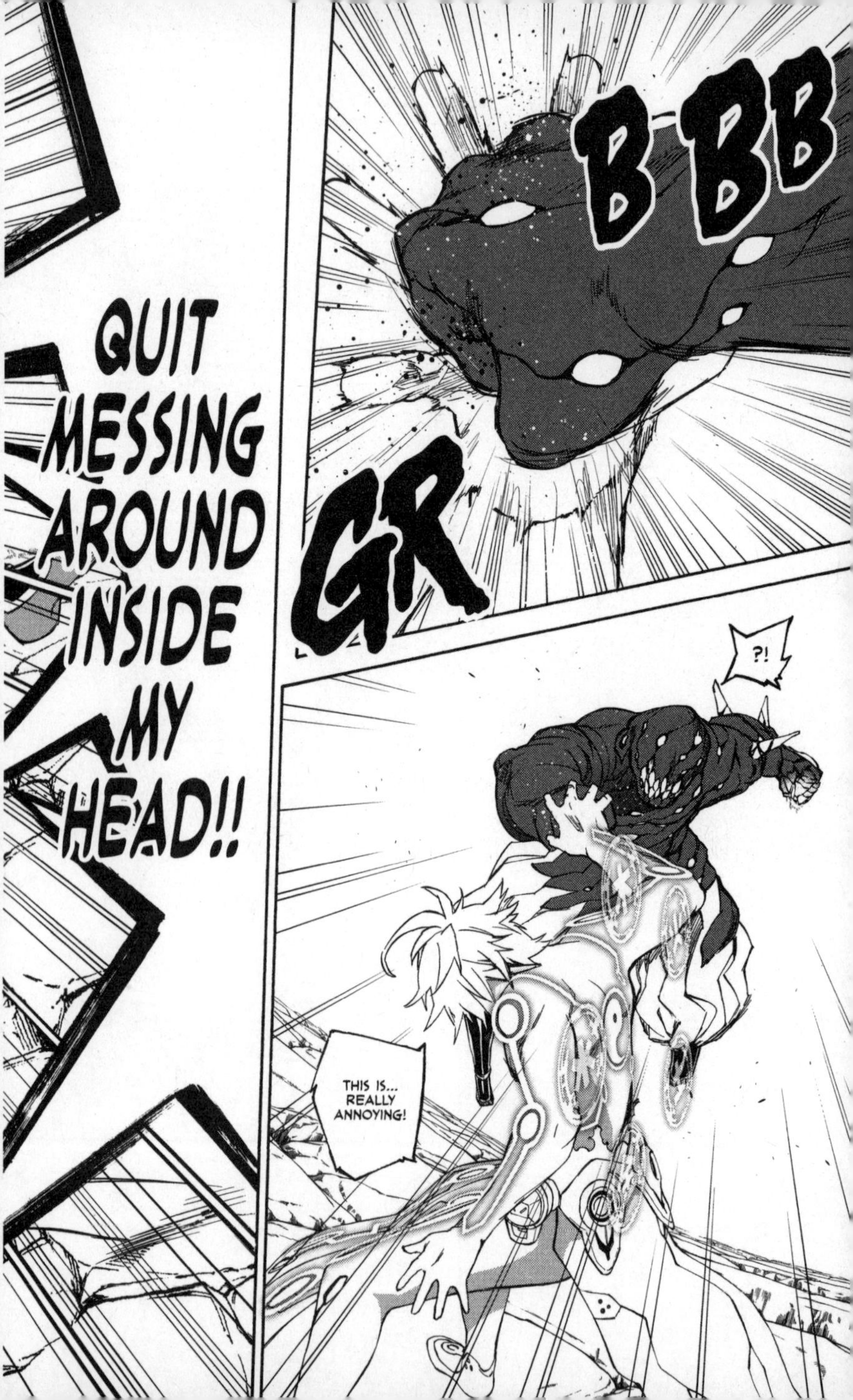
B BB
GR
?!
THIS IS... REALLY ANNOYING!
QUIT MESSING AROUND INSIDE MY HEAD!!

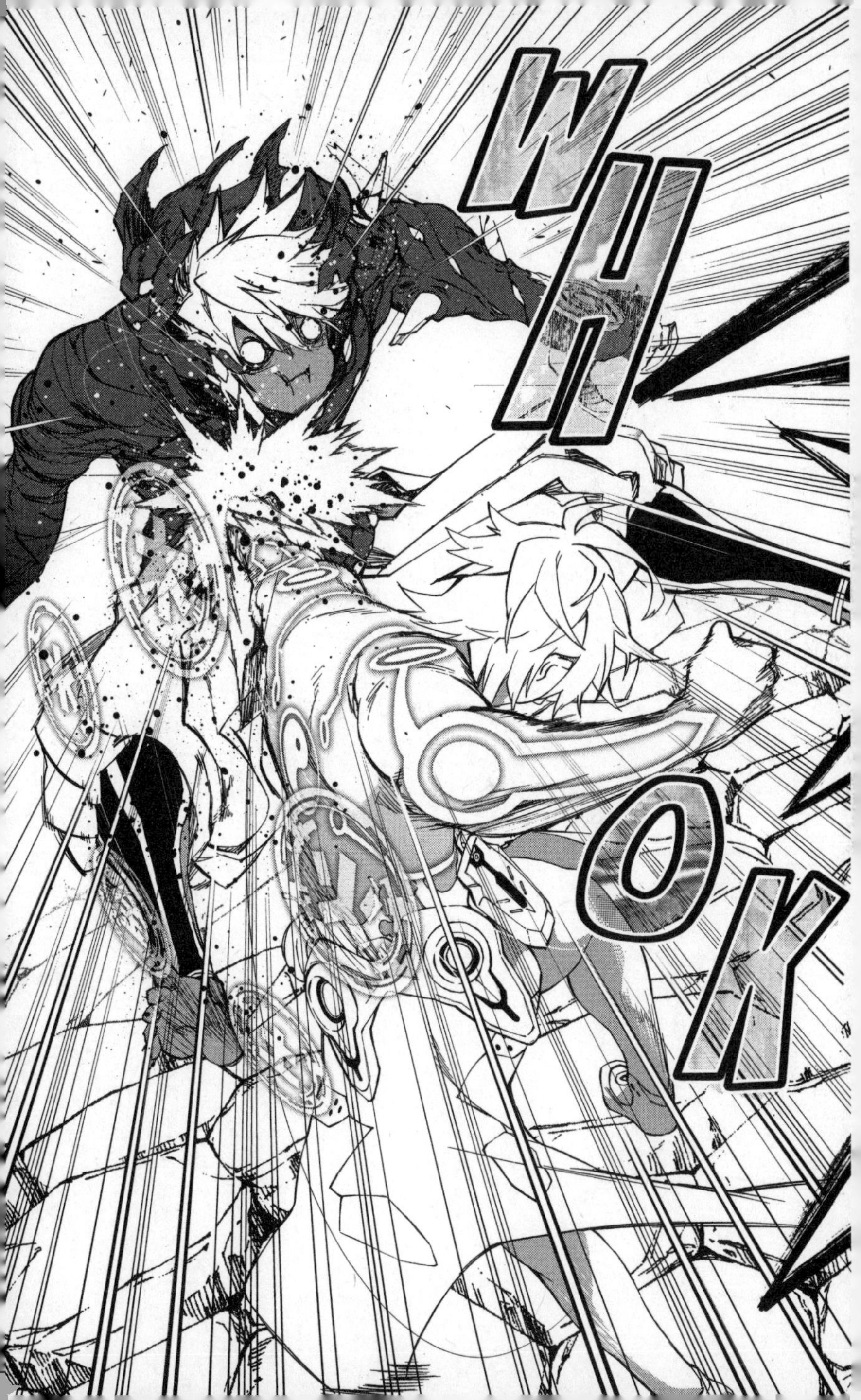
WHAOK

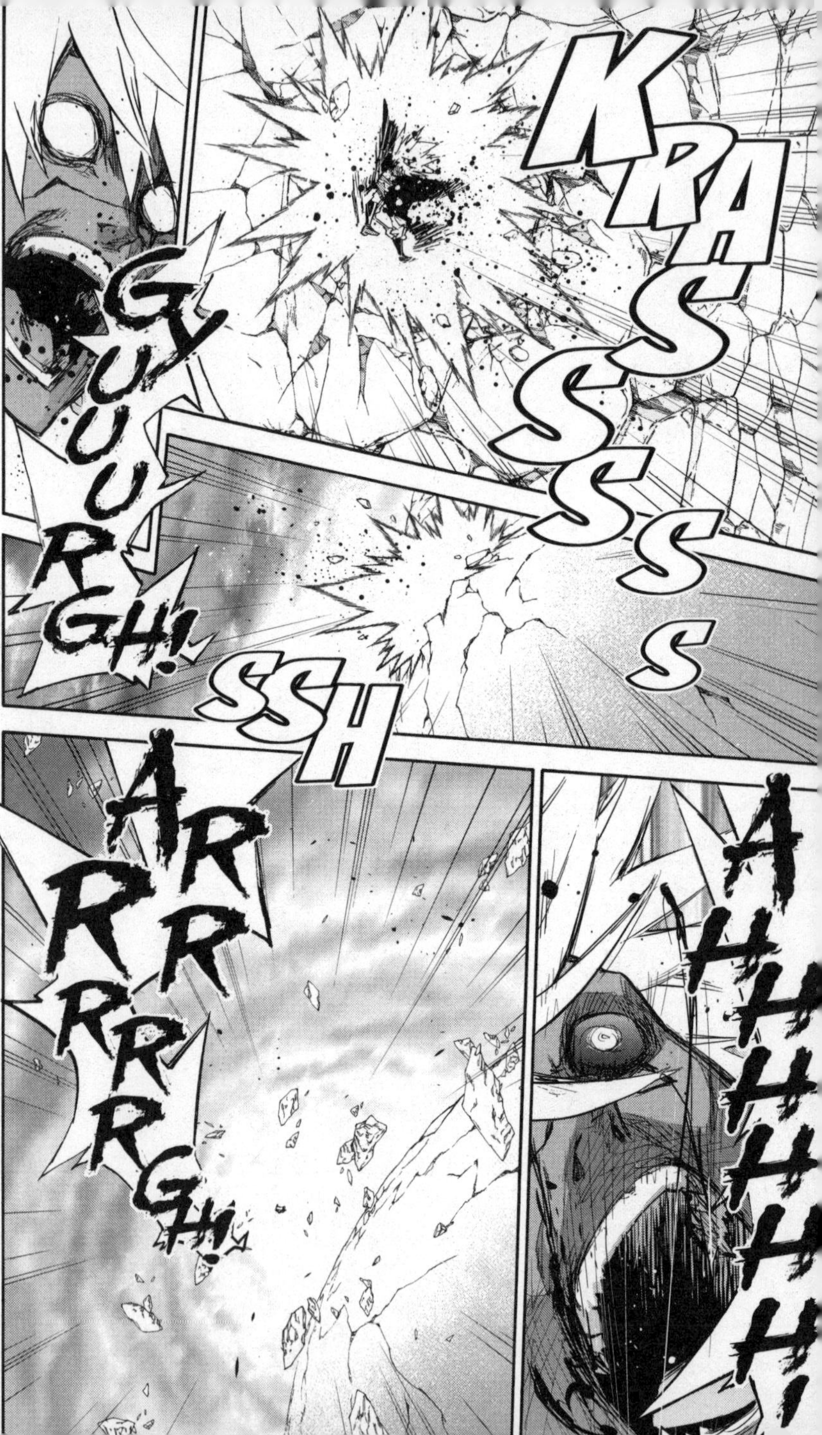
KRASSSSSS
GYUUURGH!
SSH
AHHHHHH!
ARRRRRRRRGH!

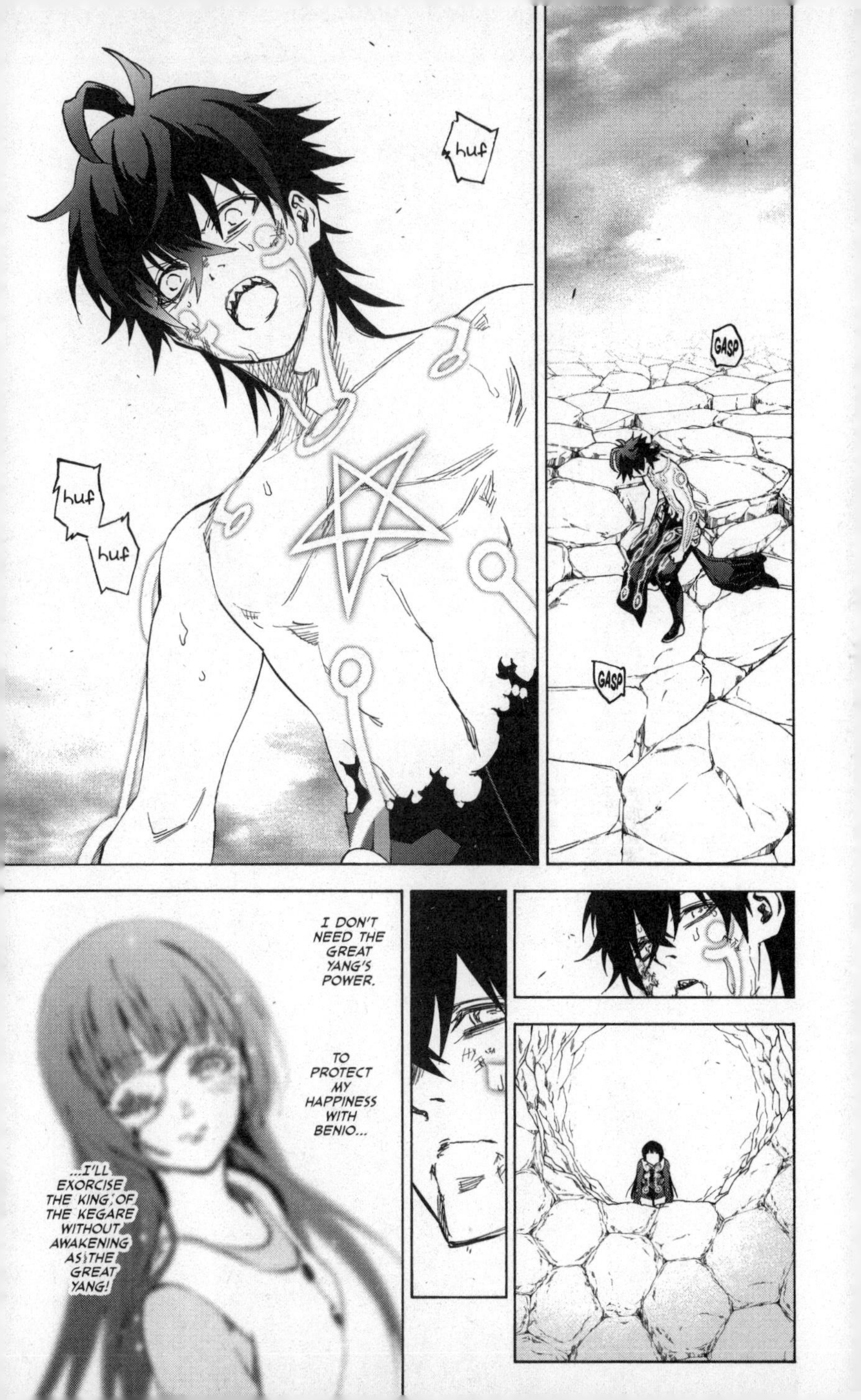
GASP
GASP
huf
huf
huf
I DON'T NEED THE GREAT YANG'S POWER.
TO PROTECT MY HAPPINESS WITH BENIO...
...I'LL EXORCISE THE KING OF THE KEGARE WITHOUT AWAKENING AS THE GREAT YANG!

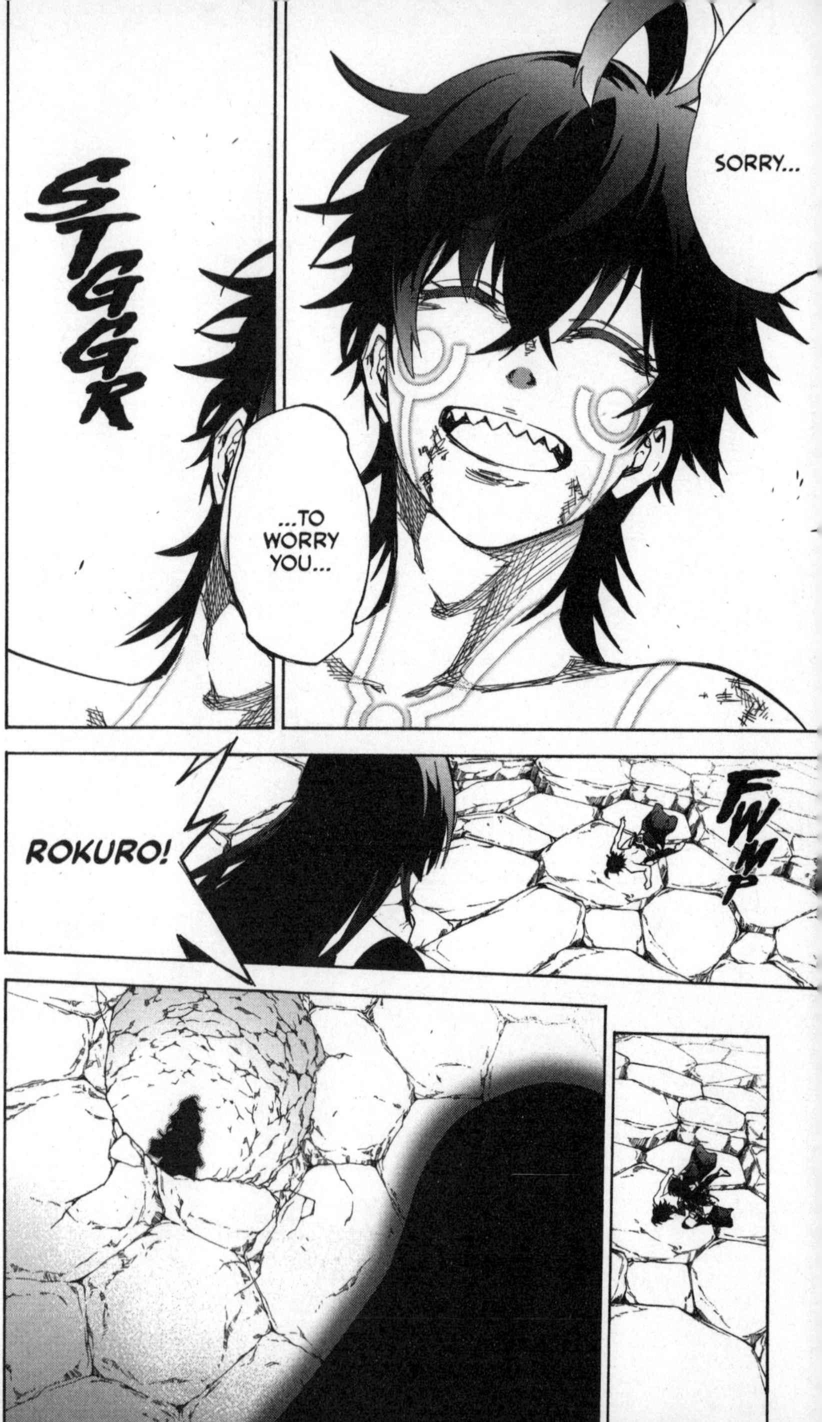
SORRY...
...TO WORRY YOU...
STGGR
FWMP
ROKURO!

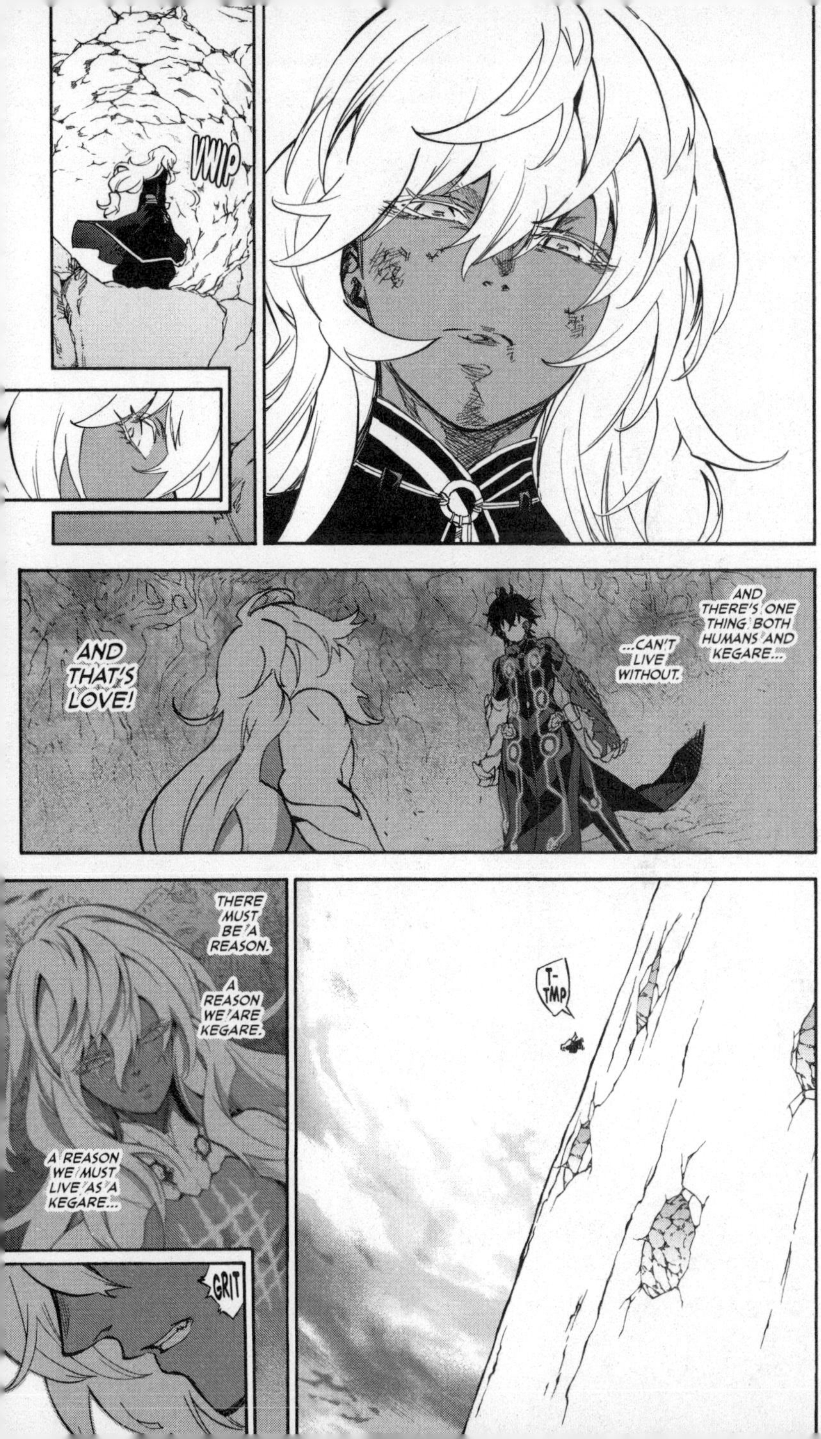
VWIP
AND THERE'S ONE THING BOTH HUMANS AND KEGARE...
...CAN'T LIVE WITHOUT.
AND THAT'S LOVE!
T-TMP
THERE MUST BE A REASON.
A REASON WE ARE KEGARE.
A REASON WE MUST LIVE AS A KEGARE...
GRIT

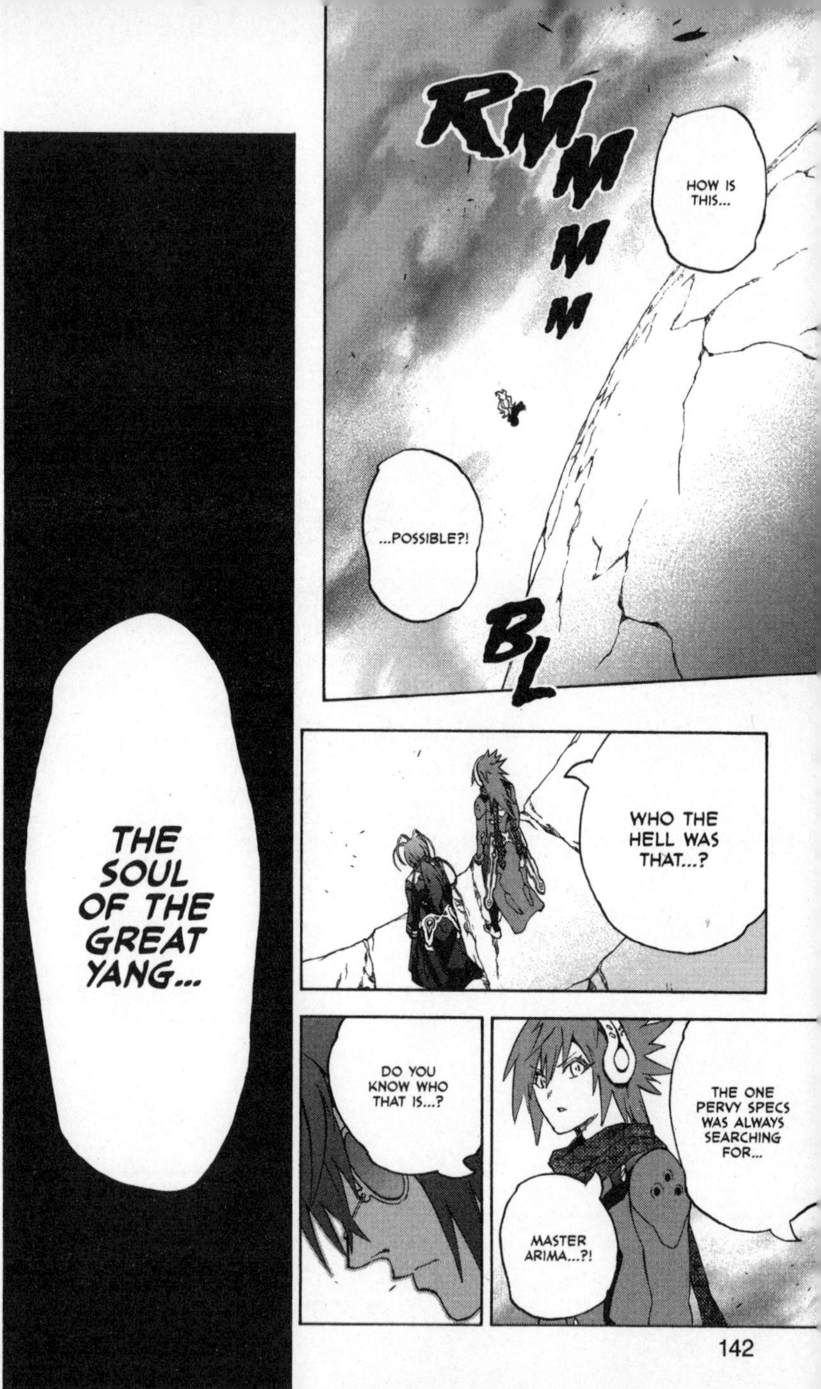
RMMMMM
HOW IS THIS...
...POSSIBLE?!
BL
WHO THE HELL WAS THAT...?
THE ONE PERVY SPECS WAS ALWAYS SEARCHING FOR...
MASTER ARIMA...?!
DO YOU KNOW WHO THAT IS...?
THE SOUL OF THE GREAT YANG...

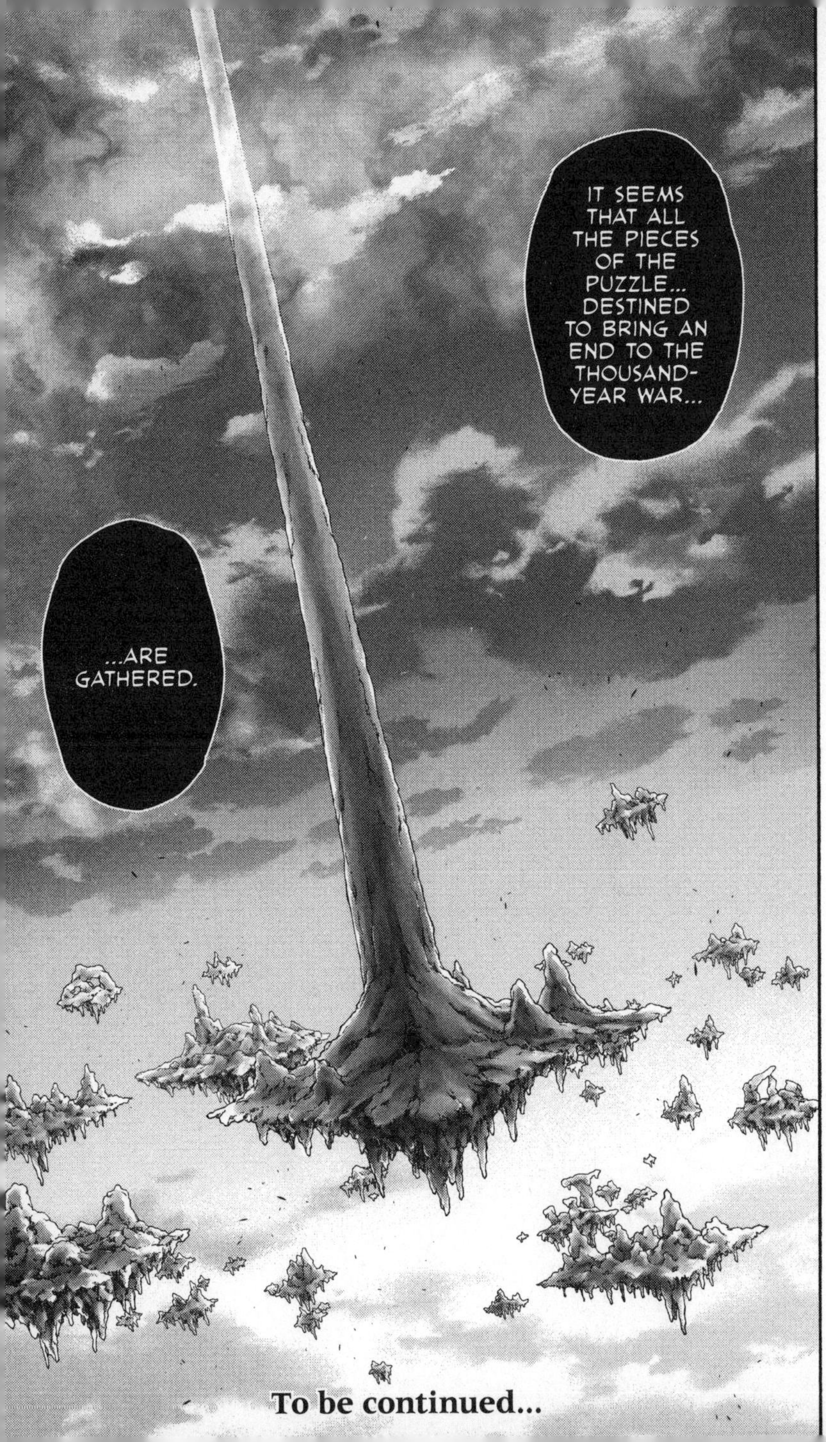
IT SEEMS THAT ALL THE PIECES OF THE PUZZLE... DESTINED TO BRING AN END TO THE THOUSAND-YEAR WAR...
...ARE GATHERED.
To be continued...

Design Ideas for New Kamui by Staff K.

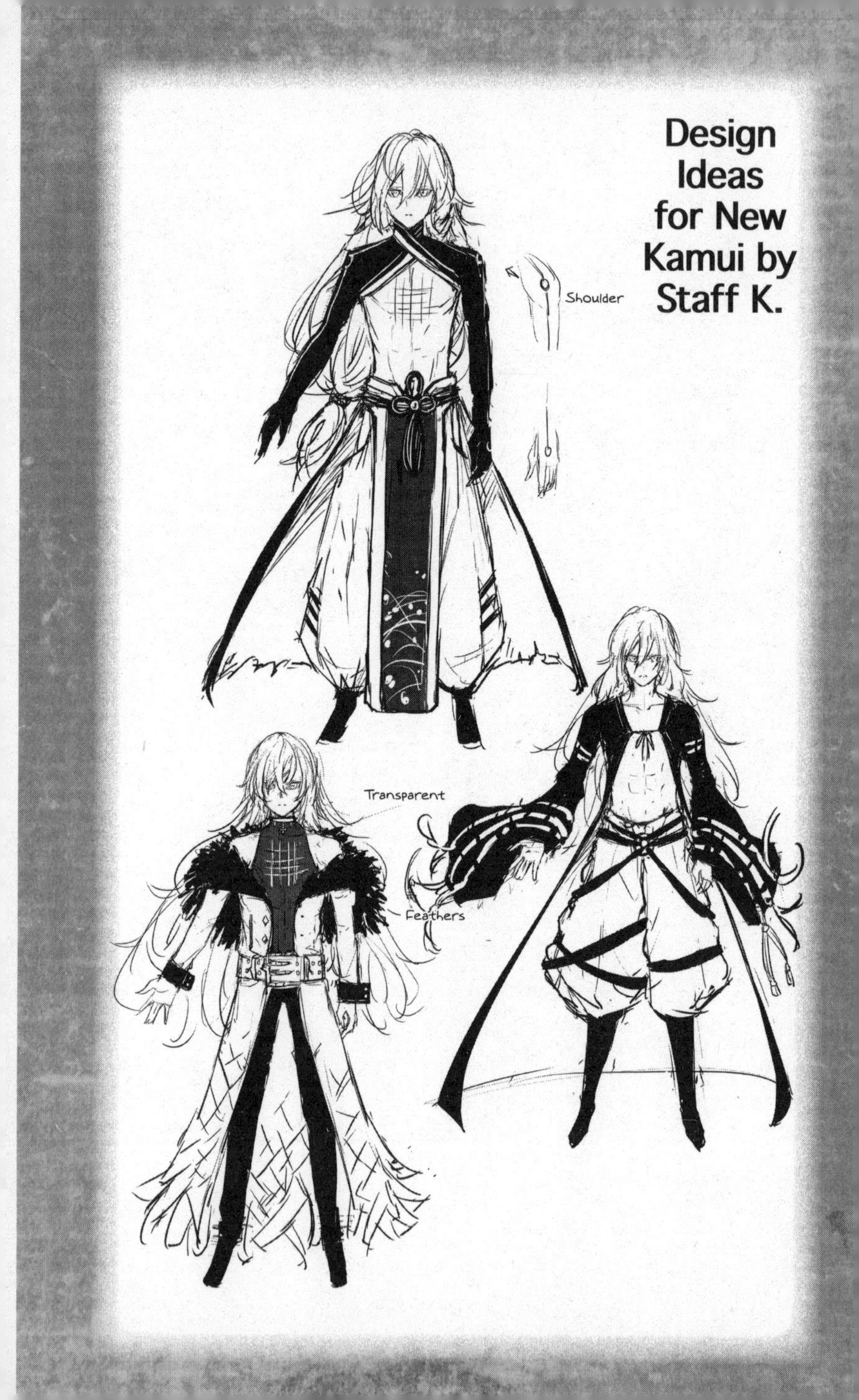
Shoulder
Transparent
Feathers

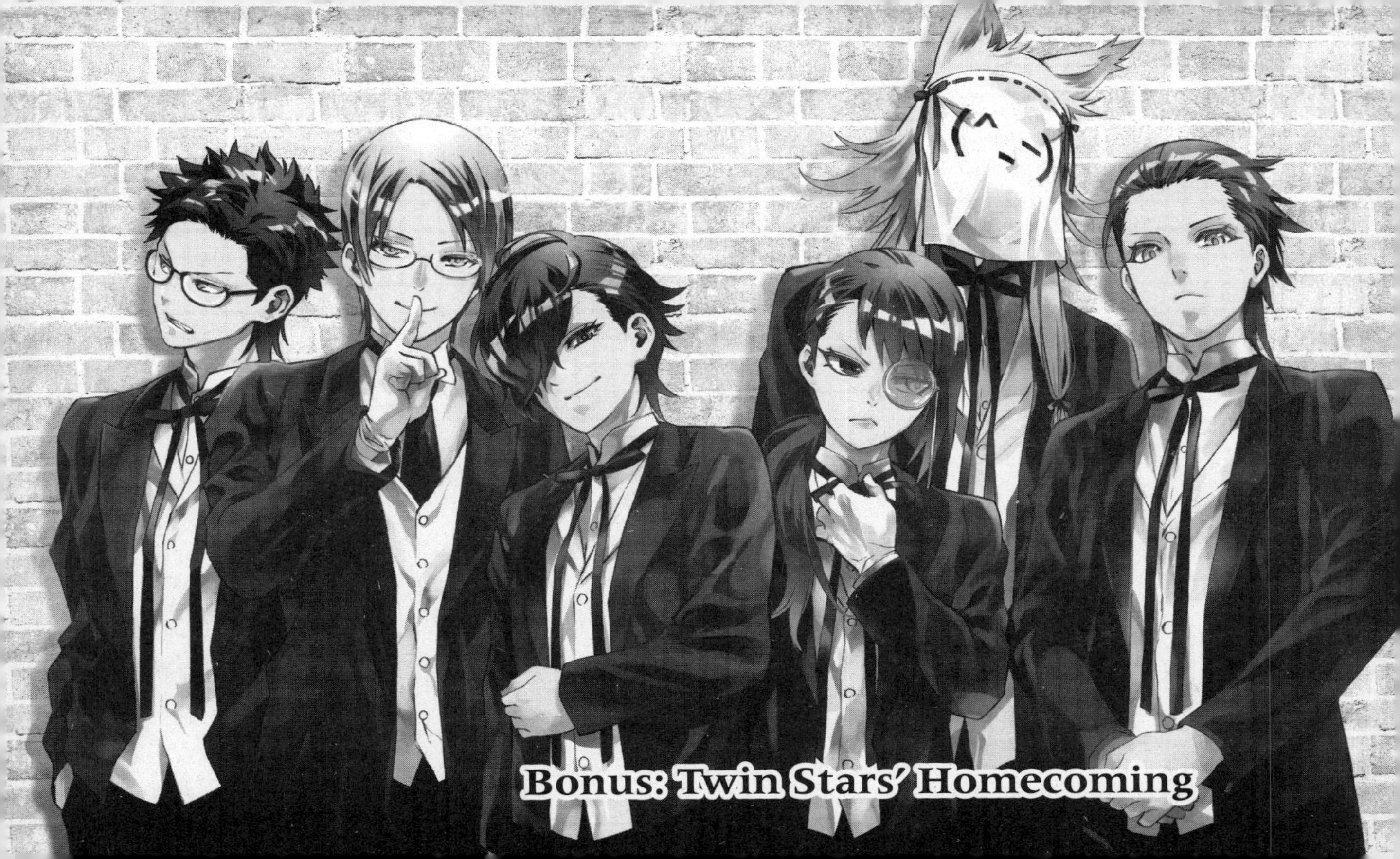
Bonus: Twin Stars' Homecoming

Twin Star Exorcists

ONMYOJI

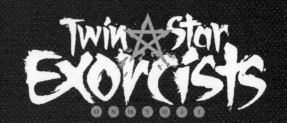

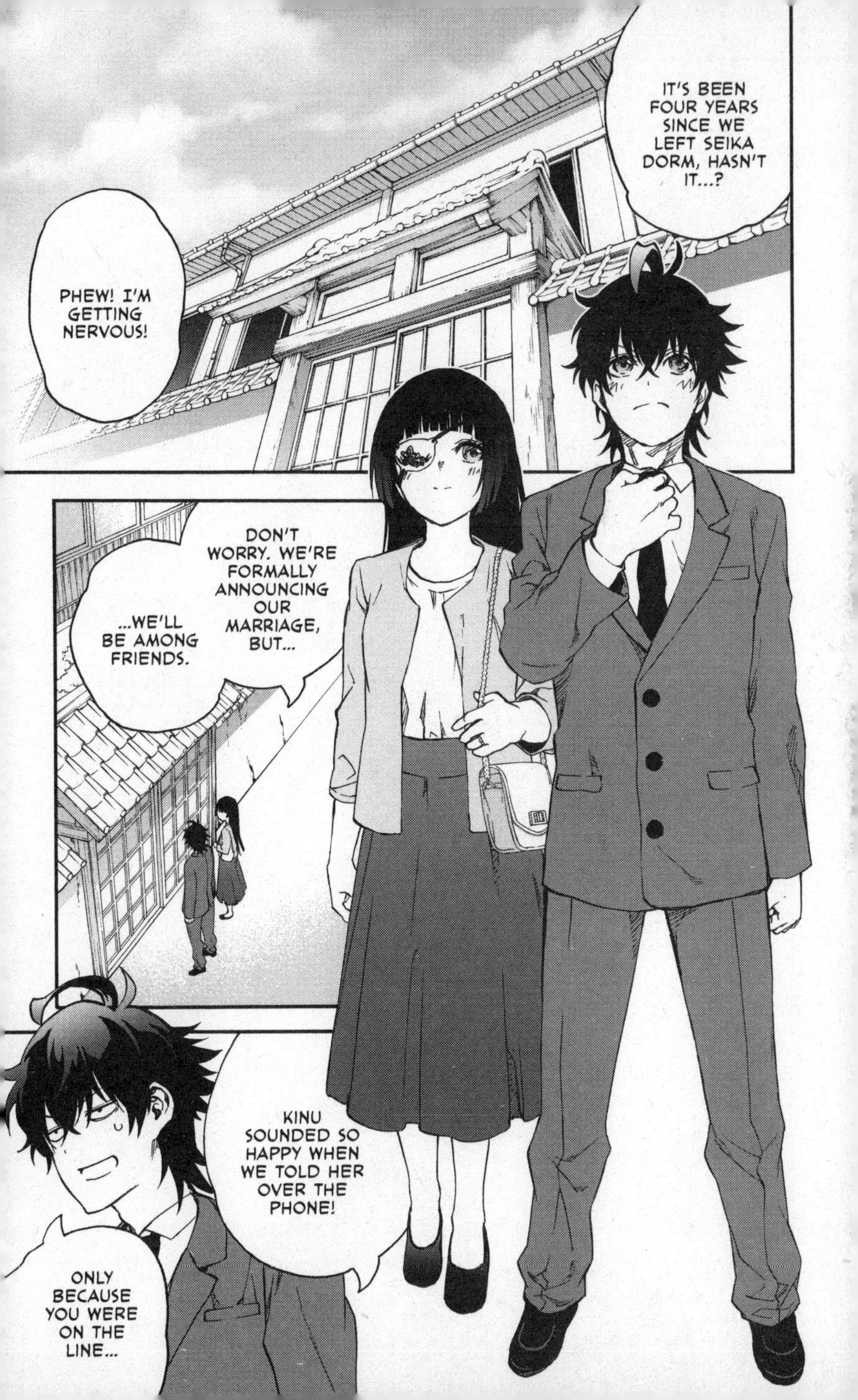
IT'S BEEN FOUR YEARS SINCE WE LEFT SEIKA DORM, HASN'T IT...?
PHEW! I'M GETTING NERVOUS!
DON'T WORRY. WE'RE FORMALLY ANNOUNCING OUR MARRIAGE, BUT...
...WE'LL BE AMONG FRIENDS.
KINU SOUNDED SO HAPPY WHEN WE TOLD HER OVER THE PHONE!
ONLY BECAUSE YOU WERE ON THE LINE...

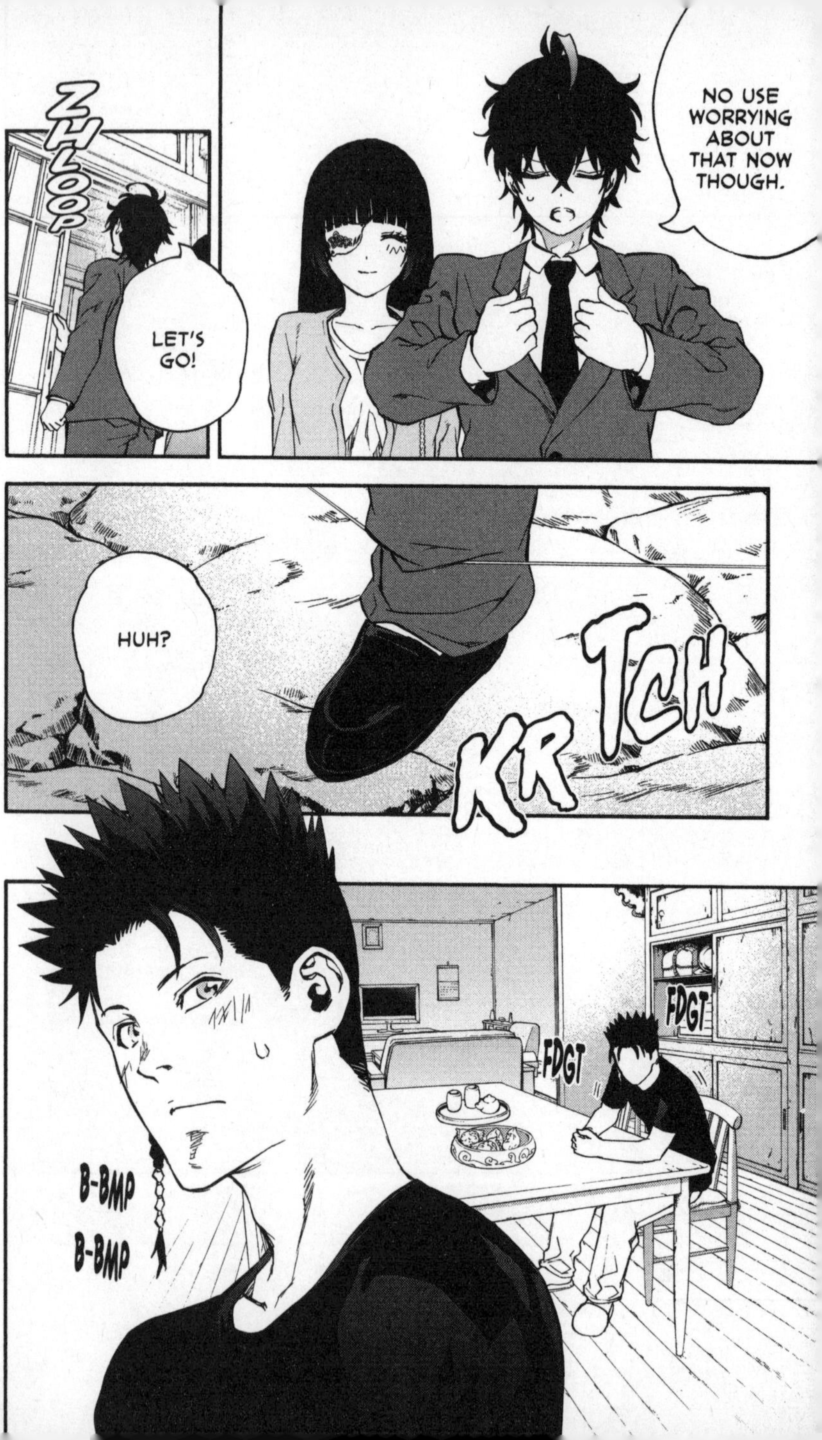
NO USE WORRYING ABOUT THAT NOW THOUGH.
ZHLOOP
LET'S GO!
HUH?
KR TCH
FDGT
FDGT
B-BMP
B-BMP

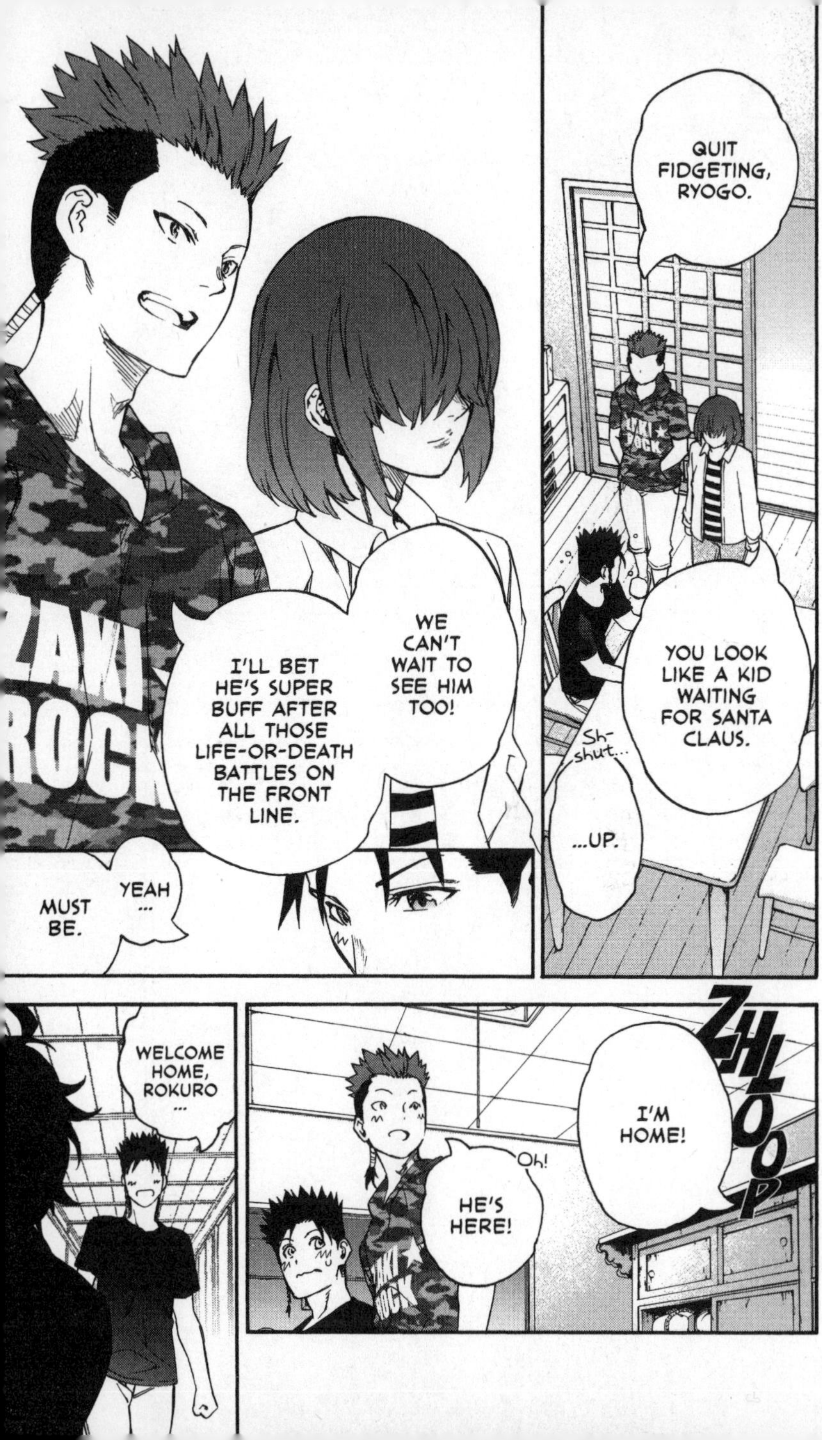
QUIT FIDGETING, RYOGO.
YOU LOOK LIKE A KID WAITING FOR SANTA CLAUS.
Sh-shut...
...UP.
WE CAN'T WAIT TO SEE HIM TOO!
I'LL BET HE'S SUPER BUFF AFTER ALL THOSE LIFE-OR-DEATH BATTLES ON THE FRONT LINE.
YEAH... MUST BE.
ZHLOOP
I'M HOME!
Oh!
HE'S HERE!
WELCOME HOME, ROKURO...

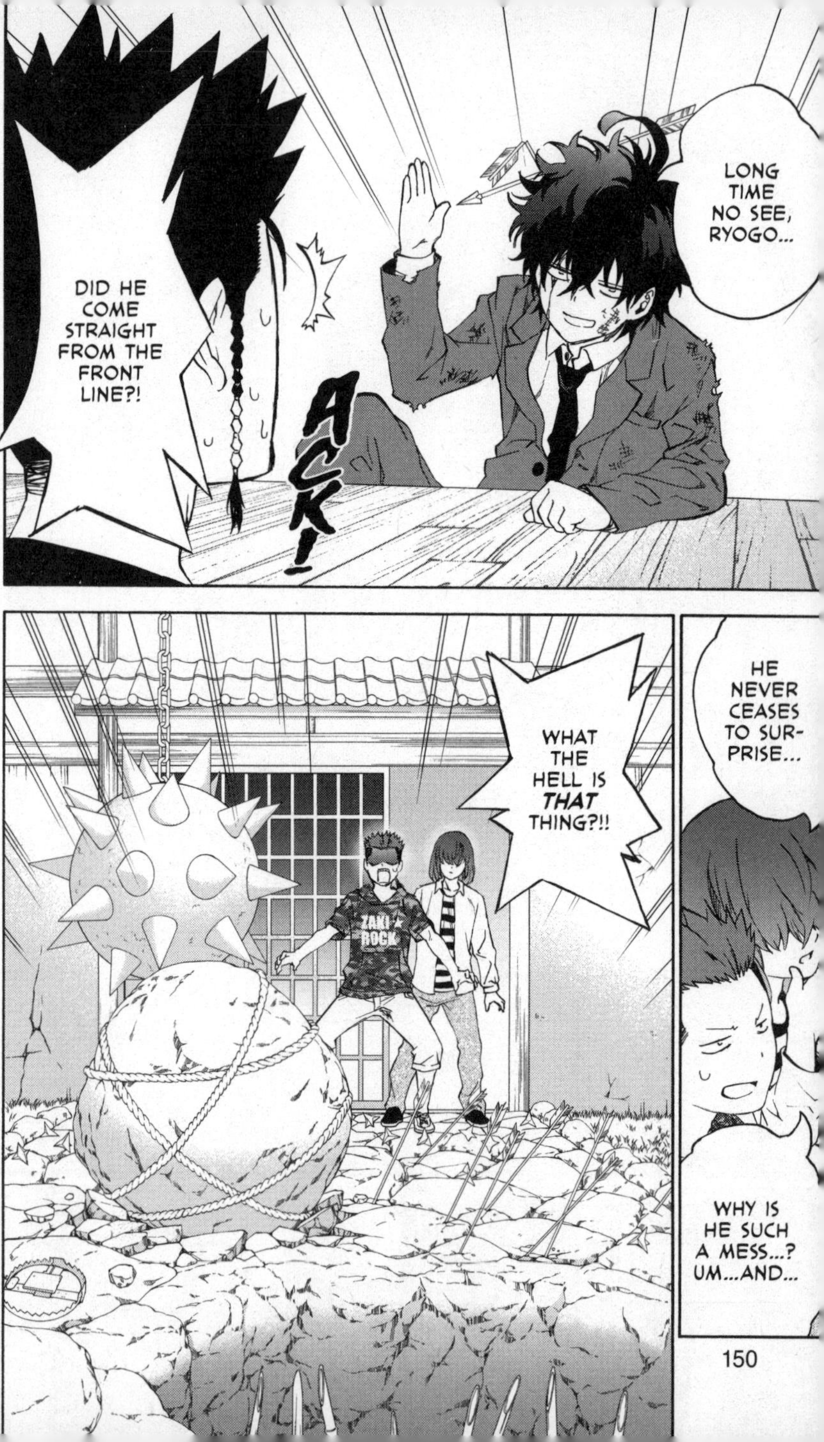
LONG TIME NO SEE, RYOGO...
ACK!
DID HE COME STRAIGHT FROM THE FRONT LINE?!
HE NEVER CEASES TO SUR-PRISE...
WHY IS HE SUCH A MESS...? UM...AND...
ZAKI ROCK
WHAT THE HELL IS *THAT* THING?!!

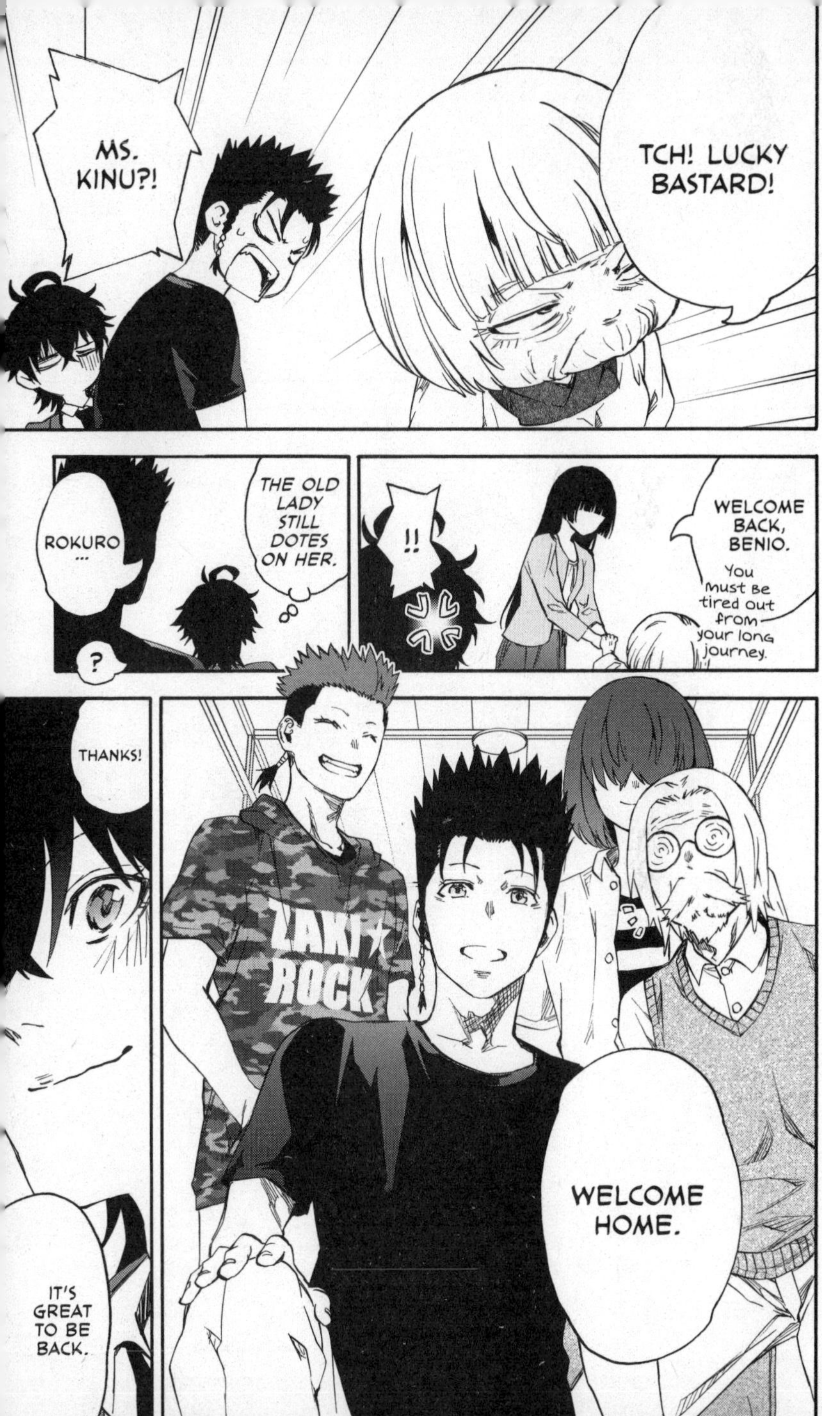
TCH! LUCKY BASTARD!
MS. KINU?!
WELCOME BACK, BENIO.
You must be tired out from your long journey.
!!
THE OLD LADY STILL DOTES ON HER.
ROKURO...
?
ZAKI☆ROCK
WELCOME HOME.
THANKS!
IT'S GREAT TO BE BACK.

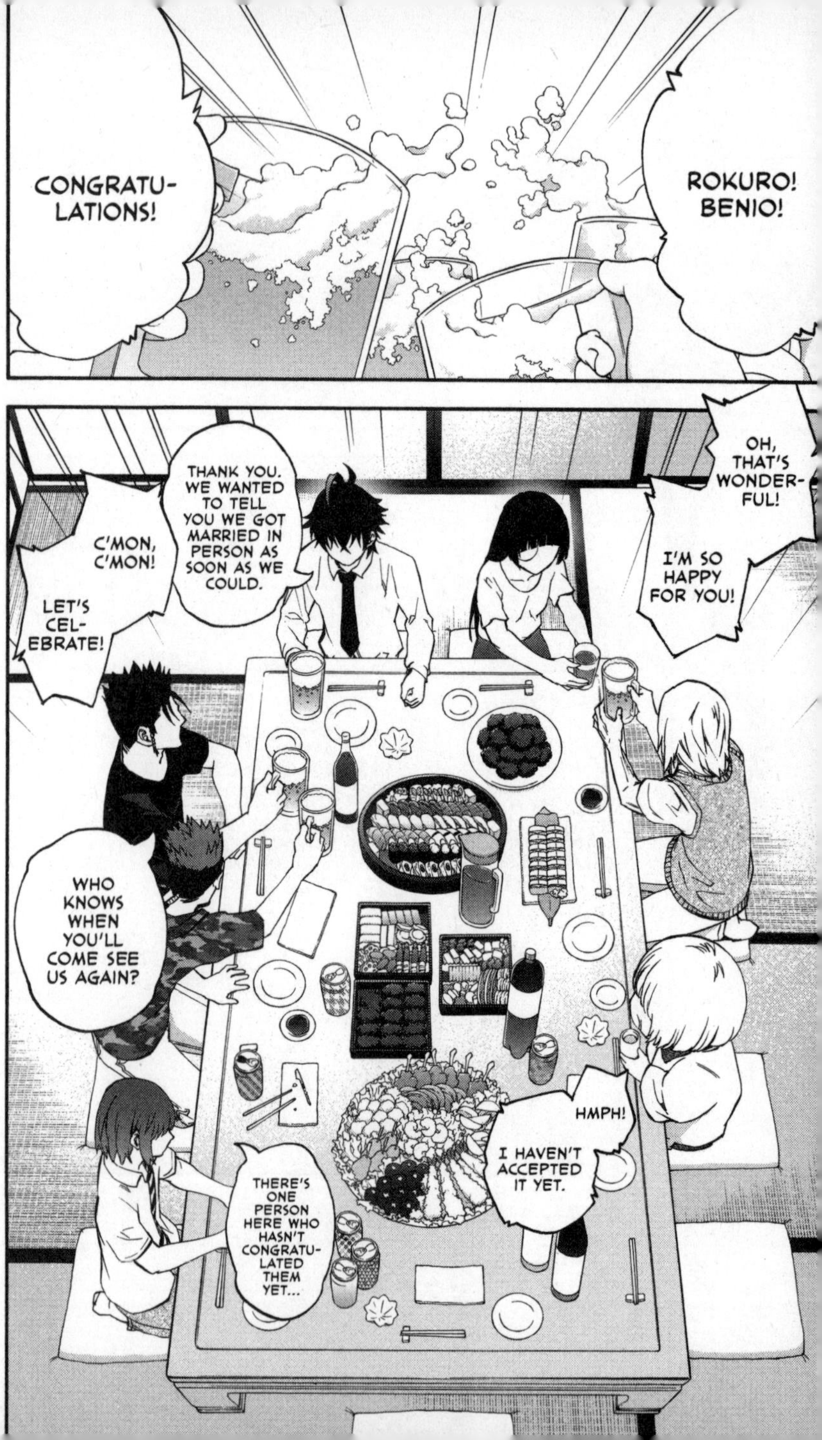
ROKURO! BENIO!
CONGRATULATIONS!
OH, THAT'S WONDERFUL!
I'M SO HAPPY FOR YOU!
THANK YOU. WE WANTED TO TELL YOU WE GOT MARRIED IN PERSON AS SOON AS WE COULD.
C'MON, C'MON!
LET'S CELEBRATE!
WHO KNOWS WHEN YOU'LL COME SEE US AGAIN?
THERE'S ONE PERSON HERE WHO HASN'T CONGRATULATED THEM YET...
HMPH!
I HAVEN'T ACCEPTED IT YET.

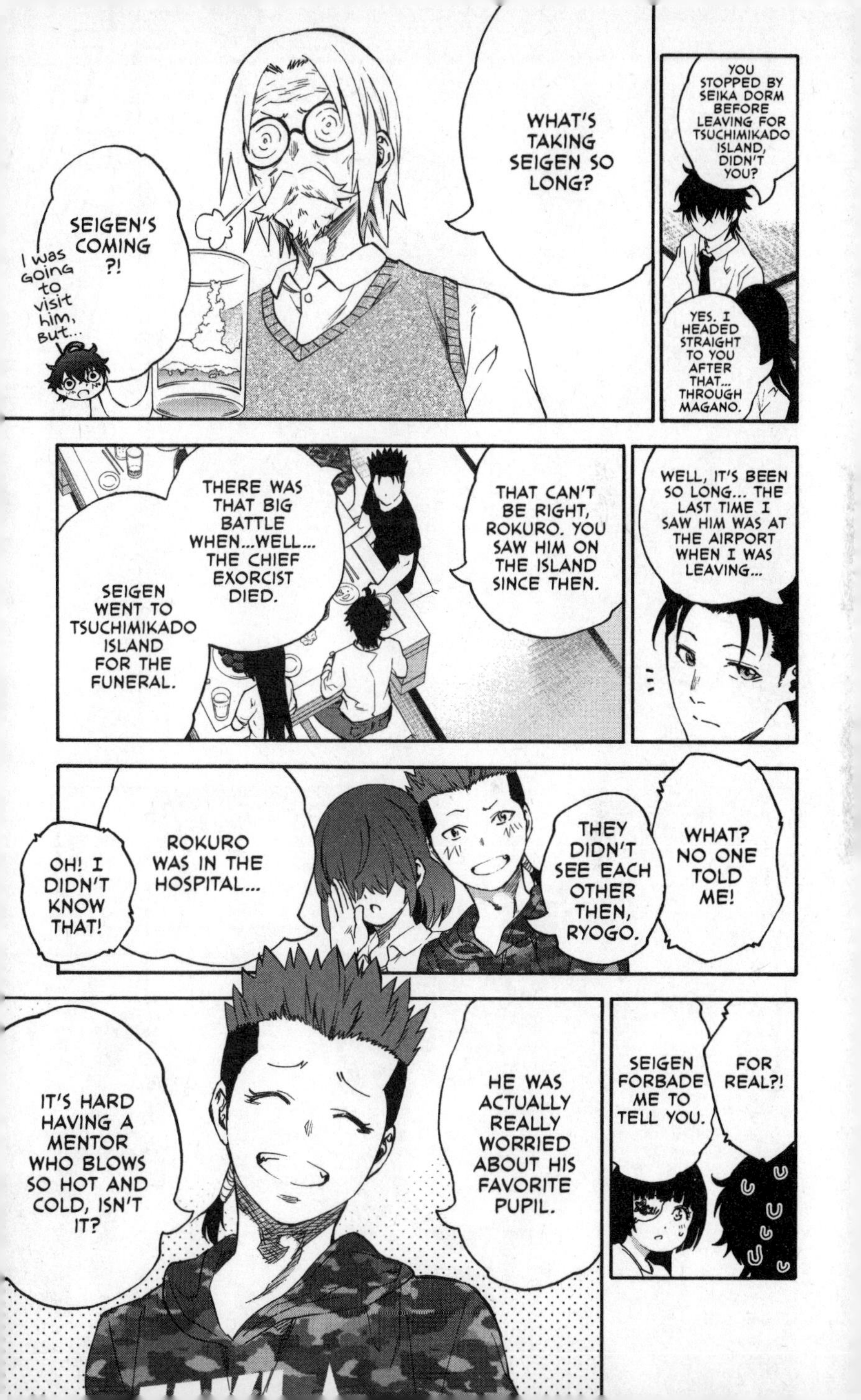
YOU STOPPED BY SEIKA DORM BEFORE LEAVING FOR TSUCHIMIKADO ISLAND, DIDN'T YOU?
YES. I HEADED STRAIGHT TO YOU AFTER THAT... THROUGH MAGANO.
WHAT'S TAKING SEIGEN SO LONG?
SEIGEN'S COMING ?!
I was going to visit him, but...
WELL, IT'S BEEN SO LONG... THE LAST TIME I SAW HIM WAS AT THE AIRPORT WHEN I WAS LEAVING...
THAT CAN'T BE RIGHT, ROKURO. YOU SAW HIM ON THE ISLAND SINCE THEN.
THERE WAS THAT BIG BATTLE WHEN...WELL... THE CHIEF EXORCIST DIED.
SEIGEN WENT TO TSUCHIMIKADO ISLAND FOR THE FUNERAL.
WHAT? NO ONE TOLD ME!
THEY DIDN'T SEE EACH OTHER THEN, RYOGO.
ROKURO WAS IN THE HOSPITAL...
OH! I DIDN'T KNOW THAT!
FOR REAL?!
SEIGEN FORBADE ME TO TELL YOU.
HE WAS ACTUALLY REALLY WORRIED ABOUT HIS FAVORITE PUPIL.
IT'S HARD HAVING A MENTOR WHO BLOWS SO HOT AND COLD, ISN'T IT?

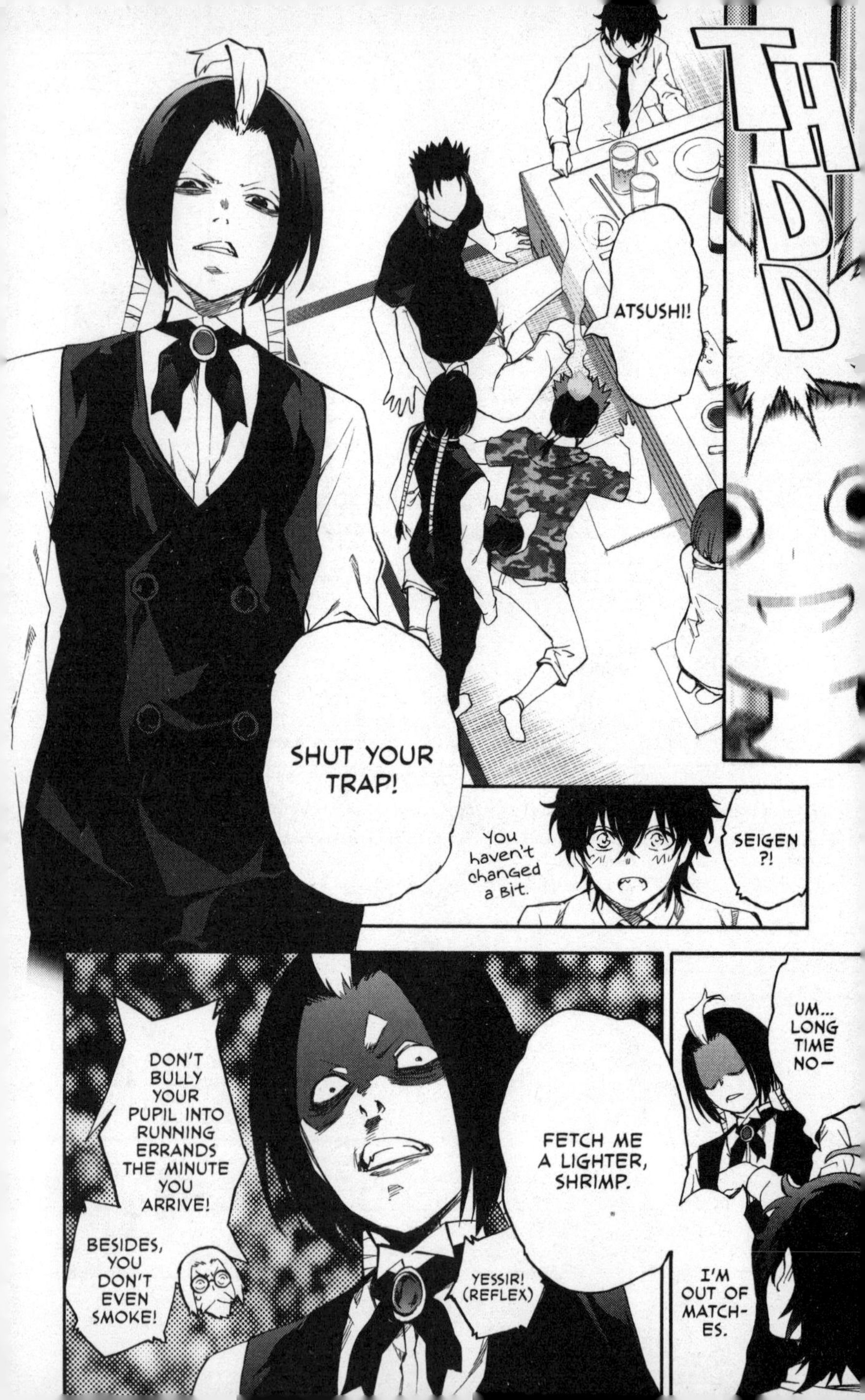
THDD
ATSUSHI!
SEIGEN ?!
You haven't changed a bit.
SHUT YOUR TRAP!
UM... LONG TIME NO—
I'M OUT OF MATCHES.
FETCH ME A LIGHTER, SHRIMP.
YESSIR! (REFLEX)
DON'T BULLY YOUR PUPIL INTO RUNNING ERRANDS THE MINUTE YOU ARRIVE!
BESIDES, YOU DON'T EVEN SMOKE!

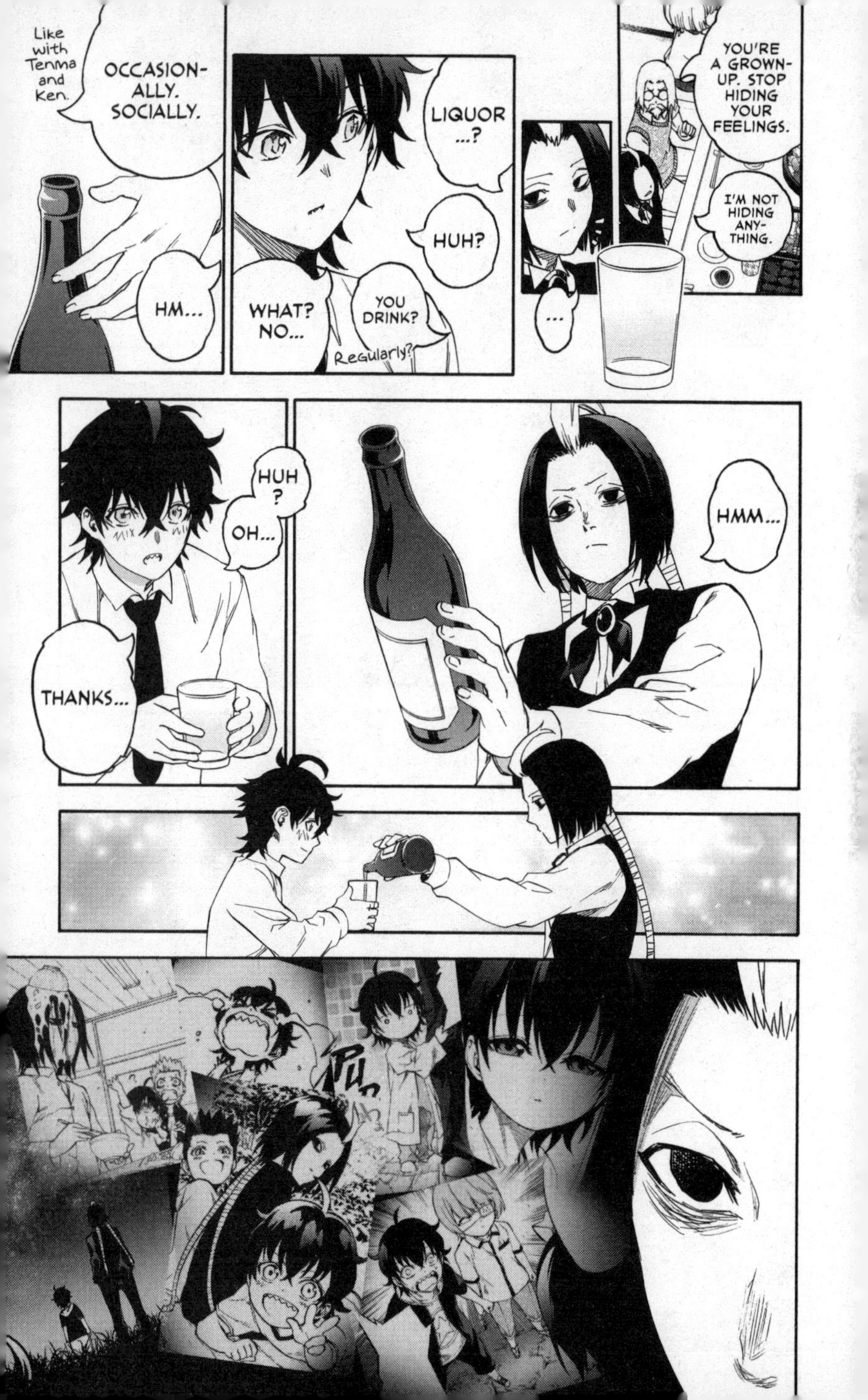
YOU'RE A GROWN-UP. STOP HIDING YOUR FEELINGS.
I'M NOT HIDING ANYTHING.
...
LIQUOR ...?
HUH?
YOU DRINK?
Regularly?
WHAT? NO...
OCCASION-ALLY. SOCIALLY.
Like with Tenma and Ken.
HM...
HMM...
HUH?
OH...
THANKS...

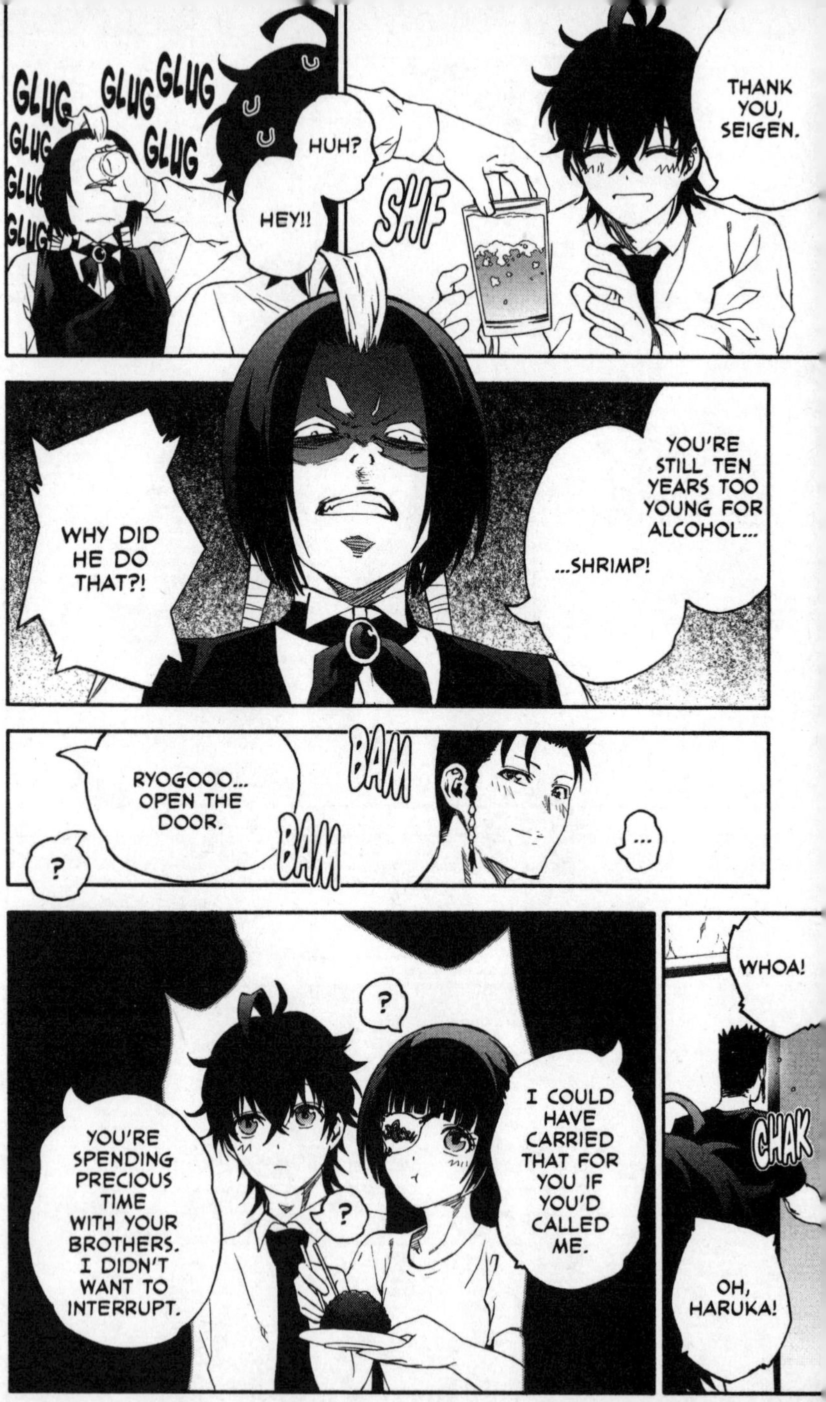
THANK YOU, SEIGEN.
SHF
HUH?
HEY!!
GLUG GLUG GLUG GLUG
GLUG GLUG GLUG GLUG
YOU'RE STILL TEN YEARS TOO YOUNG FOR ALCOHOL...
...SHRIMP!
WHY DID HE DO THAT?!
...
BAM
BAM
RYOGOOO... OPEN THE DOOR.
?
WHOA!
CHAK
OH, HARUKA!
?
I COULD HAVE CARRIED THAT FOR YOU IF YOU'D CALLED ME.
?
YOU'RE SPENDING PRECIOUS TIME WITH YOUR BROTHERS. I DIDN'T WANT TO INTERRUPT.

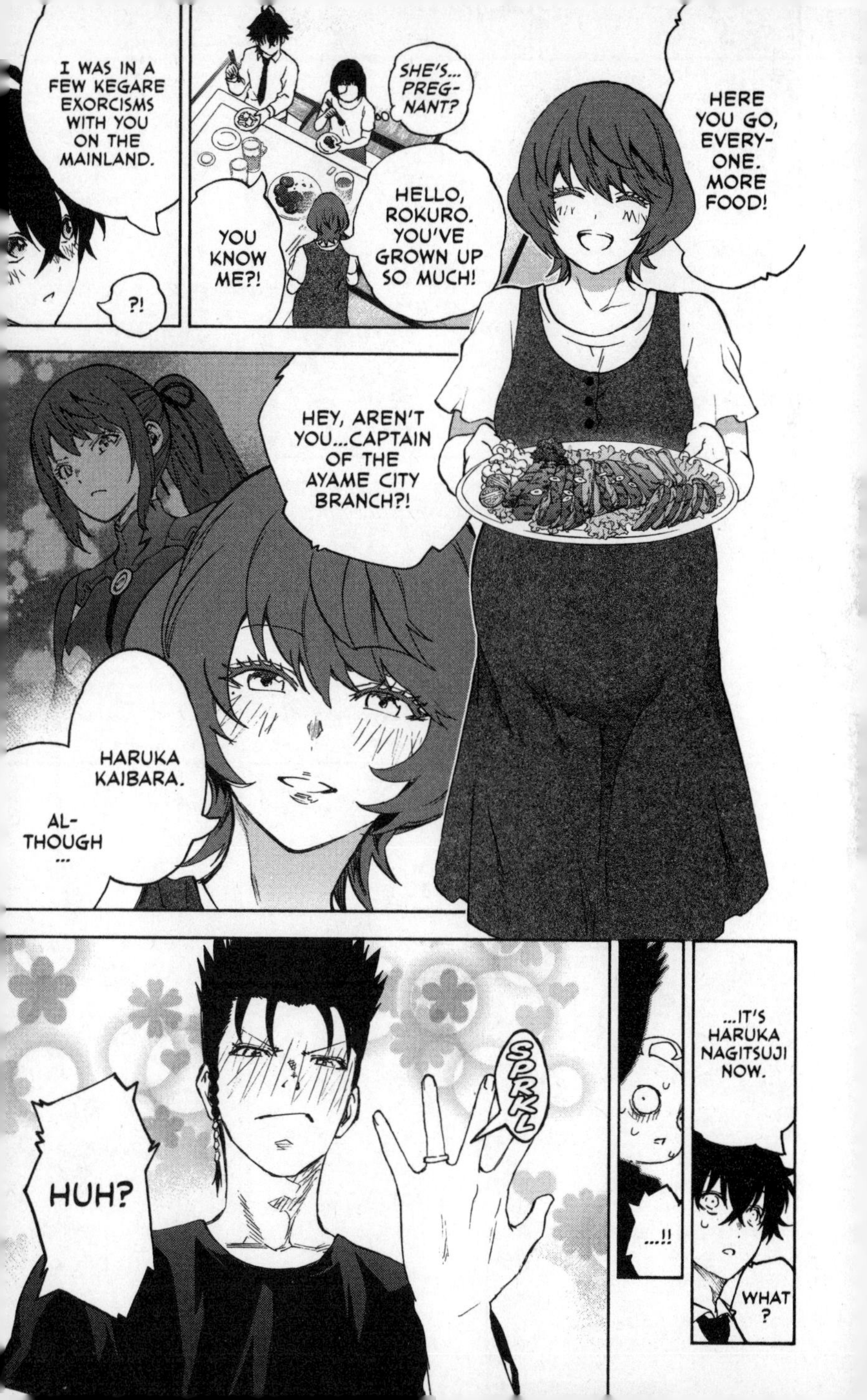
HERE YOU GO, EVERY-ONE. MORE FOOD!
SHE'S... PREG-NANT?
HELLO, ROKURO. YOU'VE GROWN UP SO MUCH!
YOU KNOW ME?!
I WAS IN A FEW KEGARE EXORCISMS WITH YOU ON THE MAINLAND.
?!
HEY, AREN'T YOU...CAPTAIN OF THE AYAME CITY BRANCH?!
HARUKA KAIBARA.
AL-THOUGH ...
...IT'S HARUKA NAGITSUJI NOW.
WHAT ?
...!!
SPRKL
HUH?

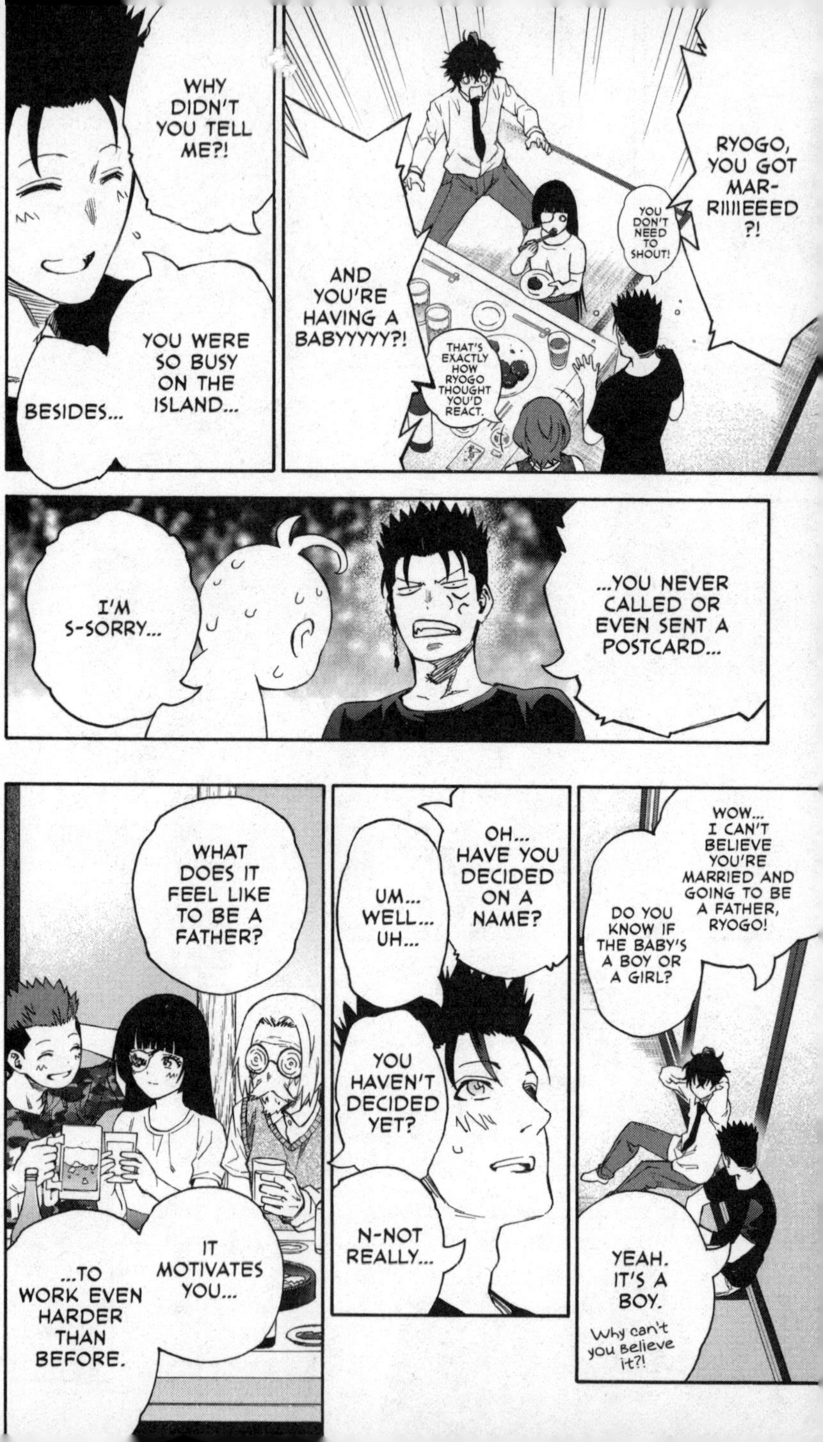
RYOGO, YOU GOT MAR-RIIIIEEED?!
YOU DON'T NEED TO SHOUT!
AND YOU'RE HAVING A BABYYYYY?!
THAT'S EXACTLY HOW RYOGO THOUGHT YOU'D REACT.
WHY DIDN'T YOU TELL ME?!
YOU WERE SO BUSY ON THE ISLAND...
BESIDES...
...YOU NEVER CALLED OR EVEN SENT A POSTCARD...
I'M S-SORRY...
WOW... I CAN'T BELIEVE YOU'RE MARRIED AND GOING TO BE A FATHER, RYOGO!
DO YOU KNOW IF THE BABY'S A BOY OR A GIRL?
YEAH. IT'S A BOY.
Why can't you believe it?!
OH... HAVE YOU DECIDED ON A NAME?
UM... WELL... UH...
YOU HAVEN'T DECIDED YET?
N-NOT REALLY...
WHAT DOES IT FEEL LIKE TO BE A FATHER?
IT MOTIVATES YOU...
...TO WORK EVEN HARDER THAN BEFORE.

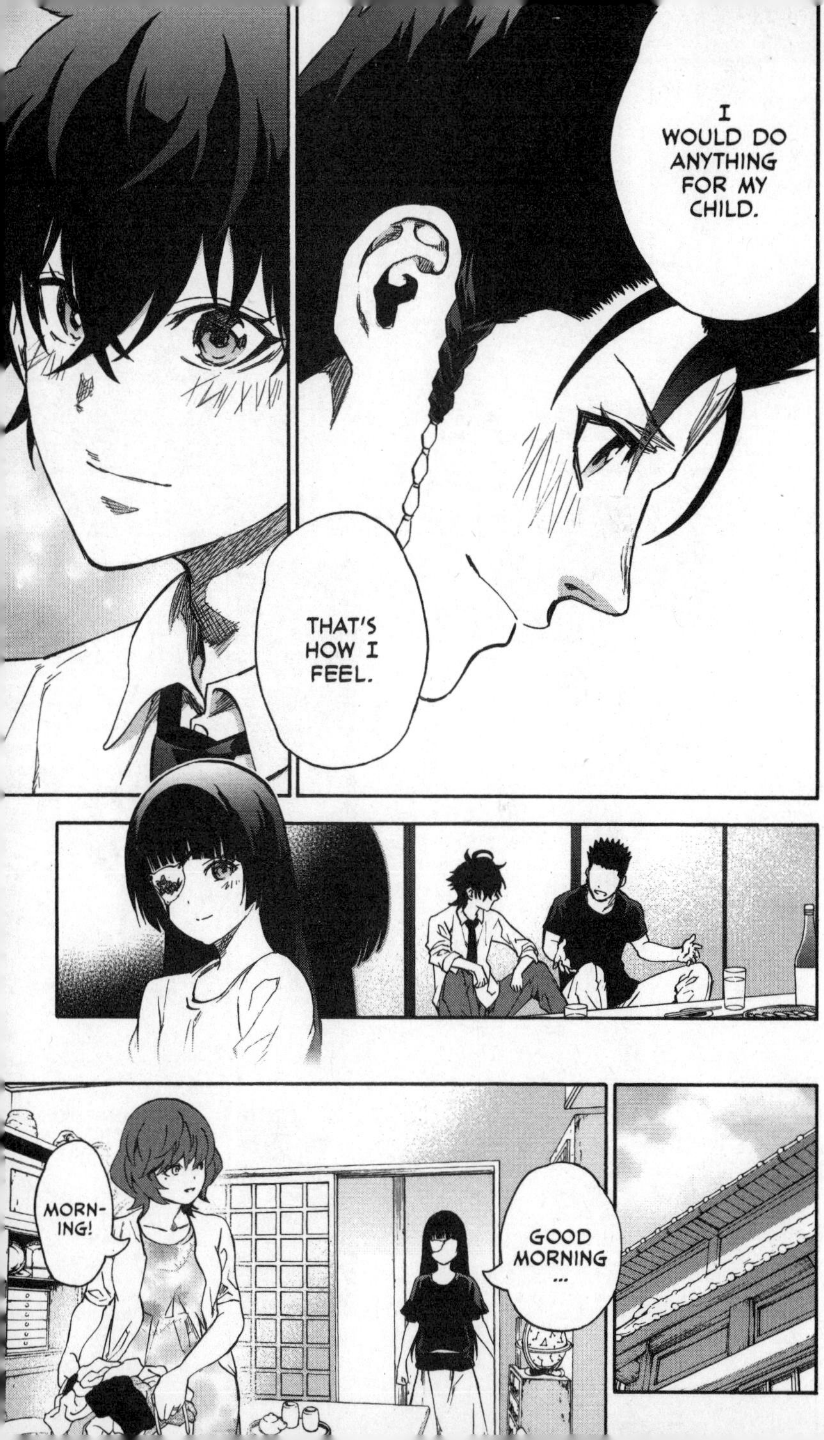
I WOULD DO ANYTHING FOR MY CHILD.
THAT'S HOW I FEEL.
GOOD MORNING ...
MORN-ING!

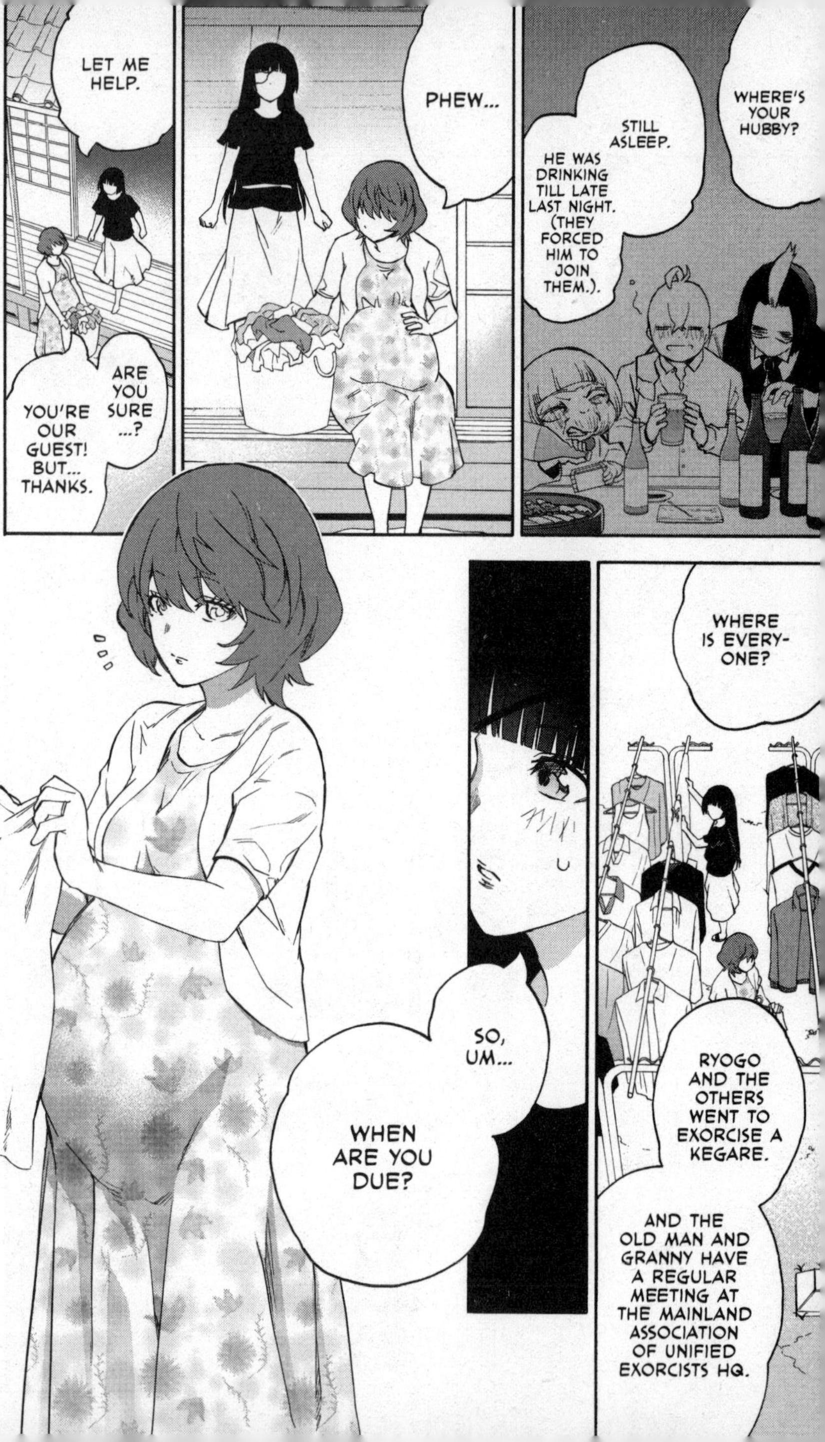
WHERE'S YOUR HUBBY?
STILL ASLEEP.
HE WAS DRINKING TILL LATE LAST NIGHT. (THEY FORCED HIM TO JOIN THEM.).
PHEW...
LET ME HELP.
ARE YOU SURE ...?
YOU'RE OUR GUEST! BUT... THANKS.
WHERE IS EVERY-ONE?
RYOGO AND THE OTHERS WENT TO EXORCISE A KEGARE.
AND THE OLD MAN AND GRANNY HAVE A REGULAR MEETING AT THE MAINLAND ASSOCIATION OF UNIFIED EXORCISTS HQ.
SO, UM...
WHEN ARE YOU DUE?

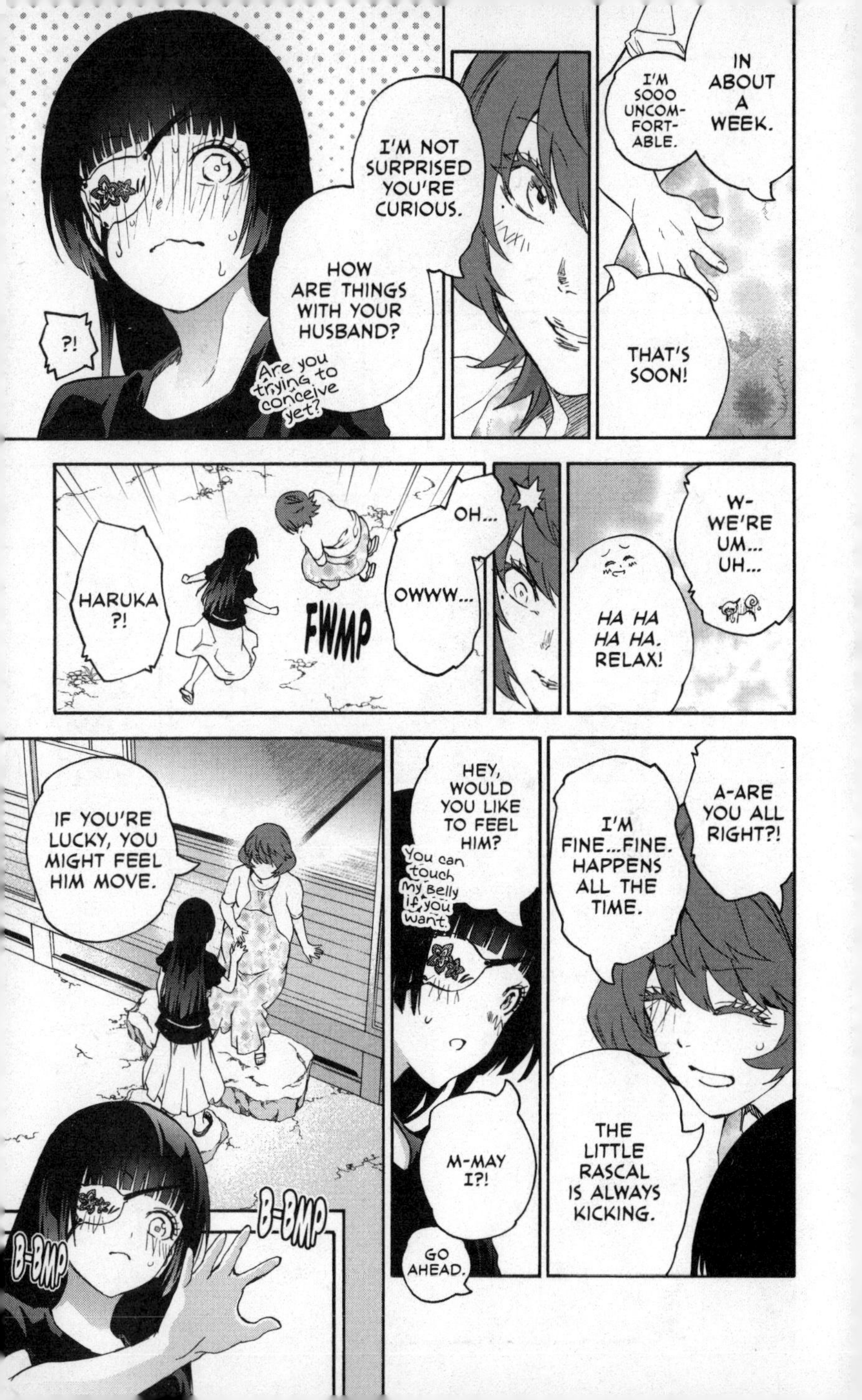

IN ABOUT A WEEK.
I'M SOOO UNCOMFORTABLE.
THAT'S SOON!
I'M NOT SURPRISED YOU'RE CURIOUS.
HOW ARE THINGS WITH YOUR HUSBAND?
Are you trying to conceive yet?
?!
W-WE'RE UM... UH...
HA HA HA HA. RELAX!
OH...
OWWW...
FWMP
HARUKA?!
A-ARE YOU ALL RIGHT?!
I'M FINE...FINE. HAPPENS ALL THE TIME.
THE LITTLE RASCAL IS ALWAYS KICKING.
HEY, WOULD YOU LIKE TO FEEL HIM?
You can touch My Belly if you want.
M-MAY I?!
GO AHEAD.
IF YOU'RE LUCKY, YOU MIGHT FEEL HIM MOVE.
B-BMP
B-BMP

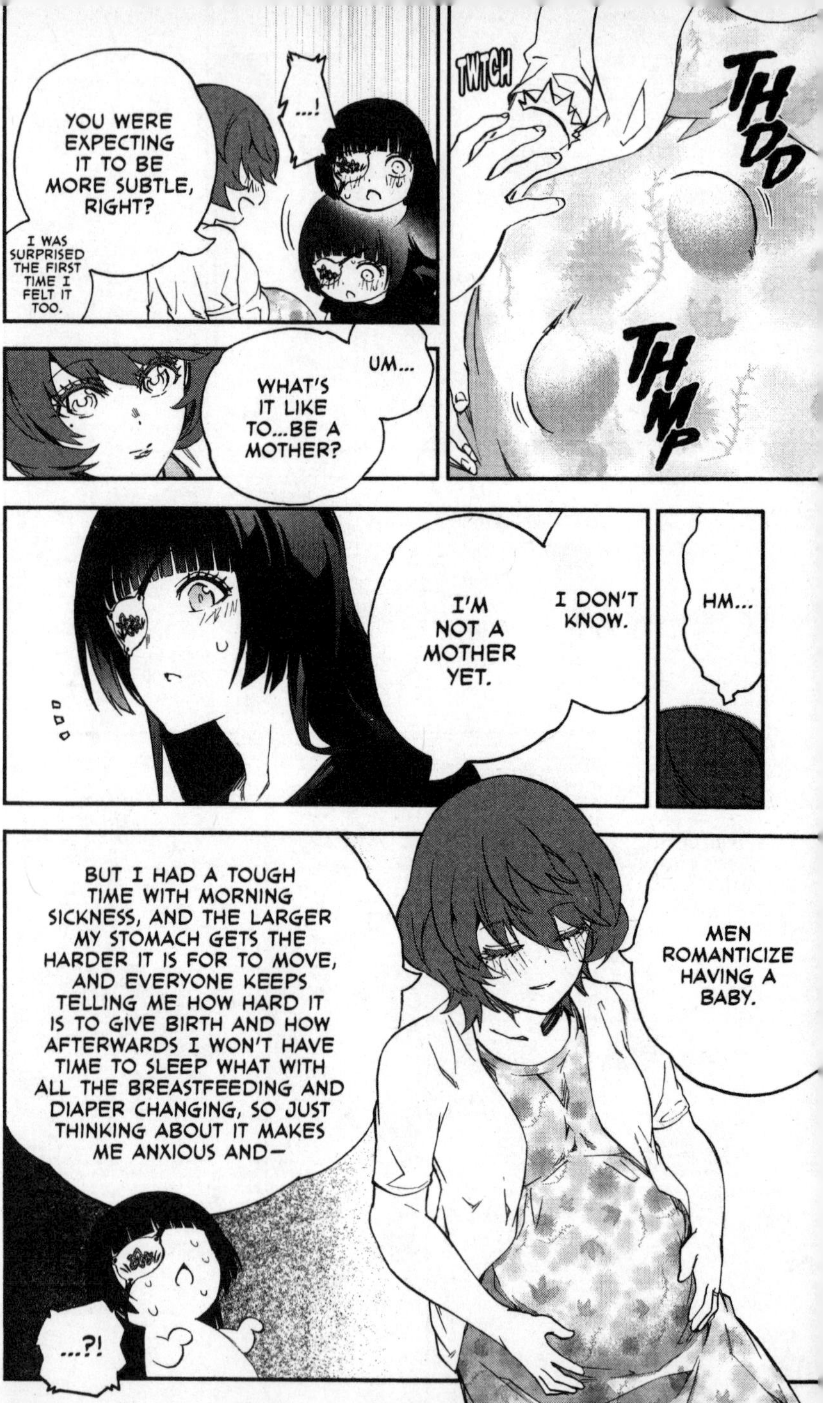
TWTCH
THDD
THMP
...!
YOU WERE EXPECTING IT TO BE MORE SUBTLE, RIGHT?
I WAS SURPRISED THE FIRST TIME I FELT IT TOO.
UM...
WHAT'S IT LIKE TO...BE A MOTHER?
HM...
I DON'T KNOW.
I'M NOT A MOTHER YET.
MEN ROMANTICIZE HAVING A BABY.
BUT I HAD A TOUGH TIME WITH MORNING SICKNESS, AND THE LARGER MY STOMACH GETS THE HARDER IT IS FOR TO MOVE, AND EVERYONE KEEPS TELLING ME HOW HARD IT IS TO GIVE BIRTH AND HOW AFTERWARDS I WON'T HAVE TIME TO SLEEP WHAT WITH ALL THE BREASTFEEDING AND DIAPER CHANGING, SO JUST THINKING ABOUT IT MAKES ME ANXIOUS AND—
...?!

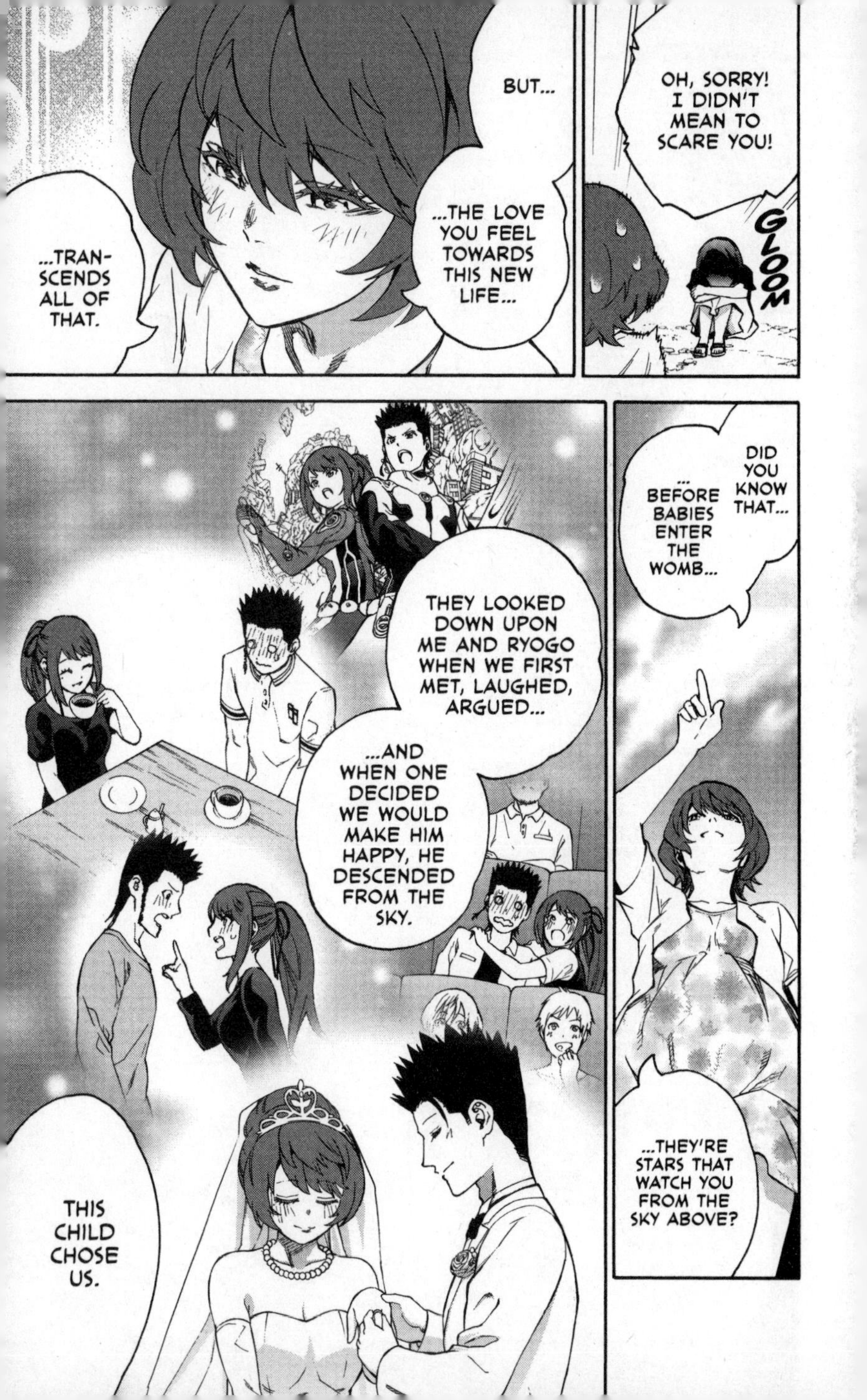
OH, SORRY! I DIDN'T MEAN TO SCARE YOU!
GLOOM
BUT...
...THE LOVE YOU FEEL TOWARDS THIS NEW LIFE...
...TRAN-SCENDS ALL OF THAT.
DID YOU KNOW THAT...
...BEFORE BABIES ENTER THE WOMB...
...THEY'RE STARS THAT WATCH YOU FROM THE SKY ABOVE?
THEY LOOKED DOWN UPON ME AND RYOGO WHEN WE FIRST MET, LAUGHED, ARGUED...
...AND WHEN ONE DECIDED WE WOULD MAKE HIM HAPPY, HE DESCENDED FROM THE SKY.
THIS CHILD CHOSE US.

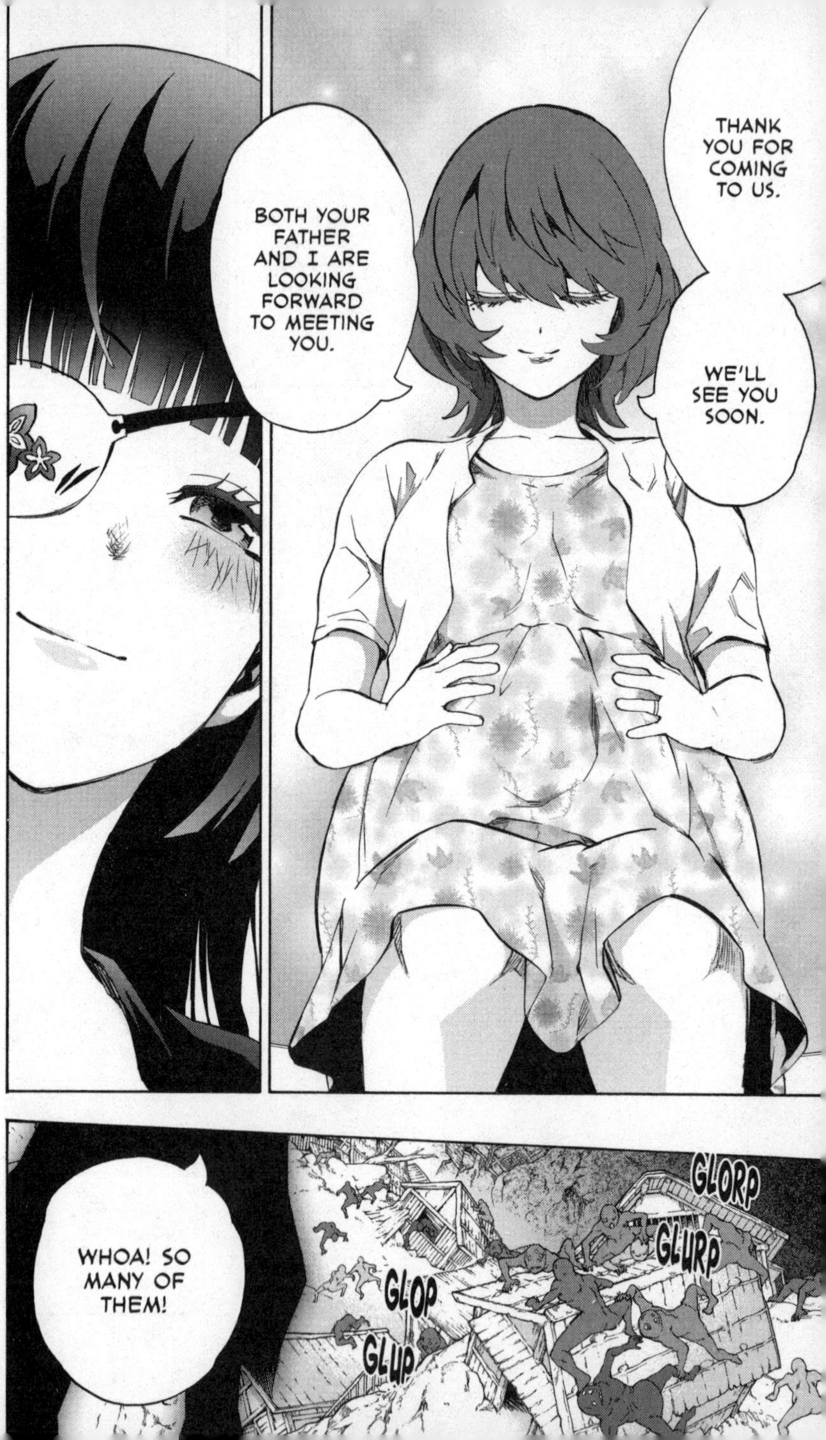
THANK YOU FOR COMING TO US.
BOTH YOUR FATHER AND I ARE LOOKING FORWARD TO MEETING YOU.
WE'LL SEE YOU SOON.
GLORP
GLURP
GLOP
GLUP
WHOA! SO MANY OF THEM!

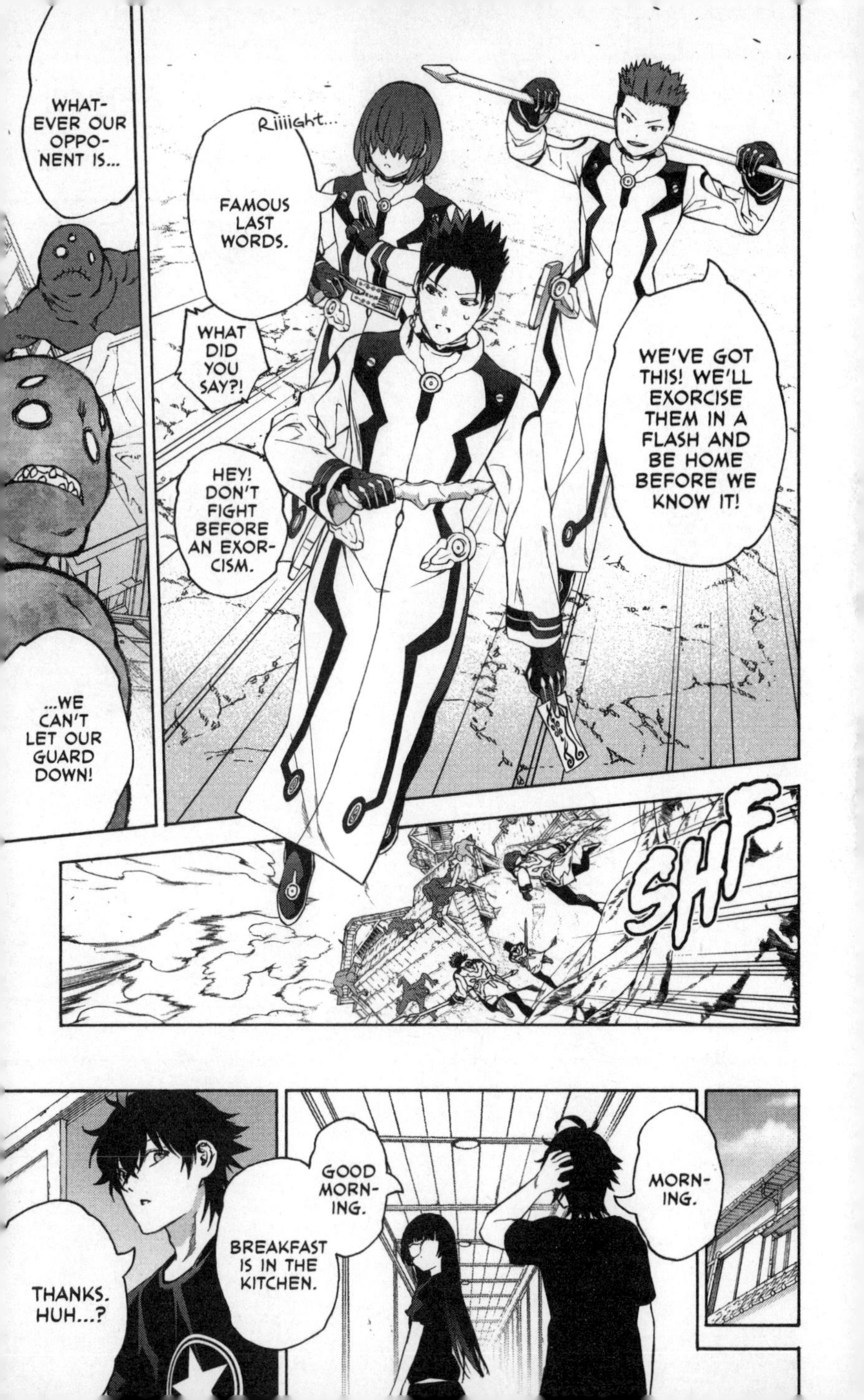
WE'VE GOT THIS! WE'LL EXORCISE THEM IN A FLASH AND BE HOME BEFORE WE KNOW IT!
Riiiight...
FAMOUS LAST WORDS.
WHAT DID YOU SAY?!
HEY! DON'T FIGHT BEFORE AN EXORCISM.
WHATEVER OUR OPPONENT IS...
...WE CAN'T LET OUR GUARD DOWN!
SHF
MORNING.
GOOD MORNING.
BREAKFAST IS IN THE KITCHEN.
THANKS. HUH...?

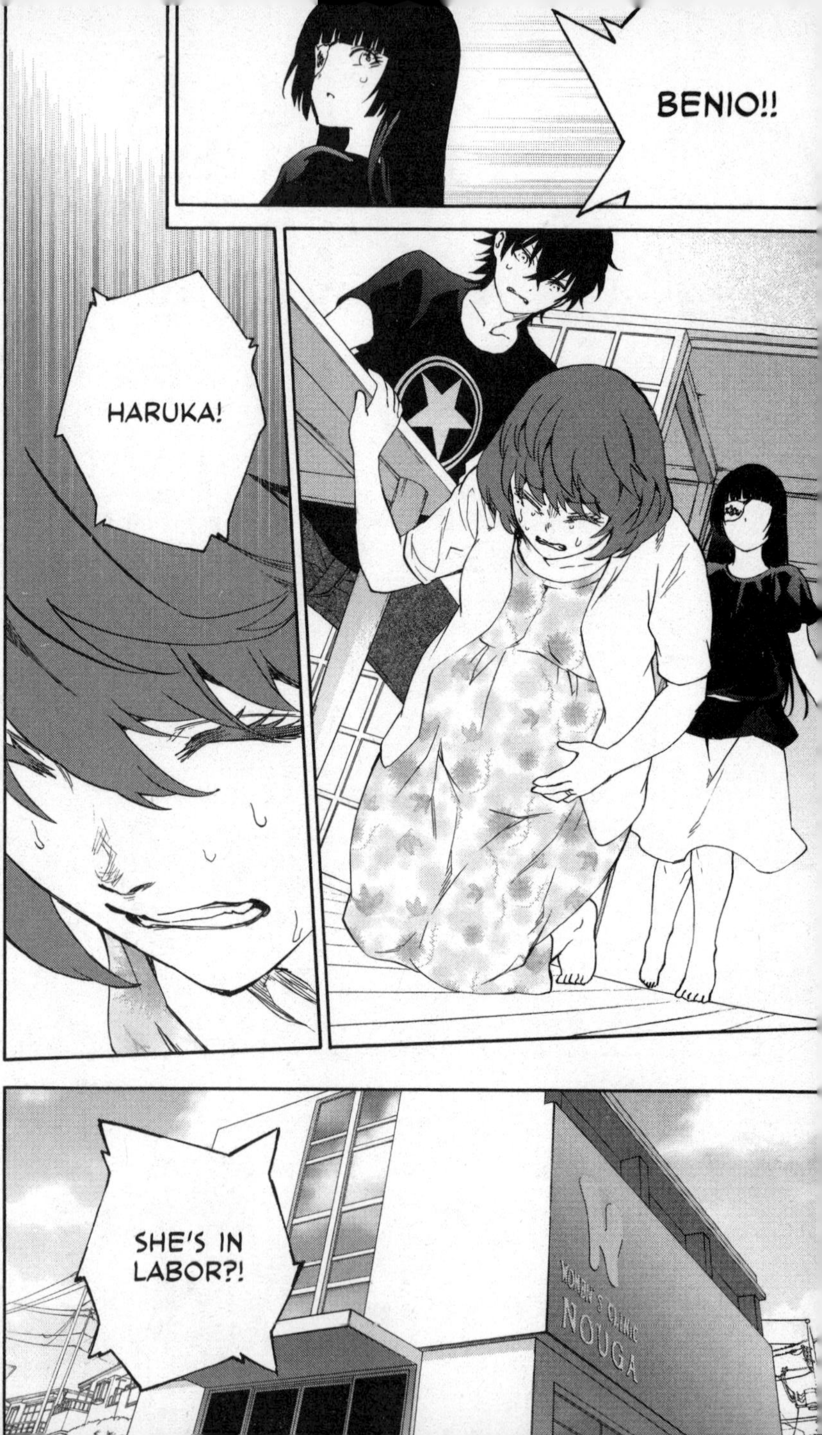
BENIO!!
HARUKA!
SHE'S IN LABOR?!
WOMEN'S CLINIC
NOUGA

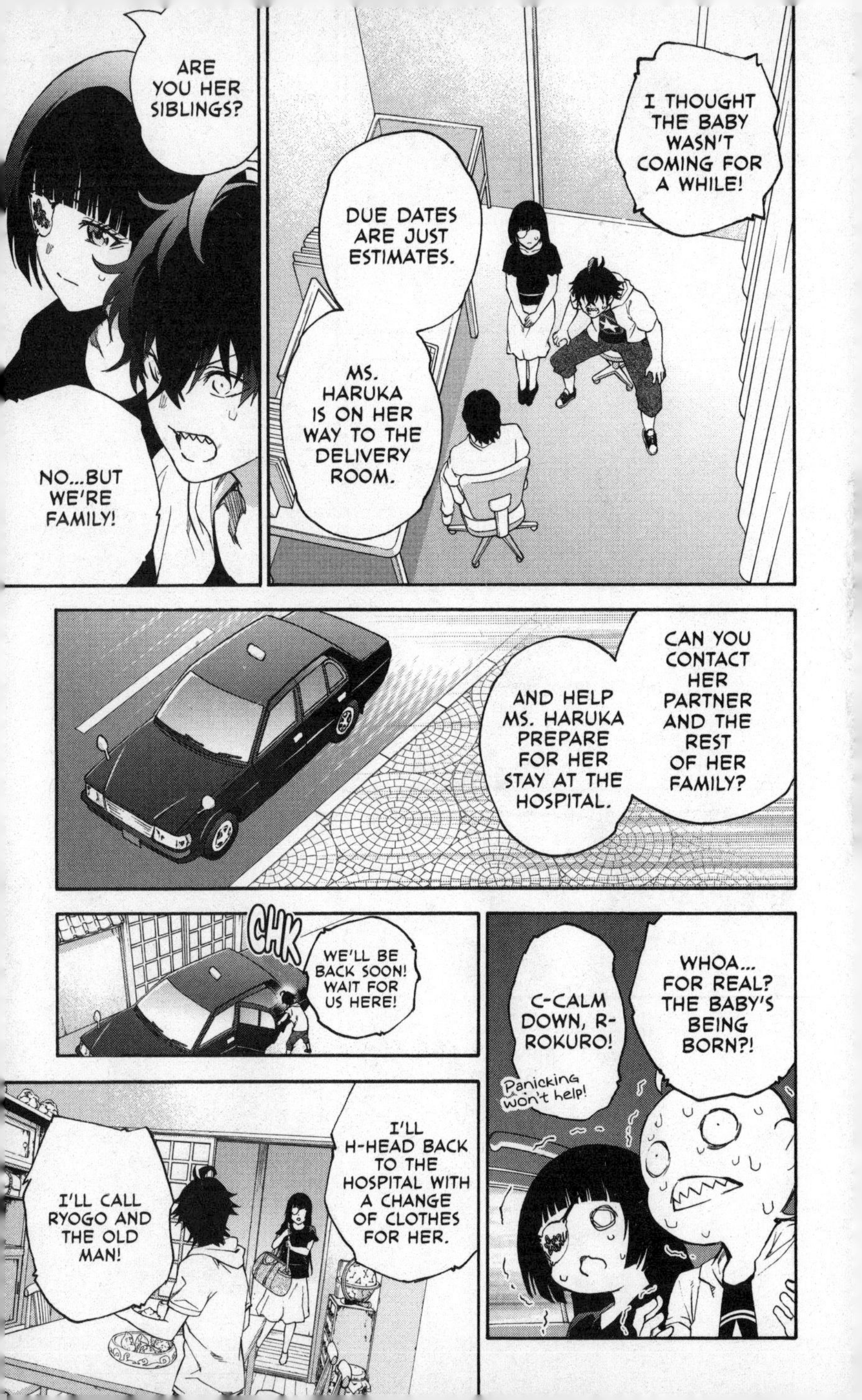
I THOUGHT THE BABY WASN'T COMING FOR A WHILE!
DUE DATES ARE JUST ESTIMATES.
MS. HARUKA IS ON HER WAY TO THE DELIVERY ROOM.
ARE YOU HER SIBLINGS?
NO...BUT WE'RE FAMILY!
CAN YOU CONTACT HER PARTNER AND THE REST OF HER FAMILY?
AND HELP MS. HARUKA PREPARE FOR HER STAY AT THE HOSPITAL.
WHOA... FOR REAL? THE BABY'S BEING BORN?!
C-CALM DOWN, R-ROKURO!
Panicking won't help!
CHK
WE'LL BE BACK SOON! WAIT FOR US HERE!
I'LL H-HEAD BACK TO THE HOSPITAL WITH A CHANGE OF CLOTHES FOR HER.
I'LL CALL RYOGO AND THE OLD MAN!

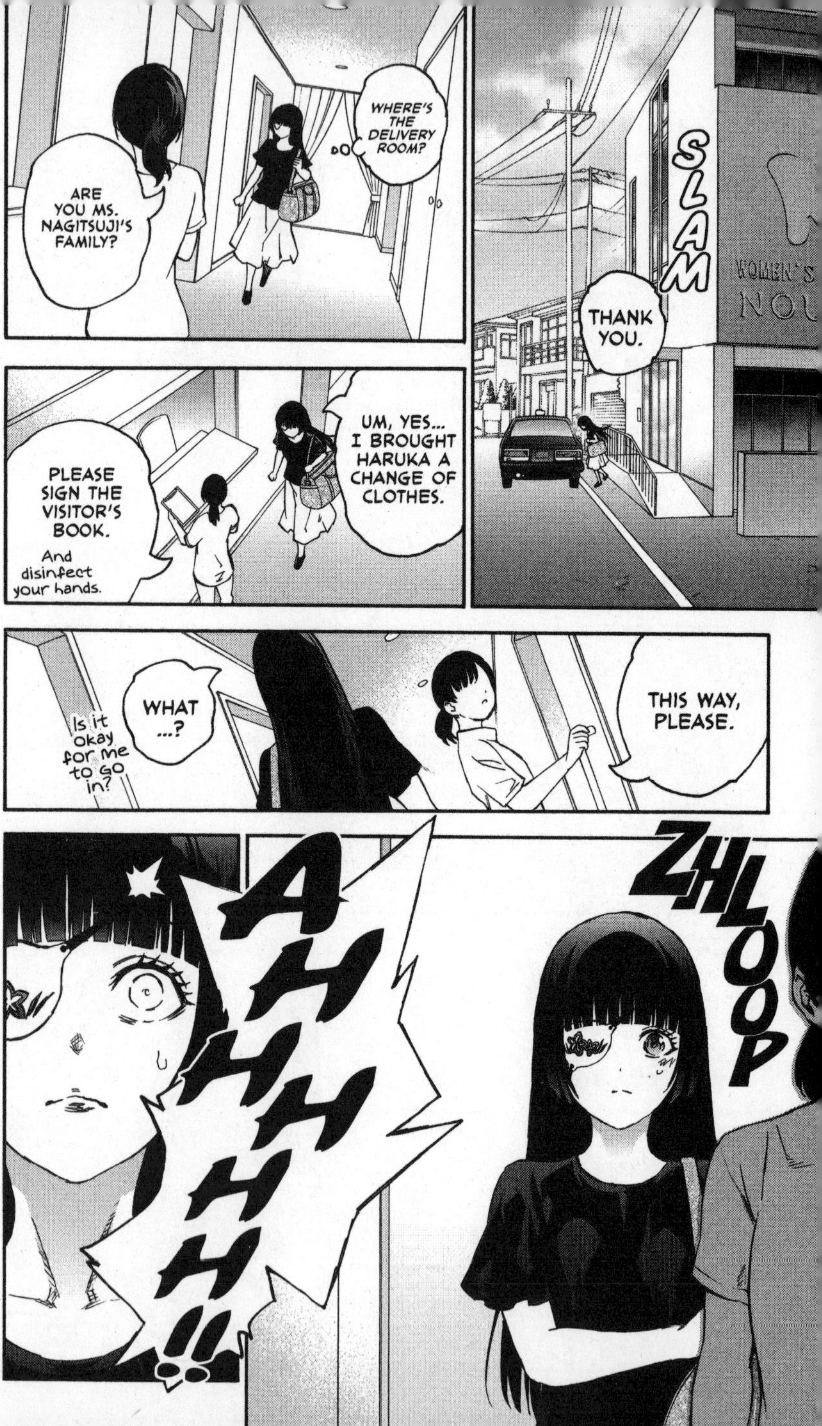
SLAM
THANK YOU.
WHERE'S THE DELIVERY ROOM?
ARE YOU MS. NAGITSUJI'S FAMILY?
UM, YES... I BROUGHT HARUKA A CHANGE OF CLOTHES.
PLEASE SIGN THE VISITOR'S BOOK.
And disinfect your hands.
THIS WAY, PLEASE.
WHAT ...?
Is it okay for me to go in?
ZHLOOP
AHHHHHH!!

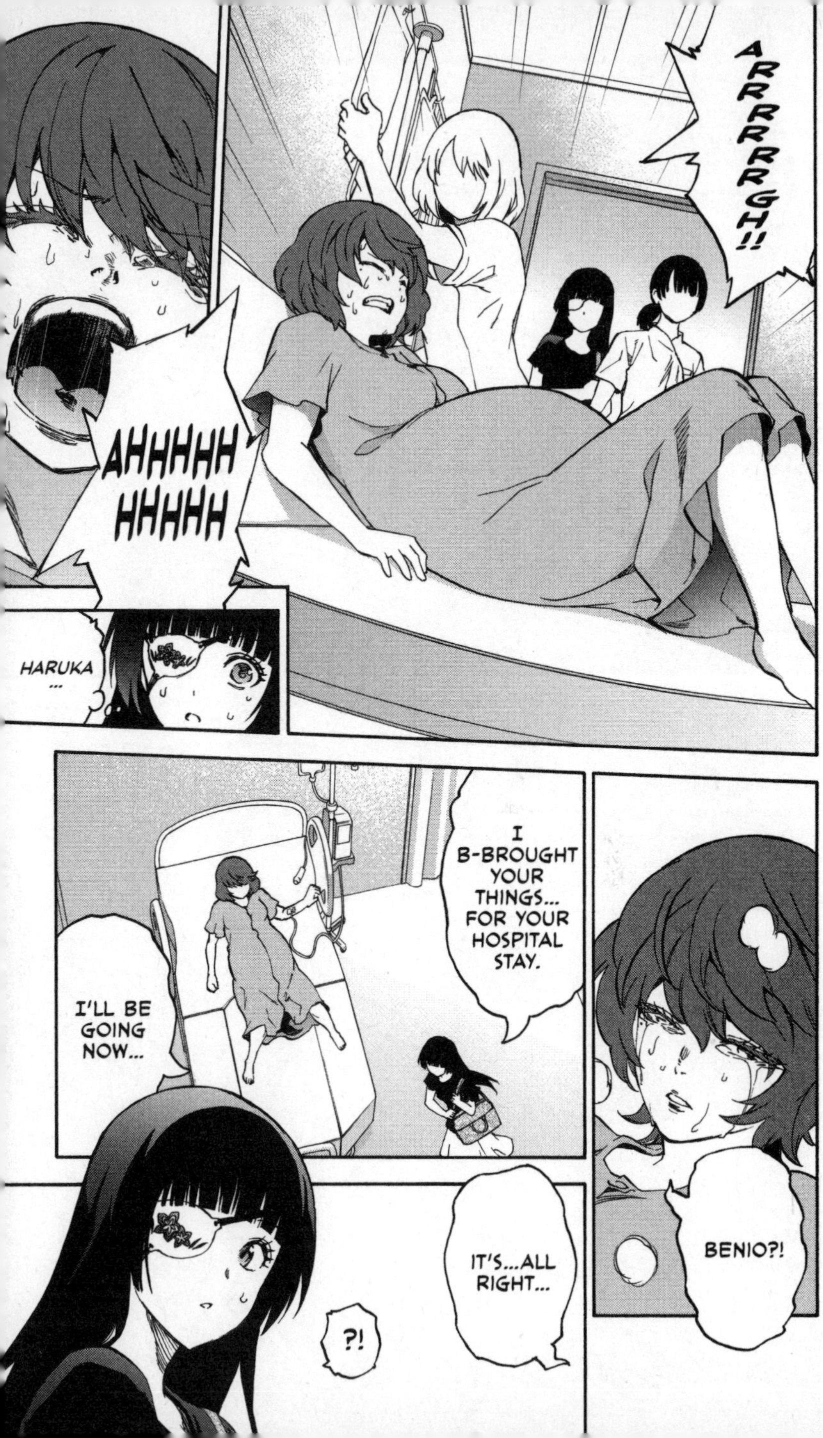
ARRRRRRGH!!
AHHHHH HHHHH
HARUKA...
BENIO?!
I B-BROUGHT YOUR THINGS... FOR YOUR HOSPITAL STAY.
I'LL BE GOING NOW...
IT'S...ALL RIGHT...
?!

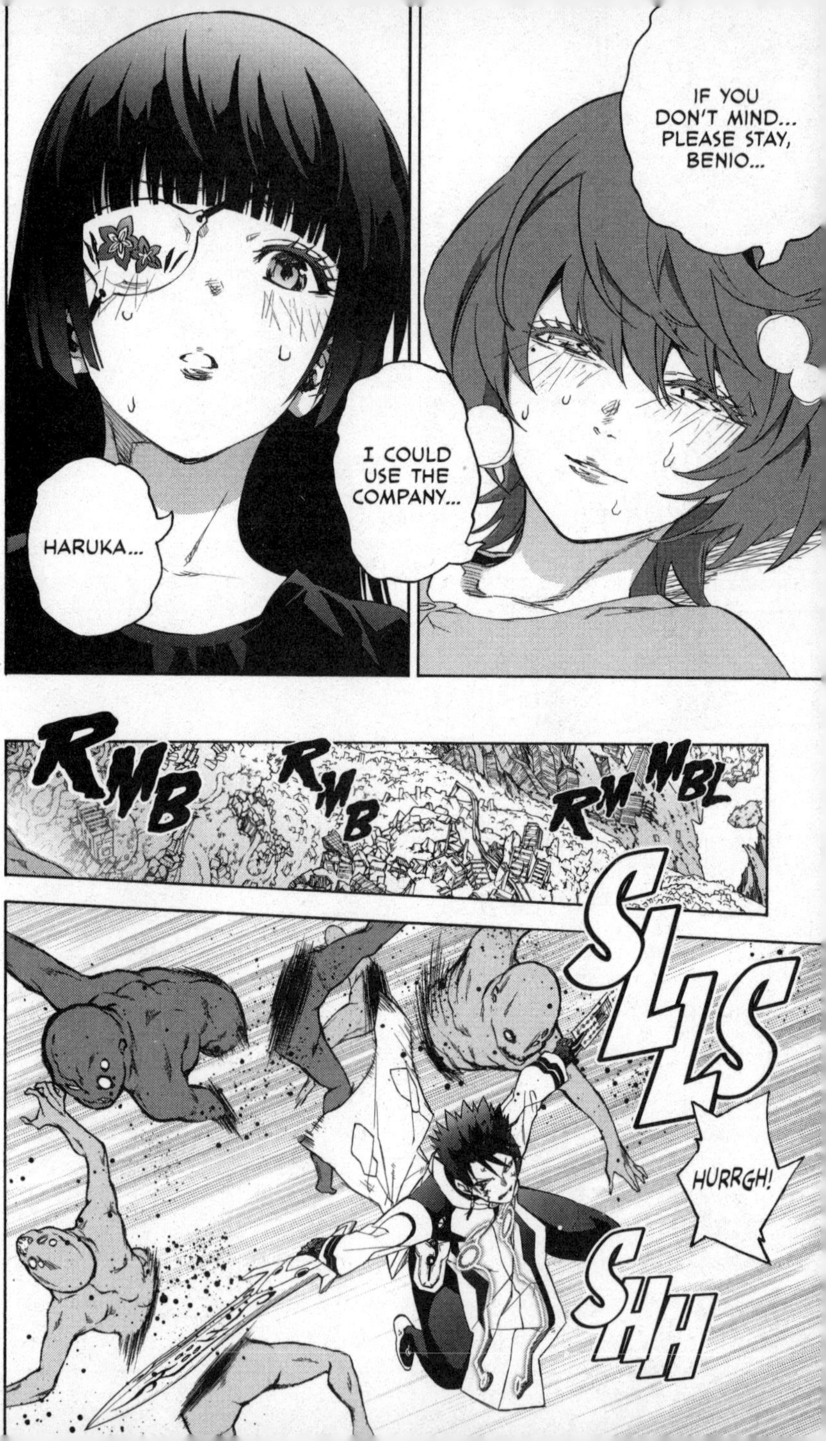
IF YOU DON'T MIND... PLEASE STAY, BENIO...
I COULD USE THE COMPANY...
HARUKA...
RMB
RMB
RMMBL
SLIS
HURRGH!
SHH

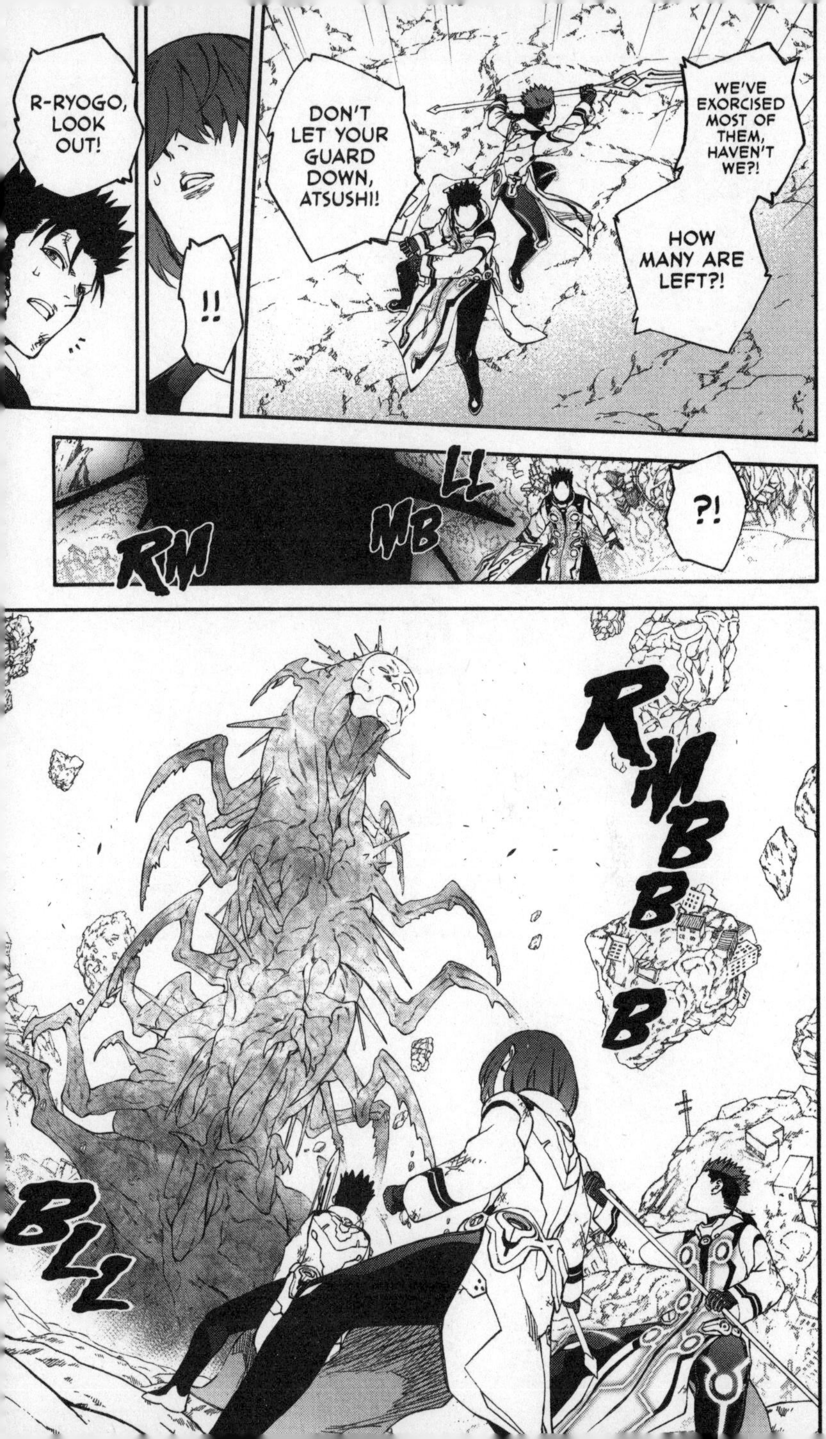
WE'VE EXORCISED MOST OF THEM, HAVEN'T WE?!
HOW MANY ARE LEFT?!
DON'T LET YOUR GUARD DOWN, ATSUSHI!
!!
R-RYOGO, LOOK OUT!
?!
RMMBLL
RMBBB
BLL

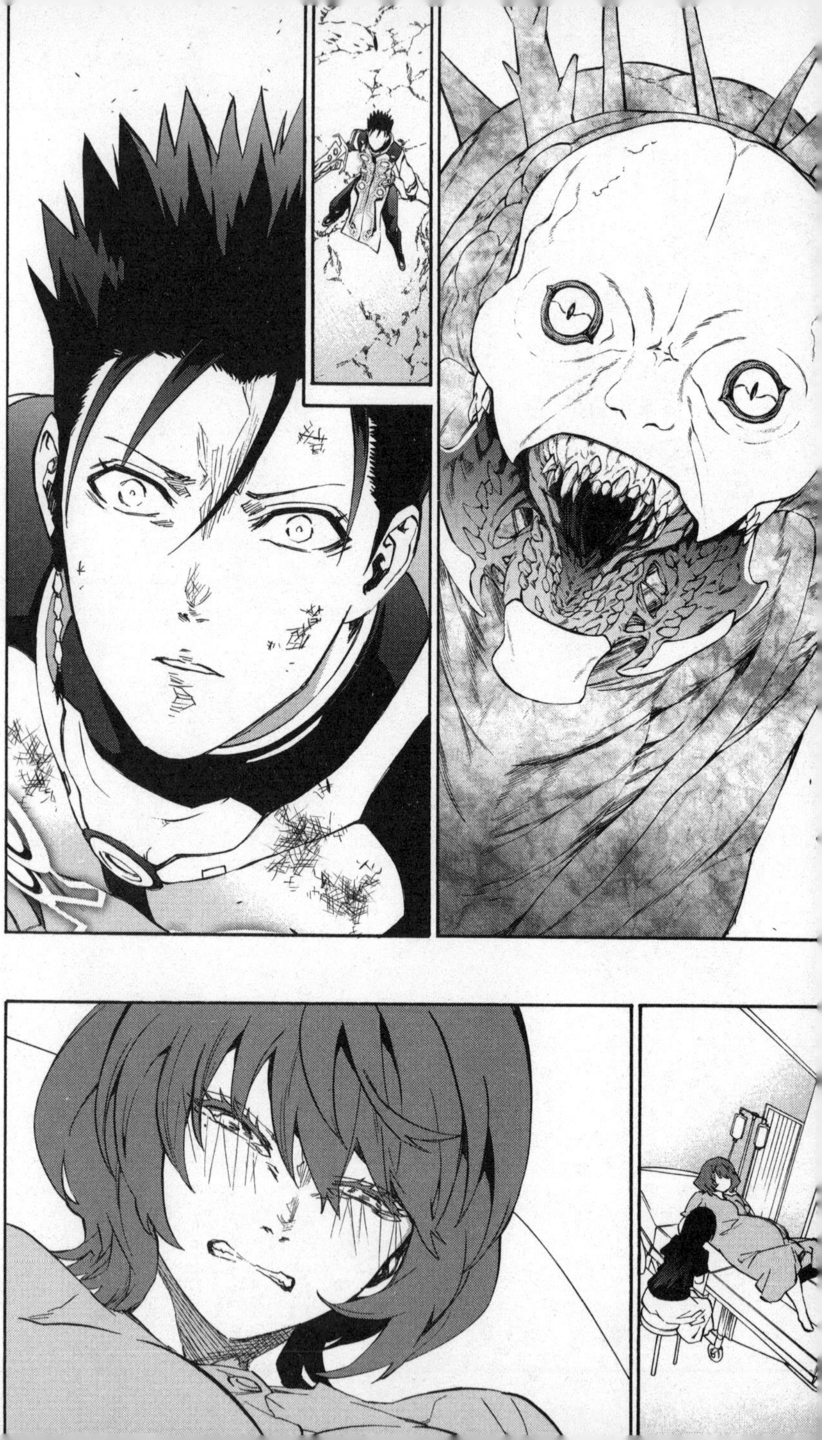

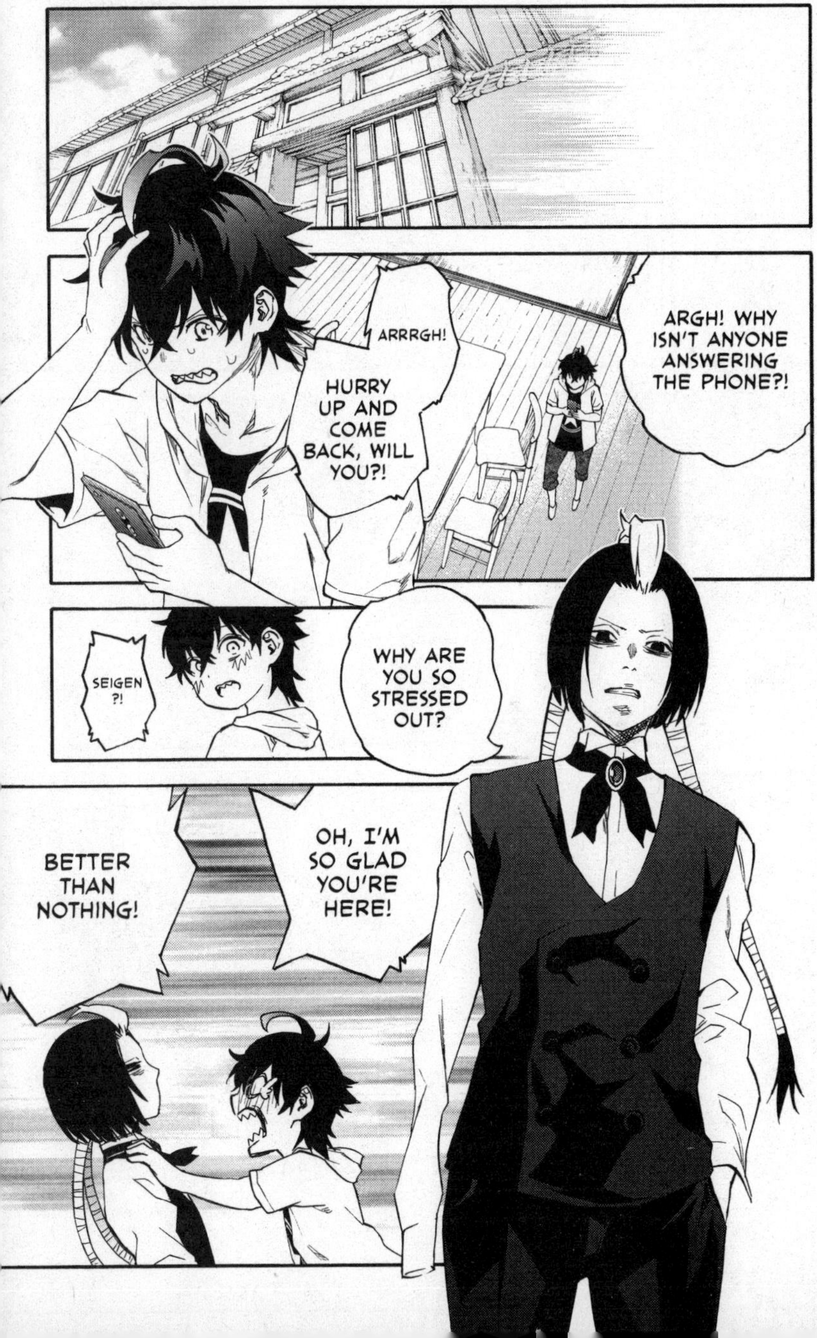
ARGH! WHY ISN'T ANYONE ANSWERING THE PHONE?!
ARRRGH!
HURRY UP AND COME BACK, WILL YOU?!
WHY ARE YOU SO STRESSED OUT?
SEIGEN ?!
OH, I'M SO GLAD YOU'RE HERE!
BETTER THAN NOTHING!

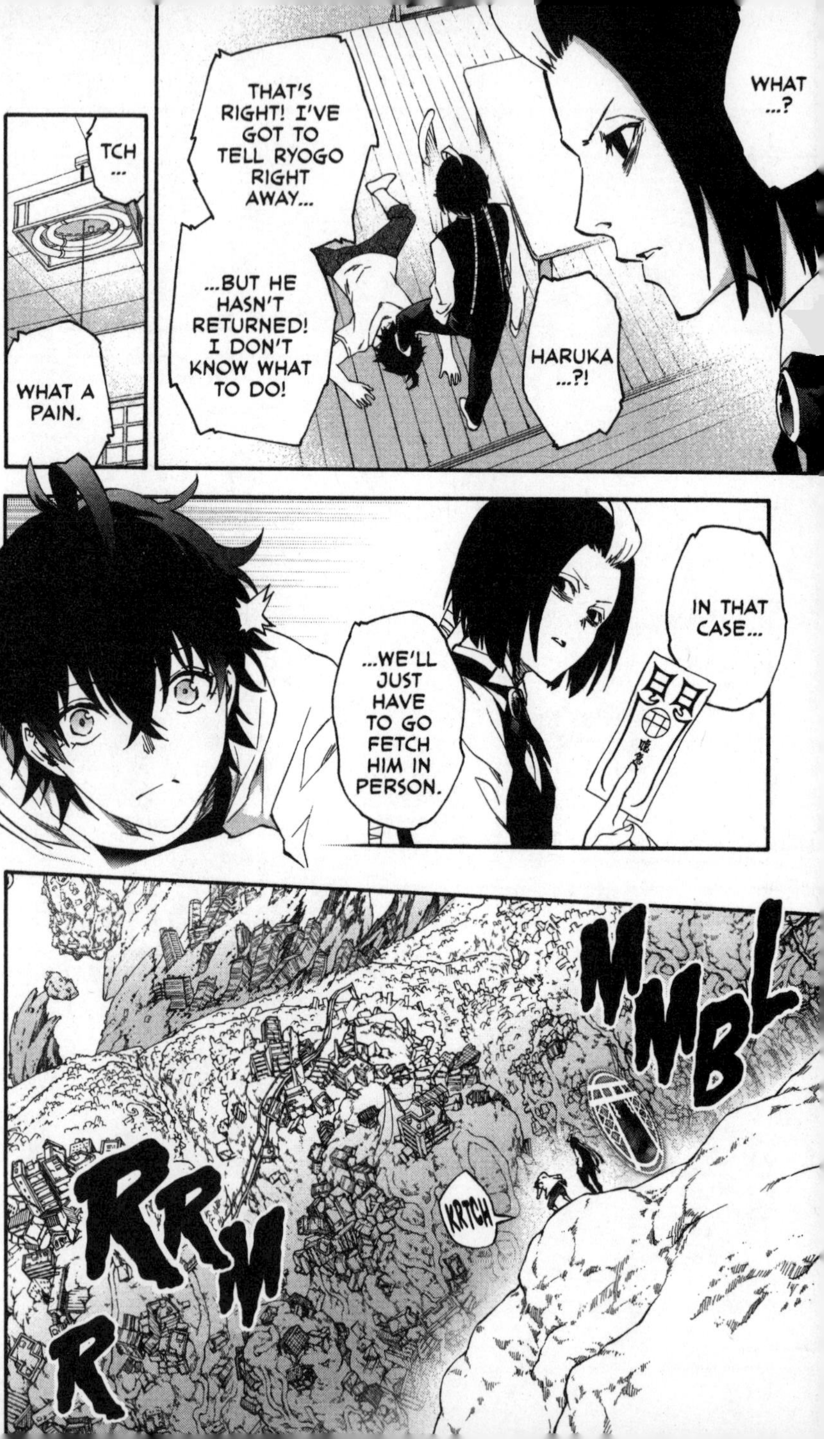
WHAT ...?
HARUKA ...?!
THAT'S RIGHT! I'VE GOT TO TELL RYOGO RIGHT AWAY...
...BUT HE HASN'T RETURNED! I DON'T KNOW WHAT TO DO!
TCH ...
WHAT A PAIN.
IN THAT CASE...
...WE'LL JUST HAVE TO GO FETCH HIM IN PERSON.
MMBL
KRTCH
RRWR

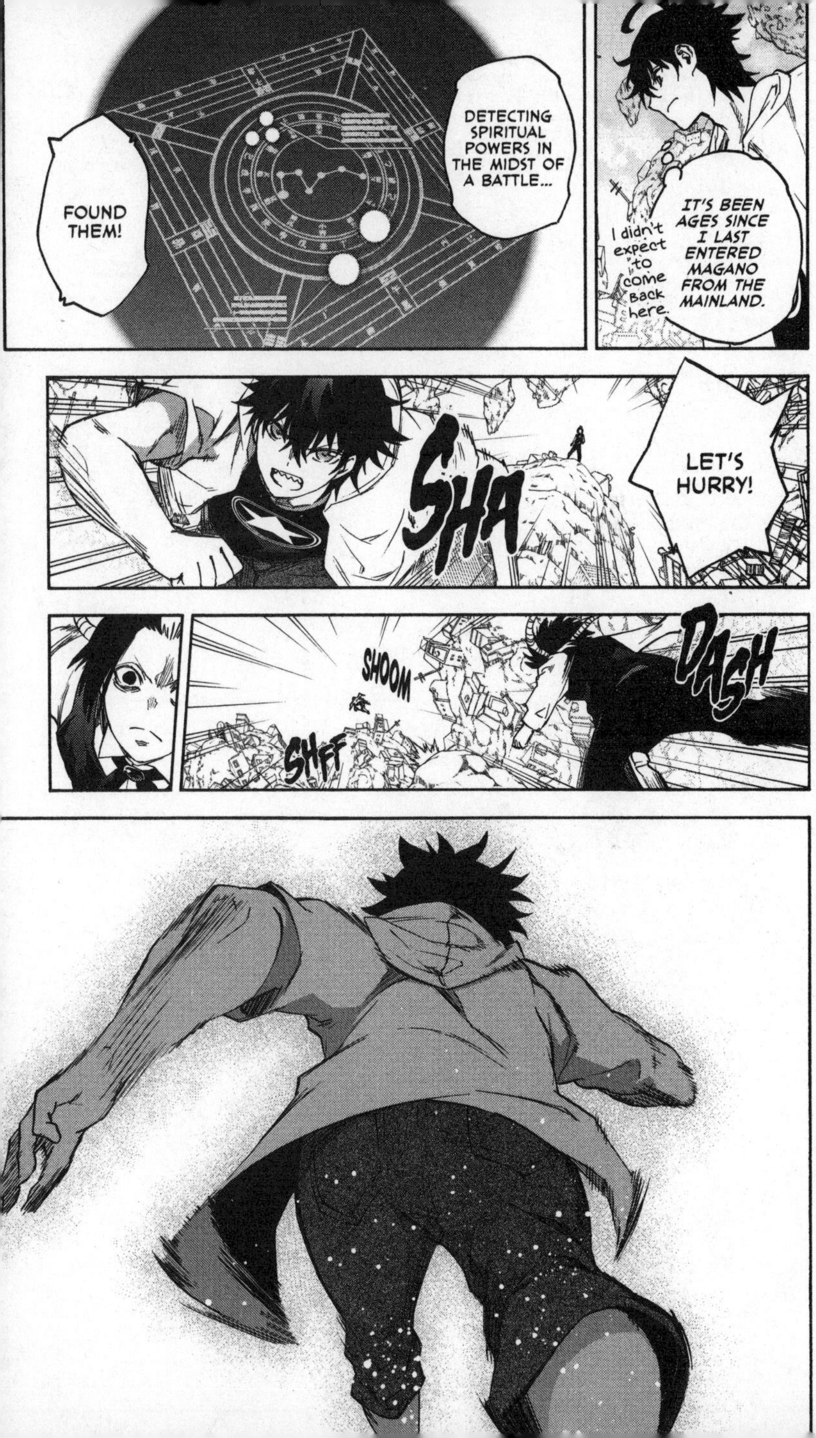
IT'S BEEN AGES SINCE I LAST ENTERED MAGANO FROM THE MAINLAND.
I didn't expect to come back here.
DETECTING SPIRITUAL POWERS IN THE MIDST OF A BATTLE...
FOUND THEM!
LET'S HURRY!
SHA
DASH
SHOOM
SHFF

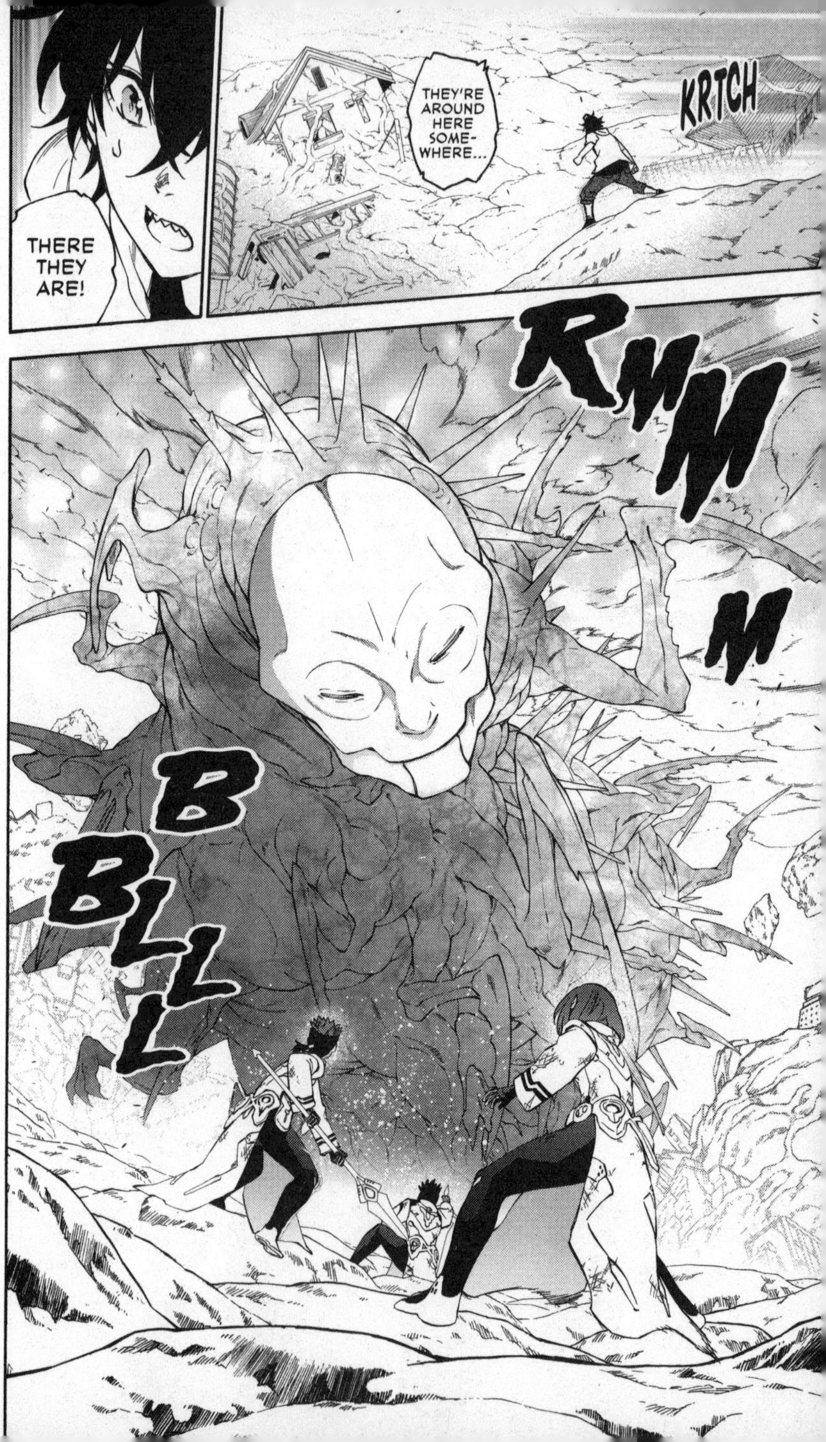
KRTCH
THEY'RE AROUND HERE SOME- WHERE...
THERE THEY ARE!
RMMM
BBLLL

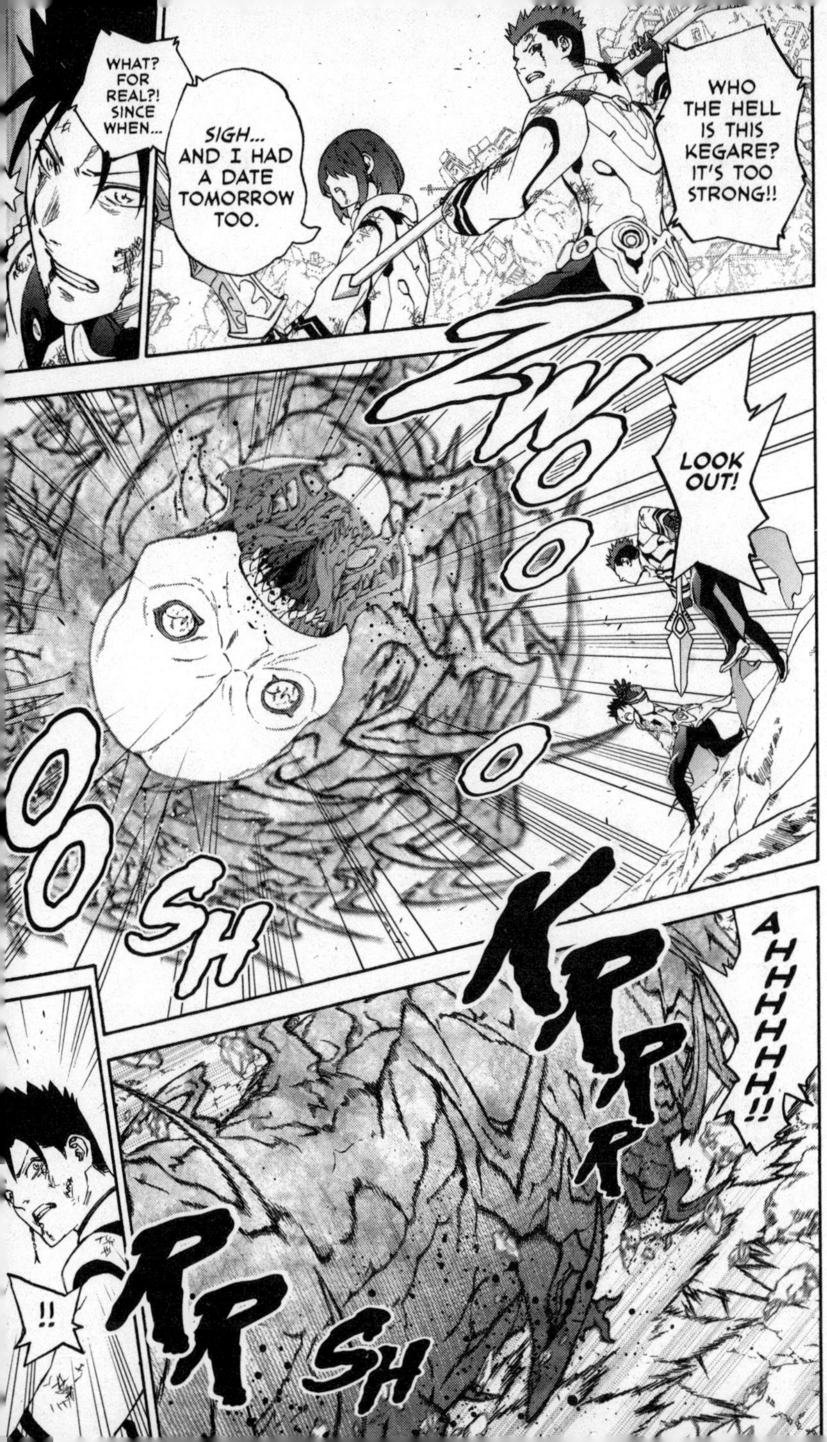
WHO THE HELL IS THIS KEGARE? IT'S TOO STRONG!!
SIGH... AND I HAD A DATE TOMORROW TOO.
WHAT? FOR REAL?! SINCE WHEN...
LOOK OUT!
ZWOOOOOOSH
AHHHHHH!!
KRRR
!!
RR SH

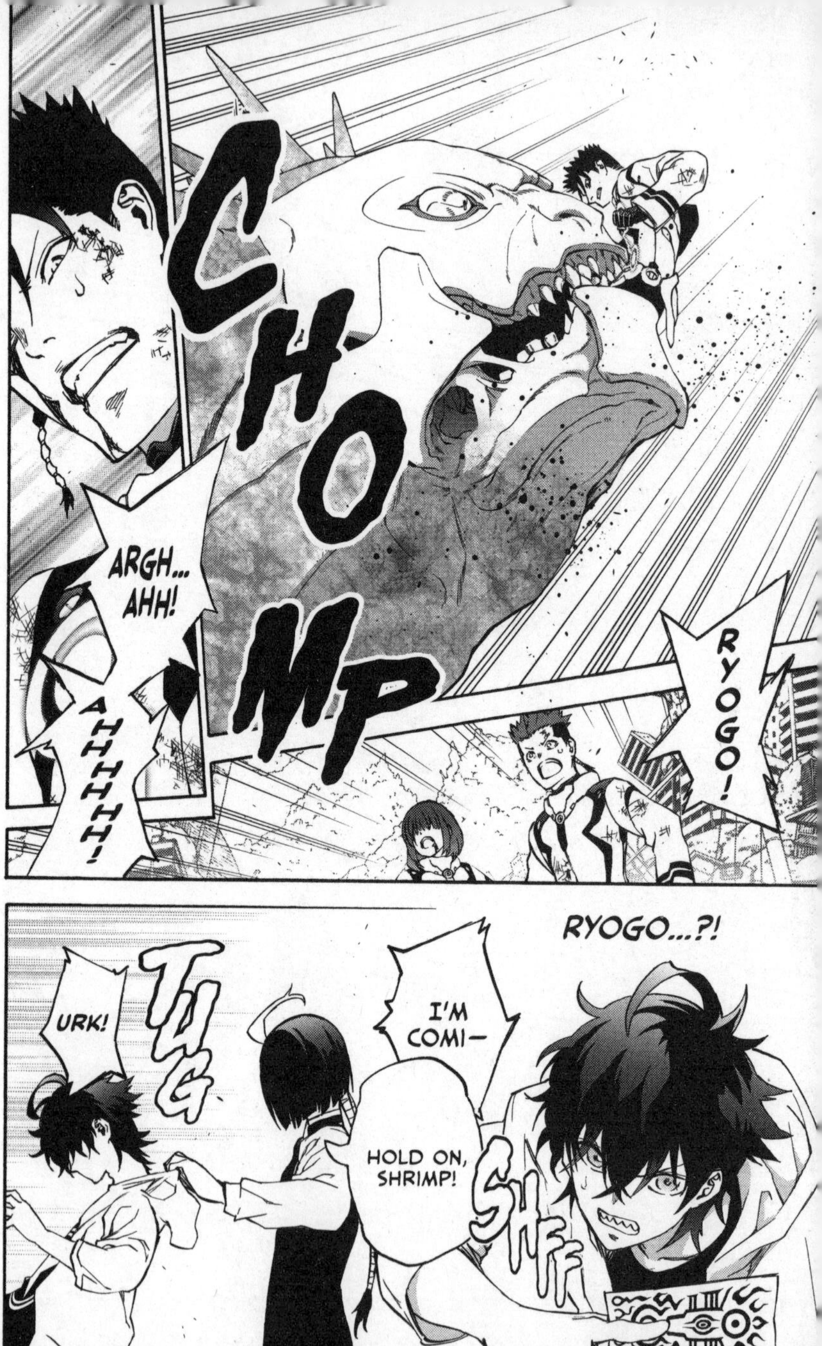
CHOMP
ARGH... AHH!
AHHHHHH!
RYOGO!
RYOGO...?!
I'M COMI—
SHFF
HOLD ON, SHRIMP!
TUG
URK!

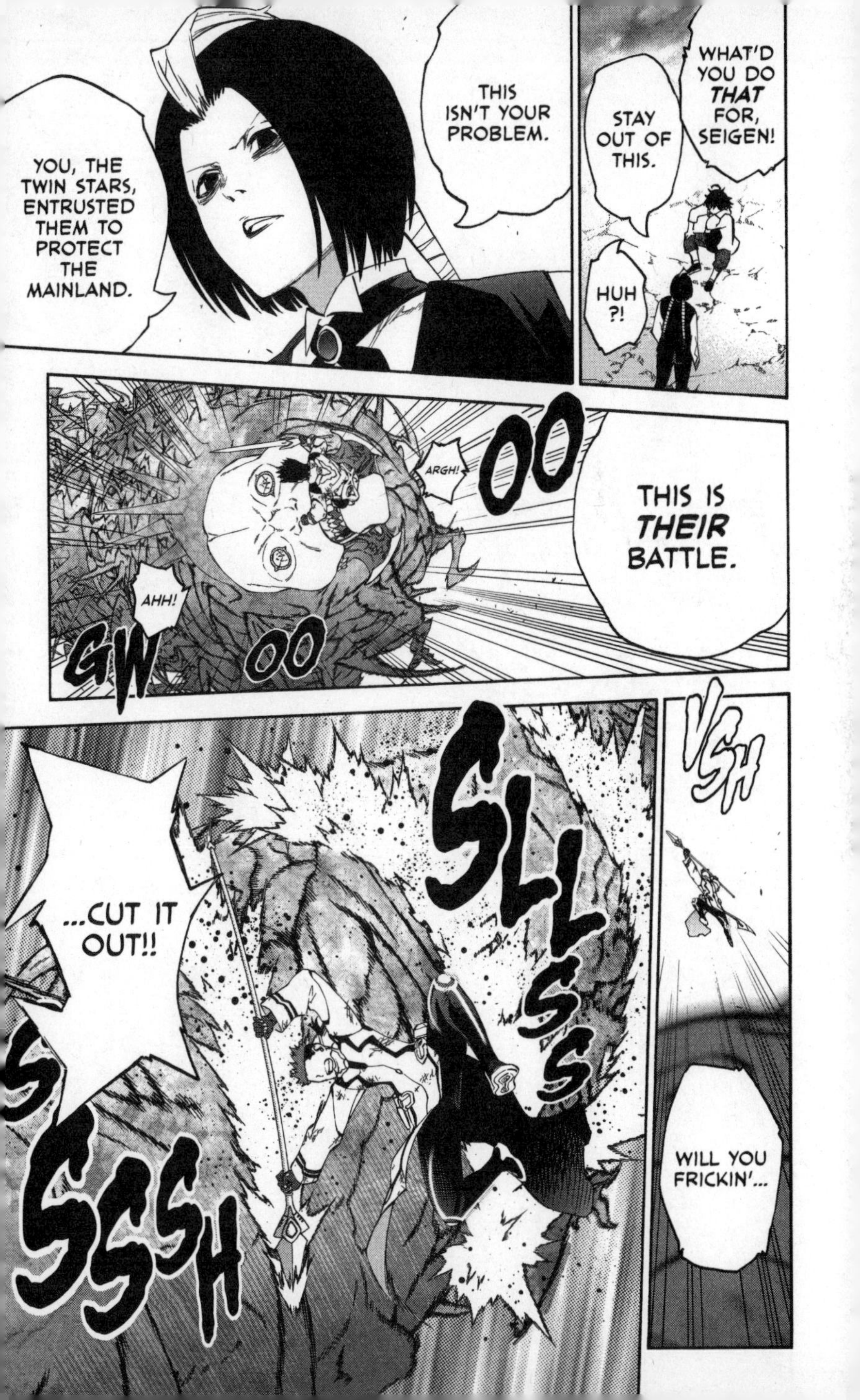
WHAT'D YOU DO *THAT* FOR, SEIGEN!
STAY OUT OF THIS.
HUH?!
THIS ISN'T YOUR PROBLEM.
YOU, THE TWIN STARS, ENTRUSTED THEM TO PROTECT THE MAINLAND.
THIS IS *THEIR* BATTLE.
OO
ARGH!
AHH!
GWOO
VSH
WILL YOU FRICKIN'...
SLLSSS
...CUT IT OUT!!
SSSSH

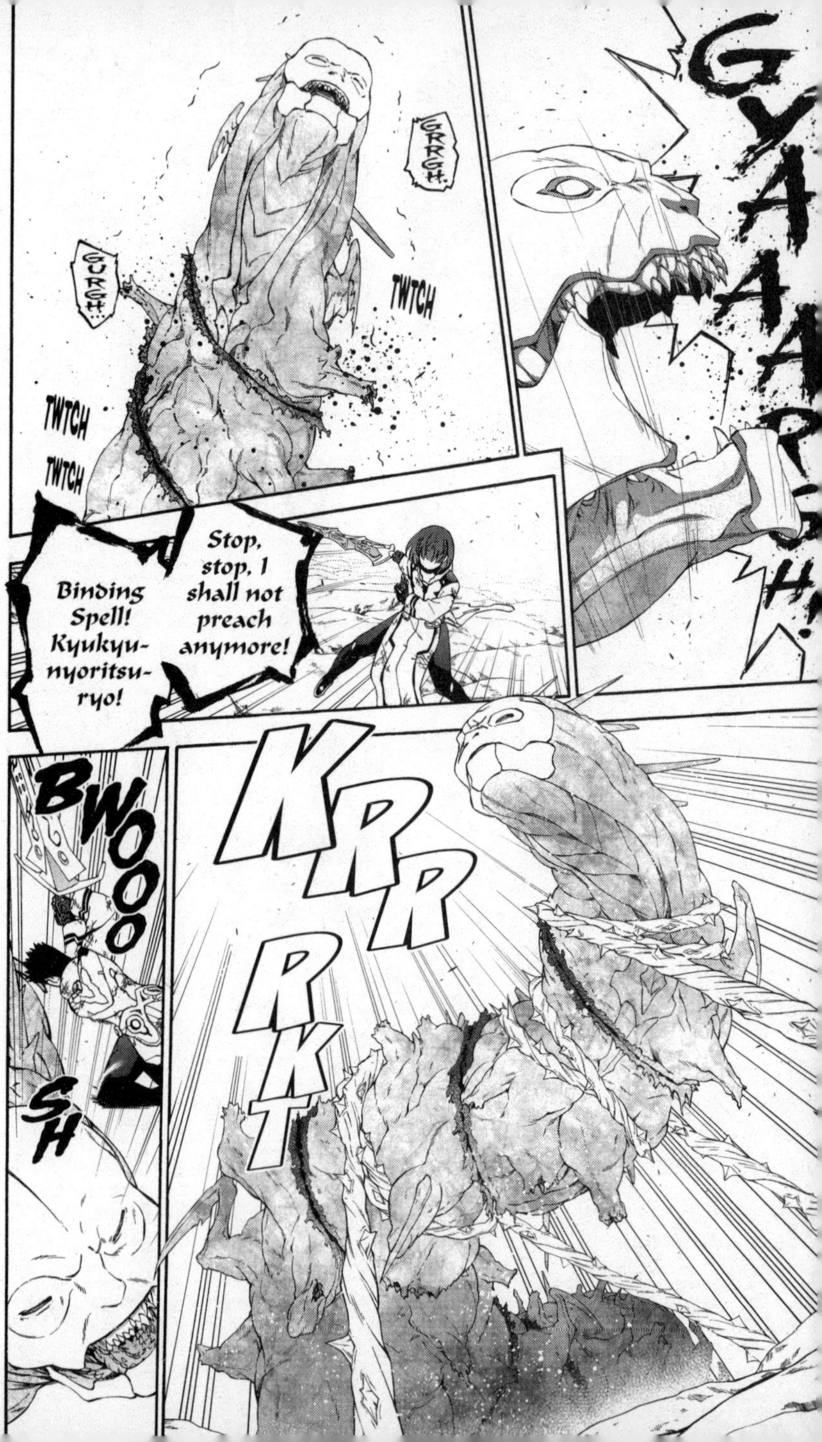
GYAAARGH!
GRRGH...
TWTCH
GURGH...
TWTCH
TWTCH
Stop, stop, I shall not preach anymore!
Binding Spell! Kyukyu-nyoritsu-ryo!
KRRRRKT
BWOOOO
SH

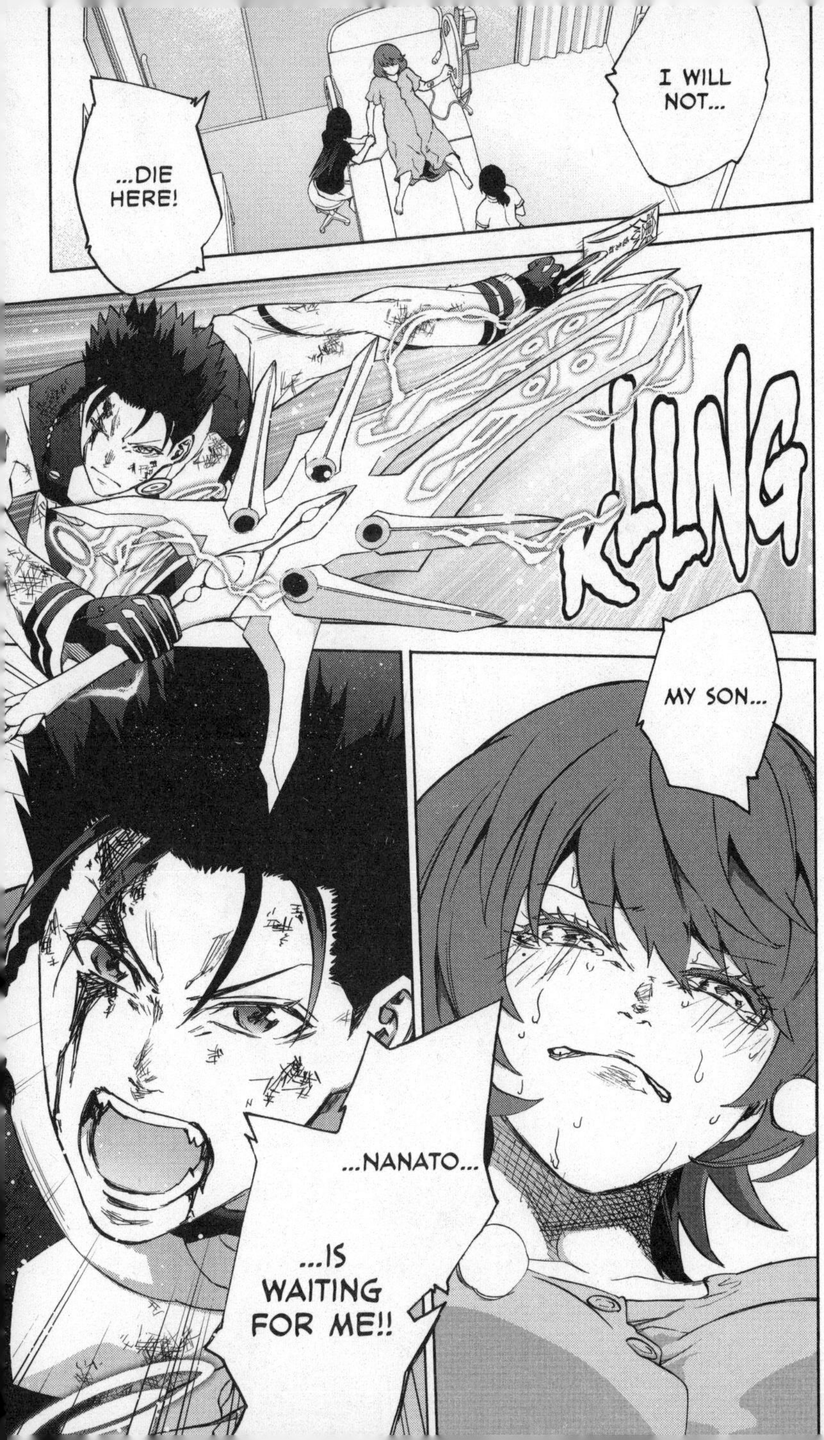
I WILL NOT...
...DIE HERE!
KLING
MY SON...
...NANATO...
...IS WAITING FOR ME!!

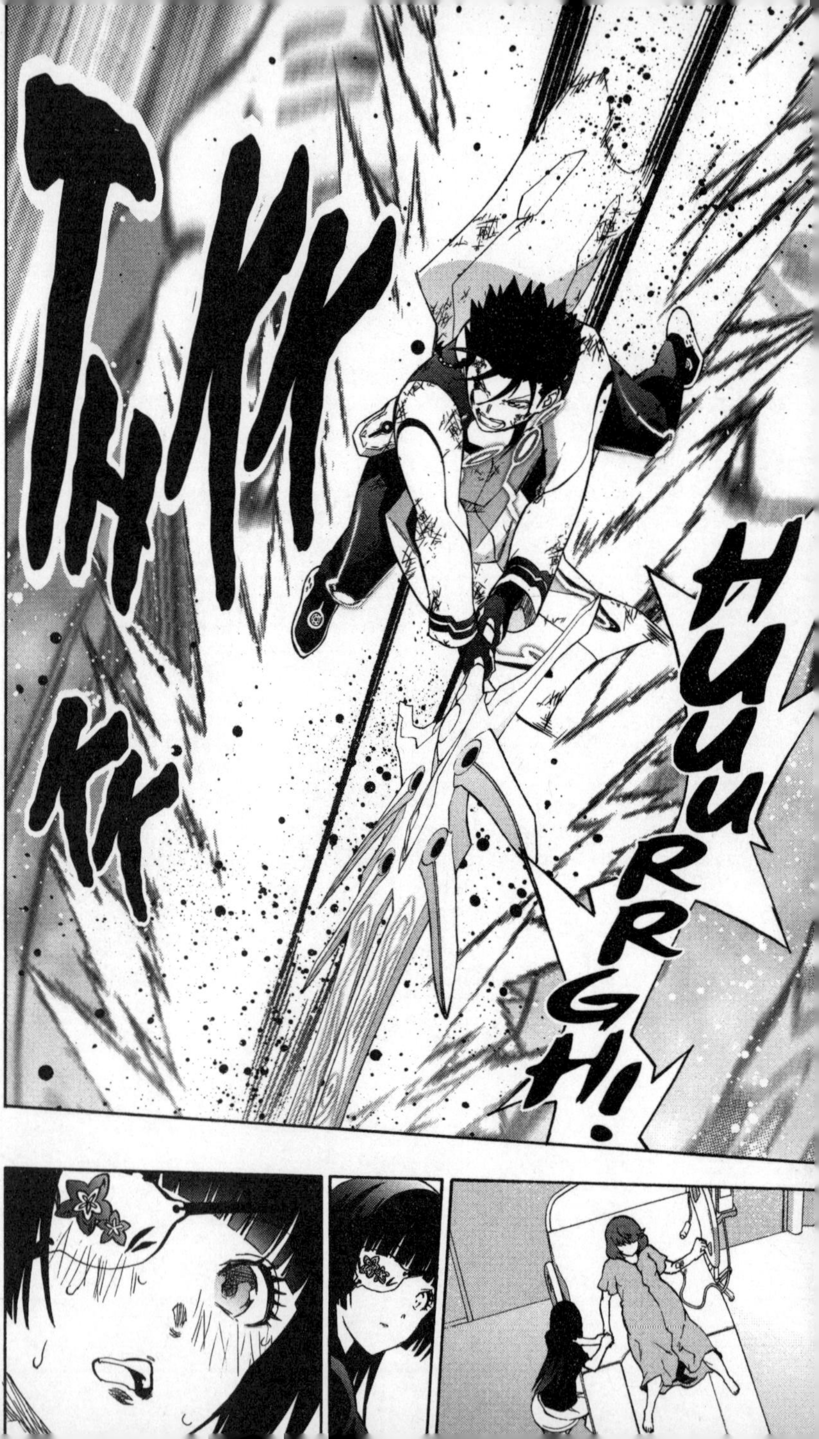
HUUURRGH!
THWKKK

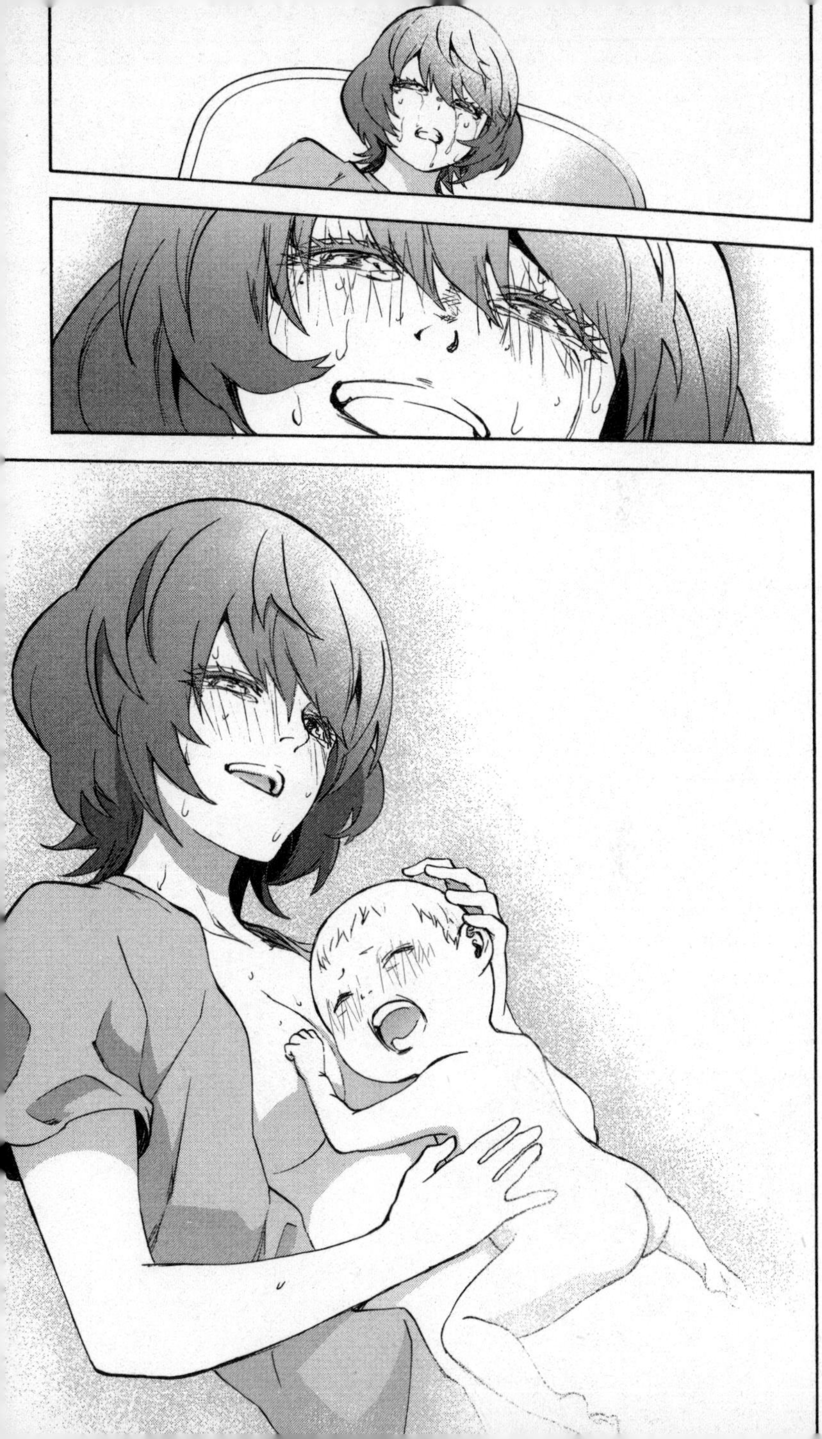

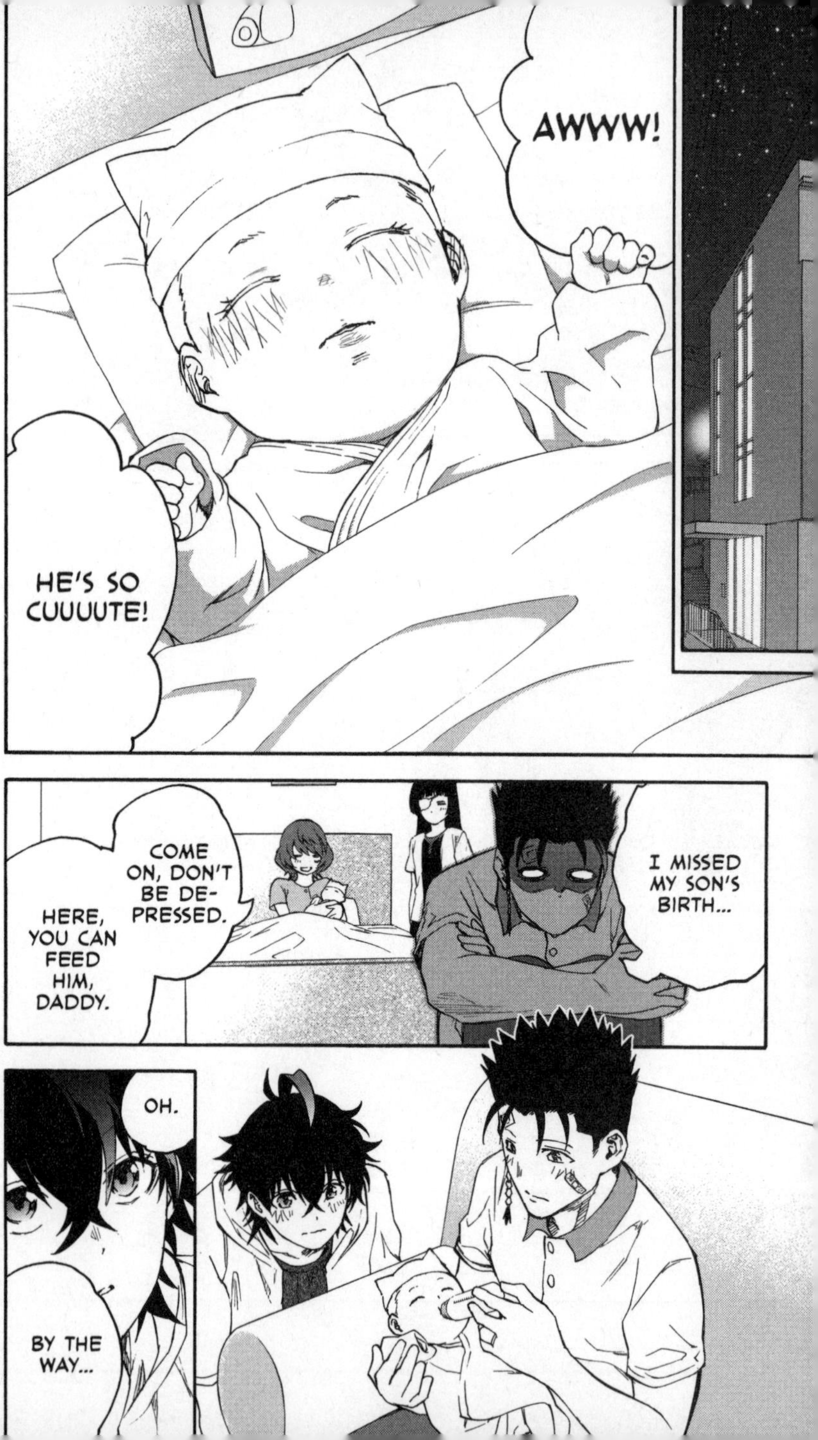
AWWW!
HE'S SO CUUUUTE!
I MISSED MY SON'S BIRTH...
COME ON, DON'T BE DE-PRESSED.
HERE, YOU CAN FEED HIM, DADDY.
OH.
BY THE WAY...

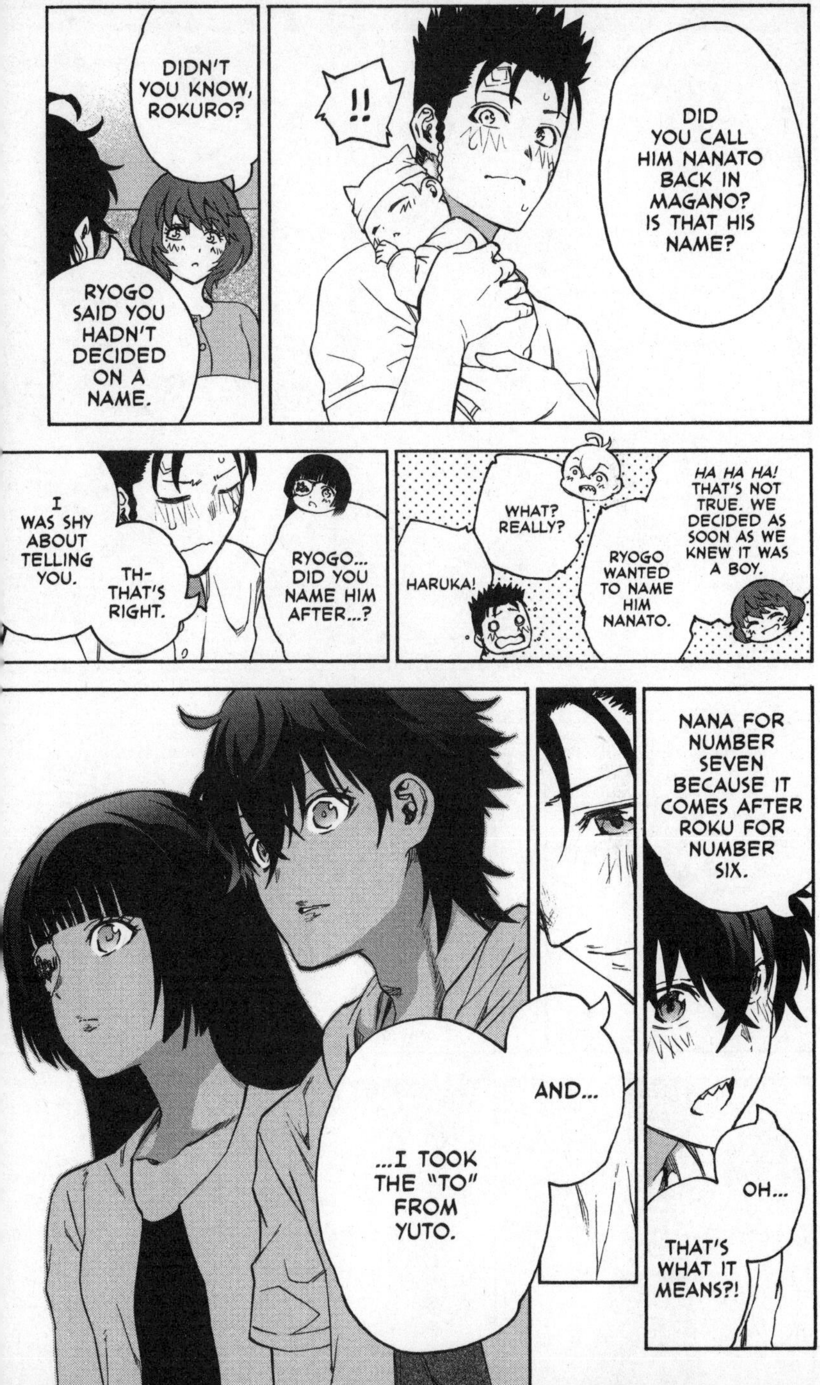
DID YOU CALL HIM NANATO BACK IN MAGANO? IS THAT HIS NAME?
!!
DIDN'T YOU KNOW, ROKURO?
RYOGO SAID YOU HADN'T DECIDED ON A NAME.
HA HA HA! THAT'S NOT TRUE. WE DECIDED AS SOON AS WE KNEW IT WAS A BOY.
WHAT? REALLY?
RYOGO WANTED TO NAME HIM NANATO.
HARUKA!
RYOGO... DID YOU NAME HIM AFTER...?
TH-THAT'S RIGHT.
I WAS SHY ABOUT TELLING YOU.
NANA FOR NUMBER SEVEN BECAUSE IT COMES AFTER ROKU FOR NUMBER SIX.
OH...
THAT'S WHAT IT MEANS?!
AND...
...I TOOK THE "TO" FROM YUTO.

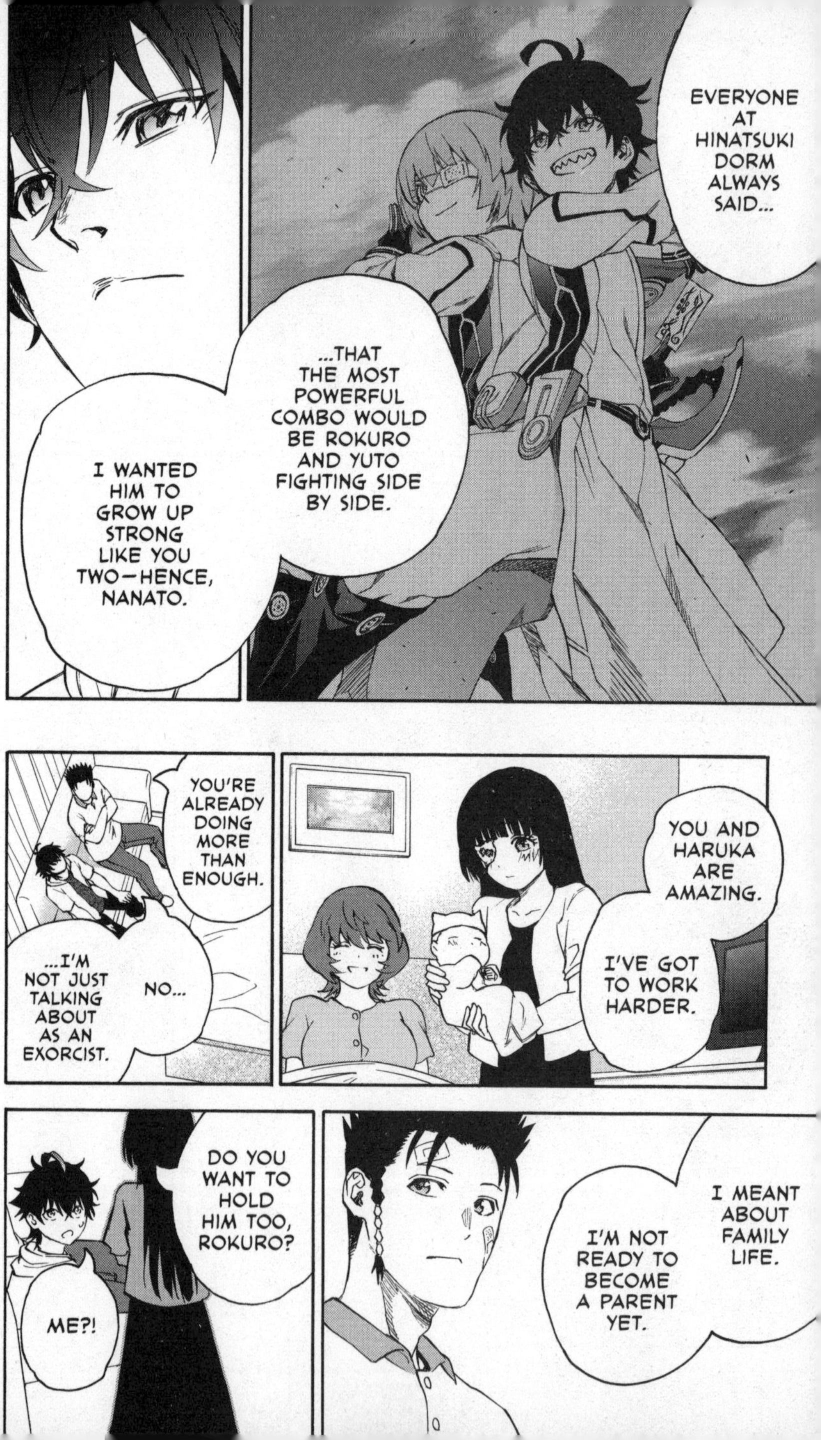
EVERYONE AT HINATSUKI DORM ALWAYS SAID...
...THAT THE MOST POWERFUL COMBO WOULD BE ROKURO AND YUTO FIGHTING SIDE BY SIDE.
I WANTED HIM TO GROW UP STRONG LIKE YOU TWO—HENCE, NANATO.
YOU AND HARUKA ARE AMAZING.
I'VE GOT TO WORK HARDER.
YOU'RE ALREADY DOING MORE THAN ENOUGH.
NO...
...I'M NOT JUST TALKING ABOUT AS AN EXORCIST.
I MEANT ABOUT FAMILY LIFE.
I'M NOT READY TO BECOME A PARENT YET.
DO YOU WANT TO HOLD HIM TOO, ROKURO?
ME?!

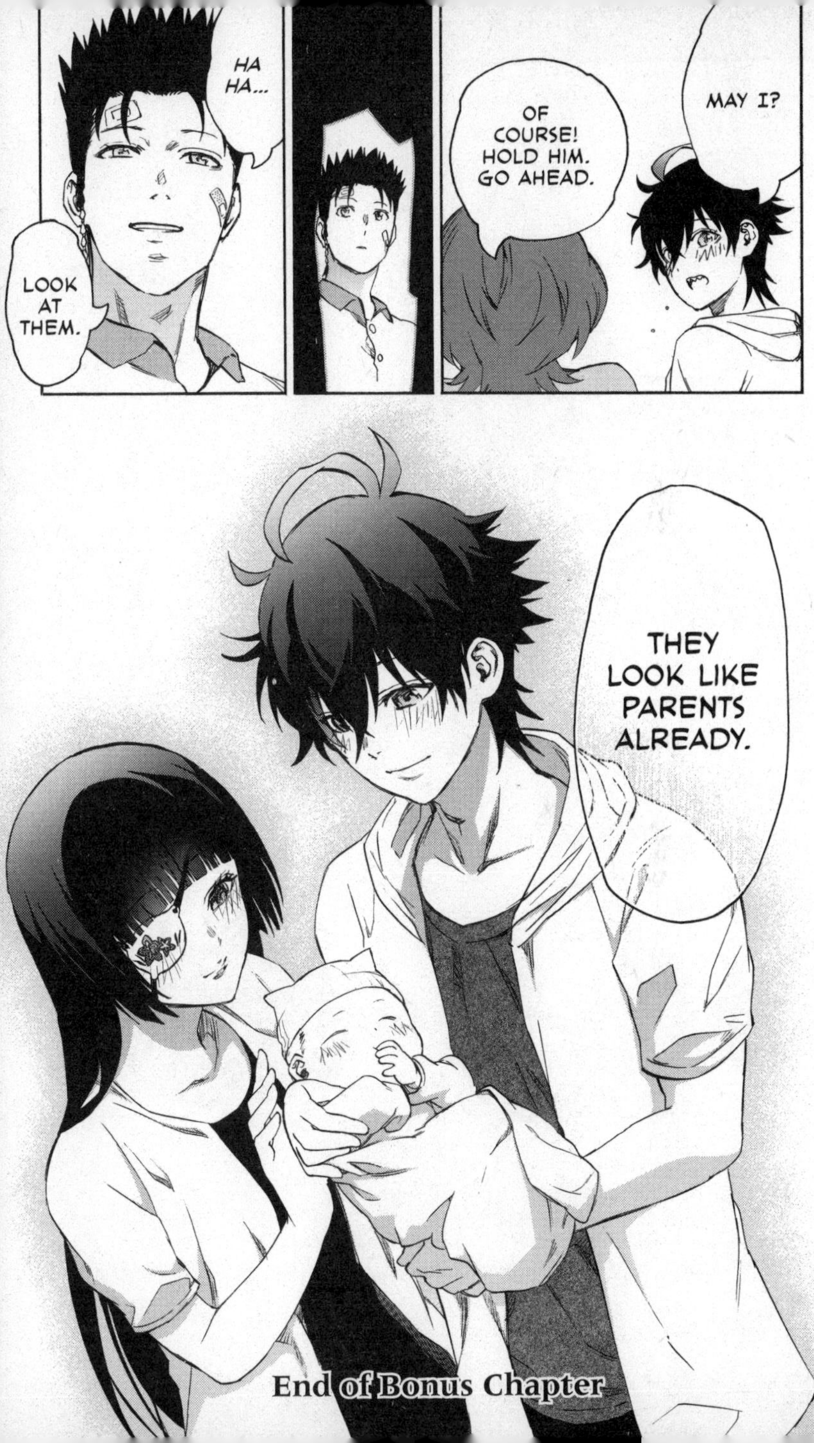
MAY I?
OF COURSE! HOLD HIM. GO AHEAD.
HA HA...
LOOK AT THEM.
THEY LOOK LIKE PARENTS ALREADY.
End of Bonus Chapter

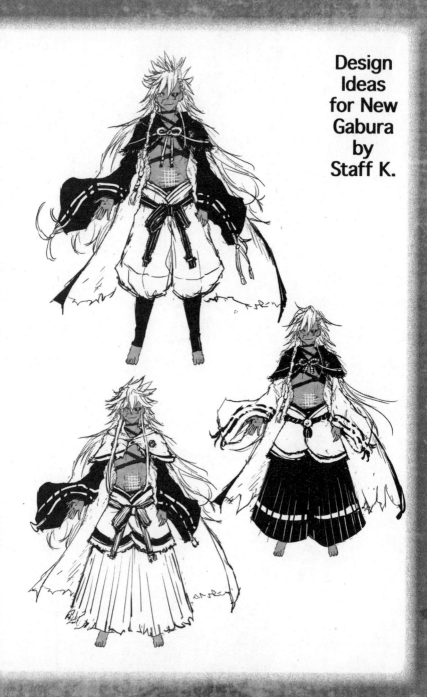

Design
Ideas
for New
Gabura
by
Staff K.

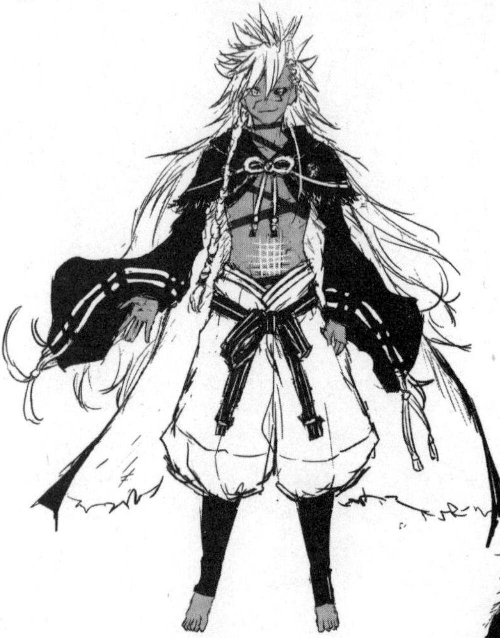

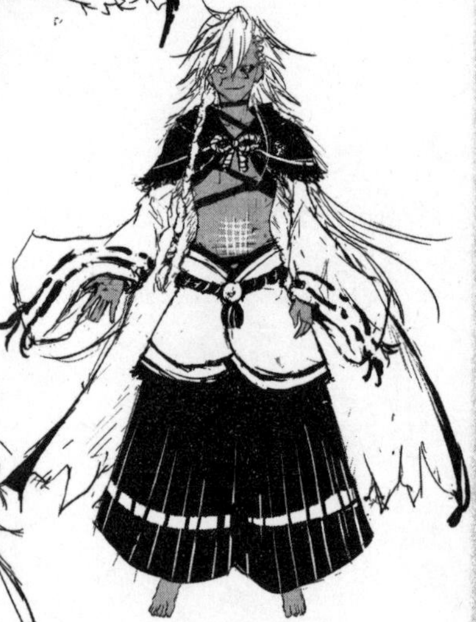

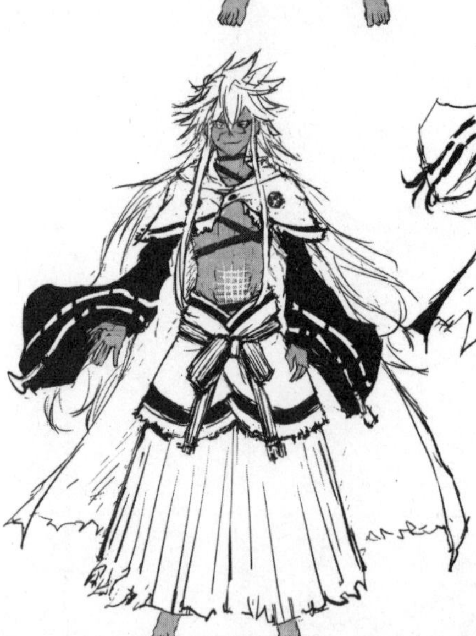

Design Ideas for New Mitejima by Staff K.

Feather

Flower

Back

Double Ribbon

Furry

Long Black Gloves

Furry

STAFF

★ Artwork ★ Takumi Kikuta / koppy
Yukiya Yamazaki / Takumi Kaba /
Natsuki Ise

Yoshiaki Sukeno

★ Editor ★ Ryota Kasai
★ Graphic Novel Editor ★ Naomi Maehara
★ Graphic Novel Design ★ Tatsuo Ishino (Freiheit)

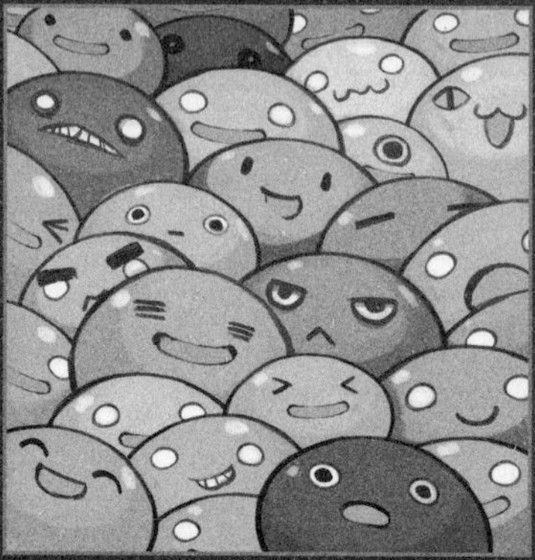

There is so much I want to work on!
Twin Star Exorcists, Senpai ga Boku wo Tori ni Kiteru
(My Senpai Is Trying to Kill Me), and drawing
for Skeb too. I want to keep drawing forever.
I want to take my family on a trip. Oh, and
I want to go on a diet too.

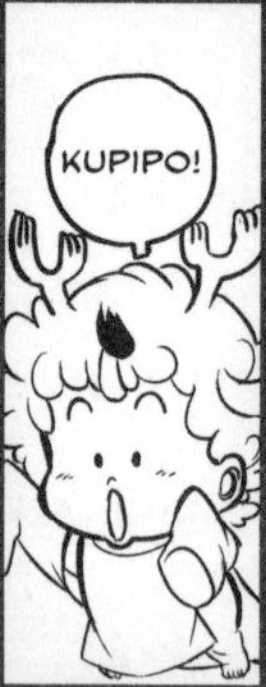
KUPIPO!

YOSHIAKI SUKENO was born July 23, 1981, in Wakayama, Japan. He graduated from Kyoto Seika University, where he studied manga. In 2006, he won the Tezuka Award for Best Newcomer Shonen Manga Artist. In 2008, he began his previous work, the supernatural comedy *Binbougami ga!*, which was adapted into the anime *Good Luck Girl!* in 2012.

Various Character-Design Concepts

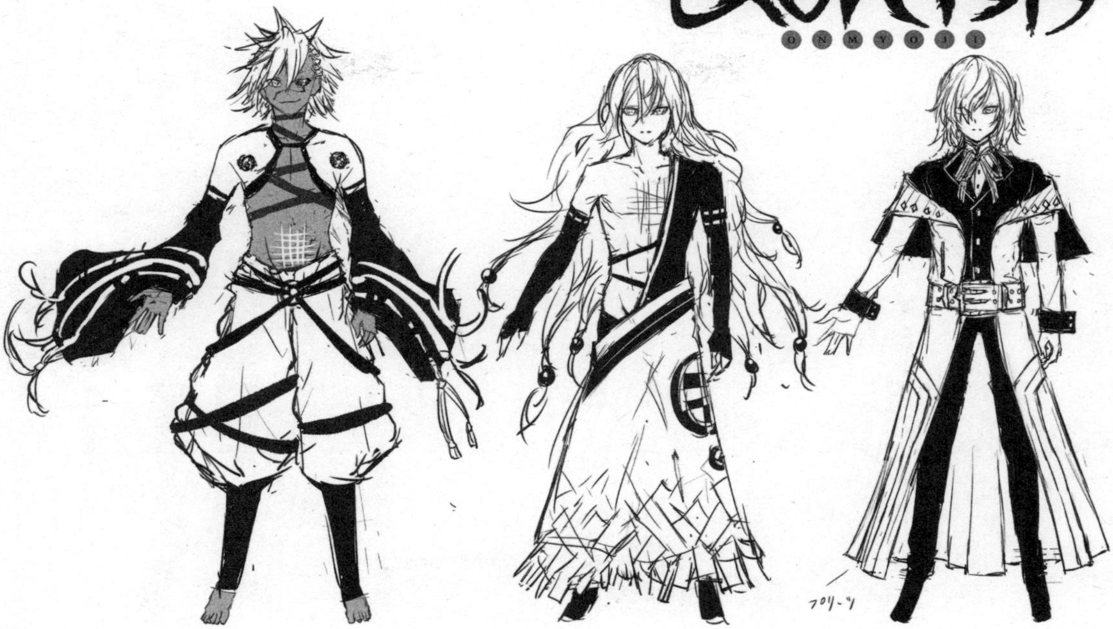

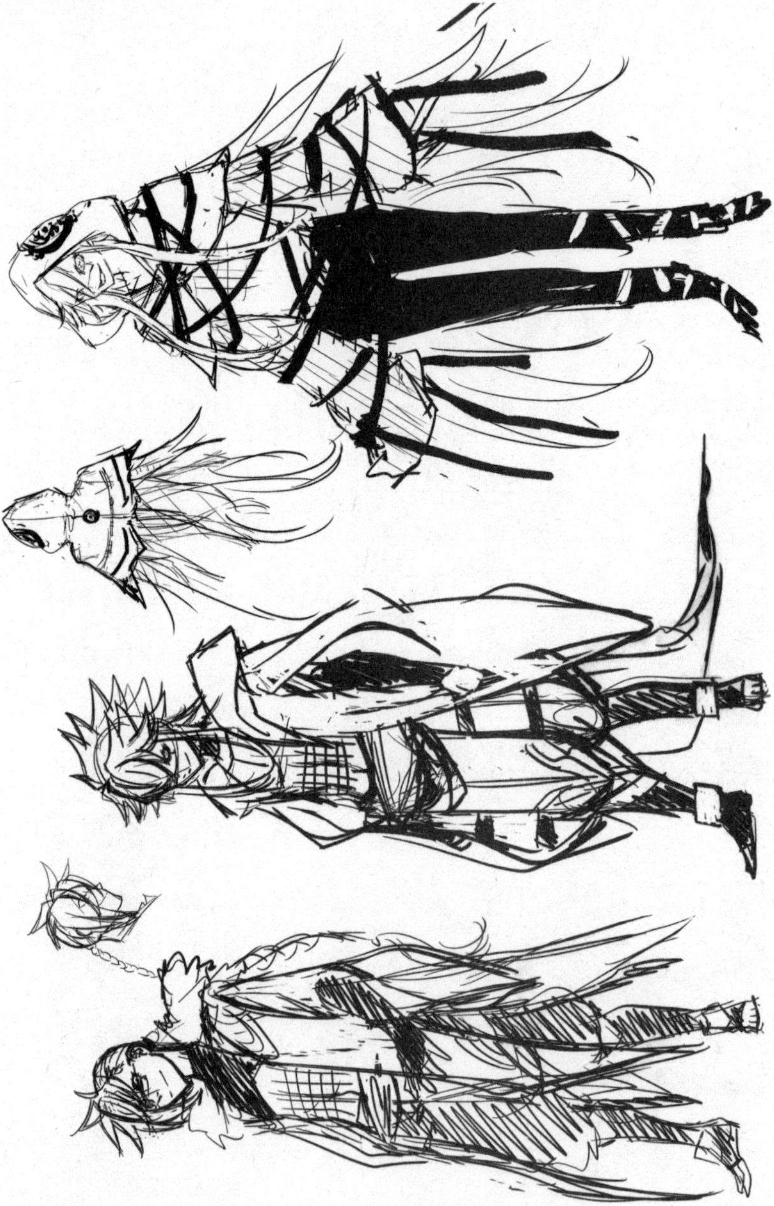

—SHONEN JUMP Manga Edition—

STORY & ART **Yoshiaki Sukeno**

TRANSLATION **Tetsuichiro Miyaki**
ENGLISH ADAPTATION **Annette Roman**
TOUCH-UP ART & LETTERING **Steve Dutro**
DESIGN **Shawn Carrico**
EDITOR **Annette Roman**

SOUSEI NO ONMYOJI © 2013 by Yoshiaki Sukeno
All rights reserved.
First published in Japan in 2013 by SHUEISHA Inc., Tokyo.
English translation rights arranged by SHUEISHA Inc.

The stories, characters and incidents mentioned in this
publication are entirely fictional.

Printed in the U.S.A.

Published by VIZ Media, LLC
P.O. Box 77010
San Francisco, CA 94107

10 9 8 7 6 5 4 3 2 1
First printing, June 2021

viz.com

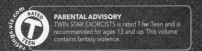

PARENTAL ADVISORY
TWIN STAR EXORCISTS is rated T for Teen and is
recommended for ages 13 and up. This volume
contains fantasy violence.

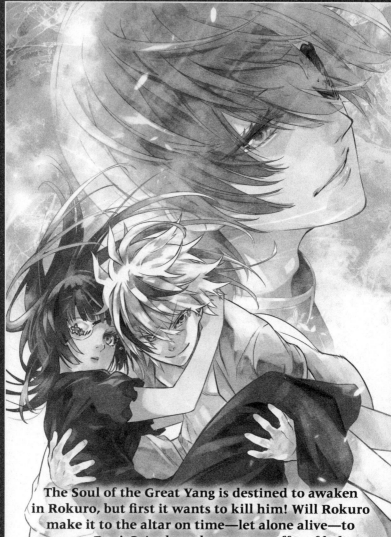

The Soul of the Great Yang is destined to awaken in Rokuro, but first it wants to kill him! Will Rokuro make it to the altar on time—let alone alive—to marry Benio? And can he trust an offer of help from a most unlikely, impossible ally?
VOLUME 23

Twin Star Exorcists

ONMYOJI

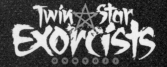

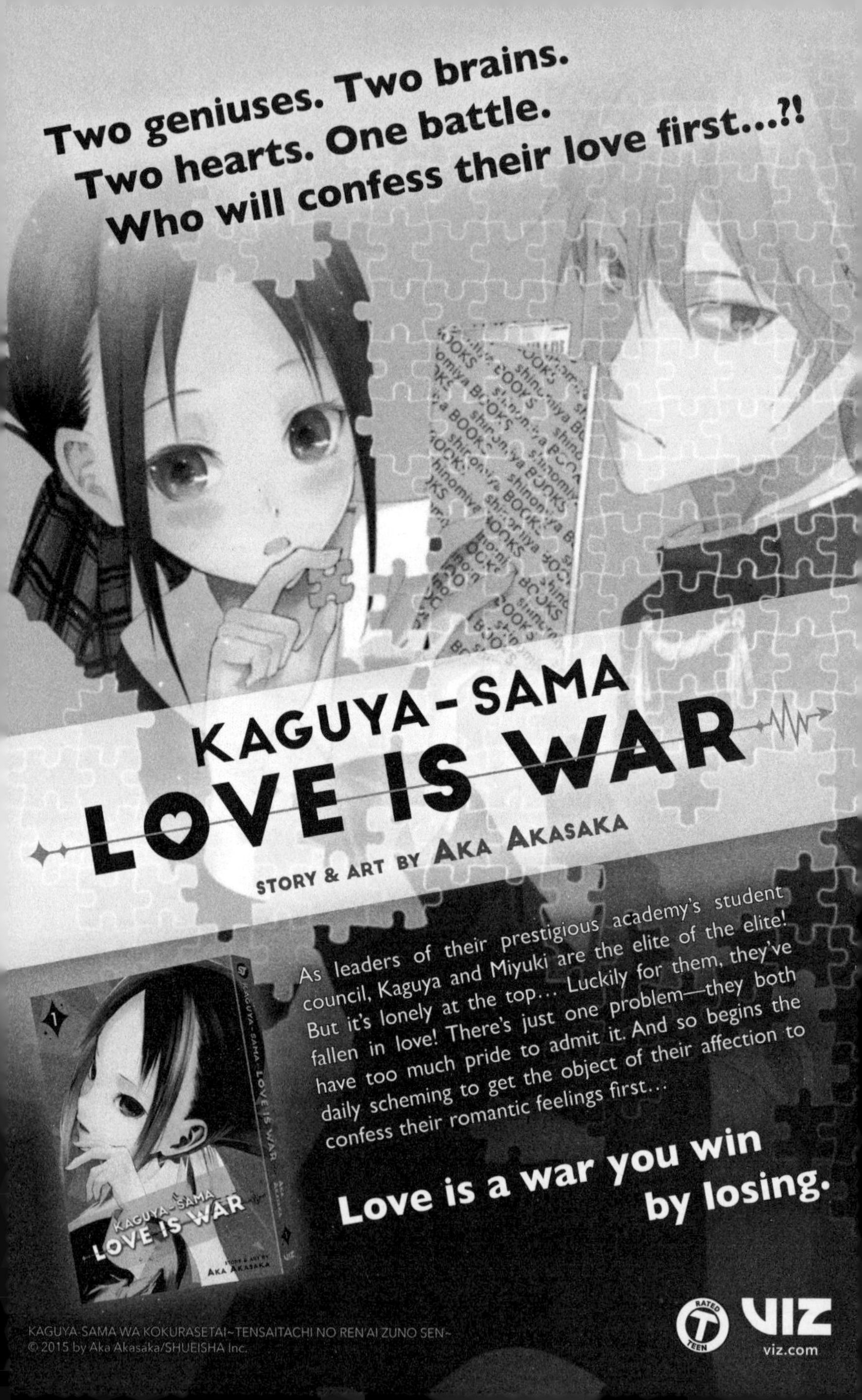
Two geniuses. Two brains.
Two hearts. One battle.
Who will confess their love first…?!
KAGUYA-SAMA
LOVE IS WAR
STORY & ART BY AKA AKASAKA
As leaders of their prestigious academy's student council, Kaguya and Miyuki are the elite of the elite! But it's lonely at the top… Luckily for them, they've fallen in love! There's just one problem—they both have too much pride to admit it. And so begins the daily scheming to get the object of their affection to confess their romantic feelings first…
Love is a war you win by losing.
KAGUYA-SAMA LOVE IS WAR
STORY & ART BY AKA AKASAKA
RATED T TEEN
VIZ
viz.com
KAGUYA-SAMA WA KOKURASETAI~TENSAITACHI NO REN'AI ZUNO SEN~
© 2015 by Aka Akasaka/SHUEISHA Inc.

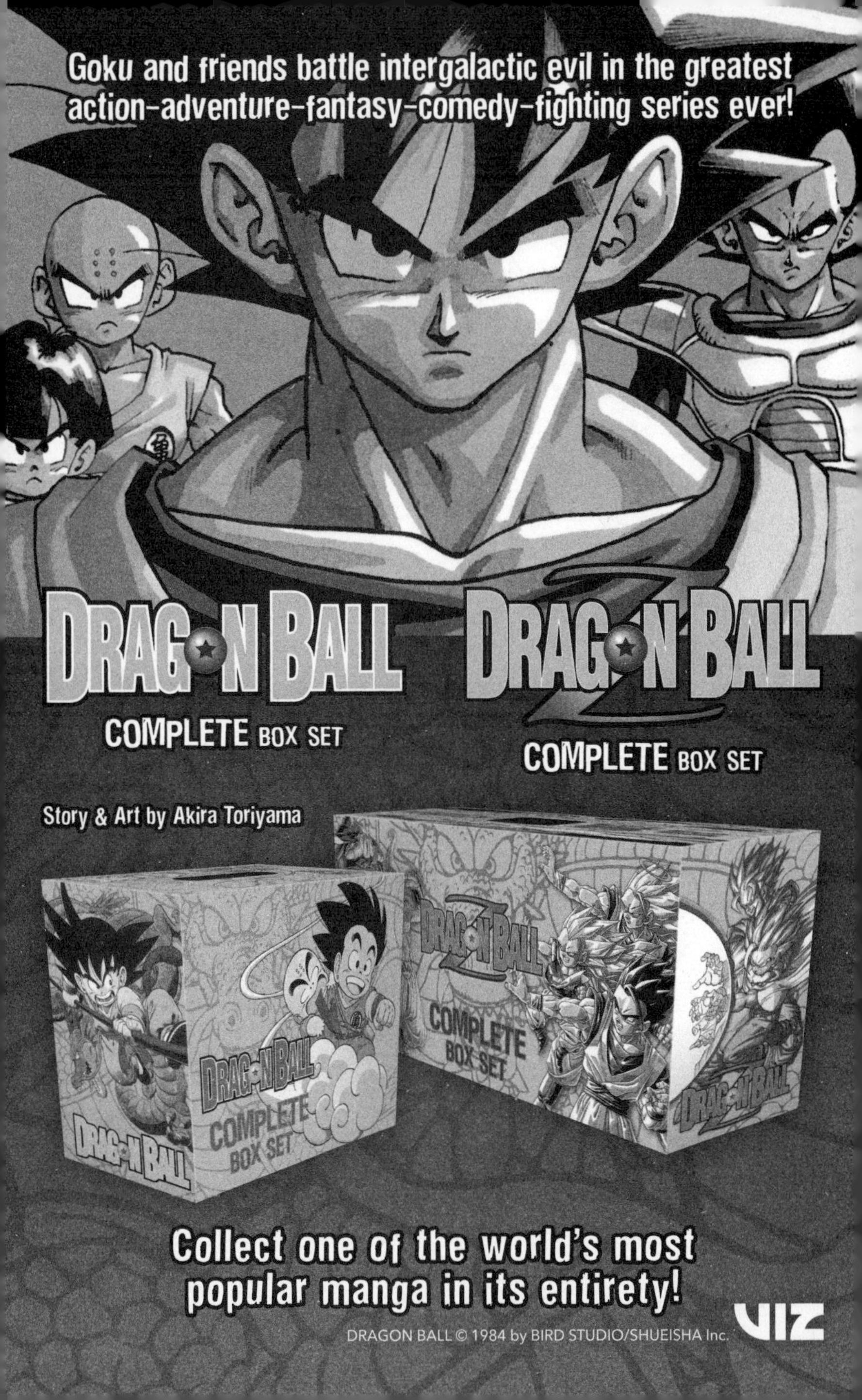

Goku and friends battle intergalactic evil in the greatest action-adventure-fantasy-comedy-fighting series ever!

COMPLETE BOX SET

COMPLETE BOX SET

Story & Art by Akira Toriyama

Collect one of the world's most popular manga in its entirety!

VIZ

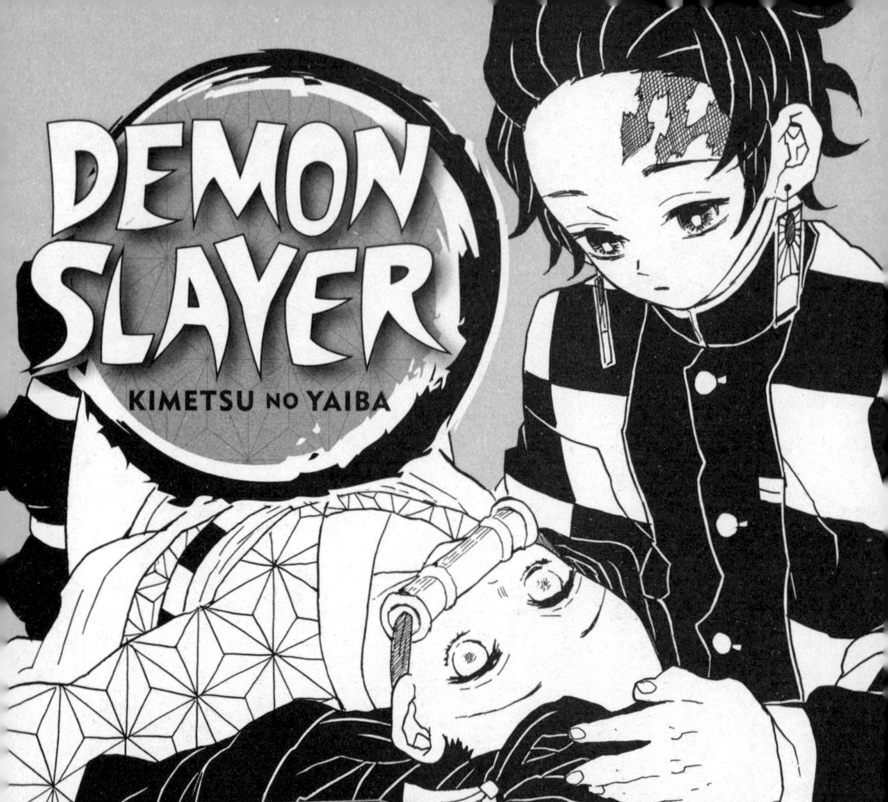
DEMON SLAYER
KIMETSU NO YAIBA

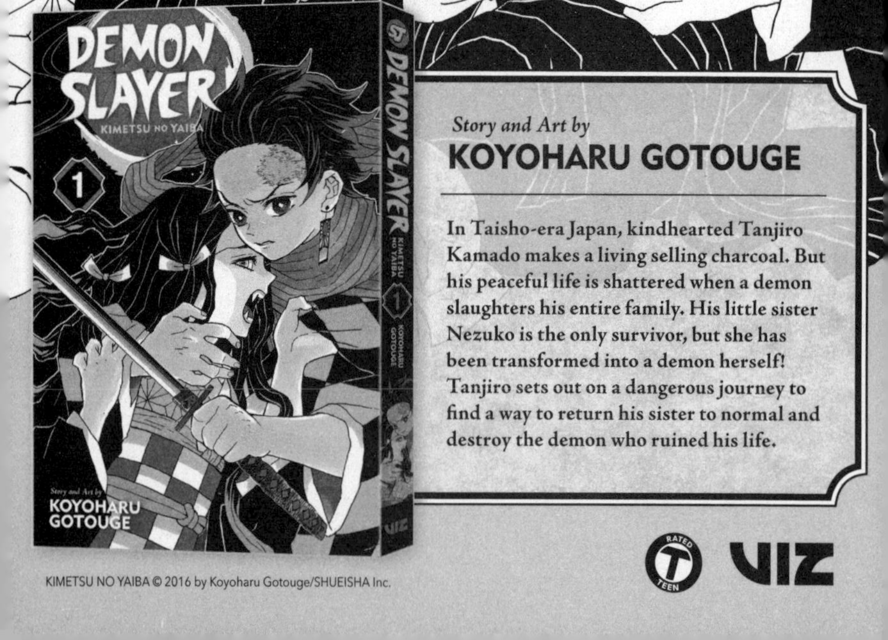
DEMON SLAYER
KIMETSU NO YAIBA
1
Story and Art by
KOYOHARU GOTOUGE
DEMON SLAYER
KIMETSU NO YAIBA
1
KOYOHARU GOTOUGE
VIZ

Story and Art by

KOYOHARU GOTOUGE

In Taisho-era Japan, kindhearted Tanjiro Kamado makes a living selling charcoal. But his peaceful life is shattered when a demon slaughters his entire family. His little sister Nezuko is the only survivor, but she has been transformed into a demon herself! Tanjiro sets out on a dangerous journey to find a way to return his sister to normal and destroy the demon who ruined his life.

RATED T TEEN

VIZ

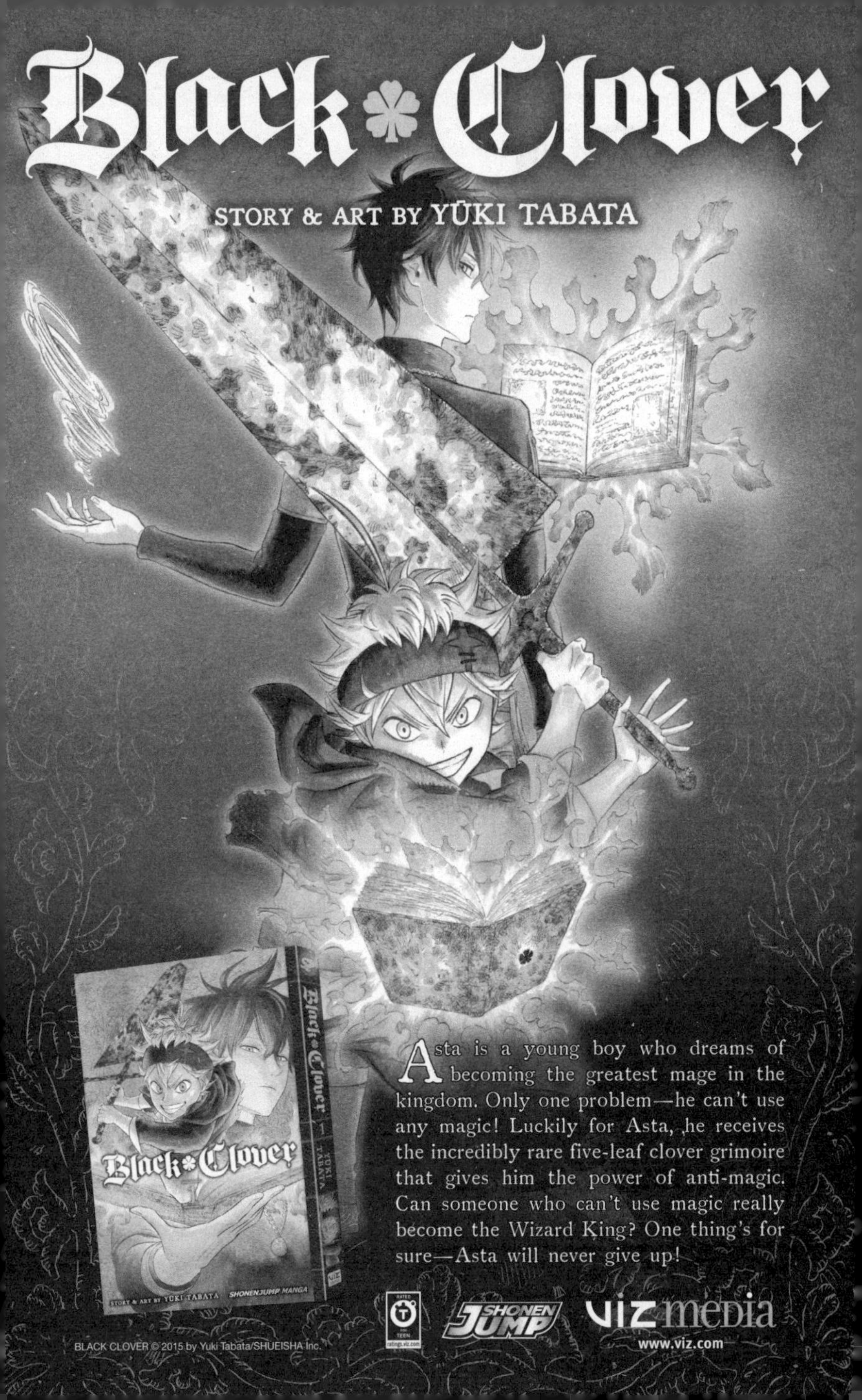
Black Clover
STORY & ART BY YŪKI TABATA
Asta is a young boy who dreams of becoming the greatest mage in the kingdom. Only one problem—he can't use any magic! Luckily for Asta, he receives the incredibly rare five-leaf clover grimoire that gives him the power of anti-magic. Can someone who can't use magic really become the Wizard King? One thing's for sure—Asta will never give up!
Black Clover
STORY & ART BY YUKI TABATA
SHONENJUMP MANGA
RATED T FOR TEEN ratings.viz.com
SHONEN JUMP
VIZ media
www.viz.com
BLACK CLOVER © 2015 by Yuki Tabata/SHUEISHA Inc.

YOU'RE READING THE **WRONG WAY!**

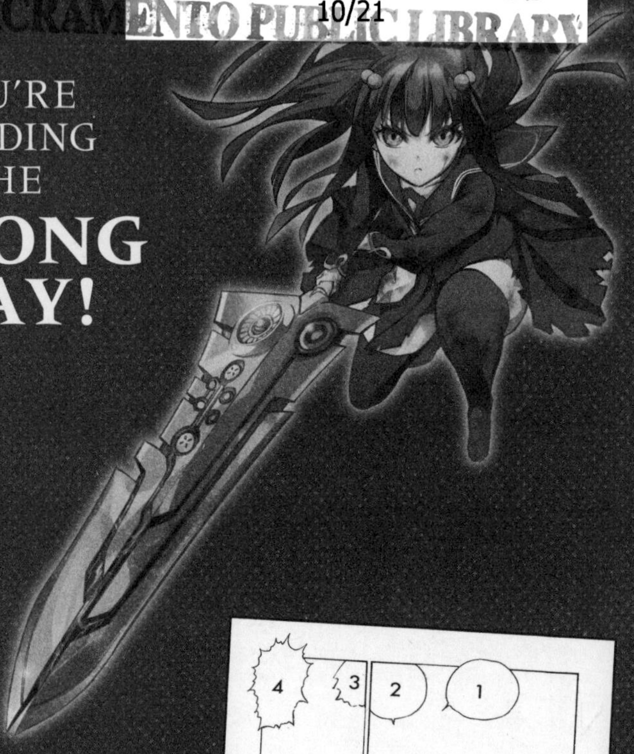

Twin Star Exorcists reads from right to left, starting in the upper-right corner. Japanese is read from right to left, meaning that action, sound effects and word-balloon order are completely reversed from English order.

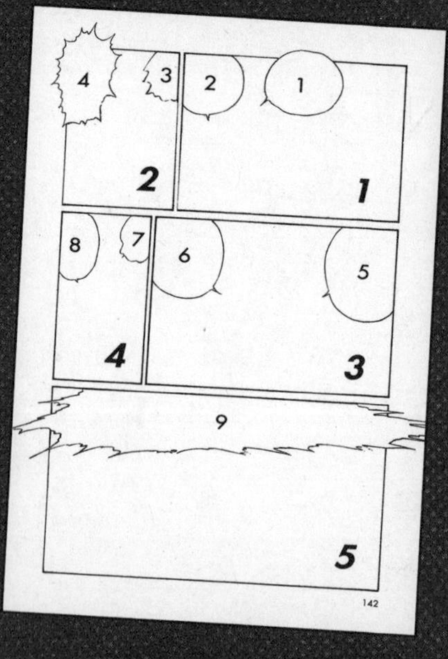